PSYCHEDELIC CULTS AND OUTLAW CHURCHES

"Backed by indefatigable research, well-organized, and astonishingly comprehensive, this remarkable work brings together into one volume the true stories of the many saints and sinners, with a preponderance of the latter, who founded organizations that proclaim or proclaimed the religious value of psychedelics and who persisted under the threat and, in many cases, imposition of harsh prison sentences and confiscation of property. What is the point of all this work Marinacci has done? Why does it matter? Consider four possible positions on the issue of the religious value of psychedelics: they are a gift from God; they are a temptation from the Devil; they are both; they are neither. Whichever of these positions you choose and whatever other reasons you may give in defense, if that view is to have any hope of being the one closest to the Truth, it will have to be consistent with the history of the individuals and groups presented in this book."

JACK CALL, AUTHOR OF *PSYCHEDELIC CHRISTIANITY*

"Mike Marinacci has made the exciting, detailed, and adventurous journey back in time to chronicle the psychonauts of the era. Mike searched, found, and explains in a highly readable fashion some of the histories of those who crave to know more of our reality and more than what we're legally allowed to find out. What's beyond the 'Do Not Enter' signs? You can now sit comfortably and vicariously journey through the lives of some of the most infamous seekers of the past half century with no risk involved. This book is a reminder of the relatively unknown yet important history of human potential that will likely help make you smile and wonder and appreciate even more the gift of life we're given on planet Earth."

"Who other than the likes of Mike Marinacci knew there were so many psychedelics-focused groups, churches, and initiatives in our recent past, and especially in the expansive and chaotic glory days of the 1960s and '70s? This is rich history in full color with a dose of bittersweet nostalgia for those who lived through and embraced the zeitgeist of the times; a cornucopia of inspiring, cautionary, and simply jaw-dropping true stories told in page-turning prose for younger readers and the rest of us. We owe a debt of gratitude to Mike for rescuing these invaluable segments and snippets of psychedelic and countercultural history from obscurity and giving them new life."

PSYCHEDELIC CULTS

AND OUTLAW CHURCHES

LSD, Cannabis, and
Spiritual Sacraments in
Underground America

MIKE MARINACCI

Park Street Press
Rochester, Vermont

Park Street Press
One Park Street
Rochester, Vermont 05767
www.ParkStPress.com

Text stock is SFI certified

Park Street Press is a division of Inner Traditions International

Copyright © 2023 by Mike Marinacci

Cataloging-in-Publication Data for this title is available from the Library of Congress

ISBN 978-1-64411-707-1 (print)
ISBN 978-1-64411-708-8 (ebook)

Printed and bound in the United States by Lake Book Manufacturing, LLC
The text stock is SFI certified. The Sustainable Forestry Initiative® program promotes sustainable forest management.

10 9 8 7 6 5 4 3 2 1

Text design and layout by Virginia Scott Bowman
This book was typeset in Garamond Premier Pro with WTC NIUNIA and Molly Sans used as display typefaces

To send correspondence to the author of this book, mail a first-class letter to the author c/o Inner Traditions • Bear & Company, One Park Street, Rochester, VT 05767, and we will forward the communication, or contact the author directly at **Mike@PsychedelicCults.com**.

*To Dean Oisboid, an honest skeptic and a
great companion on trips of all kinds.*

CONTENTS

ACKNOWLEDGMENTS

At the top of my thank-you list is my mother, Barbara Kamb Marinacci. When I was but a toddler, she awoke in me a love of books and learning and has encouraged me along every step I take as a writer and researcher. She has my deepest love and respect.

My girlfriend, Rose, has provided constant, heartfelt support during the writing of this book.

Philip Smith, who shares my fascination with this subject, gave me information about his own experiences in this spiritual demimonde and pointed me toward sources of information about it. Philip also successfully pitched this work to Inner Traditions for publication.

J. Christian Greer of Stanford University, a noted scholar of psychedelic culture, provided me with both a foreword to this book and helpful commentary about its contents.

Former Peyote Way Church of God member Carl Hassell alerted me to the fascinating story behind the sect's founder and graciously provided me with personal anecdotes and photos from his time with them.

Various founders and members of the groups I discuss in this book took the time to speak to me about their lives and missions. Those individuals are: James Flaming Eagle Mooney (Oklevueha Native American Church); the late John W. Aiken (Church of the Awakening); Tracy Elise (ONAC Goddess Temple); the late Timothy Leary (League for Spiritual Discovery); Robert Ackerly and George Kepnir (Brotherhood of Eternal Love); Natec Harijan (Shivalila); *selah* (Temple of the True Inner Light); Mother Boats and the late Jefferson Poland (Psychedelic Venus Church); Clifton Middleton and Carl Olsen (Ethiopian Zion

Coptic Church); Murray R. J. Feist (Church of the Universe); Roger Christie (THC Ministry); Steve Ryan Berke (International Church of Cannabis); Dale Gowin (Church of Gnostic Luminism); Jack Call (Church of Sunshine); Anne Armstrong (the Healing Church); Craig Everick (Lazy Nickels); Gavin Kaiser (Oratory of Mystical Sacraments); Steven Hager and Brian Spaeth (the Pot Illuminati); Norm Lubow, a.k.a. Rev. Bud Green (Religion of Drugs); Craig X. Rubin (Temple 420); Dave Hodges (Zide Door Church/Church of Ambrosia); and Rich Dorris and Rauk Zenta (Zenta).

Others who provided materials for this work include Eric Dillalogue at the University of Pennsylvania Library's Gotham Book Mart Collection; and the staff at the University of California, Santa Barbara Library's Department of Special Research Collection.

It took thousands of hours of research to unearth information about the groups and individuals described in this work, and several online tools were invaluable in this regard. One of the most useful was the fantastic "Independent Voices" collection of underground periodicals on the Journal Storage website (JSTOR). Brewster Kahle's Archive website turned up all manner of obscure data regarding the psychedelic sects, and the Newspapers website helped me track down historical local-news reports about them. The Multidisciplinary Association for Psychedelic Studies's site (MAPS) is a treasure trove for serious researchers of entheogen-related subjects, and the Chacruna Institute of Plant Medicine's site kept me abreast of legal and cultural issues regarding the "plant teachers."

FOREWORD

Over the last seven decades, hundreds of psychedelic sects have collectively reshaped America's cultural landscape. Though these fellowships have taken on a variety of institutional forms, ranging from back-to-the-land communes to libertarian hacking collectives, they all heralded psychedelic consciousness expansion as the key to humanity's salvation. Today their insistence on the spiritual value of psychedelics is achieving mainstream acceptance within scientific communities and the intellectual mainstream at large. The recent return of psychedelics raises an obvious question: Why hasn't anyone written a history of these groups? The fact that the current wave of enthusiasm is called the "Psychedelic Renaissance" offers a significant clue.

Etymologically the word *renaissance* signifies "rebirth." Therefore, the term *Psychedelic Renaissance* implies a "return to life." While psychedelic religionists faced more than half a century of persecution and condemnation on every level of the U.S. government, their numbers seem to have steadily increased during that time. Accordingly how can something that never died be reborn? The concept of a Psychedelic Renaissance reinforces the War on Drugs' extremely powerful policy of intellectual exclusion that has effaced the significance of modern psychedelic religions.

The War on Drugs was not only a militarized police and prejudicial judiciary predisposed to disproportionately imprisoning people of color for drug-related crimes. It was also a propaganda campaign concocted to manage the perception of psychedelics through after-school programs, popular entertainment, and medical associations. Moreover, this domestic government campaign dissuaded scholars from researching material related to psychedelics, and most of the research that did appear tended to present mind-expanding drugs, as well as the people who used them, in a negative light. Until very recently, scholars did not dare publish value-neutral research out of fear that their work might be construed as apologetics. Enter: Mike Marinacci's *Psychedelic Cults and Outlaw Churches.*

The book you are currently holding offers an overview of the psychedelic religions that populate modern North American history. It is the first of its kind, and along with being a wildly enjoyable read, it is destined to become a standard reference work on modern psychedelic culture. It should go without saying that the author could not account for every psychedelic religion that took shape in the postwar era, and it is certainly not my intention to fill in the blanks here. Instead, the rest of this foreword will elaborate the biases that the War on Drugs has encoded into our understanding of psychedelic religions. To be more precise, I will enumerate the ways in which Huxley's proverbial "doors of perception" remain closed with respect to the topic of psychedelic religion.

From the 1950s onward, the street-level use of psychedelics profoundly altered the production of music, literature, art, journalism, fashion, film, activism, medicine, academic research, holistic therapies, technological innovation, and religious practice in the United States. However scholars do not have a clear view of the complex entanglements between consciousness expanding drugs and American society as a result of the paucity of serious research on psychedelic religions. Instead, the same story has been told over and over again. To date, the research on psychedelic culture has focused almost exclusively on its larger-than-life heroes, chiefly Aldous Huxley, Timothy Leary, Richard Alpert ("Ram Dass"), Allen Ginsberg, and Ken Kesey. This "master narrative" of psychedelic culture is highly flawed for a number of reasons. As the aforementioned litany demonstrates, the master narrative only paints half the picture, or even less than half, considering the omission of women. If scholars are going to explain how psychedelics became a dynamic social force in modern American history, they must account for the contributions of women, indigenous communities, and people of color.

Troubling the master narrative also means pivoting away from the story of great men to a history of networks, of communities. Approaching psychedelic spirituality as the story of individuals and their unusual experiences neglects the fundamental truth that powerful psychedelics generate uniquely collective socialites. By virtue of their power to dissolve individual egos, psychedelics such as lysergic acid diethylamide (LSD) create transpersonal identities. Said more plainly, the history of psychedelic culture is a history of "groupminds," or shared consciousnesses. Seen in this light, the importance of *Psychedelic Cults* is self-evident.

Furthermore, by telling the story of religious collectives instead of individuals, the author overturns three of the patently false beliefs that undergird the master narrative of psychedelic culture. First, the movement of psychedelic religions did not disappear at the close of the sixties, but continued to grow up to the present day. The significance of this point cannot be overstated, and I will return to it shortly. Second, psychedelic culture was not born out of the "generation gap" between idealistic youths and a geriatric Establishment; rather, people of all ages have led the charge into hyperspace. Third, the history of drug culture cannot be confined to a tale of two cities, San Francisco and New York City. Psychedelic enclaves formed in rural communities, suburbs, and metropolises across the United States. By recontextualizing the people, places, and vitality of drug culture, *Psychedelic Cults* presents psychedelic experience as an integral part of North America's religious imagination, instead of a freakishly colorful and ephemeral sideshow.

Creating a new narrative of modern psychedelic religion entails a process of disassembling and reassembling the terms we use to tell the story. A few terms merit special note here. Aside from being ahistorical, the term *counterculture* is especially problematic because it homogenizes the diverse political, spiritual, and artistic groupminds that formed as a result of the psychedelic experience. Popularized as a result of Theodore Roszak's 1969 book, *The Making of a Counter Culture,* the concept of *counterculture* was, and is, intended to ostracize psychedelic spirituality. It is not a coincidence that the term was introduced into popular discourse just one year after President Lyndon B. Johnson created the Bureau of Narcotics and Dangerous Drugs, an amalgamation of the FDA's Bureau of Drug Control and the US Treasury's Bureau of Narcotics in 1968. This outdated piece of sociological jargon is an artifact of the War on Drugs and deserves to be retired. In its place, I have coined the term *psychedelicism,* a concept that emphasizes how psychedelic sects belong to a collective movement while nonetheless generating distinct doctrines and rituals. Much as Buddhism is composed of various sects, including Theravada, Mahayana, and Vajrayana, so too is psychedelicism formed out of the sects enumerated by the author.

This book offers readers a cogent overview of the religions that have animated the psychedelic movement. Most of these religious fellowships have received little, or in many cases, no attention by scholars or journalists. However, *Psychedelic Cults* is not simply a historical dictionary of drug churches; this meticulously researched account lays the foundation for a new understanding of psychedelic culture as its demographics, aesthetics, and mores shifted throughout and beyond the sixties. While it is commonly noted that psychedelic religions went "underground" in the mid-1970s, it would be more accurate to state that they refashioned themselves as a galaxy of subcultures and niche milieux. As the microhistories presented in this book indicate, the initial peak of psychedelicism was not 1969, but rather coincided with the "occult boom" of the mid-1970s. The timing is important, as the "booming" interest in magical societies, paganism, astrology, meditation, esoteric healing, and Eastern philosophies were surface-level reflections of the deep current of psychedelicism that flowed underground during the escalation of the War on Drugs. From New Age spiral dances and harmonic convergences to Satanism and black metal; from Deep Ecology to urban shamanism; UFO lore, parapsychology, and cryptozoology—all of these subcultures blossomed with the introduction of psychedelicism into the bloodstream of modern America. When openly advocating psychedelicism became too dangerous on account of the War on Drugs, psychedelicists also turned their attention to two larger mass movements.

While ecological consciousness was integrated into the LSD culture of the sixties, it was not until the late 1970s and early 1980s that psychedelicists formulated the doctrines of militant environmentalism. The foremost radical eco-activist groups of the last five decades, Greenpeace and Earth First!, were founded and led by politicized acidheads. The other tributary of psychedelic enthusiasm was channeled into the expansive musical subcultures associated with "jam bands" like Grateful Dead and Phish, which likewise came into prominence in the '70s and '80s. Among these vernacular spiritual subcultures, the funkadelic movement, centered around George Clinton's Parliament Funkadelic, represented the most imaginative psychedelic scene, attracting tens of thousands of fans who collectively recentered Black people and their struggle against racial prejudice in the psychedelicist worldview. Altogether, psychedelic musical fandom has maintained the free-wheeling experimental spirit associated with so-called "hippie" communitarianism well into the twenty-first century.

In this brief foreword, I have sketched the larger forces at work in the way we (mis)understand modern psychedelic religion. The "inside story" of this fascinating dimension of American religious experience is contained in the pages that follow. Read on, as the author has recovered a lost history that will amaze, amuse, and enlighten.

J. CHRISTIAN GREER, PH.D.
STANFORD UNIVERSITY, PALO ALTO, CALIFORNIA

J. CHRISTIAN GREER, PH.D., is a scholar, artist, lecturer, archivist, and historian of religion with a special focus on psychedelics. He holds a doctorate in Western esotericism from the History of Hermetic Philosophy Department at the University of Amsterdam and has held research and teaching appointments at Yale, Harvard, Stanford, and the University of Amsterdam. His latest book, *Angelheaded Hipsters: Psychedelic Militancy in Nineteen Eighties North America*, explores psychedelic culture within the fanzines of the late Cold War era.

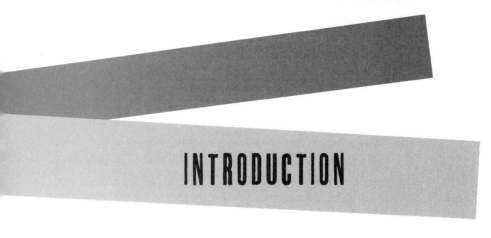

INTRODUCTION

entheogen \ *en·the·o·gen* \ *en'thēəjen* \ *noun :* a chemical substance, typically of plant origin, that is ingested to produce a nonordinary state of consciousness for religious or spiritual purposes.

OXFORD LANGUAGES

Over the last century an unusual and controversial religious underground has emerged in North America. Scores of churches, sects, and circles dedicated to using psychoactive substances like peyote, LSD, cannabis, and others as ways to experience the Transcendent and Divine, have appeared across the continent's spiritual landscape, challenging orthodox conceptions of what "religion" is, and how it can be experienced and communicated.

Although wildly diverse in their origins, creeds, and rites, these groups all see the ingestion of legally prohibited plants and chemicals as the key to personal enlightenment and the collective betterment of humanity. And they've all endured varying degrees of legal prosecution in their pursuit and promotion of this spiritual path.

PLANT-MEDICINE VISIONS AND THE MILLENNIA-LONG WAR ON DRUGS

The members of such groups maintain that precedents for their practices date back to the dawn of human history and can be found all over the planet. They point to anthropological and historical evidence that old-world shamans and priests initiated themselves and their communities into mystical states with psychoactive fungi and cannabis, and that both Paleolithic sites and ancient civilizational ruins show traces of these practices. They also argue that the peoples of the New World have used peyote, ayahuasca, and other "plant medicines" for healing practices and vision quests since time immemorial without the body-, mind-, and soul-destroying effects ascribed to these substances by prohibitionists.

The reason these practices were suppressed, they believe, is because they threatened the Abrahamic faiths. Ignorant and bigoted monotheists, they say, couldn't tolerate a spiritual path that gave its practitioners direct contact with the Divine without the mediation of formal clergy, legalistic scriptures, and unquestionable doctrines. So, the Judeo-Christian-Islamists squashed the psychedelic gnosis wherever it appeared in their religious-cultural territories and continue to inform current campaigns against psychoactive substances.

The idea that the War on Drugs is as much a religious war as it is a campaign of criminal law and public-health concerns, is a compelling one. In *The Immortality Key,* Brian C. Muraresku's study of the premodern Western entheogenic underground, the author noted that U.S. federal suppression of psychoactive substances began in 1896, when Christian missionaries on American Indian reservations begged the government to stamp out the peyote meetings that were "interfering quite seriously" with their evangelical efforts.

Indigenous peyotists fought back by uniting their circles in a formal religious organization—the Native American Church. Thus incorporated, they stood on the First Amendment right of freedom of religion to pursue their entheogen-based faith.

That right wasn't always recognized or respected. Federal, state, and tribal authorities often believed that peyote was a dangerous drug, and needed to be legally suppressed, Bill of Rights or no. In response, Native American Church members fought a century-long war in the U.S. courts, where they asserted that the plant and the mescaline-powered visions it produced were central to their faith, and that peyote's illegal status in various jurisdictions made it impossible to practice their religion freely.

Eventually the American Indian Religious Freedom Act Amendments of 1994 legalized peyotism "by an Indian for bona fide traditional ceremonial purposes in connection with the practice of a traditional Indian religion." Two years later Canada's Controlled Drugs and Substances Act exempted First Nations peoples from its prohibition of the plant. Today in both nations, Native American Church members practice their faith without legal interference.

BEATS, HIPPIES, AND NEW RELIGIONS

For other entheogen-using churches and sects, it's been quite a different story.

The Western rediscovery of the consciousness-changing potential of psychoactive chemicals began in the fifties. Although anthropologists and botanists had known of native "medicine plants'" hallucinogenic properties long before then, and scientists had isolated and synthesized their psychoactive chemicals decades earlier, it was in the Cold War era that psychedelics captured the popular imagination.

In 1954 Aldous Huxley's book *The Doors of Perception,* which described the English author's mystical visions under the influence of mescaline, became a bestseller. Three years later *Life* magazine published a photo essay by banker R. Gordon Wasson about his journey to Mexico, where a *curandera* (medicine woman) named Maria Sabina introduced him and his wife to hallucinogenic psilocybin mushrooms and their mind-expanding effects.

During that same decade, psychologists and intelligence agents alike investigated a new wonder drug called LSD that sent its users on fantastic, otherworldly inner trips and seemed to induce visions identical to those of history's great religious mystics. And Beat Generation literary figures like Allen Ginsberg and Michael McLure enchanted a generation of social rebels with their rapturous descriptions of peyote and psilocybin voyages, as well as the perception-stretching pleasures of much-demonized marijuana.

By the sixties the "consciousness revolution" spurred by the psychedelics was a worldwide phenomenon. The Beats' younger siblings, derisively referred to by the older hipsters with the diminutive

Fig. I.1. Opening the doors of perception.

slang "hippies," coalesced into a colorful global counterculture whose unorthodox attitudes about dress, money, politics, art, and sex shocked the older generation. Most scandalous of all was the hippies' embrace of cannabis, LSD, and other nontraditional intoxicants as paths to higher and stranger forms of consciousness than their parents had ever known.

Chief among the sixties counterculture's psychedelic prophets was ex-Harvard professor and psychologist Timothy Leary. A brilliant, charismatic, and media-savvy figure, Leary believed LSD and the other entheogens had the potential to bring about a revolutionary change in global awareness. He urged all who shared his vision to *Turn On* to the chemicals' mind-liberating powers, *Tune In* to the new possibilities psychedelic trips suggested, and *Drop Out* of Western society's dull and oppressive routines. The title of a 1966 booklet Leary wrote summed up his strategy to achieve this vision: *Start Your Own Religion*.

Some North Americans did just that. Imitating Leary's own psyche-delic church, the Millbrook-based League for Spiritual Discovery, sects devoted to LSD, cannabis, and other substances as keys to religious awak-ening, emerged in countercultural ghettoes and rural retreats. To the hip-pies and others who populated these groups, the Jewish and Christian faiths' traditional sacraments were inert, pale placebos; the entheogens were the true flesh of the gods that brought them to the ineffable, tran-scendent states of mind and soul formerly restricted to ascetic mystics.

Many of these sects cribbed from the Native American Church, and pursued forms of entheogenic spirituality that drew on indigenous symbology and teachings. Others looked East for inspiration and mod-eled their beliefs and practices after those of hashish-smoking Hindu saddhus and transcendence-seeking Buddhists and Taoists. Still more followed either universalist notions of nondoctrinal, nonstructured spiritual growth, or based their visions of psychedelic gnosis on the idio-syncratic insights and tastes of their often eccentric founders.

REPRESSION AND REVIVAL

The appearance of the sixties psychedelic sects was paralleled by the rise of laws that criminalized their sacraments. Responding to both real abuses of the chemicals and public hysteria about imagined ones, state and federal legislatures passed laws against the production, possession, and use of LSD, psilocybin, peyote, and mescaline.

In 1970 the Federal Controlled Substances Act placed these substances alongside heroin, cocaine, and other narcotics on the "Schedule I" list of drugs. These were drugs that the Feds deemed the most likely to be abused, with no potential for safe medical usage. Their possession and use were restricted to a small number of well-connected scientific researchers.

Cannabis also ended up on Schedule I. Proscribed decades earlier, in the wake of the thirties' racist and unscientific "Reefer Madness" panic, the plant was universally identified with the sixties counterculture. Smoking it had become a sort of hippie shibboleth that marked users as "outlaws in the eyes of America," to quote the Jefferson Airplane's psychedelic-rock song from the era. Government efforts to stamp it and "the drug culture" out were redoubled, sending countless thousands of otherwise law-abiding individuals to prison.

Unlike the Native American Church, non–Native American psychedelic sects met with no success when they tried to defend their religious practices on First Amendment grounds in court. The indigenous peyotists' rites far predated the laws against LSD, cannabis, and other favorite countercultural sacraments, and the Native American Church and its members were grandfathered into a legal exception strictly for religious use of the cactus. A fair number of self-styled psychedelic mystics went to jail when they couldn't convince juries that taking Schedule I substances was a vital part of their religious practice.

To both the courts, and to mainstream North Americans, the non–Native American psychedelic sects seemed to exist mainly as excuses to take drugs. As the hippie culture faded throughout the seventies, the concept that entheogens could allow people of all backgrounds to experience numinous states where they touched God fell out of fashion. And when the War on Drugs went into overdrive in the eighties, the handful of hallucinogen-based spiritual groups that still existed were shunted to the farthest fringes of both the religious and countercultural worlds.

By the nineties, however, things began to change. When the children of the sixties trippers dropped acid at raves, chewed up psychedelic mushrooms at music festivals, or took MDMA (3,4-Methylenedioxymethamphetamine) at the vast Dionysian Burning Man gathering, they often found themselves as deeply and as permanently transformed as their parents had been decades earlier. Many of them sought meaning and purpose for their new, psychedelicized selves, and found them in the writings of authors like Terence McKenna, Robert Anton Wilson, and Daniel Pinchbeck, who saw the "entheogenic revival" as a quest for the spiritual healing of humanity and the planet that the species dominated and abused.

With this vision, new psychedelic sects emerged. Their members reached out to a global audience via the internet, testifying to the enlightenment and transcendence that the entheogens brought them and urging others to follow their path. They also quoted the works of ethnobotanists and psychobiologists that traced the use of "teacher plants" back to prehistoric times. And they cited contemporary studies by Schedule I–approved researchers that demonstrated the psychological and spiritual healing powers of psilocybin among test subjects, looking forward to a day when such chemicals could be taken off the Federal Ugly-Drug List and offered as medicines to a hurting world.

THE CHANGING LEGAL LANDSCAPE

Legally, the new era of psychedelic spirituality was a mixed bag. Thanks to decades of hard work by activists and attorneys, cannabis was eventually legalized in several American states for all uses—medical, recreational, and religious alike. Other states have slowly and grudgingly decriminalized the herb for medical or industrial purposes, while a select few still penalize possessors of any amount with jail time and fines. And the plant is still a Schedule I substance, as illegal as heroin in federal jurisdictions. (In contrast, the Canadian federal government legalized cannabis across the board in 2018.)

As of this writing, LSD, psilocybin, peyote, mescaline, DMT, and a variety of both natural and synthetic entheogens all remain on the Schedule I list. Courts have ruled DMT-bearing ayahuasca tea legal for the American missions of two Brazil-based sects, but the Drug Enforcement Agency hasn't approved religious exemptions for its use by other groups. Several recent court decisions have recognized that the religious use of organic psychedelics by non–Native Americans is protected by the First Amendment, but their rulings have limited scope, and have not affected the drug laws.

Perhaps the most encouraging sign for psychedelic religionists has been the rapidly changing legal status of psilocybin. Several American cities and counties have decriminalized possession and use of the mushrooms that bear the chemical, and in 2020 Oregon's voters approved an initiative that legalized it for medical usage. As evidence mounts as to its potential medicinal value, other jurisdictions will undoubtedly follow the Beaver State's lead, and perhaps even sanction "healing circles" where the magic fungus is used for not only medical, but spiritual purposes.

THE PSYCHEDELIC SECTS

This book is an informal survey of various North America–based groups that have treated entheogenic substances as spiritual sacraments. No judgments are made about the sincerity of their beliefs or practices, nor of their legitimacy as organized religious groups.

Part I of this book is an in-depth examination of eighteen different churches, sects, and spiritual circles that the author has designated as "major" groups. These are entheogen-using organizations that existed for at least several years, produced substantive literature about themselves, were covered extensively in academic or popular media, and had noticeable impacts in the areas of religious-freedom case law or the psychedelics world.

Part I starts with a chapter about the Native American Church's history. Chapters 2 through 4 cover three other peyote-using sects and their founders, practices, and legal struggles. Next in chapter 5 comes a look at Timothy Leary's League for Spiritual Discovery, and the other organizations he founded to promote his entheogenic gospel. This is followed by chapters 6 through 9 about four distinctly different spiritual groups that made the LSD experience the center of their respective faiths. Next are chapters 10 and 11 about sects whose sacraments of choice exist in a legal gray area, neither explicitly prohibited nor totally approved by the state. Six cannabis-using organizations are covered in chapters 12 through 17, four of whom are currently active in this era where the noble weed is being rediscovered as an aid for meditation, prayer, and general spiritual enhancement. And finally, chapter 18 covers a prominent sect devoted to ayahuasca, the South American plant medicine.

Part II covers the "minor" groups in alphabetically ordered short entries. These forty-odd psychedelic sects are smaller, more obscure, and less historically significant than the ones covered in Part I, but peopled with equally engaging individuals, beliefs, and practices. Most of them have never been mentioned outside of specialized academic journals, long-defunct underground newspapers, or local-media stories, and their stories appear here in book form for the first time.

An appendix is provided that organizes in a concise list the entheogens used as sacraments by each of the sects addressed in this book. For those readers wishing to learn more about existing entheogenic groups and psychedelic spirituality in general, please visit my page at www.instagram.com/psychedeliccults.

I have chosen to use the terms "Native American" and "American Indian" interchangeably when describing the eras within which they were most commonly used. I do so with utmost respect for the indigenous peoples of the United States.

A PERSONAL NOTE

This book originated over forty years ago, in a cramped dorm room where I took my first trip on psilocybin mushrooms and saw God—or at least, a vision of the transcendent and eternal. Although I was raised as a secular humanist, I had several similar experiences later with both psilocybin and LSD and became interested in both nontraditional spirituality and the far frontiers of human consciousness and perception.

In the mideighties, I learned of the psychedelic-spirituality movement—or what was left of it. When I reached out to a few groups, I found that most of them were dormant or hiding from the War on (Some) Drugs during the era. My interest in the topic remained though, and when the "Entheogenic Revival" of the nineties arrived, I began to collect data about this spiritual underground, along with publications and ephemera its members had produced.

When I realized that nobody had ever produced a book about this strange yet compelling subculture, I got to work compiling my research into a manuscript, and eventually interested a long-established publisher in the project. This book is the result of years of study about a modern religious and social phenomenon that nobody else has examined quite as broadly or as deeply; I hope readers will be both informed and entertained by it.

Of course, no endorsement of any of the substances or groups described here is implied by either me or the publisher. May the reader use caution, prudence, and common sense while walking their Path, whatever it may be.

PART I

MAJOR SECTS

*Superstars of the Entheogenic
Spiritual Underground*

Following are the stories of eighteen "major" psychedelic cults and outlaw churches. These are formally organized sects with written creeds, discernable membership numbers, and a presence in both the academic and popular literature about North American entheogenic history. They are the stars of this ecclesiastic underground.

ONE

THE NATIVE AMERICAN CHURCH

Trouble and Triumph on the Long Peyote Road

The Native American Church is the *original* North American psychedelic sect.

Most of the other groups profiled in this book would never have emerged without the spiritual, cultural, and legal precedents that this organization has set over the last century. Founded officially in 1918, but with roots that stretch back thousands of years into prehistory, the NAC is overwhelmingly the oldest, largest, and most established of all past and present North American religious groups that have used psychoactive sacraments in their ceremonies. It is also easily the most persecuted of them, having spent nearly a century in federal, state, and tribal courts fighting for the religious rights of its members to seek healing and visions with the peyote cactus.

THE DIVINE CACTUS

Known to botanists as *Lophophora williamsii,* peyote is a small, flowering, button-like cactus that grows throughout the interior of northern Mexico, as well as in the South Texas deserts. The plant contains several psychoactive alkaloids, chief of which is mescaline—a powerful hallucinogen that, when ingested either in plant cells or as a synthetic compound, can induce a ten- to twelve-hour psychedelic trip. Users report that the experience features intense and often strange visual and auditory effects, and feelings of peace and interconnectedness with all nature and the Universe.

Peyote use in North America dates to prehistoric times. In 2005 the *Journal of Ethnopharmacology* published a study of two cactus specimens taken from an ancient indigenous cave near what is now Texas's Rio Grande. Radiocarbon analysis showed that the mescaline-bearing samples were "the oldest plant drug ever to yield a major bioactive compound upon chemical analysis . . . evidence that native North Americans recognized the psychotropic properties of peyote as long as 5700 years ago."[1]

Fig. 1.1. A cluster of peyote cacti.
Photograph by Paolo Neo.

Indigenous Americans believed that the cactus bore a special spirit that took those who ate it into a dimension of the Timeless and Divine. Peyote use was common among the indigenous tribes of what is now central and northern Mexico for healing and divination, as well as in community religious ceremonies.

Most early written accounts of peyotism come from Spanish

Catholic missionaries. The clerics associated the plant with the bloody rites and conquests of the Aztecs and called it *Raiz diabolica* ("the devil's root"), seeing its use as "sorcery" and "superstition." The church staged dozens of Inquisitions across Mexico in the seventeenth century to stamp out its usage among converts to the faith. Yet the Mexican Native Americans continued to use the plant, particularly in remote areas where church and government had only limited influence, and where the peyote experience was a community rite that bonded together those who sought its medicine and visions.

Perhaps the most famous Mexican peyote rites that survived to present times are those of the Sierra Madre Mountains' Huichol Indians. At the end of rainy season in October or November, Huichol villages send a band of representatives into the peyote-growing desert country to gather the plant. The peyote hunters take vows of purity and fasting and embark on a sacred journey of over 300 miles (in old times, the Huichol might not return to the village for a month; now they set off in automobiles). Prayers and rites are performed during the hunt, and when the first plants are found, the pilgrims celebrate a special ceremony of thanks.

Upon their return to their village, the Huichol peyote hunters are greeted with dancing and celebration, and the peyote is dried, and consumed in a festival that goes on for days. Anthropologist Peter Furst noted that during the ceremonies, "Huichols will literally saturate themselves with peyote, chewing it incessantly for days and nights on end, getting little sleep and eating little normal food, until the entire social and natural environment and the individual's relationship to it take on a wholly mystical dimension."[2]

PEYOTE COMES TO *EL NORTE*

Peyote usage remained mostly south of the Rio Grande until the mid-nineteenth century, when Plains tribes raided Mexico, and brought the cacti back to their territories in the American West. The Apache, Comanche, Kiowa, and Tonkawa tribes adopted peyote and developed rituals around its usage, and by the 1880s its use was spreading among other North American tribes.

Around this time, the remnants of North America's Indian nations faced a spiritual crisis. Four centuries of wars, diseases, and outright genocide at the hands of the European conquerors had wiped out indigenous populations from Newfoundland to Florida to Alaska and had left a hunger for a sense of identity and purpose among the continent's remaining indigenous peoples.

After most American Indian territories were lost in the face of the colonizers' superior numbers and technology, Native Americans staged one final and mostly symbolic religious and political rebellion against the White man: the Ghost Dance. The cross-tribal movement, where celebrants circle-danced and prayed for tribal unity and the return of their lands, ended barely a year after it had begun, with the death of resistance leader Sitting Bull and the massacre of over 150 American Indians by government troops at Wounded Knee in late 1890.

As in Mexico, Christian missionaries had worked extensively among the North American Indian populations—usually backed up by the laws and arms of the colonizers. Although many American Indians accepted the White man's faith, perhaps seeing in Jesus's crucifixion and resurrection a reflection of their own peoples' horrific sufferings and hopes for renewal, the old ways never died out completely. Indigenous peoples from the Rio Grande to the Arctic Circle continued to tell the same stories of Great Spirits, venerate the same totems, and perform the same sacred rites that their ancestors had since creation.

Many of the practices continued despite disapproval or persecution from churches and governments. Often, they were combined with Christian worship to create new forms of religiosity much as Catholic-syncretistic sects like Santeria and Santa Muerte had done in multiracial Latin America. Among North American Indians, peyote became a particularly potent element in this process.

JOHN WILSON, QUANAH PARKER, AND THE PEYOTE ROAD

The first major figure to develop the peyote ritual in America was John Wilson. Of mixed Lenape, Caddo, and French ancestry, Wilson was a medicine man and former Ghost Dance leader who first learned about the sacred plant from a Comanche peyotist. Seeking its knowledge,

Wilson and his wife went on a two-week retreat where he consumed as many as fifteen peyote buttons every day.

During the experience, Wilson had a vision of a road that led from Christ's grave, through the stars to the Moon, and the Sky Realm where the Savior dwelt. This was the Peyote Road, he realized, and he was charged to follow its path and stay true to its precepts for the rest of his life. The visions also taught Wilson how to construct and celebrate a ritual that would help others walk this sacred way, and he learned the songs that are still chanted today in peyote rites.

From these visions came the Big Moon, or Cross Fire, peyote ceremony, which emphasizes Christian spirituality and faith. Interestingly, many Native American Christian peyotists believe that Christ's crucifixion was the White man's sin, and that Native Americans had no need to atone for it. Peyote had been their medicine since creation, they maintain, and through the plant they communed directly with their Savior.

Another important early American peyotist was the half-Comanche warrior Quanah Parker. One of the last holdouts in the Plains Indians' resistance against the American settlers, Parker fell deathly ill in 1884, but recovered when a Mexican curandera treated him with peyote tea. Parker then renounced violence and became the best-known proponent of peyotism as a way of life that could unite Native American peoples and give them a sense of purpose and destiny in the White man's world.

Appointed chief of the Comanche by the federal government, Parker spent the rest of his life as an influential figure in both secular and sacred American Indian circles. He was a proponent of the Half Moon peyote ceremony, which de-emphasized the Christian elements of John Wilson's Big Moon rite and oriented itself more to indigenous myths and symbols.

THE HALF MOON CEREMONY

The Half Moon ceremony is an all-night prayer meeting, usually held in a tipi, although hogans and lodges can be used as well. It is scheduled when a sponsor presents sacred tobacco to a Roadman—the ceremonial leader, and so called because after years of attending meetings and learning every detail of the rite, he is empowered to lead others along

Fig. 1.2. Quanah Parker, Comanche chief and Half Moon ceremonial peyotist.
Photograph courtesy of the National Archive, taken between 1909 and 1932.

the Peyote Road. Not merely a ceremony or religion, the Peyote Road is a way of life that encourages healing, sobriety, family unity, self-sufficiency, and brotherly love among those who walk it.

The gathering may be held to celebrate, honor, mourn, bless, cure, or protect individuals within the community. Ceremonies are always dedicated to the Creator who advises and aids the faithful, and are usually held on Fridays, Saturdays, or holidays, but can also be per-formed simply when the Spirit moves peyotists.

Once the Roadman accepts the offering and sets a date, a meeting place is erected (or chosen), a firepit is dug, and firewood is stacked so that the sacred fire can burn through the night. A mound of earth sev-eral inches high is created at the center of the tipi or lodge and shaped into a crescent altar that symbolizes the mountain range where the mythic Peyote Woman discovered the sacred plant and brought it to humanity. The altar is oriented to the east and inscribed with a line that symbolizes the Peyote Road.

On the evening of the ceremony, the participants follow the Roadman in a ritual circuit around the outside of the meeting place, then file quietly into the structure and sit cross-legged on blankets. The Roadman sits in the westernmost spot of the meeting place, opposite the eastern door. Sitting to his right is the Drum Chief, who plays along during songs on the water-filled, resonant water drum. On his left is the Cedarman, who places cedar on the fire as an incense. On either side of the eastern door are the fire-tending Fireman or Fire Chief, and the Water Woman, who brings blessed water to the meeting.

Once all are seated, the Roadman produces the sacred instruments. These include a gourd rattle, a ceremonial staff, a feather fan, an eagle-bone whistle, corn husks, tobacco, and medicine bags that contain peyote, cedar, and sage. Every item symbolizes a different aspect of the Peyote Road and is used during the night's ceremonies.

The Roadman then opens the meeting with a statement of its purpose, and an invocation. During this period, the celebrants smoke sacred tobacco rolled in the corn husks, and meditate prayerfully on the altar, the fire, and the single "Grandfather" peyote button the Roadman places on a bed of sage.

Peyote in the form of either raw buttons, ground powder, or tea is then passed around to the attendees, who partake of the medicine. The plant's bitter taste often causes nausea or vomiting, and some meetings provide attendees with buckets if they get sick during the ceremony.

When the Roadman takes up his staff, fan, and gourd rattle, he sings the Opening Song, accompanied by the Drum Chief. This part of

the meeting focuses attendees' attention on its intent, and on the sacredness of the ceremony. The staff, fan, and rattle are then passed through
the circle to the left, and each recipient sings four peyote songs, accompanied by the beat of the water drum. Personal rattles and fans are also
brought out for use in the ceremony, as well as a pail of water, which is
prayed over and censed, and used to bless the four corners of the meeting space and all within it. Then the song/drum cycle is repeated, while
the Roadman steps out of the tipi to blow the eagle-bone whistle four
times, toward each sacred direction.

When the Roadman reenters, there's usually a short break, during
which the celebrants can stretch, or relieve themselves. On their return
the singing, drumming, and praying continues, accompanied by more
rounds of peyote ingestion.

At around midnight, the Cedarman recites prayers for the purpose of the meeting, and then censes the attendees with cedar smoke.
Sometimes, the Roadman may perform a healing ritual; at other times,
people may make confessions, begging tearfully for forgiveness, or ask
for blessings or guidance in their lives. All are heard and accepted without judgment by the attendees, who are in the mind- and soul-delving
intensity of the mescaline trip.

The singing, drumming, praying, and testimonies continue until
dawn. As the first light of day shows through the eastern door, the
Roadman sings the Dawn or Water Song. Then the Water Woman,
who represents the archetypal Peyote Woman, carries in a pail of spring
water, gives thanks to the Creator, and offers drinks to the thirsty celebrants. Participants may be allowed to speak briefly at this time.

Finally, the Water Woman and several helpers bring in the morning meal. Foodstuffs vary in different tribes, but usually include corn,
beans, fruit, and sometimes beef or sweets, and are passed around the
circle while the Roadman sings four more songs, and delivers an inspi-
rational talk, and perhaps a Bible reading. During this part of the ritual,
the Fireman sculpts the fire's embers and ashes into the shapes of spirit
animals or sacred symbols.

When the repast is done, the circle sings the Quitting or Moving-On
Song, to mark the end of the ceremony. The Fireman leads the attendees out the east door, and under the morning sky all raise their hands

to the Four Directions in gratitude for the healing and visions they have experienced. A period of fellowship follows, during which the people return to the tipi, express their feelings, and eat a breakfast prepared by the host.

With some variations in the Big Moon rite and in local usages, this is the basic peyote ceremony developed by Wilson, Parker, and others in their wake. In the three decades after the Ghost Dance ended, the ceremony spread through North America's Indian nations, giving indigenous peoples a faith based not in recited scriptures or memorized liturgies, but in the direct experience of the Divine. Quanah Parker famously contrasted the practices of the Christian missionaries with his own when he quipped, "The White Man goes into church and talks *about* Jesus. The Indian goes into his tipi and talks *with* Jesus."

A CHURCH IS BORN

Still, the modern world required some form of organization for the peyotists. They had been under fire from Christian authorities since Spanish colonial times, and U.S. government suppression began in 1896, when the Bureau of Indian Affairs, misidentifying peyote as "the mescal bean," instructed its agents to seize and destroy any quantity of the plant that appeared on American Indian reservations, since the medicine was "interfering quite seriously with the work of the missionaries."

Oklahoma, with its many displaced Native American tribes, became the birthplace of legally organized peyotism. In 1906 a group of peyotists there banded together under the name "The Union Church." Eight years later, Sac/Fox Roadman Jonathan Koshiway incorporated the Firstborn Church of Christ in Oklahoma, filing a statement of purpose that didn't mention peyote at all and that stressed its promotion of Christianity and its prohibition of tobacco. A former Mormon and Presbyterian, Koshiway limited church membership to the Otoe-Missouria Nation, although it was later reported that his peyote proselytizers were active in Utah as well.

The real impetus for a transtribal peyote church, though, came from a White man. In 1891 anthropologist James Mooney of the Smithsonian Institution became one of the first non–Native Americans to participate in a peyote ceremony, and he studied the religion and its practitioners extensively for nearly three decades. Sympathetic to peyotism, he believed that the best way for the Native Americans to protect their right to use the plant was to form a national religious organization that admitted members of all tribes, and that could be defended on First Amendment, freedom-of-religion grounds.

In 1918 Mooney drew up the articles of incorporation for an organization that would unite American Indian peyotists under a single body. Its stated purpose was:

> to foster and promote the religious belief of the several tribes of Indians in the State of Oklahoma, in the Christian religion with the practice of the Peyote Sacrament as commonly understood and used among the adherents of this religion in the several tribes of Indians in the State of Oklahoma, and to teach the Christian religion with morality, sobriety, industry, kindly charity and right living and to cultivate a spirit of self-respect and brotherly union among the members of the Native Race of Indians, including therein the various Indian tribes in the State of Oklahoma.[3]

On October 18, 1918, representatives of the Cheyenne, Otoe-Missouria, Ponca, Comanche, Kiowa, and Apache tribes signed and filed the papers of incorporation in Oklahoma. The Native American Church was born.

The church grew quickly, and by 1922 it was estimated that it had about 13,000 members. Several state branches were incorporated as well, and over fifty American Indian nations had organized peyote groups under its authority as a religious corporation.

EARLY OPPOSITION TO PEYOTISM

Not everyone recognized the church's authority, though. Alcohol abuse had become a serious problem in the Oklahoma Territory, and many White and Native American authorities alike thought that an 1897 law that prohibited supplying Indians with liquor should be amended to include peyote.

Department of the Interior Agent William E. "Pussyfoot" Johnson, who'd busted thousands of alcohol traffickers throughout Oklahoma and other states, also aggressively pursued peyote commerce in the territory, raiding suspected possessors and lobbying government officials to ban all shipments of the plant to American Indian reservations. His efforts to characterize peyotism as a menace were largely thwarted though, partly due to an influential article by James Mooney in the *Handbook on American Indians* that testified to the plant's "varied and valuable medicinal properties," and its use in "a ceremony of prayer and quiet contemplation."

Opposition to peyotism came from physicians and health experts as well. In 1921 Thomas S. Blair, M.D., chief of the Bureau of Drug Control of the Pennsylvania Department of Health, published a paper in the *Journal of the American Medical Association* where he called the American Indian peyote religion a "habit indulgence in certain cactaceous plants" and accused peyote suppliers of being "dope vendor[s]." Dr. Blair urged Congress to pass a bill that would ban the possession and use of peyote, claiming that:

> commercial interests involved in the peyote traffic are strongly entrenched, and they exploit the Indian. . . . Added to this is the superstition of the Indian who believes in the Peyote Church. As soon as an effort is made to suppress peyote, the cry is raised that it is unconstitutional to do so and is an invasion of religious liberty. Suppose the Negros of the South had Cocaine Church![4]

Although federal laws against peyote were proposed from the 1920s to the 1950s, none were signed into law. Different tribal, state, and local statutes across America prohibited peyote, though, and arrests for its possession continued throughout the period, particularly on the Navajo Reservation, where there was strong sentiment that peyotism was foreign to the Diné people and had no place on the land. Still, the relative obscurity of the plant shielded it from a nationwide moral panic like the one directed against the era's cannabis users, and the church continued to hold discreet ceremonies on American Indian reservations.

"A BEAUTIFUL AND UNUSUAL CEREMONY"

By 1944 the Native America Church had changed its name to the Native American Church of the United States. At that time the church was headed by Mack Haag and Alfred Wilson of the Southern Cheyenne Nation, Joe Kaulity (Kiowa), Truman Dailey (Otoe), and Frank Takes Gun (Crow).

Frank Takes Gun, who later became church president, was one of the most vigorous proponents of religious freedom for peyotists. During his presidency he encouraged tribes to incorporate state Native American Church branches for legal protection, worked to legalize peyote on the Navajo Reservation, and sought the American Civil Liberties Union's help in various First Amendment cases involving church members.

President Takes Gun also helped peyotists north of the border. Since the 1930s Native Americans in Canada's Blood, Cree, Ojibwa, and Assiniboine Nations had been using peyote, and in 1954 they organized as the Native American Church of Canada. Fearing that the Canadian government would prohibit importation of the desert-grown entheogen, Takes Gun and other church officials invited medical experts to an all-night ceremony in Saskatchewan, hoping to show the trained observers that the plant was a medicine and sacrament integral to their faith.

After spending a long night inside a Fort Battleford tipi with church celebrants, the White Canadian observers reported that the peyotists emerged from it unharmed. One attendee, Dr. Humphry Osmond, who would later coin the term *psychedelic,* called the meeting "a beautiful and unusual ceremony." And the Canadian press published favorable articles about the church.

On the eve of the sixties, peyotism and the Native American Church were attracting more attention—and controversy. *The Doors of Perception,* Aldous Huxley's 1954 bestseller about his visionary mescaline trip, brought the psychedelic experience into mainstream consciousness, and stimulated interest in the stubby cactus that produced the potent hallucinogen. Beat Generation figures such as poets Allen Ginsberg and Michael McClure and novelist Ken Kesey experimented with peyote.

And early accounts of LSD and psilocybin's potential medical uses often included speculation about whether mescaline could heal the psychological and spiritual complaints of non–Native American users.

PEYOTISM IN THE SIXTIES

The decade dawned with a landmark legal case for the church. On October 29, 1959, Navajo peyotist Mary Attaki called police to report that her brother Jack was drunk and causing a disturbance in her Williams, Arizona, home. When police arrived, Jack retaliated by informing the arresting officer that Mary had peyote in her home. The peyote was found, and Mary was taken to jail along with Jack, and charged with possession, illegal under Arizona law.

When her case came to trial in July 1960, ACLU attorney Herbert L. Ely represented Attakai with a religious-freedom defense. The expert witnesses he called included anthropologist Omer C. Stewart, later the author of the book *The Peyote Religion,* and Native American Church president Frank Takes Gun, who told the jury that the church had 225,000 members across North America.

After a two-day trial, Judge Yale McFate found the Arizona statute against peyote possession unconstitutional in cases of religious use, dismissed the complaint, and freed Attaki. The prosecution appealed *State of Arizona v. Mary Attaki* to the Arizona Supreme Court, which upheld the ruling in April 1961. Although peyote remained illegal in Arizona state law, the case set an important precedent for the church, and for First Amendment rights regarding peyote use.

The following year, the church fought an even more important legal battle for peyotist rights. On April 28, 1962, Jack Woody and two other Navajos were arrested during a Native American Church service in a hogan near Needles, California. Charged with violation of California's Health and Safety Code section 11500, which prohibited unauthorized possession of peyote, the three men were tried in San Bernardino Superior Court, with Omer C. Stewart and Frank Takes Gun again testifying for the defense. The defendants were found guilty, and the Los Angeles County District Court of Appeals upheld the ruling several months later.

An appeal to the California Supreme Court was made and accepted. On August 24, 1964, the court ruled in the defendants' favor, stating that peyote presented "only slight danger" to the state of California, and that its compelling interests were outweighed by the defendants' First Amendment rights.

In the ruling, Justice J. Tobriner opined that:

[T]he right to free religious expression embodies a precious heritage of our history. In a mass society, which presses at every point toward conformity, the protection of a self-expression, however unique, of the individual and the group becomes ever more important. The varying currents of the subcultures that flow into the mainstream of our national life give depth and beauty. We preserve a greater value than an ancient tradition when we protect the rights of the Indians who honestly practiced an old religion in using peyote one night at a meeting in a desert hogan near Needles, California.[5]

As in Arizona, California's state law against peyote remained unchanged by the ruling. One year earlier, State Assemblyman Nicholas C. Petris had introduced a bill to legalize peyote for the Native American Church, and although the bill passed in the California Assembly, it was killed in the State Senate's Committee on Public Health and Safety. Still, *People v. Woody* set a precedent in California cases where church members were arrested and could prove the peyote they held was for a legitimate religious purpose.

By the midsixties, America's burgeoning psychedelic underground had taken note of peyote. The 1966 cult film *Chappaqua* featured a scene where its narrator related how a mescaline vision led him to quit alcohol and heroin. Two years later *The Teachings of Don Juan,* an apocryphal account of anthropologist Carlos Castaneda's experiences with a peyote-using Yaqui shaman, became a bestseller. And in that same year Kiowa author N. Scott Momaday's novel *House Made of Dawn,* which described a nontraditional urban peyote meeting, won the Pulitzer Prize for literature.

The hippie world romanticized American Indian culture and spirituality, and during the era some counterculturalists sought admission to traditional peyote meetings. Although serious and sincere non–Native Americans were often allowed to attend them, the church, now called the Native American Church of North America, restricted membership to only people who could document that they were of at least one-quarter Native American descent. A nonracially exclusive "Native American Church of the United States," based on the original Oklahoma charter, emerged among dissident state and local church bodies, and the participation of non–Native Americans in peyote ceremonies remains a controversial topic among indigenous peoples to this day.

A BATTLE FOR RELIGIOUS FREEDOM

Entheogenic consciousness expansion went out of fashion in the seventies, and during that era peyote and the NAC were largely ignored by government prohibitionists far more concerned with stopping cannabis, cocaine, and heroin use. In 1978 the American Indian Religious Freedom Act was signed into law, and its blanket protection of indigenous sacred sites and "traditional native religious practices" was generally assumed to include NAC peyotism.

But that assumption proved to be false in 1984. That year Al Smith, a Klamath Indian alcohol and drug counselor, was fired from his job in Roseburg, Oregon, when his supervisor learned he had participated in an NAC peyote ceremony. When Smith and a non–Native American coworker, who'd also been fired for attending a peyote meeting, filed for unemployment, their claims were denied. On appeal, Oregon's Employment Department ruled against them, saying that religion or no, they'd violated the state's drug laws, and weren't entitled to compensation.

After a protracted legal battle, the Oregon Court of Appeals ruled in favor of the two peyotists. When the state attorney general challenged the ruling, Oregon's State Supreme Court upheld it, saying the two men had been unjustly dismissed and deserved compensation. Still dissatisfied, the Oregon attorney general took the case to the U.S. Supreme Court.

On April 17, 1990, the Supreme Court ruled against the defendants in *Employment Division v. Smith*. The ruling stated that, contrary to previous American religious-freedom cases, government agencies no longer had to prove a "compelling state interest" for them to intervene in religious activities. The court also maintained that First Amendment protections did not apply to violations of criminal laws, and that its guarantee of religious freedom wasn't effective unless other rights, such as speech and association, had been infringed.

The ruling dealt a bad blow to Native American peyotists, and to the First Amendment in general. Frightened by the precedent it set to sanction government repression of minority faiths, a broad coalition of American religious organizations sponsored the Religious Freedom Restoration Act, which restored the compelling-state-interest test to First Amendment adjudication. The act was passed by Congress in 1993, but the Native American Church felt it still allowed loopholes for prohibitionists to legally persecute peyotists.

The church then began a national campaign to guarantee the religious right of its members to use peyote. American Indian Movement leader Reuben Snake organized a new alliance of Native American and non–Native American religious groups, as well as American Indian nations and their allies, to educate the American public about the plant, and push for a law that would legalize its religious usage once and for all at the federal level.

Spurred by the upswelling of Native American activism, then-Congressman Bill Richardson of New Mexico introduced H.R. 4230 (RH)—the American Indian Religious Freedom Act Amendments of 1994—to the House. The bill stated that:

> the use, possession, or transportation of peyote by an Indian for bona fide traditional ceremonial purposes in connection with the practice of a traditional Indian religion is lawful, and shall not be prohibited by the United States or any State. No Indian shall be penalized or discriminated against on the basis of such use, possession or transportation, including, but not limited to, denial of otherwise applicable benefits under public assistance programs.[6]

Passed overwhelmingly by the House and Senate, the bill was signed into law by President Bill Clinton on October 6, 1994. Two years later

Canada's Controlled Drugs and Substances Act specifically exempted peyote from its prohibitions. The century-long persecution of Native American peyotists was over.

THE NATIVE AMERICAN CHURCH TODAY

Today, the Native American Church continues to hold peyote ceremonies on American Indian reservations and rancherias across the continent. Nobody is sure of exactly how many members it has; estimates usually range between 250,000–500,000; although it's possible that as many as one-quarter of all living Native Americans—well over a million people—have attended its ceremonies.

One current concern of the church is the ever-dwindling supply of peyote. Writing in the *American Indian Law Journal,* legal scholar James D. Muneta noted that the plant was rapidly disappearing from both American and Mexican deserts, and that Texas's government-licensed peyote vendors might soon be unable to meet the church's demand for the cactus. Muneta blamed the situation partly on the rise of groups that called themselves "Native American Churches" but were made up of non–Native Americans to whom First Amendment protections didn't apply, and who were poaching peyote from both vendors and wild sources.

In the piece, Muneta noted grimly that such organizations were beginning to win court cases based on the hard-fought precedents set by the NAC and Native Americans. He also said that some of these groups maintained that not only peyote, but cannabis, psilocybin mushrooms, and other entheogens were "religious sacraments" to them, violating both the letter and spirit of the religious-freedom exemption granted to Native American peyotists.

It is to those non–Native American panentheogenic religious organizations we now turn our attention.

TWO

THE CHURCH OF THE AWAKENING

Heartland Explorations in Mescaline Awareness

John and Louisa Aiken were two of history's most unlikely entheo-genic evangelists.

The married, retired physicians were old enough to be the grandparents of the hippies and students they met on the sixties-counterculture lecture circuit, where they discussed peyote as a path to spiritual enlightenment and higher consciousness and shared the psychoactive cactus with select individuals. Yet they found a ready audience for their accounts and ministrations and are recognized today as the first non–Native Americans to formally incorporate and promote a psychedelics-using religious organization—the Church of the Awakening.

TRAGEDIES AND TRANSCENDENCE

Both born in 1902, the Aikens became practicing osteopaths in 1937, and moved twelve years later to Socorro, New Mexico, where they founded a clinic. The two doctors soon settled into small-town life and became dedicated members of community groups and the local Presbyterian church. John Aiken even served terms as both the Socorro Rotary president, and as a city councilor.

But their peaceful lives were shattered by two tragedies. In 1951 their younger son, David, a U.S. Navy aviator, was killed in a plane crash in the Mediterranean. Six years later their other son, Don, also a doctor, drowned in a Lake Huron boating accident. The grieving couple sought healing and meaning for their pain and loss but found none from their church.

Distraught, the Aikens explored alternative spiritual paths. On October 12, 1958, they held the first of what would be several years of weekly meetings at their house, where they and other seekers discussed the meanings of life and death, and whether the human spirit survived the physical body's demise. Devotees of Christian medium Arthur Ford and his Spiritual Frontiers Fellowship, the group also wondered if such things as transcendent consciousness, extrasensory perception, and psychic healing powers were real, and they delved heavily into metaphysical literature, as well as writings from the great religious and philosophical traditions.

As the Aikens' circle explored the deeper mysteries of life, consciousness, and the universe, they alarmed their Socorro friends, as well as local clergy, one of whom warned they were treading dangerous territory without the guidance of a credentialed minister. The seekers responded that unlike the orthodox religionists, who treated spiritual growth as a belief-based intellectual endeavor, they sought direct experience with the Divine and the Infinite. But the path to that experience seemed to elude them.

In 1959 the Aikens read a scientific journal article by Dr. Humphry Osmond that discussed how such substances as LSD and mescaline seemed to produce deeper and fuller awareness in human consciousness. Dr. Osmond disliked the term *hallucinogenic* for the chemicals, and instead coined the term *psychedelic*, "mind-manifesting," to describe the effects they had on patients. Intrigued, the Aikens corresponded with Dr. Osmond and other early entheogen researchers, and found out that mescaline-bearing peyote, a cactus that grew wild in their Rio Grande Valley backyard, was used by the Native American Church to induce mystical states.

The Aikens suspected that peyote was the key to their spiritual quest, and their circle began to experiment with the plant. One member of the group, an atheist, took peyote and told the Aikens, "I have experienced God! I know that reality is there, that it is desirable above all things, and that it is attainable . . . I know that I, too, may become the way, the truth, and the life."[1]

John Aiken noted that various members of the group experienced similar, wholly positive, life-changing experiences under peyote's influence, often after more orthodox forms of spiritual devotion and discipline had failed them. Significantly, the Aikens' group reported none of the "bad trips" that later bedeviled psychedelics users; there were unpleasant episodes, to be sure, but nothing permanently traumatic or harmful.

NARCOTIC OBLIVION VS. PSYCHEDELIC GNOSIS

In an essay in the book *Psychedelics: The Uses and Implications of Hallucinogenic Drugs,* John Aiken stated that the group continued to explore the use of peyote as a sacrament, albeit carefully and with proper setting and intent. "We were more and more impressed with the importance of the effects of this substance," he reported, "when taken by people with a motivation toward better understanding of themselves and of life, and when given by one with similar motivation and an awareness of the hazards of improper use."[2]

In May 1963 the occult-oriented *FATE* magazine published an article by John Aiken. Titled "Can Drugs Lead You to God?" it examined the historical uses of plants and fungi to expand consciousness and produce spiritual awakening and brought the Aikens' work to national attention.

Aiken decried media and government attempts to lump the entheogens in with genuinely addictive and dangerous substances like cocaine and heroin and described how different the psychedelic gnosis was from the dulling oblivion of narcotics. Aiken admitted that using chemicals to stimulate a mystical experience "is a shortcut, and perhaps in a sense, cheating. But it can prove beyond any shadow of a doubt the reality of Spirit, of God; and then we may be willing to earn, by way of effort, the right to always live in this Reality. . . . If you choose to start your search for the Path through psychedelic chemicals," he asserted, "do so proudly."[3]

John Aiken also penned several articles about psychedelics for the Borderland Sciences Research Foundation's journal. The BSRF was run by Riley Crabb, a retired U.S. Navy employee and Theosophist who had a particular interest in UFOs and their alleged contactees. Although he initially opposed the use of drugs, Crabb was open-minded enough to travel to Socorro in the spring of 1963, where the Aikens dosed him with 500 mg of mescaline while his wife, Judy, tape-recorded the seven-hour session. Recalling the experiment many months later in a letter to Timothy Leary, Crabb called it a "positive, a very deep and satisfying spiritual experience."

THE CHURCH OF THE AWAKENING

At around this time the mainstream media discovered LSD and started to broadcast sensationalized stories about the misadventures of less responsible psychedelics users. Fearing that public panic would bring the legal hammer down on serious entheogenic explorers, the couple consulted with friends and decided that their group needed to be incorporated as a church, so that they could receive the same First Amendment legal protections that the Native American Church had for peyote use.

On October 14, 1963, the Church of the Awakening was incorporated in New Mexico as a nonprofit religious organization. John Aiken later described it as "a fellowship of those who are dedicated to conscious participation in their own spiritual evolution and who are aware of the importance of the proper use of psychedelic plants or chemicals as a factor in that growth. We believe that the real purpose of life is growth in awareness, or the unfolding, the actualizing, of our inner spiritual potential."[4]

Aiken was careful to add that it was "not a psychedelic church in the sense that its only or even its chief function is to promote the use of psychedelic chemicals." The entheogens, he insisted, were a means to growth, rather than an end in themselves. The name "Church of the Awakening," he said, came from the experience common to mystics of all ages, where the transcendent unity of life and the universe was revealed, "awakening" one to a new, higher state of being.

In the church the "psychedelic sacrament" would be restricted to people over twenty-one years of age, or eighteen if they had parental permission. Potential communicants had to be evaluated by certified ministers or monitors, demonstrate an interest in spiritual growth and the motivation and discipline to attain it, spend three months as probationary church members, and attain approval by its board of directors before they could ingest peyote in a ceremony. To discourage thrill-seekers from joining the church as an excuse to get high, the Aikens recommended that members consume the sacrament only once every three months and process their experiences and insights between trips.

John Aiken said that the church wouldn't define itself by a body of beliefs. He maintained that the individual psychedelic experience was more immediate, direct, and effective than doctrines and dogma, and that "doubt, questioning, and experiment" were vital to spiritual growth. The church encouraged each member to grow his or her inner life as fully as possible, and to see failures or setbacks as opportunities for reflection. As for religious forms and rituals, they were mainly useful as aids to spiritual growth, and could be discarded when they no longer served the purpose of personal enlightenment.

Eventually the church produced a set of six Affirmations that encapsulated their mission and goals:

1. WE AFFIRM the unity of all mankind, of whatever nation, race or religion.
2. WE AFFIRM the reality of man's spiritual nature, called Christ, Light, Life, Atman or Buddha, and the importance of our recognition of this Light or Christ as our real Being, rather than the physical or intellectual form.
3. WE AFFIRM the importance of achieving a personal experience of this Reality and its oneness with Universal Reality, through the Unitive Experience.
4. WE AFFIRM the importance of a properly directed psychedelic sacrament (through the use of peyote or other sacramental substance approved by the Board of Directors) as a means toward the achievement of the Unitive Experience.
5. WE AFFIRM the importance of the practical application of the Unitive Experience in our daily lives, through the loving acceptance of each person, and the recognition of the Being of each as this Reality of Christ.
6. WE AFFIRM the importance of extending the awareness of the reality of man's spiritual Being, both in ourselves and in others, as a major factor in the solution of both personal and world problems.[5]

At its founding, the church hoped to create a cadre of trained ministers who agreed with their philosophy and could administer the sacrament safely, legally, and responsibly. Candidates for the ministry had to have logged a minimum of five peyote experiences and monitored a group of five or more trippers at least once under supervision by a church pastor. Aiken stressed that he wanted neither dryly scientist researchers nor druggy hedonists for the clergy, but sensitive, conscientious leaders who could help form a community around the sacrament and minister a support network for its members. Leaders would not impose authoritative teachings, but instead encourage the development of individual seekers and guide the organization through what promised to be a challenging journey.

ADVENTURES IN THE MOBILE PEYOTE TENT

And challenges were coming. Less than two months after the church's founding, federal Food and Drug Administration agents raided the Aikens' clinic, and confiscated a bottle of mescaline sulfate, forty unlabeled capsules of the same substance, and 217 grams of powdered peyote. The mescaline, which the Aikens used as a more palatable substitute for peyote, had been ordered from a British chemical company, whereas the peyote came from a Texas farm. The Feds maintained that the mescaline was ordered without the proper application for investigative use, while the capsules and peyote didn't display the descriptive, usage, and warning labels required of all legal drugs.

Recalling the incident to a reporter years later, John Aiken said that the FDA agent in charge had a warrant to pick up 275 grams—about 10 ounces—of mescaline. Unfamiliar with metric weights, the agent wondered if his car could carry a 275-gram payload. "I assured him it could," said Aiken, "gave him a bit of it and some of our peyote, and he seemed very happy!"[6] The FDA eventually destroyed the chemicals, recording the case as Issue No. 7883 in their *Notices of Judgment Under the Federal Food, Drug, and Cosmetic Act.*

With their clinic on the Feds' radar, the sexagenarian Aikens gave up their osteopathic practices and retired in February 1964. They purchased a VW microbus, converted it into a mobile peyote tent, and spent the next three years touring North America, visiting far-flung correspondents who'd joined the Church of the Awakening and desired to take the sacrament with the Aikens. They also spoke on psychedelics and spirituality to audiences across the continent, billing the lectures with titles like "Exploring Inner Space," "Psychedelic-Religious Revolution Today," and "Psychedelics: Felony or Freedom?"

By 1966 the church claimed an organized chapter in Los Angeles, as well as groups of followers in San Jose, Chicago, Philadelphia, and Vancouver and Calgary in Canada. Aiken reported that over 300 people across the continent had joined, many of whom the Aikens had personally initiated with peyote buttons or mescaline.

Although the Aikens resembled acid-avatar Timothy Leary in that they were mature, well-educated professionals uninfluenced by the Beats and other pre-sixties, drug-using subcultures, all parallels ended there. Unlike the ex-Harvard academic, they had no desire for a media spotlight, nor a mission to convert the masses to psychedelic spirituality through performative "happenings," or enticements to "drop out" into communal clans. They limited their sacramental circles to approved church applicants, and held them in safe environments, under the supervision of experienced mentors.

Speaking to a reporter in Berkeley, California, where psychedelics were a vital part of the nascent hippie counterculture, John Aiken warned off dilettante trippers from the church: "Not everyone likes to listen to what we have to say. Although we use psychedelics, we consider it only a means to spiritual growth, not an end in itself. . . . We preach the doctrine of hard work, not the easy answer."[7]

EXPLORATIONS IN AWARENESS AND THOMAS MERTON ON ENTHEOGENS

Aiken articulated his philosophy in a little book titled *Explorations in Awareness*. Self-published in 1966, when LSD was still legal and the "drug culture" hadn't yet become a menace to Middle America, *Explorations* described the nature and process of spiritual awakening, and how entheogens—when intelligently used—could spur and enhance it. Aiken drew from such disparate sources as the Bible, the teachings of Buddha and Krishnamurti, and the writings of occult scholar Manly P. Hall to demonstrate the essential unity of the numinous experience, and how the wisdom of history's great mystics and philosophers gave the psychedelic seeker a framework in which to grow a newly expanded consciousness.

In 1967 Aiken contacted Thomas Merton, the Trappist monk and Christian mystic who had achieved worldwide fame with his books on monastic life and spirituality. Merton had opined that all drug use was a substitute for self-transcendence or love, and Aiken sought to present a different view to the Catholic author. Eventually Merton told Aiken that he'd corresponded with Aldous Huxley and Gerald Heard about psychedelics, was interested in using peyote to "sacramentally" connect with Native Americans, and admitted, "you are right in saying that 'careful and occasional use' of psychedelics can be quite helpful."[8]

By the sixties' end, the low-key Church of the Awakening had been almost wholly overshadowed by the youth-oriented, hedonistic, and chaotic psychedelic counterculture, whose freewheeling attitudes toward entheogens were such a stark contrast to that of the Aikens. Yet the couple, now in their late sixties, continued to quietly proselytize for the peyote sacrament, confident that their church could attain the same religious-use exemption for the cactus that the Native Americans had years earlier.

"THE CONTROL OF CERTAIN HALLUCINOGENIC DRUGS"

On May 17, 1967, the church petitioned the Food and Drug Administration under the Drug Abuse Control Amendments of 1965 for an exemption to use peyote for religious purposes. The petition was rejected, as was another one the following year.

Then, in May 1969 John Aiken and thirteen church members approached the Bureau of Narcotics and Dangerous Drugs (the BNDD, now known as the Drug Enforcement Agency [DEA]) as co-petitioners to amend §320.3(c)(3) of Title 21 of the Code of the Federal Regulations, to obtain an exemption for the church "to permit them the nondrug use of peyote in bona fide religious ceremonies." Aiken also enlisted the help of an American Civil Liberties Union lawyer in the case, since he believed that the church members' First Amendment freedom to practice their religion was being violated—especially since the Native American Church had been already granted the peyote exemption.

The BNDD responded that the Native American Church was a special case. Its members were indigenous peoples with a unique legal and cultural relationship to the rest of the United States, said the bureau, and as semi-sovereign entities American Indian tribes could be granted legal exemptions regarding traditional practices. Their peyote ceremony, the bureau maintained, was "essential and central to the religion in that without peyote their religion would not and could not exist." On the other hand, the Aikens had stated that the cactus "is not the only way to find God," which to the bureau meant that "peyote obviously is not essential to the existence of the Church of the Awakening. The Church has existed and does exist without the use of the drug."[9]

On September 23, 1970, the Federal Register published the Bureau's ruling against the Church of Awakening. It stated that

> the Government has direct responsibility and interest in the control of certain hallucinogenic drugs. . . . Peyote has been designated as a drug with a potential for abuse because of its hallucinogenic effect and it is subject to control. . . . The Government's interest for the public welfare is sufficient to override the inconvenience that refusal of the exemption might cause to the petitioners.[10]

The report took a parting shot at the church, stating that unlike the Native American Church, "the Church of the Awakening is not a religion in the true sense of the word, but a loose confederation of kindred souls whose purpose is to explore the mystical boundaries of humanity through the use of hallucinogenic drugs and other means." Granting a religious exception to it, in the bureau's opinion, "would create serious breaches in drug abuse legislation and open the door to pseudoreligions conceived for the purpose of circumventing drug laws intended to control the misuse of drugs."[11]

The Aikens and the church fought the decision, appealing it before the U.S. Ninth Circuit Court. The court's 1972 ruling, *Kennedy v. Bureau of Narcotics and Dangerous Drugs,* upheld the

BNDD's decision, stating "that the governmental interest sufficiently outweighed the First Amendment rights of the petitioners," and that "Congress may prescribe and enforce certain conditions to control conduct which may be contrary to a person's religious beliefs in the interest of the public welfare and protection of society."[12]

BARTHOLOMEW SPEAKS AND THE *PIHKAL* TRIP

The ruling killed the Church of the Awakening as a legally viable entity. Now in their seventies, the Aikens returned to Socorro, where they continued to hold metaphysical study and healing circles in their home, with peyote and other entheogens shunted to the fringes of their work.

In the midseventies one of their friends, Mary Margaret Moore, came to John Aiken for healing of her back troubles. When he laid his hands on her, she began to speak as an entity named "Bartholomew," who described himself as an "energy vortex." Eventually Bartholomew became one of the most popular channeled entities of the New Age movement, his pronouncements on self-knowledge and harmlessness anthologized in books like *I Come as a Brother* and *From the Heart of a Gentle Brother*. The Aikens became especially devoted to him, helping others to contact the entity, and distributing cassette tapes of his talks.

The Aikens' last documented journey into psychedelia happened on December 22, 1980. That day the seventy-eight-year-old couple and four other people at the Aikens' house each ingested 120 mg of MDMA and recorded the details of the day-long trip. Although the Aikens reported at the end that they saw no use for the chemical, being satisfied with Bartholomew as their sole spiritual guide, the data was entered into the research for *PiHKAL,* Alexander Shulgin's classic account of the psychedelic and empathogenic properties of MDMA and other phenethylamines.

When John Aiken passed on in 1993, and Louisa followed him five years later, few took note of their deaths. And like so many other groups covered in this volume, the Church of the Awakening, which never attained a following of more than about 400 members, was consigned to the footnotes of academic studies about the sixties psychedelic scene and nontraditional religious groups.

POSTHUMOUS RECOGNITION

Yet the church hadn't been completely forgotten. On the fiftieth anniversary of *Explorations in Awareness*'s publication, Ronin Publishing of Berkeley, California, issued a revised and expanded edition of the book. The 2016 edition featured previously uncollected articles and essays by John Aiken about psychedelic spirituality, as well as an introduction by me that placed the Aikens and the Church of the Awakening in the context of the greater entheogenic religious revival. The back-cover copy noted that the church had predated Timothy Leary's League for Spiritual Discovery and Art Kleps's Neo-American Church (OKNeoAC) (see chapter 6) by two years, although it had never attained the influence or notoriety of the Millbrook-based sects.

In retrospect, it seems that the staid, low-key Aikens and their church were at least as important as Leary, Kleps, and other better-known entheogen advocates in challenging the legal status quo about psychedelics and their use as religious sacraments. They demonstrated that "respectable" middle-aged Middle Americans could be just as passionate about hallucinogens, and the First Amendment issues regarding their usage, as any hippie or indigenous person.

Unsuccessful as they may have been in changing the laws, the Aikens' work stands as early battles in the ongoing—and increasingly fruitful—efforts to recognize entheogens as legitimate tools for healing, insight, and growth among the United States' 300-million-plus non–Native Americans.

THREE

THE PEYOTE WAY CHURCH OF GOD

Outlaw Stewards of the Magic Cactus

Forty miles northeast of Tucson, Arizona, in the high desert country shadowed by soaring Mount Graham, is a remote ranch that boasts one of the largest peyote-growing operations on Earth. Tens of thousands of the cactus buttons bloom in three large greenhouses there, safe from the casual pickers who've denuded the American Southwest of the sacred plant over the last half century.

The ranch is the headquarters of the Peyote Way Church of God, the first religious organization to provide the psychedelic cactus to non–Native Americans with the blessing—or at least tolerance—of the law. Since its founding, the church has taken hundreds of people from across the globe on peyote-infused "Spirit Walks" in the desert country, guiding them with teachings and practices adapted from the Native American Church, Mormonism, and the insights of church founder Immanuel Trujillo.

WOUNDED WARRIOR, PEYOTE PRIEST

Tracing the origins of Immanuel Pardeahtan Trujillo, who also went by the names Mana Pardeahtan, Mana Truhill, and others, is challenging. Church sources give his birthdate as May 25, 1928, but other records list his birth year as 1930. A 1955 news story says that he was born in Pennsylvania to a Roman Catholic mother, given up for adoption to a

Catholic couple, and named "James Coyle." Several years later, however, Trujillo told the *Arizona Daily Star* that he was born on the state's San Carlos Indian Reservation.

At various times Trujillo claimed to be either one-quarter, one-half, or full-blooded Apache. A 2014 *Village Voice* article about the church stated that his mother was "French-American . . . of Jewish descent," and that his Indian father came from Mexico—two pieces of information that never appeared in earlier accounts of his life.

According to the church, Trujillo ran away from his adoptive home and tried to join the U.S. Army to fight in World War II. The army rejected the underaged Trujillo, so he joined the British Merchant Marine, which had a long tradition of accepting teenage males as apprentices. From there, he was inducted into the Royal Marines, and after he was badly wounded in a raid on a German ammo dump, "[h]is face was rebuilt, his teeth were blown out; he had a piece of steel in his head and a piece of steel in his leg."[1] Trujillo also claimed that the incident gave him PTSD and traumatic brain injury.

Somehow, upon his return to the States the grievously wounded teenager managed to be accepted into the elite U.S. Army Rangers unit, where he became a sergeant and trained postwar recruits. (No records of his service can be found, although a photo of a smiling young Trujillo in an army uniform dated "1947–48" exists.) Trujillo said that during this period, he took to art as a post-trauma therapy, became a skilled potter and painter, and was discharged from the army in 1948 after a disastrous parachute jump left him with fresh injuries.

Around this time, Trujillo also located his long-dead birth father's will, which left him a $30,000 estate. The document requested that he get in touch with two of his father's old friends back in Arizona: Eugene Yoakem and Bill Russell. These men would lead Trujillo to the plant that would help define his life mission.

Yoakem, a White Spanish-American War veteran, and Russell, a half-Apache World War I vet, were both peyotists, dedicated to ingesting the cactus buttons as a spiritual communion. Russell himself was a Roadman—a ceremonial leader in the Native American Church (see chapter 1)—and owned a nursery out on Oracle Road north of Tucson where he cultivated peyote. Both men introduced Trujillo to the plant and the Native American Church, and during a three-day vision quest and fast in the Arizona desert, the young soldier experienced a life-changing trip on the cactus. For the rest of his life, according to his official biography, Trujillo dedicated himself to spreading the message of spiritual healing and transcendence through peyote.

BIKERS, NAZIS, AND A "VIOLENT NYMPHOMANIAC"

Trujillo's worldly career began in 1948 when he founded Mana ("spirit of life") Pottery. Until his death in 2010, pottery making would serve as Trujillo's main source of income. Mana Pottery pieces, which depict traditional peyotist and southwestern American Indian themes, have been featured in the Smithsonian's Museum of the American Indian Collection, were sold for many years in arch-conservative Arizonan Barry Goldwater's family department store, and appear in the homes of celebrities like Whoopie Goldberg and Bill Walton. Today, the stone-ware work continues as a for-profit business.

Trujillo married during the early 1950s and fathered two children before the marriage collapsed (later, he was briefly jailed for nonsupport of his estranged family). Shortly thereafter he relocated to New York to continue his artistic career and sell his work to the city's moneyed art collectors. But his doings there, as reported in the news stories and FBI records of the time and place, reflected little of his creative or spiritual leanings.

Around 1953 the peyote-promoting potter started riding with local biker gangs and calling himself "Cochise," or "Mana Truhill." Under the latter name he joined New York's neo-Nazi National Renaissance Party, where he organized the party's uniformed stormtrooper squads, networked the organization with European fascist groups, and penned a virulently anti-Semitic work titled, "Is Communism Really Jewish?"—odd activities indeed for a peyote-using Native American artist.

Strangely enough, during the same period, Truhill/Trujillo also enrolled in the NYC Communist Party's Jefferson School of Social Science. According to one account, the eclectic Manhattanite made his Audubon Avenue apartment a haven for "Communists, uniformed

Nazis, motorcycle gang hoodlums, some ballet dancers [he] had acquired in Greenwich Village, and a Jamaican medical student who kept parts of cadavers in the icebox."[2] His flat sported a large picture frame that housed a portrait of either Hitler or Stalin, depending on the political sensibilities of his guests.

When he was confronted later about these doings, Trujillo claimed that he'd infiltrated the NRP as an informant for the Anti-Defamation League, which monitored anti-Semitic and neo-Nazi activities during the period. FBI records obtained through the Freedom of Information Act showed that the Feds were aware of Trujillo's odd allegiances and kept close track of his activities in the era. Today, at least one source maintains that not only "Mana Truhill," but "Immanuel Trujillo" itself was a pseudonym, and that he may have been a government-connected, deep-cover double- or triple-agent, a charge that's also been leveled at such key figures in psychedelic-spirituality history as the Brotherhood of Eternal Love's Ronald Stark, the Church of Naturalism's George Peters, and even Timothy Leary.

In 1955 the hallucinogenic Hitlerian found himself mixed up in Manhattan's "Café Society" scandal. Mickey Jelke, the free-spending playboy heir to an oleomargarine fortune, had been charged with prostituting his fiancée, Pat Ward, to various upper-crust johns to cover his mounting debts. Jelke was tried and convicted twice for pimping, and eventually served twenty-one months in state prison.

After Pat Ward left Jelke in early 1954, she took up with Trujillo, whom she met while she was slumming with his biker friends. Their affair lasted six weeks, and the next year, when Jelke's second trial again put Ward in the public eye, Trujillo cashed in on his brush with fame by writing a book about his time with the high society call girl. Titled *I Love You! I Hate You!* (Andre Levy, 1955), the now-scarce book featured Trujillo's accounts of life with Ward, where he revealed that she accompanied him to National Renaissance Party meetings, stunk up his apartment with her inattention to personal hygiene, and was a "violent nymphomaniac" who paraded around in front of his Nazi and Communist comrades clad in nothing but an SS officer's cap and black leather jackboots.

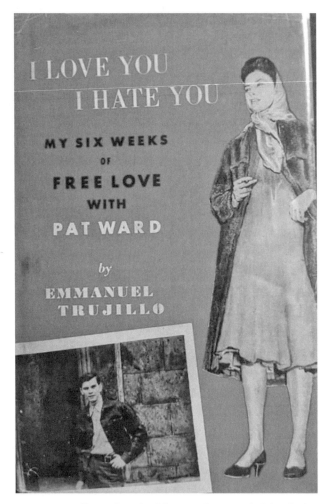

Fig. 3.1. Trujillo, rockin' the fifties Marlon Brando-biker look,
wrote this 1955 book about his involvement in a NYC sex scandal.

CANADIAN CONTRABAND AND
THE ALL-RACE NATIVE AMERICANS

Trujillo next surfaced in Canada. On January 4, 1956, the *Calgary Herald* reported that the New Yorker, who'd been going by the name "Mana Pardeahtan," had been busted for narcotics trafficking in Montreal. The peyotist, who had spurned psychedelic cactus for the more profitable, and more prohibited, cannabis trade, was caught by an undercover policewoman when he tried to sell her over 300 joints.

In May a Quebec court found him guilty, and Trujillo, who had married again and fathered another child, reportedly did two years in a Canadian prison.

By 1960 Trujillo was back in Arizona. A front-page article in the Tucson *Arizona Daily Star* featured a photograph of him wearing an Indian headband and long hair and creating a ceremonial dish for kiln-firing. Referring to himself only as "Mana," the erstwhile Canadian drug-runner and neo-Nazi propagandist said that he designed pottery for the gift-shop trade and looked to both his Apache elders and historical sources for inspiration.

Trujillo was also active again in the Native American Church. In August 1961 he was promoted to Roadman, and led a fourteen-person ceremony that month for the first time. Around this time, he also petitioned the church to drop its required one-quarter–Native American ancestry for communicants, stating that his own mixed-blood grandchildren—assuming they had non–Native American parents—would someday be turned away from the peyote ceremonies if the regulation stood. The church, which was still struggling with the courts over its religious use of the plant, denied his request.

Unfazed, the Roadman chartered his own chapter within the Native American Church. Called the Native American Church All-Race Group, it was made up largely of World War II and Korean War vets, and accepted people of any ethnic background as members. The chapter lasted for a year before the Native American Church leaders revoked its charter and ordered it to disband, and Trujillo returned to selling Mana pottery to ethnic-arts outlets in the western United States.

MILLBROOK'S INDIAN IN THE WILD WEST

But by the midsixties, the psychedelic potter was on the Peyote Road again—this time at the very center of the fledgling American entheogenic-spirituality movement. Trujillo moved back to New York State and joined Timothy Leary and Richard Alpert's Millbrook psychedelic commune near Poughkeepsie. The peyotist, who claimed he originally met Leary in 1962 and gave the Harvard psychologist his first taste of the cactus, occupied the Millbrook estate's Gate House—the fortress-like building that was later the home of Neo-American Church (see chapter 6) "Chief Boo Hoo" Art Kleps. There he fired and glazed his pottery and acted as a sort of token representative of Native American peyote spirituality to both the residents and the New York underground press.

On February 7, 1966, Trujillo, who was again calling himself "Mana Pardeahtan," spoke at a well-attended New York meeting of Leary's Castalia Foundation. Addressing the ex-Harvard professor's recent legal troubles, as well as those of the whole psychedelic subculture, Mana/ Trujillo described himself as a Native American Church member, likened using psychedelics in the chaotic Manhattan environment to "driving on the sidewalk," and said that the Castalia Foundation could serve as the non–Native American equivalent of the NAC, sanctifying and supervising trippers' experiences.

Mana/Trujillo later told *East Village Other* publisher Walter Bowart that to be a peyotist, "You have to get out of the brown paper lunchbag, going to fight the subway scene, working with terrible people. Eating hasty lunches. Doing the city thing."[3] He asserted that various "Anglo" chapters of the NAC existed throughout the Southwest, and that the church itself took the same hard line against LSD and cannabis that the U.S. government did. They only wanted, he said, to be left alone to use peyote as a sacrament.

Weeks later, Duchess County lawmen under the command of Deputy D.A. and future Watergate burglar G. Gordon Liddy raided the Millbrook commune in search of illegal drugs. Although Mana/ Trujillo somehow avoided getting caught in the mass arrest, he realized that the community was vulnerable to more raids and teamed up with estate co-owner Billy Hitchcock to find a home in a more remote location. Trujillo, acting as an agent for Hitchcock, relocated to the U.S. Southwest and bought three properties that were earmarked for use by Leary's League for Spiritual Discovery (see chapter 5).

Trujillo soon found out the Wild West was no friendlier to psychedelic spirituality than the staid eastern states. On December 21, 1966, the potter, who was still going by the name Mana Pardeahtan, was arrested at his Denver, Colorado, studio and charged with illegal possession of peyote.

When the case came to court in June 1967, the judge ruled in favor of Trujillo. In the ruling, Denver County Judge Julian Conley said that the potter/pastor used the cactus "in honest and good faith in the practice of peyotism, a bona fide religion,"[4] and that Trujillo's First Amendment rights had been violated in the bust. *People v. Mana Pardeahtan* provided the foundation for the legalization of sacramental peyote in Colorado, and to this day the state officially tolerates its use in religious ceremonies by non–Native Americans.

Trujillo dodged yet another bullet in the Haight-Ashbury. When he traveled to the San Francisco hippie stronghold in the early spring of 1967, locals grew suspicious of the pottery-bearing, suit-wearing stranger, and the Communication Company, the publishing arm of the anarchist Diggers collective, issued a public broadside with his portrait bearing the words: "Is Mana the Heat [police]? BE CAREFUL." The Diggers later circulated another document where they scotched rumors that Trujillo was an undercover cop, and reprinted a statement signed by Walter Bowart and other counterculture figures attesting to his countercultural bona fides.

HOLY LIGHT IN ARIZONA

The next year, Trujillo returned to Arizona. After a stint at Mellon heiress Peggy Hitchcock's well-appointed "artist commune" in Tucson, he migrated to a 360-acre former dude ranch outside of Benson, where Millbrook residents Bill Haines and his Sri Ram Ashrama had fled after being expelled from the New York estate. Trujillo set up a pottery studio there, enlisted other residents as helpers, and provided much-needed income for the desert commune with stoneware sales.

During his time at the Ashrama, Trujillo met and married his third wife, Jane. In 1971 the Trujillos and two other couples co-purchased the 160-acre "Peaceful Valley Ranch" in the remote Aravaipa Valley, fifty miles up a washboard road from Willcox, Arizona. There Trujillo established the Church of Holy Light and dedicated it to the "Open Hand Rehabilitation Program," which sought to reform alcoholics and drug addicts by teaching them the discipline and art of pottery making.

Over the next few years, Trujillo also discreetly continued his peyotist mission and envisioned the church as an independent sect wholly free of the Native American Church's racial strictures (he had made his final break with the NAC in late 1966). Although the period was marred by the death of his four-year-old son Byram James in a freak vehicle accident, and the dissolution of his third marriage, the middle-aged Trujillo nevertheless kept busy with his stoneware business and his rehabilitation ministry.

THE PEYOTE WAY CHURCH OF GOD

In October 1977 newlywed hippies Matthew Kent and Anne Zapf arrived at the ranch. Introduced to Trujillo by a mutual acquaintance, they spent several days there, hanging out with the middle-aged peyotist and learning about his devotion to the plant. Intrigued, they ingested some buttons under his guidance.

Like countless humans throughout history, Kent and Zapf were transformed by the experience. And like their host had done nearly thirty years before, they dedicated their lives to guiding others on the Peyote Road. Years later, Kent would say that first trip "reversed" a vasectomy he'd had and allowed him to father three children by Zapf.

The couple moved onto the ranch and joined Trujillo's ministry. He took on the title Reverend Trujillo and designated his lieutenants as "Rabbi" Kent and "Reverend" Zapf, even though neither of them had ministerial training. The couple became the pastor's most loyal and valuable associates and helped transform his church from an obscure one-man mission in the Arizona outback, into an organization that would openly—and in a limited sense, legally—take the peyote experience into the non–Native American world.

Now calling themselves the Peyote Way Church of God, the three made their first move in December of 1977. That month they registered a Declaration of Intent in the Graham County Recorder's office stating that they were stewarding, ingesting, distributing, and growing "the Holy Sacrament Peyote" as an essential part of their church's beliefs and practices. They also gave a live peyote plant to a local judge, who advised them to carefully document church activities.

In May 1979 the church, which now boasted a board of stewards and bylaws, was registered as an Arizona State corporation. Two months later it sent a letter to President Jimmy Carter calling for a removal of the federal Native Americans–only stricture on peyote use, saying that "no one race can own a sacrament of God for we are all children of one Holy Mother and Father."[5]

THE GREAT TEXAS PILGRIMAGE BUST

The church ran into its first legal troubles in Texas. In November 1980 Kent, Zapf, and Deaconess Nora Booth traveled to the Lone Star State in a truck emblazoned with the words "Peyote Way Church of God, Texas Pilgrimage, 1980" and paintings of peyote buttons and firebirds. A cop in Richardson pulled them over and discovered that they were carrying four peyote buttons each in their medicine bags. (Church bylaws required clergy to always have this amount on their person when traveling "in the event of imminent martyrdom.")

The officer arrested the trio, and the truck and the load of Mana pottery it carried was impounded. The church clergy were charged with unlawful possession of a dangerous drug and impeding traffic and released on bond the next day. When the case came to court in December 1981, the judge called the arrest "an obvious case of subterfuge," and it was dismissed.

The following year the church sued both the state of Texas and the federal government, claiming that their clergy's First, Fifth, and Fourteenth Amendment rights had been violated by the arrest, and by the legal prohibition on non–Native American peyote possession. The court ruled against the church, and while they waited on an appeal, Trujillo and his associates contacted state and federal agencies and elected officials, urging them to lift the racially restrictive peyote laws.

Meanwhile, back at the ranch, construction began on communal buildings and domiciles to house the resident clergy and visiting peyotists. Mana Pottery was also formally incorporated as Mana Inc., with marketing efforts expanded to raise money for church activities.

VICTORY IN GLOBE, DEFEAT IN DALLAS

By 1986 the church's suit against Texas and the Feds was still unresolved, and it had a new case to contend with as well.

In May of that year, a police officer in Globe, Arizona, pulled Trujillo's vehicle over for speeding. When the officer examined Trujillo's ID, which gave his Peyote Way Church of God address, he asked if the reverend had any plants on his person. Trujillo then pulled a dried peyote button from his medicine bag; when a piece fell on the ground, he put in in his mouth as an act of sacramental respect. The officer arrested Trujillo, who was later released on his own recognizance.

Charged with ingestion of a dangerous drug, Trujillo went on trial in Gila County Superior Court on February 14, 1987. Witnesses for the defense included Dr. Andrew Weil, a famed psychedelics researcher and alternative-medicine advocate whose books *The Natural Mind* and *Chocolate to Morphine* revolutionized popular thinking about "the drug problem." After three hours of deliberation, the nine-member jury returned a not guilty verdict, and Trujillo's peyote and medicine bag were returned to him.

Four months later the church's suit against the Texas and federal governments finally came to Dallas's Federal Court. After many months of testimonies, briefs, and deliberations, Judge Robert Maloney of the Fifth Circuit issued his ruling in *Peyote Way Church of God, Inc. v. Thornburgh* on October 28, 1988.

The judge ruled against the church, stating that Texas and federal laws against non–Native American peyote use were "political" and not "racial" in nature, since Native American tribes were legally considered sovereign nations rather than ethnic groups. Furthermore, he said that regarding peyote possession, state and federal authorities were authorized to prioritize public safety over religious freedom, and the preservation of Native American culture over the needs of wildcat peyotists. Three years later an appeals court upheld the ruling, and several other church lawsuits against government figures and agencies were similarly unsuccessful.

THE SPIRIT WALK

Still, the church continued to use peyote in its ceremonies at the ranch. Arizona, along with five other western states, allows residents of any race to legally ingest the cactus so long as they can demonstrate a sincere belief in its sacramental nature, and if the usage is an integral part of an accepted religious ritual. But the Arizona law places the burden of proof on defendants, and non–Native American peyotists occasionally face legal persecution in the Grand Canyon State.

Accordingly, the church developed a ritual for using peyote that requires the commitment and discipline of a sincere religious seeker. Called the "Spirit Walk," the ceremony spans a three-day period from arrival at the ranch to departure.

In the Spirit Walk, a prospective peyotist ideally arrives at the remote ranch on 5 p.m. of the first day. They are given a tour of the property, and then either sleep indoors, or camp out on the land for the first night. Spirit Walkers are forbidden from bringing meat, alcohol, tobacco, coffee, firearms, or drugs onto the property. They are expected to fast for twenty-four hours before ingesting the sacrament, so that they can purify themselves for the peyote experience.*

After the fasting period, a church steward directs the Spirit Walker to a campsite. There, the steward lights a campfire and sets up a tented site for the peyotist-to-be, complete with chair, sleeping bag, and a flashlight for the dark desert night. The church recommends that novice peyotists bring plenty of water to keep hydrated during the twelve-hour trip, as well as a notepad and pen to record their experiences.

When all is ready, the Spirit Walker is given the sacrament: twelve

---

*Interestingly, the church's dietary strictures are based in Mormonism. Anne Zapf, who served as church president for eight years, joined the Latter-Day Saints in college, and Peyote Way literature itself says that "both the Mormon faith and the entheogenic path rely on the concept of Divine Revelation, wisdom revealed to those with pure hearts and open ears,"[6] and therefore demand an unadulterated body and soul—the "Peyote Way of Living," as the church calls it. The basis is section 89, or the "Word of Wisdom" from the Mormon *Book of Doctrine and Covenants,* which proscribes alcohol, tobacco, and "hot drinks" among the faithful. Spirit Walkers are also advised to eat only organic foodstuffs for several days before they arrive at the ranch.

fluid ounces of peyote-infused tea. The brew is made with 21 grams of powdered peyote tops—according to Rabbi Kent, the measure is used because it's the reputed weight of the human soul. The tea is ingested slowly, to acclimate the stomach to the bitter, nauseating cactus, and to allow the hallucinogen to gradually take the Spirit Walker into the place of wonderment and transcendence produced by mescaline intoxication.

The next morning, Spirit Walkers are offered a repast of organic pinto beans to break their fast and are allowed to consume whatever foods they brought to the ranch. They are also counseled to reflect on their peyote experience, and to process any feelings of "penitence, forgiveness of self and others, renewed confidence, desire for self-improvement and improved health and a healthy attitude" that may have emerged from it.

The Spirit Walk is offered for a donation of at least $500 and is only available to registered members of the church. Church membership is open to all races and faiths, and the annual $50 required dues are used to maintain church land and buildings and finance its publications and internet presence. Members are also allowed to download the *Peyote Way Church of God Anthology,* which includes church legal and historical documents and writings on spirituality.

Like so many other entheogenic sects, the Peyote Way Church of God is deliberately vague about doctrine, saying that it was not founded "to create more dogma. Our purpose was to make the Holy Sacrament Peyote available to seekers in a safe environment." The church states, "we enthusiastically support personal revelation and encourage you to be faithful to the Light within. . . . We encourage individuals to create their own rituals as they become acquainted with the great mystery and believe that the Holy Sacrament Peyote, when taken according to our sacramental procedure (Our 3-Day Spirit Walk) and combined with a holistic lifestyle (Peyote Way of Living), can lead an individual toward a more spiritual life."[7]

In the years since the *Peyote Way Church of God, Inc. v. Thornburgh* decision, the church has faced additional difficulties, but has survived. Hundreds of people from all over the world have gone on Spirit Walks at the ranch, and hundreds more support the church as dues-paying members.

THE ENTHEOGENIC ELDER

As for the church founder, he spent his last years growing into a new role as an entheogenic elder. At the end of 1989 Rev. Trujillo took a sabbatical to New York, to help care for his ailing adoptive uncle Bill. There he revived his biker lifestyle of four decades earlier, riding with the Ching-a-Lings motorcycle club, firing his pottery in the club's garage, and running a free after-school pottery program for children in their South Bronx neighborhood.

When Rev. Trujillo returned to Arizona, he continued to oversee activities on the ranch. Rev. Zapf yielded the church presidency to her husband in 1993, and the two became the main representatives of the Peyote Way, addressing the ever-growing public interest in "plant medicines" with media interviews and appearances at entheogen-related conferences.

Californian Carl Hassell, a former church member, told me that he visited the ranch several times during this period for Spirit Walks. Hassell often hung out with Rev. Trujillo, whom he described as an entertaining raconteur, ever ready to drop names and tell tales about his long, action-packed life in a style that reminded the Californian of "a beatnik Captain Beefheart on acid."

Like other psychedelic-sectarians, Rev. Trujillo wasn't averse to privately enjoying unsanctified entheogens or sensual pleasures. Although the aging peyotist suffered from breathing difficulties and toted an oxygen tank in his last eight years, he happily smoked the fistfuls of cannabis Hassell smuggled onto the ranch. And the reverend, along with his younger cohorts, often strolled the grounds of their entheogenic Eden in the nude, particularly during hot summer days.

On July 24, 2010, the ailing, octogenarian Rev. Immanuel Trujillo passed on from congestive heart failure. He was buried on the ranch alongside the grave of his four-year-old son Byram James, under a mound of stone and gravel. Ranch visitors are encouraged to pay their respects at his resting place, where they can meditate on the life and work of one of the most colorful and complex figures to ever emerge from the entheogenic underground.

THE GRANDCHILDREN'S GREENHOUSE

Several years before the reverend's death, the church took on its most ambitious project yet: the replenishing of North America's peyote supply. For years the population of *Lophophora williamsii* had been declining rapidly in the western deserts, due mostly to its unauthorized harvesting by individuals not connected to traditional Native American peyotism. One scholar labeled the shortage a "crisis" for the Native American Church, and proposed greenhouse cultivation of the plant as a possible solution, since a 1994 amendment to the federal peyote-exemption law allowed farming the cactus on Native American land.

In the early 1980s the Peyote Way Church began construction of the first peyote greenhouse on the ranch. Two more of the structures have been erected on the land since then, and they currently house tens of thousands of seedlings, juvenile plants, and mature cacti. The "Sustainable Peyotism Project," as it is called, has raised almost $100,000 to date from donors in its mission to save the plant from extinction.

The greenhouse project requires long-term planning and commitment, not only because of the logistical hassles of getting workers and supplies out to the remote ranch, but because peyote cacti can require up to twenty years of growth before they mature fully. One of the structures is called "The Grandchildren's Greenhouse," since the patiently cultivated peyote there will someday be offered to Rabbi Kent and Reverend Zapf's grandchildren when both the plants and the kids reach maturity.

Now approaching their seventies, the couple carry on the late Immanuel Pardeahtan Trujillo's mission, both at the ranch and elsewhere. They are training a new generation of clergy and stewards to take on the duties of cultivating peyote, shepherding Spirit Walkers on the land, and disseminating the Peyote Way message to the world via the church's website, social media, and psychedelics-related meetings and conferences. The church remains a contentious subject among Native American Church faithful, many of whom regard Trujillo and his successors as cultural appropriators, but in recent years some traditional peyotists have reached out to Peyote Way clergy, seeking common ground and open communication.

With its well-stocked greenhouses, its ever-improving ranch facilities, and its (generally) unmolested legal status in Arizona, the Peyote Way Church of God is a testament to the vision and hard work of its creative, passionate, and sometimes-enigmatic founder. There's no doubt that seekers will continue to travel the long, rough road to the Aravaipa Valley for many years to come, to partake of the plant and walk in Spirit, much as North America's original inhabitants have since time immemorial.

FOUR

THE OKLEVUEHA NATIVE AMERICAN CHURCH

Bringing Many Medicines to the White Man

James Warren "Flaming Eagle" Mooney may be the most prolific psychedelic-church planter in history.

The Utah resident and retired cop is the founder of the Oklevueha Native American Church, an organization that has established hundreds of local chapters across the United States, all chartered under his authority.

Despite its name, the Oklevueha Native American Church has no formal connection to the far older, larger, and better-known indigenous American peyote sect. In fact, representatives of the "official" Native American Church network have denounced Mooney and his organization and charged him with everything from faking his Native American heritage, to profiting from religion, to pandering to non–Native American druggies with his multientheogen ministry. As Mooney succinctly put it, "Most of the Native American Churches hate my guts."[1]

The law has been no kinder. His status as a former policeman notwithstanding, Mooney has been arrested for violating Schedule I drug prohibitions and was even the defendant in a landmark Utah State Supreme Court ruling on religious peyote possession and use.

FLAMING EAGLE

So, who is the man behind the Oklevueha Native American Church—the psychedelic sect that endorses not only peyote, but a wide variety of entheogens as official sacraments, and whose local chapters have experienced everything from the creation of "temples of sexual healing," to deadly shootouts?

According to his testimony, James Mooney was born on January 3, 1944, in Grass Valley, California. At the age of three, when he was visiting his grandparents in Missouri, he was assaulted and beaten by a gang of boys, who tried to drown him in a pond. Although his grandmother rescued him, the little boy was comatose and near death, so she and her husband erected a small sweat lodge and carried the child into it.

After many hours inside the lodge sweating, chanting, and praying, James's grandmother and grandfather saw that the boy had returned to full consciousness. Picking up the child, his grandfather lifted him skyward, prayed to the Four Directions, and said, "We present our grandson, 'Flaming Eagle,' . . . Mary Ella and I have done our part. He is now yours to do with what you may."[2]

When James's mother remarried, they moved to Southern California. Mooney recalled that in his childhood, his stepfather Walt Perkins painted artwork depicting buffalo-hunting Indians on his bedroom wall, as if to remind him of his roots. The young boy took his stepfather's surname, and went by "Jim Perkins" until 1969, when a background check on him revealed his birth family name. Since then, he's been known as James Warren Mooney.

James Mooney spent his early adulthood in Hawaii's restaurant and hotel industries. Later, he branched out into business consulting, and soon became an in-demand advisor for enterprises on three continents. He also joined the Mormon church when he moved to Utah.

But Mooney's career and personal life fell apart in the eighties. During that period his wife Irene developed cancer and died after a nine-month struggle. Mooney suffered from severe bipolar disorder, and it eventually got so bad that the 1800 mg of lithium he took daily to treat it didn't make him functional enough to hold a job or raise his seven children, who were taken away from him and made wards of the Latter-Day Saints church.

Mooney was unemployed and living at the home of a friend when a call came for him. The caller was Chief Little Dove Buford of the Oklevueha Band of Seminole Indians, who told him her tribe had been looking for him for over twenty years. The chief informed Mooney that according to a complex family tree, he was a direct descendant of both Osceola, a.k.a. William "Billy" Powell (1804–1838), the Seminole Indian war chief and medicine man, and James Mooney (1861–1921), the White cofounder of the Native American Church. Chief Little Dove said that if she could connect her lineage to his, it would fill a gap in the historical and genealogical record and allow her tribe to receive federal recognition.

NATIVE AMERICAN MEDICINE

When Mooney described his dismal situation to the chief, she told him that Native American medicine could cure him. Skeptical, he nevertheless accompanied his housemate Linda to a Long Dance ceremony in southern Utah. There he met Gwen, a massage therapist who introduced him to a local Native American Church Roadman named Clifford Jake, who had treated her successfully with peyote.

Mooney attended six Half Moon peyote ceremonies on the Paiute Shivwits Band Reservation with Jake. Although they revived his spirits, nothing seemed to address his deeper psychological pains until he traveled south to the Navajo Reservation and took the Medicine. As Mooney remembers it:

> The Diné Tipi Half Moon ceremony was conducted very similarly to Clifford's ceremonies with one exception: the Roadman's wife was the cedar person. She did most, if not all, of the healing works. For the first time, I made a ceremony intention to live a much more balanced life.
>
> Up until the midnight water blessing, my experience of this particular ceremony was very similar to my previous ceremonies. However, when the water was finally taken out of the Tipi, I

suddenly became extremely ill, vomiting uncontrollably. My body, all of its muscles, joints, ached excruciatingly. I rolled around in this pain for four to five hours. I sensed people were very concerned for my wellbeing. I was aware of the Cedar Woman coming to my aid a number of times. When the Roadman attempted to give me more medicine, I refused to receive it.

As soon as the sun came up, the pain and anguish suddenly left my body, leaving me feeling more exalted and peaceful than I had ever experienced before in my life.[3]

Mooney told Jake about the meeting, and the Roadman accompanied him to three more peyote ceremonies. At each one Mooney writhed in agony for several hours, and relief came only with sunrise. Finally, Clifford staged a private peyote healing for Mooney, and during yet another excruciating episode, the Roadman gave his suffering friend a peyote button that he'd blessed personally.

Years later, Mooney said that from the moment he put the plant in his mouth, he was overwhelmed by an indescribable feeling of peace that has stayed with him since that night. He also married Gwen, his third wife, and the two spent several years living in a tipi in Utah's Snow Canyon.

THE BIRTH OF A MEDICINE MAN

When Mooney visited Clifford two months later to thank him for the healing, he asked permission to take the Medicine to the White man. Clifford refused, saying that if Mooney did so, "the Indians will try to kill you and the white man will throw you into jail." It turned out to be a fairly accurate prediction.

The Roadman did take him on as an apprentice and spent over a decade teaching Mooney his medicine ways. Mooney also took counsel from LDS church leaders on how to practice American Indian spiritual path in a way that didn't conflict with his Mormon faith. And he was told by Chief Little Dove that although the Seminole didn't do peyote ceremonies, she approved of his path, and charged him to never refuse anyone asking for help or healing.

Mooney's first work as a fledgling medicine man was in prison. He volunteered to conduct sweat lodge ceremonies at Utah's Central Utah Correctional Facility, helping Native American inmates purge the physical and psychic poisons that had landed them there. So effective was his work there that then-Governor Michael Leavitt honored him with a Citizen's Award of Commendation in 1994. That same year he accepted a full-time position with the Utah Department of Corrections and married his fourth wife, Linda.

Mooney did undercover work for the department on drug cases. Although he never used the medicine in the prison or on the job, his superiors disapproved of the private peyote ceremonies he held for any-one who requested them. Mooney withdrew from narc work when he learned that a band of Huichol Indian peyotists who had been forced to grow cannabis for Mexican drug cartels were about to be busted with the help of his agency. Fired in 1997, he sued the state for wrongful termination, later accepting a $50,000 settlement.

That year also saw the end of Mooney's relationship with the Native American Church of North America. A member of the church's Salt Lake City branch, he became its vice president, and acted as "Custodian of the Medicine" when he traveled to Texas to buy peyote from autho-rized vendors there. But when church president Emerson Jackson ordered Mooney to call the cops on any peyotists who weren't rec-ognized American Indian tribe members, he again chose the role of entheogenic healer over institutional enforcer and quit the NAC.

"TO UNEARTH THE CREATORS SPIRIT"

Determined to bring peyote healing to the world at large, Mooney and his wife, Linda "Bright Hawk," formed the Oklevueha Earthwalks Native American Church of Utah that year. Incorporated on April 11, 1997, as a nonprofit Utah corporation, the ONAC, as it is popularly known, stated in its charter that it "Exists to Unearth the Creators Spirit, in Our Hearts and Heritage, for all of our Relations," and that its ideology was one of "Charity, Forgiveness, Humility, Gratitude, Faith, Respect, and Honor."[4]

The ONAC maintained that it celebrated all indigenous ceremonies, including "Birth, Breath, Holy Anointing, Marriage, Passing Over, Prayer Pipe, Sacrament, Spirit Dance, Sun Dance, Sweat Lodge, and Vision Quest." Because many of these ceremonies would "facilitate extreme mental, emotional and physical transformations," members and medicine people alike were held to a strict code of understandings and responsibilities designed to guarantee the health, safety, and personal dignity of all participants, especially regarding the vulnerability and suggestibility commonly experienced by entheogen users.

Two aspects of ONAC belief and practice would make Mooney and the church the objects of much controversy. One was that although the church's prime sacrament was peyote, it also recognized cannabis and other "sacred plant medicines" in its healing practices. Mooney, who'd received a blessing for his work from famed Huichol shaman and peyotist Guadalupe Rios de la Cruz, noted that the Mexican Indian tribe often used cannabis in conjunction with its healing rites, and reasoned that it, and psychoactive substances like ayahuasca, psilocybin, San Pedro cactus (*Trichocereus* species), and others were all provided by the Earth for sacramental use by her children.

The ONAC also welcomed people of all races, religions, nationalities, and lifestyles to not only its ceremonies, but to train and work as medicine men and women, and to establish local branches of the church. American Indian tribes had fought a century-long legal battle with federal and state governments for the right to conduct peyote ceremonies, and it was felt by many NAC members, and American Indians in general, that their First Amendment victories had been won for their community alone, and that bringing non–Native Americans into peyotism disrespected the struggles of indigenous peoples to preserve their ways.

"TAKE THIS MEDICINE TO THE WHITE MAN"

Within a year after founding the ONAC, American Indians had twice threatened Mooney with death for allowing White people into Native American ceremonies. When a third threat promised death to Mooney, his wife, and children unless he ceased his spiritual activities, the ONAC chief sought advice from a licensed peyote vendor, who told him to get a blessing from Leslie Fool Bull, the leader of the Rosebud Sioux Tribe's long-established Native American Church.

Mooney and an associate traveled to Rapid City, South Dakota, where the aging, ailing Fool Bull was bedridden in hospital. When Mooney approached his hospital bed, the elderly Lakota Sioux Roadman recognized that his visitor needed help and accepted an offering of a bag of peyote buttons from him. Tears in his eyes, Fool Bull held the bag to his heart, uttered a blessing in Lakota, and then translated his words for Mooney: "Take this medicine to the White Man." A simple "Blessing for Peyote Church" card, witnessed and dated by Fool Bull's son and Mooney's cohort, is displayed on the ONAC website as proof of this authorization to administer the sacrament outside Native American circles.

For the ONAC, this was a vital endorsement. According to Mooney, the Rosebud Reservation has a unique legal status with the U.S. government where the land and people are considered legally inseparable. Because of this, the Rosebud Native American Church was considered an organic part of the reservation, and not bound to American

Fig. 4.1. An Oklevueha Native American Church peyote ceremony.
Photograph by James Mooney.

laws that governed religions or organizations. Although its NAC later legally incorporated, Mooney says that Fool Bull's blessing, and a later relationship he established with Ogala Chief Richard "He Who Has the Foundation" Swallow, gave the ONAC an unassailable legal and spiritual pedigree—one that means they're exempt from having an IRS 501(c)(3) authorization.

FIFTEEN FELONIES

Thus sanctified, Mooney continued his medicine work, offering peyote and other ceremonial healings to all who requested them. A corporate executive, grateful for the six months of healing work Mooney had done with him, donated $500,000 to the ONAC, and the church leader used most of the money to buy a large house in Benjamin, Utah. Although he insisted the property would eventually be used as an ONAC retreat and spent $25,000 on plans for a healing facility that could host over 1,000 people on its six acres, about half of Mooney's followers abandoned him, angered by what they saw as a televangelist-style misappropriation of donations.

The law began to take interest in Mooney's doings as well. In 1997 the Utah County Sheriff's Office investigated a report that the ONAC head was administering peyote illegally. Although the investigation cleared Mooney of any wrongdoing, a second one in 2000 reported that Mooney had lost his membership in the Florida Seminole tribe, and could no longer be considered a registered Native American, authorized to hold peyote ceremonies.

The ONAC leader said a schism in the Seminole tribe had led some, but not all, of its members to disavow his membership, and investigators had gotten their information from one of the anti-Mooney members. The sheriff's office nevertheless issued a warrant to search his home, and when they arrived, they seized a package of peyote Mooney had received in the mail, along with computers, donation slips, and cash. Although Mooney warned the officers that the items were church, rather than personal property, and that the raid was illegal, the district attorney instructed them to continue the search, and Mooney and his wife were arrested and charged with fifteen felonies.

The Utah County Attorney's Office also issued a report that said there was no genealogical evidence Mooney was an American Indian. Mooney countered, saying that many of his lighter-skinned ancestors had declared themselves White on birth certificates and census forms, since Seminoles often believed that the U.S. government's war on them had never ended, and they stood to be persecuted or even murdered if they were identified as American Indians.

Whatever the truth of his ancestry, Mooney and his wife were still charged with being drug traffickers. Mooney was excommunicated from the Mormon church, and when his own church was labeled as an illegal enterprise, donations dried up, and it was forced to declare bankruptcy.

In September 2001 a district court ruled against the Mooneys. Rejecting their religious-freedom defense, it held that neither of the couple were registered with a federally recognized Indian tribe, and that the exemption provided to Native Americans for peyote use didn't apply to non–Native Americans.

THE SUPREMES RULE

The next year, Mooney appealed to the Utah State Supreme Court. His attorney Kathryn Collard argued that membership in a "Native American church," rather than one's race, was the key element of the religious-peyote exemption. The court agreed, and *State of Utah v. Mooney et al.* ruled that membership in such a church alone guaranteed the right of an individual to use the cactus sacrament.

But Mooney and the ONAC weren't out of the legal woods yet. After the state ruling was issued, the federal government charged the Mooneys with possession and distribution of a Schedule I drug. Oddly enough, the charges were dropped on February 22, 2006—the day after the Supreme Court ruled in *Gonzales v. O Centro Espírita Beneficente União do Vegetal* that a Brazilian sect's New Mexico branch could legally use sacramental hallucinogenic ayahuasca tea in its rites, in federal jurisdictions.

Although it's tempting to draw a connection between the cases, Mooney believes otherwise. He told me that he thinks the federal government, which thoroughly researched his family tree and confirmed his American Indian ancestry, realized that any attempt to bring the case to court would expose not only the appalling history of the government's attempts to destroy American Indian religious culture, but the ultimate unconstitutionality of *all* U.S. drug laws. The Feds, he said, opted to quietly ignore the ONAC.

THE PSYCHEDELIC CHURCH PLANTER

Remembering his charge by Leslie Fool Bull to bring medicine to the White man, and Chief Little Dove Buford's to never refuse anyone in need of healing, Mooney pressed forward with the ONAC. Taking advantage of twenty-first-century communication technology, he started a website for the church that explained its beliefs and practices and listed his own qualifications as a Native American healer and spiritual leader. Anyone who sent in $200 and agreed to abide by the church's code of ethics received an ONAC membership card that made them "'members' of a bona fide Native American Church [who] have the constitutional rights and protection to worship with any and all earth-based Sacraments 'especially Peyote.'"[5]

Of course, it was impossible for Mooney and his close associates to travel all over the United States to conduct ceremonies with members. So, the church also offered a "Native American Branch" package "for those seeking to grow the church and conduct sacred ceremonies as well as providing a place for others to learn and grow in the Native American Indigenous culture."

For a donation of $2,495 the ONAC provided a portal website based on its main site but customized for a local branch. The package included a shopping cart that allowed the branch to sign up affiliate members for a share of the $200 fee, and an online store platform where it could sell its own wares alongside official church merchandise using a PayPal account.

In other words, anyone with $2,495 who signed on with the church could create their own local chapter of it, share in donations, and run their own entheogenic ceremonies under the First Amendment protections the ONAC claimed. Looking back, Mooney told me that he was so committed to his mission of unconditionally spreading medicine healing, that he didn't realize what potential trouble this system would cause for him and the church.

Many local ONAC branches were started by sincere individuals committed to ceremonial plant-medicine work. Typically, they were located on existing rural retreats, and offered a wide variety of healing practices ranging from sound therapy to Reiki, to yoga, along with the more traditional Native American ceremonies. In keeping with ONAC policy, entheogenic ceremonies would be offered to paid church members, and many local branches used a variety of sacraments, ranging from peyote, to ayahuasca, to cannabis.

SCHISMS AND TROUBLES

Other branches, however, spun off from the mother church body to create religious corporations that diverged from Mooney's Native-American healing ideals. In New Mexico, Gavin Kaiser's ONAC chapter reincorporated as the Oratory of Mystical Sacraments (see page 303), a psychedelic sect that drew its inspiration from Western-esoteric teachings rather than American Indian wisdom. In Florida, Anthony B. James's ONAC group reinvented itself as the Native American Indigenous Church (see page 299), and became part of a diverse network of spiritual, educational, and medical organizations James managed or affiliated with, ranging from an Ayurveda medicine school to a non-papal "Catholic" church.

The most painful schism of all came when Mooney's son, Michael Rex "Raging Bear" Mooney, split with the ONAC in 2009 to start his own Native American Church of Hawaii. The younger Mooney, who spent several years fighting the Hawaiian state and federal governments over the right to use cannabis in church ceremonies, left the ONAC since he felt that his father's group had "cheapened itself" by selling memberships and church charters to anyone on the internet. In response, the elder Mooney called his son a "thug," further distancing their familial and ecclesiastical connections.

Some California ONAC branches were raided when local law enforcement suspected they were using their nonprofit status to dodge taxes or circumvent the laws that regulated the state's legal cannabis sales. Costa Mesa's ONAC chapter was shut down when police charged it with being an illegal cannabis dispensary rather than a religious organization. San Jose's Oklevueha Native American Church in South Bay was also charged with selling pot for tax-free "donations." And Antioch's local branch was closed when authorities said its center violated zoning ordinances by being within 600 feet of two elementary schools.

SHOOTOUTS, TOPLESS CARWASHES, AND TEMPLES OF SEXUAL HEALING

Far worse troubles plagued Sacramento's "ONAC Sugarleaf Rastafarian Church." Started by antiprohibition activist Heidi Grossman-Lepp, the chapter set up a network of local affiliate churches where its cannabis sacrament was both grown and consumed. At one of them, an itinerant laborer who'd been hired to harvest the property's plants got into a gun battle with two sheriff's deputies; when the smoke cleared, he was dead, and the two officers were hospitalized.* Over the next few weeks lawmen raided Sugarleaf-connected farms across the state, destroying plants and arresting eighteen people.

Perhaps the most unusual ONAC branches that Mooney chartered during this period were four "temples of sexual healing." One of them, Tracy Elise's Phoenix Goddess Temple, got raided when Arizona authorities decided it was not a house of worship, but one of prostitution where male patrons gave cash donations for intimate contact with the temple's priestesses.

When Elise went to trial, Mooney testified in her defense. During his testimony, he demonstrated how the traditional Indian pipe ceremony symbolized sexual congress, since it was a "tantric combination of male, represented by the pipe, and female, represented by the pipe's bowl." He also said that the temple practiced "the anointing oil ceremony that native people have been doing forever"[7] in its rites and was therefore a legitimate religion. The court disagreed, and sentenced Elise to four and a half years for a variety of felonies.

---

*The injured deputies were the beneficiaries of a Yuba City strip club's fundraiser for their medical bills. A story about the benefit began with what must have been 2017's greatest news headline: "Topless Carwash Raises Cash for Deputies Wounded in Gun Battle at Rastafarian Pot Farm."[6]

Even unluckier than Elise was thirty-three-year-old Lindsay Poole. During an ayahuasca ceremony at ONAC of the Peaceful Mountain in Berea, Kentucky, she fell and died from her injuries. The local courts declined to press criminal charges, but the incident further stained the ONAC's image in the public eye.

"ANYTHING THAT CAN PRODUCE A MIND-ALTERING STATE IS PROTECTED"

The ONAC found few friends among traditional American Indian peyotists, or defenders of indigenous spiritual practices. Sandor Iron Rope, the president of the National Council of Native American Churches, condemned the ONAC in a 2016 interview, where he said the group's endorsement of cannabis and sex temples disrespected his own church's "tribal teachings that come down from our grandma and grandpa. We're not in a New Age paradigm where we create our own religion and grab anything and put it on our altar and say it's sacred. You can call anything sacred, but we have a tribal lineage and teaching that tells us what actually is and isn't."[8]

Iron Rope was one of several Native American Church leaders who signed a statement to publicly "oppose the attempts of non-Natives to come in and misuse government protection of traditional Native American religion to conduct illegal activity that has nothing to do with our traditional ways." Without specifically mentioning the ONAC, the signees stated,

> We reject and condemn any claim by these illegitimate organizations that marijuana or any other plant serves or has ever served as a sacrament in addition to peyote in indigenous Native American Church ceremonies," and asserted that "the mere use of the term Native American Church does not entitle any of these illicit organizations to any legal protection under federal law.[9]

When Michael Mooney's Native American Church of Hawaii came before the Ninth Circuit Court in a dispute over their legal right to use sacramental cannabis, the National Council of Native

American Churches filed an amicus brief with the court. The brief, which asked the court to designate peyote as the only legitimate sacrament in Native American Church doctrine, was an obvious legal strike at not only Michael's Hawaiian sect, but at his father's panentheogenic church. The filing was tabled, but the Court ruled against the younger Mooney anyway.

Another strong critic of the Mooneys and their sects was Native American Rights Fund attorney Steven Moore. In a series of articles about the churches' legal troubles, he told *Courthouse News Service* reporter Karin Brown that the father and son were "creating a new set of religious doctrine here under a belief system where anything that can produce a mind-altering state is protected. And they're saying it's protected under their status as a Native American Church." He maintained that the Mooneys were "conjuring up self-proclaimed religions for their own profit and ego-gratification, under the guise of the 'Native American Church,' when that name carries real weight and legitimacy under federal law. Their motives are transparent and illegitimate."[10]

For his part, Mooney denounced the Native American Rights Fund as a "corrupt" organization, and his Native American critics as malcontents living in an ethnocentric bubble. He pointed out that the ONAC was the only church authorized to conduct Indigenous Native American ceremonies within the U.S. Navy. Mooney also asserted that the Mexican government recognized the church's cultural exchange program with the Huichol Nation, and that the ancient and prestigious Military and Hospitaller Order of Saint Lazarus of Jerusalem had chosen him as its official representative to the world's indigenous peoples and cultures. The endorsements of these august, well-established institutions were enough for Mooney.

MEDICINE MAN EMERITUS

Still, the septuagenarian peyotist was getting tired of answering his critics and dealing with ONAC's trouble-ridden chapters. In 2016 he retired from the church's temporal activities and declared himself Medicine Man Emeritus—an elder and adviser.

ONAC administration is now handled by a committee, and the

screening process for prospective new branches has been tightened up immensely. The church's website now emphasizes the duties and responsibilities of new members, with Codes of Ethics and Conduct designed to discourage anyone seeking to use the ONAC as an excuse for recreational drug use or exploitative behavior.

The ONAC's website currently lists only about forty branches in good standing with the mother church and warns against organizations that fraudulently use the Oklevueha name. One of them is the so-called ONAC of Antelope Valley, a Southern California "Cannabis Church" that makes the sacrament available at a drive-thru kiosk.

Mooney shared with me that even though he no longer works in ONAC's day-to-day operations, the reformed church is doing better than ever, with paid members all over the world. He looks forward to the day when there are global church branches dedicated to ceremonial use of indigenous entheogens, whether they be South American ayahuasca, European *Amanita muscaria* mushrooms, or African and Asian cannabis.

To Mooney, the idea that one ethnicity or nation legally "owns" a plant medicine is abhorrent and absurd. Someday, he hopes, the peoples of the world will reject the authority of the state and other institutions that seek to circumscribe and control the entheogenic experience and find healing and spiritual rebirth with the aid of Earth's cornucopia of "teacher plants."

FIVE

THE LEAGUE FOR SPIRITUAL DISCOVERY

Turning On and Tuning In with Timothy Leary

No human being in history has ever been more closely identified with entheogens, and their use as spiritual sacraments than Timothy Francis Leary (1920–1996). The revolutionary psychologist, whom President Richard Nixon would call "the most dangerous man in America," began the tumultuous sixties as a respected Harvard academic and mental-health researcher. He ended the decade as the face of the global psychedelic movement, beloved by the counterculture, loathed by the establishment, and facing a ten-year prison sentence for the possession of a tiny quantity of cannabis.

Along the way he founded no fewer than three different organizations dedicated to the research and pursuit of consciousness expansion through chemical means. The first was oriented to scientific study, the second to psychological growth, and the third to the use of LSD as a religious sacrament.

TIMOTHY LEARY: PSYCHOLOGY, PHYSICS, AND PERSONALITY

Leary, who grew up in a middle-class Boston Irish Catholic household, attended both West Point and the University of Alabama in his young adulthood. After a stint in the U.S. Army during World War II, he earned a bachelor's in psychology, married, and fathered two children.

In the spirit of the postwar era, Leary looked with favor on the rapid advances in peacetime science and technology. Modern physics especially intrigued him, and Leary attained a UC–Berkeley psychology doctorate with a 1950 dissertation where he posited that psychotherapists should be able to classify and quantify any behavioral characteristics or interpersonal change, as precisely as physicists did for elements in the periodic table.

Leary settled into fifties life as a comfortable, accomplished family man and professional. He became an assistant professor of psychology at UC–San Francisco, and cofounded Kaiser Hospital's psychology department, where he also ran a pioneering study of psychoneurotic patients. In that study he coined the term *psychlotron* to describe the group-therapy sessions he ran where "human elements could be freed, accelerated to higher states of intensity, and recorded."[1]

Yet Leary felt increasingly like a misfit in the regimented, conformist worlds of academia and health care. Both he and his wife, Marianne, began to drink heavily and have extramarital affairs, and her suicide in 1955 sent Leary into an existential tailspin that not even the heralded publication of his book *Interpersonal Diagnosis of Personality* two years later could shake. A sojourn to Spain with his children, where he attempted to write another book, resulted in a full-scale nervous breakdown, accompanied by excruciating physical symptoms that Leary later likened to a near-death experience.

THE MEXICAN MAGIC MUSHROOM TRIP

In 1959 Leary accepted a position at Harvard as a clinical lecturer and joined the university's Center for Personality Research. One of his center sponsors, a former UC–Berkeley colleague named Frank Barron, knew of Leary's interest in new behavioral-change techniques, and told him about a bag of mushrooms he'd brought back from Mexico that gave him "William Blake revelations, mystical insights, and transcendental perspectives"[2] when he consumed them.

Two years earlier, *Life* magazine had published a photo essay by retired banker and amateur mycologist R. Gordon Wasson that described his 1955 experience taking psilocybin mushrooms in a Mexican Mazatec ceremony. Wasson, who was given the fungi by a Mazatec shaman named Maria Sabina, was one of the first Whites to describe its hallucinogenic effects after ingesting it. The 1957 *Life* article created interest in the mushrooms among scientists as well as tourists, and Barron was just one of many people who brought the fungi back from Mexican vacations.

Although initially skeptical of Barron's claims, Leary was open-minded enough to try the fungi for himself. While on summer break at a Cuernavaca, Mexico, villa, he was visited by East German scholar Lothar Knauth, who had obtained a supply of psilocybin mushrooms from a local. Remembering Barron's testimony, on August 9, 1960, Leary, along with Knauth, his girlfriend, and her adult daughter, all gathered around the villa pool and chewed up handfuls of the earthy, foul-tasting fungi.

Fig. 5.1. Psilocybin mushrooms. Timothy Leary took his first trip into psychedelic space with this type of mushroom in Mexico on August 9, 1960.

Photograph courtesy of AirGrib.

When the effects of the seven mushrooms he'd consumed hit, they initially reminded Leary of nitrous oxide. As the trip deepened, however, he began to feel as if he was floating through an "air-sea" on rubber legs. Then Leary began to see "jeweled patterns, swirling tapestry work in closed eyes,"[3] as well as fantastic visions of Egyptian palaces, Chinese temples, Babylonian harems, flaming mosaics, and bejeweled reptiles. At the height of the trip, he envisioned himself as Earth's first living creature, writhing up from a bed of slime into the dark depths of the primeval ocean.

The experience changed the thirty-nine-year-old academic forever. The next day when fellow Harvard lecturer Richard Alpert visited the villa, Leary told him, "I learned more in the six or seven hours of this experience than in all my years as a psychologist."[4] To Leary, the trip was an ego-shattering destruction of the perceptual, mental, and emotional "machinery" that had trapped him in a world of surface appearances, meaningless abstractions, and petty desires—a "classic visionary voyage" that would soon make him the most famous and influential entheogenic evangelist in history.

THE HARVARD PSILOCYBIN PROJECT

When he returned to Harvard, Timothy Leary set up a series of experiments with then-legal synthetic psilocybin supplied by Sandoz Pharmaceuticals. Later known as the Harvard Psilocybin Project, the eighteen-month-long study examined the effects of the chemical on artists, writers, graduate students, and "normal people" alike, and was run by Leary, Richard Alpert, and Frank Barron. Subjects who took the chemical completed questionnaires and wrote accounts about their experiences that were entered in the study's database.

Some of the study participants were leading lights in the Beat subculture. Poets Allen Ginsberg and Peter Orlovsky, novelists Jack Kerouac and William S. Burroughs, and future Merry Pranksters bus driver Neal Cassady all took psilocybin as part of the project. So did *Darkness of Noon* author Arthur Koestler and Aldous Huxley, whose 1954 bestseller *The Doors of Perception* had described his experience with mescaline.

Test subjects would eventually number 167 trippers. Among them were a group of 32 inmates at Concord State Prison, whom Leary and a German-born graduate student named Ralph Metzner suspected might be less inclined to continue "the cops 'n' robbers game" if psilocybin trips were added to their rehabilitation programs. Although the recidivism-rate results of the prison experiment were disputed, an astonishing 95 percent of project participants overall reported the chemical had changed their lives for the better.

THE MIRACLE AT MARSH CHAPEL

The project's most famous experiment took place at Boston University's Marsh Chapel. Walter Pahnke, a Harvard Divinity School graduate student, wanted to know if psilocybin could induce the same mystical states in educated American Christians that it did in Mexican Indian campesinos.

So, under the supervision of Leary and Richard Alpert, Pahnke assembled twenty Andover Newton Theological School grad students in Marsh Chapel on Good Friday of 1962. Half of the students—the control group—were given a placebo of niacin, while the other half received 30-mg doses of Sandoz psilocybin. Leary, who believed that therapists should lead by example and undergo the same treatment as their charges, was present, and dosed with psilocybin.

Soon it was obvious who had gotten the psychedelic secret sauce, and who hadn't. While minister and civil-rights leader Howard Thurman, resplendent in robes and vestments, conducted a three-hour worship service, ten of the subjects sat attentively, while the other ten lay sprawled out on the benches and the floor, or wandered around the chapel murmuring prayers, chanting hymns, or playing weird tunes on the chapel organ. One of the tripping students received a message from God to the world, wandered out onto the street to proclaim it, and had to be walked back to the chapel and restrained.

Twenty-five years later, psychedelics researcher Rick Doblin followed up on the Marsh Chapel subjects and reported that save for the man who'd wandered out of the chapel, every single psilocybin recipient remembered the day as "a genuine mystical experience . . . [with] positive long-lasting impact on their lives."[5]

As for Leary, he hosted a party that evening at his house for the subjects, still "high and glowing and talking about God." Looking back on what was later known as the Marsh Chapel, or Good Friday, Experiment, Leary claimed that day, he and Pahnke had obtained "proof—scientific, experimental, statistical, objective [that] Psychedelic drugs were sacraments."[6]

A SPECIAL JAR OF SUGAR

Leary's new role as a psychedelic missionary alarmed many of his Harvard cohorts. One particularly strong critic was Center for Personality Research head David McLelland, who'd heard "horrific stories" about what went on at Leary's rented Newton Center home—stories that made the project sound less like a disciplined scientific enterprise, and more like a months-long drug party. In a memo he delivered to a faculty meeting, McLelland noted the project leaders' "repeated casual ingestions of the drug," and inferred that it was making them sloppy and irresponsible with their subjects and findings.

Part of the trouble may have been due to a new, volatile element that had appeared in the lives of Leary and his associates. In October 1961 a mysterious Englishman named Michael Hollingshead got in touch with Leary, and told him he was hugely interested in psychedelics, was broke, and needed a place to stay. After Leary got Hollingshead a job teaching a Harvard graduate course, and let him move into his house's attic, the Englishman brought over his few possessions, one of which was a mayonnaise jar filled with a white, sugary paste.

The paste was a few ounces of confectioner's sugar laced with a gram of Sandoz Laboratories LSD-25. Developed by Swiss chemist Albert Hofmann in 1938, and known chemically as lysergic acid diethylamide, LSD's properties were not discovered until April 19, 1943, when Hofmann accidentally ingested about 250 micrograms of the chemical. The tiny dose rocketed the chemist into the world's first acid trip, where he experienced overwhelming feelings of joy, paranoia, and hilarity, as well as bizarre distortions of his senses and perceptions.

Four years later Sandoz introduced LSD to the pharmaceutical market and promised physicians and hospitals it would cure everything from schizophrenia, to alcoholism, to sexual perversion. The drug's biggest buyer was the CIA, who purchased Sandoz's entire supply in the early 1950s and began to distribute the drug through its front organizations to doctors, scientists, and psychologists.

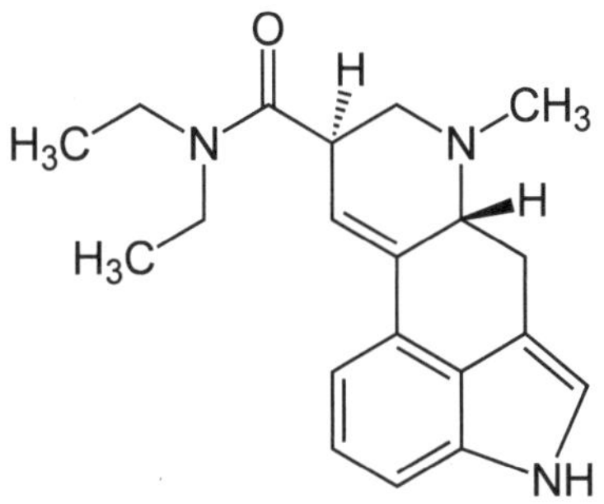

Fig. 5.2. The chemical structure of lysergic acid diethylamide (LSD)
Image courtesy of Jü.

The CIA was interested in LSD's potential to manipulate human consciousness, so that it could be weaponized for military or intelligence uses. Through a network of connected physicians and academics, the agency ran extensive experiments on human subjects ranging from ordinary citizens to military personnel, to prostitutes and prisoners, most of whom were unaware that they'd been dosed with the world's most powerful hallucinogen.

The program, which the spooks called MKULTRA, was only revealed to the public during 1975 congressional hearings about the CIA. Countless program records were destroyed before investigators could get to them, and the full extent of its doings is still unknown. And although nobody has ever definitively linked Hollingshead to intelligence-agency skullduggery, his arrival in Leary's world with the equivalent of 5,000 doses of LSD, precisely when the psilocybin experiments were going full blast, has raised eyebrows among historians.

"THE WHIRLING DANCE OF PURE ENERGY"

Metzner and Alpert mistrusted Hollingshead and called him a "con man" and "evil," but Leary was smitten by the enigmatic Englishman. Hollingshead gleefully told Leary of his acid experiences and urged him to try the chemical, but the Harvardian was apprehensive at first. He didn't trust a chemical that lacked the organic basis or long history of safe human usage that psilocybin had.

Finally, at his house in December 1961, Leary gave in, and sampled a spoonful of Hollingshead's sugar paste. Within an hour, the Harvard academic went "out beyond life into the whirling dance of pure energy, where nothing existed except whirring vibrations, and each illusory form was simply a different frequency."[7]

Leary later called the all-night trip "the most shattering experience of my life." It was a death-and-rebirth journey where he envisioned and embodied the entirety of human existence, and "moved beyond the game of psychology, the game of trying to help people, and the game of conventional love relationships."[8] Psilocybin had been merely the preparatory stage for a total transformation of his mind and soul, and Leary now believed lysergic acid could turn the world on to a new, higher form of consciousness and living.

When Sandoz stopped sending Leary and his cohorts psilocybin, they replaced it in both their scientific and recreational usages with Hollingshead's LSD. Things began to get very weird around the Newton Center house, with days-long psychedelic parties and acid-fueled sexual couplings between random attendees. Rumors that undergrads— off-limits to the experiment—were visiting the house and sampling the chemical wares swirled through Cambridge.

The project and Leary were becoming major points of contention on the Harvard campus. On March 15, 1962, Center for Personality Research head David McLelland held a meeting to determine the current nature of Leary's work, and whether it constituted either a legitimate scientific study, a hedonistic drug cult, or an unstable melding of the two.

Government agencies began to get involved as well. Even though psilocybin and LSD were legal at the time, agents from the State Health Department, the FDA, and the FBI alike investigated Leary, who invited them to participate in the experiments and decide for themselves if they were legitimate. Under pressure from the investigators and McLelland, Leary agreed to turn the project and its supply of psilocybin over to the university and a "sober" physician.

ZIHUANTANEJO, IFIF, AND CARIBBEAN CAPERS

Perhaps feeling that the sunny climes of southern Mexico would be more conducive to such research work than cold, uptight Massachusetts, Leary and Alpert, along with Mellon family heiress Peggy Hitchcock, decamped to the then-sleepy fishing village of Zihuantanejo in April 1962. There the trio located a hotel manager who said he could let them take over his property, the Catalina Hotel, during the slow months of July and August.

The three agreed to his terms and returned that summer with a supply of LSD, and thirty-three people who had signed up to explore higher consciousness under the Harvard professors' supervision. Every day, one-third of the hotel guests would take the chemical, while another third would guide them, with the remaining third recovering from their previous day's trips and providing data and reports to the research team. Leary later described the scene as idyllic, with trippers "walking along the beach, body surfing, meditating, or lazing in hammocks strung along the terrace. At night the grounds were alive with color, fires burned in the sand, guitars and flutes filled the air."[9]

At the end of six weeks, Leary said goodbye to Zihuantanejo with an all-night farewell party, and an acid-and-beer-powered softball game between the visitors and the locals. When they returned to Cambridge, Leary and a dozen of the retreat attendees moved into a new, large house in Newton Center, where they lived together and continued to explore the psychedelic world under the auspices of psychological study.

Feeling increasingly constricted by Harvard, Leary and his associates formed their own psychedelic nonprofit organization, independent of university oversight. They called the group the International Federation for Internal Freedom, more often referring to it with the possibility-pregnant acronym, IFIF.

In its Statement of Purpose, IFIF said it was formed as a collection of "small research groups—assemblages of six to ten persons who share the general goal of consciousness expansion and who are involved in a common research project."[10] The organization committed itself to form such research groups, maintain centers and obtain drugs for them, and publish a journal and "instruction manuals" that would disseminate information about the consciousness-expansion experience.

Running IFIF soon became Leary's full-time job. Tired of repeated bad press about the project and the "drug scene" at Harvard, as well as Leary's increasing absence from his academic duties, the university fired him on May 6, 1963. Soon afterward, Richard Alpert was dismissed from his own position for giving psilocybin to an undergraduate. From that point on, the two psychologists would spend the rest of their lives as self-employed advocates of consciousness expansion and spiritual awakening, and forever identified with LSD as the key to the journey.

Undaunted by their Harvard dismissals, Leary and Alpert worked to get Zihuantanejo's Catalina Hotel ready for another summer of LSD research. Over 1,500 people had applied to attend IFIF's Summer 1963 program there, where they would pay $200 a week for acid experiences. Although Leary had been warned by other scientists and professors to be discreet about the gathering, the ex-academic, who was beginning to show a distinct talent for self-promotion, invited the national media to the Mexican village. Understandably, the Mexican government was alarmed by the possibility of Oaxaca being overrun by druggies, and soon expelled Leary and his cadre of followers from the country.

Leary then turned his eyes to Dominica, a then-largely undeveloped, mountainous island in the Caribbean. Invited there by John "Jud" Presmont, a New York guru who led a communal-sex sect called "Kerista," Leary visited the little UK Commonwealth, only to be deported when local officials learned of his LSD research. Still seeking a tropical retreat to continue their work, Leary and his followers migrated to the island of Antigua, but they were soon made unwelcome there as well.

MILLBROOK AND THE CASTALIA FOUNDATION

Then heiress Peggy Hitchcock came to the rescue. She told Leary and Alpert that her brothers Billy and Tommy had just purchased a 2,500-acre estate near Millbrook, New York, as a tax shelter. The property sported lush lawns, a chalet with its own bowling alley, a four-bedroom bungalow where Billy and Tommy came on weekends to unwind, and—most importantly—an uninhabited, four-story, sixty-four-room neo-Baroque mansion that could house dozens of visitors.

That August, Leary and Alpert signed a dollar-a-year lease on the property with the Hitchcocks and moved their associates and furniture into the "Big House," as the mansion was called. They settled in for the cold season, taking LSD as a group once a week and planning to run Zihuantanejo-style retreats at Millbrook. Leary again alerted the national media about his doings, and during the late fall of 1963, the *New York Times, Look, Esquire, Newsweek,* and the *Saturday Evening Post* all ran stories on the former Harvard academic, his magic consciousness-changing elixir, and the scene that was developing at the big house in Millbrook.

Back in Cambridge, the first issue of *Psychedelic Review* appeared. This was IFIF's academic journal, dedicated to publishing "original reports, scholarly and historical essays, outstanding phenomenological reports of spontaneous or induced transcendental experiences, and reviews of relevant pharmacological and other literature."[11] Contributors to the journal would eventually include Alan W. Watts, Gerald Heard, Huston Smith, R. D. Laing, and many other notable figures. Although the *Review* published through 1971, IFIF itself soon faded from view as a new Leary-run psychedelic-enlightenment group took its place.

The new organization was called the Castalia Foundation. Named after the fellowship of mystic, mind-gaming monks in Herman Hesse's novel *Magister Ludi,* a favorite book at the Newton Center house, the foundation was organized by Leary and Ralph Metzner to conduct psychedelics research and raise money for the Millbrook community.

The foundation shifted Leary's focus from scientific research to guided group therapy. Spurning the analytical researcher/subject model of his earlier work, Leary told paying participants at Millbrook's weekend Castalia Foundation seminars: "There will be little interest manifested in your thoughts . . . nor in the history and complexity of your personality. You will find total acceptance but little verbal reassurance. 'Good' is what raises the ecstasy count of all persons present and 'bad' is what lowers the ecstasy count."[12]

For attendees, the "ecstasy count" didn't include LSD use. Still gunshy from their tropical misadventures, Leary and his associates instead

Fig. 5.3. A 1902 *New York Tribune* article about the Daheim estate.
Sixty years later it would become the home of Timothy Leary and
a community of psychedelic researchers.

used sensory-confusion techniques cribbed from Gurdjieff and other sources, hoping to give attendees a drug-free psychedelic high. One program, the Castalia Foundation "Psychedelic Training Course," admitted that although "[p]sychedelic plants and drugs are the most powerful releasers of neurological energy ever known to man . . . [a]lmost no one in our society . . . has the specific knowledge and general wisdom to use these agents."[13]

Instead, the course hoped,

1. To produce psychedelic experiences (without drugs).
2. To teach methods of running psychedelic sessions.
3. To teach recognition of different levels of consciousness and how to direct consciousness in order to reach specified levels.
4. To teach psychedelic language—techniques of communicating psychedelic experiences.[14]

THE PSYCHEDELIC EXPERIENCE AND THE MERRY PRANKSTERS

Privately, Leary and his associates continued to use LSD, and by mid-1964, the Castalia Foundation had produced the "psychedelic manual" earlier promised by IFIF.

Shortly before his death, British author and mescaline user Aldous Huxley had introduced Timothy Leary to the Evans-Wentz English translation of the *Tibetan Book of the Dead,* a fourteenth-century Buddhist work that guided readers through the stages of death, the interim "Bardo" states, and rebirth. Leary saw parallels between its accounts and the psychological transformations of someone on an LSD trip. He began to view the individual tripper as an "initiate" who must experience a death of the ego and a series of surreal and perhaps frightening visions before they could be reborn into a new spiritual life. With Alpert and Metzner's assistance, he retranslated Evans-Wentz's rendition into "psychedelic" language.

Published in August 1964 by University Books, the book, titled *The Psychedelic Experience,* became the bible of sixties LSD users. Dedicated to Aldous Huxley, it went through several editions, and is still in print today. Perhaps the greatest tribute to the book came from the Beatles, who adapted its imagery of ego-death, rebirth, and transformation to the lyrics of their 1966 song "Tomorrow Never Knows," an early example of the musical genre later known as "psychedelic rock."

Yet Millbrook wasn't quite ready yet for the nascent psychedelic counterculture. When Ken Kesey and his LSD-gobbling Merry Pranksters roared onto the estate grounds that September in their brightly painted Furthur bus, with mad beatnik-hero Neal Cassady at the wheel, no Dionysian acid-parties materialized. The Big House residents were scared by the loud, anarchic Pranksters, who in turn saw the Millbrookians as straitlaced East Coasters so ashamed of being psychedelians that they took their trips in the mansion's basement, out of sight of the drug-free weekend guests. Eventually Leary met privately with Kesey, and had his photo taken aboard Furthur with a bare-chested Cassady, but the visit played up the contrast between the staid, serious Millbrook community, and the emerging California psychedelic scene.

At the end of the year, Leary married his third wife, Swedish supermodel Nena von Schlebrügge, whom he'd met through the Hitchcock brothers. After an adventurous six-month honeymoon in Asia, it became obvious the two were a mismatch, so in the spring of 1965 he left her and took up with Rosemary Woodruff, who moved into Millbrook with Leary and gave him and his children the heartfelt, maternal support they hadn't gotten from the Swedish model.

With Alpert and many of the others gone from the estate, Leary spent the summer working on another "psychedelic" translation of an Eastern spiritual classic, Lao Tzu's *Tao Te Ching,* as well as an autobiography. During 1965 Leary and others noted that the property seemed to be under surveillance from mysterious observers, and rumor had it that the Dutchess County D.A. planned to raid the property.

THE LAREDO BUST AND THE THIRTY-YEAR SENTENCE

Not wanting to spend the winter in snowbound upstate New York, Leary, Rosemary, and his children Jack and Susan headed for Mexico. After they crossed the border, they discovered they lacked proper tourist visas, and headed back to the United States to get one. At the Laredo border their luggage was searched, and customs agents found a small quantity of cannabis hidden in Susan's underwear.

Leary took responsibility for the contraband and was convicted on March 11, 1966, for violation of the Marihuana Tax Act of 1937. Facing a potential thirty-year sentence and $30,000 fine, he appealed the conviction on the grounds that cannabis was his sacrament, and that the bust violated his First Amendment religious-freedom rights.

The sentence shocked Leary's cohorts, who rose to his defense, offering support and funds for the appeal. In response, the press ran sensationalized accounts about Leary, LSD, and cannabis, and the topics began to rival the growing Vietnam War as front-page topics. After reports appeared that LSD use had resulted in cases of insanity, blindness, and even death, Sandoz removed the chemical from the market, and bills to make its production and possession a felony were introduced in state and federal legislatures.

SENATE TESTIMONIES AND "SEVERAL HUNDRED ORGASMS"

On April 16, 1966, law enforcement upped the ante against Leary and Millbrook. That night the estate was raided by armed deputies under the command of County Sheriff Larry Quinlan and Assistant District Attorney G. Gordon Liddy. Liddy, who would later attain infamy as a Watergate burglar/bungler, found a small amount of cannabis and charged Leary and several other Millbrook residents with possession—a felony in New York State. Although the charges were eventually dropped, the bust was just the beginning of Millbrook's troubles with the local law.

Now at the center of the national LSD controversy, Leary appeared in May 1966 before a U.S. Senate subcommittee that Senator Thomas Dodd had convened to address the "drug crisis." There, Leary testified that LSD and other psychedelics were "nonaddictive, nontoxic, and antinarcotic," and that criminalizing them would create even more problems. But he ran into trouble when Senator Ted Kennedy aggressively cross-examined him about just what kind of alternatives he proposed to prohibition. Unprepared for the senator's attack, Leary admitted that the LSD situation was out of control, and that some form of "licensing" was needed for its use—a striking contrast to his previous enthusiastic promotion of entheogens for all and sundry.

The Senate hearings, and Leary's increasing public notoriety, made him an in-demand speaker at college campuses during 1966. That year he also recorded an LP of readings drawn from *The Psychedelic Experience* and gave an interview to *Playboy* magazine where he claimed that in "a carefully prepared, loving LSD session, a woman will inevitably have several hundred orgasms."[15] And Leary's translation of the *Tao*

Te Ching was published as *Psychedelic Prayers: And Other Meditations,* with Ralph Metzner and Michael Horowitz listed as coauthors.

"TURN ON, TUNE IN, DROP OUT"

On September 19, 1966, the Castalia Foundation yielded to a new— and now explicitly religious—organization under Leary's command. That day, the League for Spiritual Discovery was formed, with Nina Graboi, a middle-aged Holocaust survivor and entheogen enthusiast as Leary's cofounder and manager of its storefront center in Greenwich Village. The organization's initials left little doubt as to the method of "spiritual discovery" it favored.

Although it lacked a statement of doctrine, Leary later said in his book *The Politics of Ecstasy* that the league strove to teach three actions:

- Drop Out—detach yourself from the external drama, which is as dehydrated and ersatz as TV.
- Turn On—find a sacrament that returns you to the temple of God, your own body. Go out of your mind. Get high.
- Tune In—be reborn. Drop back in to express it. Start a new sequence of behavior that reflects your vision.[16]

Leary later abbreviated these commandments to the "Turn On, Tune In, Drop Out" soundbite that became his most famous quote. He advocated that those on the psychedelic path "form that most ancient and sacred of human structures—the clan" with each other, and that the clan had to be defined by "religious goals . . . religion is the turn on, tune in, drop out process."[17]

The day after the league was formed, Leary was interviewed by the *New York Times'* Robert E. Dallos. In the article, Leary claimed that the league had a total of 411 members. Of these, fifteen were full-time "guides" who had "resigned from their jobs and were dedicating their lives to the religion," and were living at Millbrook.

Later, Leary told another reporter that "religious leaders through-out history have used chemical methods for turning on," and that the league was working on a court order "allowing our priests, whom we call our 'guides,' to import and distribute the psychedelic chemicals marijuana, LSD, and peyote only to initiated League members." The chemicals were intended for "sacramental use in League shrines,"[18] in other words, the homes of the group's members.

DEATH OF THE MIND AND THE HUMAN BE-IN

Leary took the league's message to America's cities via his *Death of the Mind* stage show. Loosely based on the novel *Steppenwolf,* by Herman Hesse, *Death of the Mind* starred Ralph Metzner as Harry Hall, the hero of Hesse's book, to whom a white-robed, beatific Leary gives drugs that "spin him into multiple reality." In the manner of the era's "happenings," a psychedelic trip through the hero's body and mind followed that featured a dazzling light show, kaleidoscopes of projected images, the sounds of gongs, flutes, electric guitars, and string music, and Rosemary Woodruff as an Everywoman whom Hall symbolically "killed" to "play the game of Death."

Reviewed glowingly in the *New York Times, Death of the Mind* was a perfect vehicle for the hallucinogenic gestalt that Leary sought to communicate to the world. The show played for many weeks at the Lower East Side's Village Theatre and was appended by two other psychedelic pieces: *The Reincarnation of Christ,* which featured Leary talking Jesus down off the cross, and *The Vision of Hieronymus Bosch.*

Leary eventually took the act on the road to hip urban centers across America, to mixed reviews. When his friend, author and *Playboy* editor Robert Anton Wilson, saw the show in Chicago, he later remarked that Leary resembled "an Oriental Billy Graham," and that "it seemed a brilliant scientist had turned himself into a second-rate messiah."[19]

Leary's biggest audience during the tour was at San Francisco's Human Be-In. On January 14, 1967, over 30,000 people gathered at the Golden Gate Park Polo Fields to hear Leary, along with a galaxy of countercultural heroes ranging from Allen Ginsberg, Alan Watts, and Jerry Rubin to rock bands like the Grateful Dead and the Jefferson Airplane, bring the psychedelic/hippie culture to a mass audience. As Leary recited his "Turn on, tune in, drop out" mantra to the attendees, underground chemist Owsley Stanley III moved through the crowd,

Figure 5.4. Timothy Leary, family, and band on a lecture tour
Photograph courtesy of Dr. Dennis Bogdan, 1969.

handing out tabs of his now-illegal "White Lightning" LSD to all takers.

MILLBROOK SUMMER, CALIFORNIA SPRING

By the time Leary returned to Millbrook, the estate boasted two other resident sects. The league shared the Big House with the Sri Ram Ashrama, a meditation group that had been expelled from the nearby Ananda ashram when yoga guru Bill Haines and his devotees turned on to LSD. And former psychologist and irascible psychedelic contrarian Art Kleps ran his psychedelic-absurdist Neo-American Church (see chapter 6) from the estate's formidable gatehouse.

The sects, and the burgeoning New York hippie scene, brought new life to Millbrook. During 1967 the estate's buildings and grounds housed scores of colorfully dressed young people, to whom Millbrook was a real-life enchanted wonderland, especially if they sampled the sacrament that its unofficial patriarch was still so tirelessly promoting. Visitors who couldn't find room in the estate's buildings erected tipis out in the woods, sleeping under the stars during that idyllic Summer of Love.

But as that summer gave way to fall, local law enforcement became more determined than ever to stamp out the "Millbrook drug menace" and put its most visible public advocate out of business. Roadblocks and raids continuously vexed the estate, and not only Leary and his family, but even multimillionaire Billy Hitchcock were harassed and busted by sheriff's deputies. The psychedelic dream was quickly turning into a nightmare for the remaining Millbrookians.

Finally in February 1968 the Hitchcock brothers, tired of the constant hassles and bad publicity, evicted Leary, the league, and the rest of the guests and squatters from the estate. Leary migrated to California, where he married Rosemary and sought sanctuary with Laguna Beach's Brotherhood of Eternal Love (see chapter 7). From that point on, the League for Spiritual Discovery was essentially defunct, although a website currently exists under its name that collects information about the history and practice of psychedelic spirituality.

START YOUR OWN RELIGION

Leary would never attempt again to lead an entheogenic sect. He spent the next twenty-eight years living not one but several lives: as a psychedelic politician, an international fugitive, a hard-time prisoner, an advocate of space travel, a standup entertainer, a cyberspace enthusiast, and an elder statesman of the Western counterculture who still packed college auditoriums in his seventies. One of the most controversial American cultural figures of the postwar era, he remains the single person who most embodied what his old Harvard associate Charles Slack later called "the Madness of the Sixties."

As for the league, perhaps its ultimate legacy came in the form of a booklet Leary wrote for it, titled *Start Your Own Religion*. In the 1966 work, Leary said that the most effective way to "drop out" was to form one's own psychedelic sect, legally incorporate it, reverently consume the sacrament in a home "shrine," and sincerely and steadfastly fight for the First Amendment religious right to chemically expand one's consciousness as a spiritual path.

It was advice that would be followed for the next six decades by a wild variety of entheogenic visionaries, to varying degrees of success.

SIX

THE NEO-AMERICAN CHURCH

The Chief Boo Hoo Presents Massive Doses of Acid Absurdity

If Timothy Leary was the ringleader of the sixties' Psychedelic-Spirituality circus, then Arthur J. Kleps (1928–1999), founder and "Chief Boo Hoo" of the Neo-American Church was its clown and wild man.

THE "MAD MONK" OF PSYCHEDELIA

Although the two men and their organizations lived alongside each other at Millbrook, they shared little common ground otherwise. While Leary acted as the glib, photogenic public representative of LSD and all its usage entailed, Kleps struggled largely behind the scenes to define and articulate the true nature of the hallucinogenic experience and support himself as a self-chosen guru of the iconoclastic, life-is-a-dream philosophy he called Solipsistic Nihilism.

While Leary carefully crafted his image and message for maximum media-friendliness, Kleps openly, bluntly, and hilariously sneered at both Middle America and hippiedom's sacred cows, as well as Eastern and Western religions, most philosophical schools, human sentiment, and social niceties.

And while Leary continuously reinvented his various post-sixties personae, Kleps doggedly remained what Leary called "the Martin

Luther of the psychedelic movement"—a "mad monk" and an "ecclesiastical guerrilla" possessed of a powerful *Truth* that he broadcast and defended at all costs.

Said Leary of his rival:

> Art Kleps came on the scene before the cool, gentle love-heads . . . [he] is a clumsy manipulator, a blatant flatterer, a bully to the willingly weak, the world's most incompetent con-man. He is, in short, a sodden disgrace to the movement . . .
>
> Art Kleps is a not-wholly Holy, Funny Man.[1]

"THE ULTIMATE VOCABULARY OF THE MIND"

The son of a New York Lutheran pastor, Kleps served in the army after World War II, and later became a school psychologist. In 1960, while living in upstate New York, he became intrigued by Aldous Huxley's classic account of mescaline intoxication in *The Doors of Perception* and ordered a gram of then-legal mescaline sulfate from a chemical supply company.

About a month before Timothy Leary sampled his first dose of psychedelics in Mexico, Kleps swallowed 500 mg of the chemical, and journeyed into the inner landscape that would become familiar terrain for millions of trippers in the years to come.

As he described the experience many years later in his memoir, *Millbrook:*

> All night, I alternated between eyes-open apprehension and eyes-closed astonishment. With eyelids shut I saw a succession of elaborate scenes each of which lasted a few seconds before being replaced by the next in line. Extra-terrestrial civilizations. Jungles. Animated cartoons. Displays of lights in abstract patterns. Temples and palaces of a decidedly pre-Columbian American type, neither grim nor pretty, but beautifully delineated, textured, colored, and always in perfect perspective . . .
>
> What I was seeing was a kind of language of the gods, the ultimate vocabulary of the mind.[2]

Kleps may have Turned On and Tuned In, but Dropping Out was not an option . . . yet. Although the trip greatly intrigued him, he nevertheless returned to his "normal" life the next day as a husband, father, psychologist, school employee, and citizen. That same day, the Democratic Party chose John F. Kennedy as its presidential nominee, and the New Frontier beckoned.

MILLBROOK AND SOLIPSISTIC NIHILISM

Perhaps it was mere coincidence, but Kleps's reentry into psychedelia came just days after Kennedy's Camelot was blown apart in Dealey Plaza. Idly scanning the *New York Times* December 14, 1963, issue, Kleps spotted an article about odd goings-on at a huge, rambling estate in upstate New York. It seemed that three renegade Harvard psychologists named Timothy Leary, Richard Alpert, and Ralph Metzner had established a community at a place called Millbrook, where they and a group of followers were experimenting with a mind-expanding chemical called LSD. From what Kleps read, their LSD experiences sounded very much like the mescaline trip he had taken three years earlier. Intrigued, he vowed to visit the retreat.

His first trips to Millbrook were discouraging. A garrulous, hard-drinking, barroom intellectual who resembled a beatnik John Wayne, Kleps had little tolerance for the estate's prevailing pseudo-Eastern and "occultist" mindset and clashed with several of the academic acidheads on points of doctrine and practice. Kleps was particularly critical of Leary's plan to issue the *Tibetan Book of the Dead* as a guide for psychedelics users, since he saw it as a "stupid, ignorant, crazy, and evil book" whose grim, morbid content would guarantee a bad time for anyone reading it during an acid trip.

Kleps instead advocated a philosophy and practice he later dubbed *solipsistic nihilism*. Claiming that he had received full-blown *Enlightenment* while stone-cold sober and walking the Millbrook grounds, Kleps denied the existence of an "external world," and maintained that not only human life but all seeming circumstance around it was part of each individual's own private dream, and that "death" was merely the passing from one state of dreaming consciousness, into another. Kleps believed that Nagarjuna in the East, and David Hume in the West, had fully understood and properly described this metaphysical and philosophical truth, and that LSD was the key to awakening individuals to it, and bringing them to the rich, synchronicity-laden state of awareness such an ontology created.

To many Millbrook residents, however, Kleps was a drunken, opinionated pain in the ass who needed to be taught a lesson. Shortly after the "enlightenment" experience, persons unknown spiked Kleps's morning brandy shot with a massive dose of LSD-25, sending him on a twelve-hour trip that, although shattering and disturbing, still paled next to his earlier, drugless vision of "the externality of relations" as an illusion, and life as a symbol-laden dream.

The involuntary dosing just confirmed Kleps's suspicions that the estate was a lair of passive-aggressive "cosmic minders" who wanted to preserve their ideologies and egos at all costs. Angered and frustrated, he left Millbrook—for the time being.

MORNING GLORY LODGE
AND THE NEO-AMERICAN CHURCH

After acid and enlightenment, life would never be the same for Kleps. Fired from his school-psychologist job for advocating changes in New York State's draconian marijuana laws, he bought a run-down resort property on the shores of Cranberry Lake in the Adirondack Mountains and converted it into a psychedelic retreat. Kleps dubbed the settlement Morning Glory Lodge, in an homage to lysergic amide-bearing morning glory seeds. He also grew closer to Timothy Leary, who by this time was becoming notorious across America as the foremost promoter of psychedelia.

In April 1965 Kleps established the Neo-American Church at Morning Glory Lodge. Although the organization's name was based on the Native American Church, and the lodge was modeled after Millbrook, Kleps rejected both the racial exclusivity and Christocentric doctrines of the former, and the intellectual pretensions and oh-so-spiritual solemnity of the latter. Kleps instead envisioned the Neo-American Church as an inclusive, invisible *Kingdom of Wise Fools* who, while seriously pursuing enlightenment via chemical means, could also laugh at themselves and the silliness of consensus reality as they tripped in the safety and beauty of the lodge's sylvan setting. For a start, he dubbed Neo-American clergy "Boo Hoos," and appointed himself to the post of "Chief Boo Hoo"—a lysergic Lord of Misrule for the burgeoning psychedelic underground.

The church had no stated creed, and its three principles reflected the personalized subjectivity of the psychedelic experience and the solipsistic-nihilist philosophy:

1. Everyone has the right to expand his consciousness and stimulate visionary experience by whatever means he considers desirable and proper without interference from anyone.
2. The psychedelic substances, such as LSD, are the True Host of the Church, not drugs. They are sacramental foods, manifestations of the Grace of God, of the Infinite Imagination of the Self, and therefore belong to everyone.
3. We do not encourage the ingestion of psychedelics by those who are unprepared.[3]

Beyond that, the Neo-American Church employed no set rituals, nor regulated the frequency or intensity of members' sacramental experiences. It confessed that:

[m]any of our members are damned fools and miserable sinners; membership in the church is no guarantee of intellectuality or of spiritual wisdom . . . it has never been our objective to add one more swollen institutional substitute for individual virtue to the already crowded lists. We are, however, somewhat dismayed by the prevailing habit of "doing" (really not doing) things through institutional identification, and have, accordingly, injected massive doses of absurdity into our embryonic social fantasy.[4]

"VICTORY OVER HORSESHIT!"

The "massive doses of absurdity" were central to church culture, and reflected both Kleps's solipsist philosophy, and the playful side of the psychedelic experience. The church symbol was a three-eyed toad, and its newsletter was called *Divine Toad Sweat*—allusions to common psychedelian knowledge of certain amphibians secreting hallucinogenic venom. The church's motto was "Victory Over Horseshit!" Its hymns were "Puff, the Magic Dragon" and "Row, Row, Row Your Boat" "Life is but a dream," and the Sacred Church Key was—what else?—a bottle opener.

Neo-Americans who went above and beyond the call of lysergic duty earned honorary titles like, "Keeper of the Divine Toad," "Disease Simulator of California," and "Metaphrast of Emanations." And, spurning the Eastern mantras and iconography favored by more conventional psychedelic sects, the Chief Boo Hoo recommended that his tripping faithful instead meditate on television programs and commercials, whose most seemingly banal offerings, he maintained, were packed with synchronistic symbolism and folk wisdom for those with Third Eyes to see.

For over a year, the church and Morning Glory Lodge operated unmolested in the peaceful Adirondacks. Access to the lakeside property was by boat, and Kleps ferried groups of visitors to the lodge and the woods where, surrounded by the gorgeous scenery and supervised by the trained, if periodically crochety, psychologist, most of them happily tripped on then-legal LSD. (Paradoxically, mere possession of cannabis was then a felony in New York State, and the Chief Boo Hoo always advised his guests to hide well their stashes of what he called "the Lesser Sacrament.")

No less a bohemian icon than *On the Road* author Jack Kerouac once showed up at Morning Glory Lodge to share wine and acid with Kleps. Timothy Leary and Millbrook estate co-owner Billy Hitchock, a young scion of the hugely wealthy Mellon family, made an appearance there as well, although bad weather dogged their flight to the Cranberry Lake airfield, and they declined to partake of the lysergic Greater Sacrament.

The few lodge visitors who went on bad trips nevertheless emerged without long-term physical or psychological traumas. And their experiences gave the Chief Boo Hoo valuable intelligence about how different types of people handled LSD, as well as amusing anecdotes he later related to Neo-Americans for their edification and entertainment.

"ARE YOU REALLY CALLED A BOO HOO?" "I'M AFRAID SO."

As whimsical as the church might have seemed, Kleps was serious enough about it to plead the case for psychedelic sacramentalism before the United States Senate in May 1966.

When he appeared before the Subcommittee on Juvenile Delinquency, which was investigating the dangers of the growing LSD underground, Kleps's first question from the senators was, "Are you really called a boo hoo?" "I'm afraid so," answered Kleps, who then delivered a 2,500-word address making the case for lysergic acid as a mind-expanding holy sacrament, and Timothy Leary as a spiritual leader akin to Jesus or Buddha under whose banner the young and aware would fight if the anti-LSD juggernaut rolled forward.

"On the day the prison doors close behind Tim Leary," warned the Chief Boo Hoo, "this country will face religious civil war. Any restraint we have shown heretofore in the dissemination of psychedelics will be ended."[5]

Years later, Kleps said that he regretted giving Leary such a stirring buildup, as the normally ebullient Harvard academic, who followed him, withered under an interrogation by Senator Ted Kennedy. A philosophical anarchist, the Chief Boo Hoo also opposed Leary's proposal before Congress to license and regulate LSD use and maintained that intelligent adults didn't need the oversight of the state or the medical establishment to explore the mysteries of their own minds.

RETURN TO MILLBROOK

After a series of personal disasters left him broke, divorced, and homeless—Morning Glory Lodge was sold in a vain effort to save his marriage—Kleps sought refuge at Millbrook in early 1967. By that time, the estate was no longer the acid-washed grove of academe that it had been on his first visit, but the home of two psychedelic gurus and dozens of their followers.

While Millbrook co-owner Billy Hitchcock took refuge in the property's spacious "Bungalow," Timothy Leary and his League for Spiritual Discovery, and Bill "Sri Sankara" Haines's Sri Ram Ashram occupied the estate's four-story, sixty-four-room Big House, housed their respective members in its quarters, and gathered therein for meals, meetings, group trips, and parties.

Meanwhile, Kleps and his new wife, Wendy, established Neo-American Church headquarters at Millbrook's Gate House, the arched stone building that guarded entry to the grounds. There they processed church membership applications and pocketed donations, produced, and mailed out issues of *Divine Toad Sweat,* and compiled Kleps's various screeds and diktats into the book-length *Neo-American Church Catechism and Handbook.*

Later revised and updated as *The Boo Hoo Bible,* the *Handbook* gathered pronouncements by the Chief Boo Hoo on LSD, marijuana,

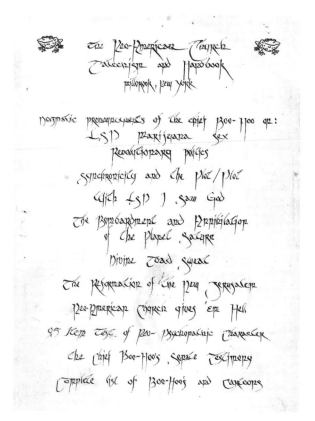

Fig. 6.1. The 1967 *Neo-American Church Catechism and Handbook.*
Note the three-eyed toads at the top corners.
Authors Timothy Leary and Art Kleps.

sex, revolutionary politics, and other issues germane to Neo-Americans. It also featured articles like "Synchronicity and the Plot/Plot," "The Bombardment and Annihilation of the Planet Saturn," "The 95 Item Test of Neo-Psychopathic Character," and similar pieces that merged Kleps's solipsistic-nihilist philosophy with psychedelic sensibilities and goofy absurdist humor, all accompanied by cartoons and comically altered clip art.

The *Handbook* also named Timothy Leary, Richard Alpert, Allen Ginsberg, and other high-profile acidheads as church directors and ranking clergy and included a directory of Boo Hoos across North America. To help raise funds, it featured a catalog of items for sale to readers, ranging from "destruct boxes" that would automatically immolate their contents if opened improperly, to dartboards targeting anti-drug "master horseshitter" and church enemy Guru Meher Baba.

Although Kleps claimed a following of between five and ten thousand Boo Hoos and laity, money was always tight at the Gate House. Having neither the Hitchcocks' vast family wealth, nor Leary's connections and abilities to finagle funds from well-heeled patrons, the Chief Boo Hoo and his wife lived in genteel hippie poverty, and regularly dunned church members, most of whom were in similar circumstances, for dues and donations. Eventually Kleps used his skills as a psychologist to have himself declared mentally unfit for work and lived mostly off Social Security largesse for the rest of his life.

A HIGH, WHITE SUMMER WITH *DIVINE TOAD SWEAT* AND THE GRATEFUL DEAD

Poverty aside, Kleps later looked back on 1967 as the golden era of the Neo-American Church and Millbrook. During that year the estate sported the greatest East Coast tribe of acidheads, freaks, and eccentrics outside of Greenwich Village—a hedonic hippie haven that rivaled Ken Kesey's La Honda Ranch and the Grateful Dead's Olompali property as a countercultural playground.

Kleps's memoir, *Millbrook: The True Story of the Early Years of the Psychedelic Revolution,* described the madness and ecstasy of the estate during what Hunter S. Thompson later called the "high white summer of 1967." Neo-Americans, Leary-Leaguers, ashramites, and guests both formally invited and otherwise, freaked freely through the grounds, their food and lodging provided by the Mellon millions and simpatico donors, and their spiritual and recreational needs supplied with Dr. Hofmann's magic elixir, as well as copious amounts of cannabis, speed, and booze. Thus equipped, the estate became a 24/7 psychedelic circus.

In *Millbrook,* Kleps recounted the tale of when Richard Alpert, already easing into his role as robed Western-guru "Ram Dass," took some LSD, convinced himself he could fly, jumped out of a second-story window in the Big House . . . and shattered his ankle when he hit the ground. He also told of the morning when he awoke to find two naked, giggling teenage girls romping through his Gate House sanctuary . . . and put them to work collating *Divine Toad Sweat.* And he described the Millbrook Fourth of July party where the Grateful Dead serenaded both the resident acidheads and the Hitchcocks' upper-class guests as they tripped happily on LSD-spiked champagne, skinny-dipped in Billy's pool, and even managed to "bomb" magnate Huntington Hartford's drink with genuine Owsley acid (luckily, the middle-aged multimillionaire enjoyed the experience). As with so many other scenes during that era, Millbrook seemed to be an idyllic, endless party, where lysergic acid was melting away old habits and strictures, and its acolytes were exploring new possibilities and sensations daily.

THE FALL OF MILLBROOK

But Kleps, whose Gate House residence was the estate's entry point, could tell the party wouldn't last forever. Increasing numbers of casual visitors from New York City and other urban centers strained both the estate's and the nearby town's tolerance; some were crazies and criminals who caused ugly scenes and eroded the trust Millbrookians shared with each other, and with the local community.

And local and state cops increasingly harassed and raided the community, in search of drugs and general misbehavior. Eventually not only Kleps, but Timothy Leary, his children, and even the patrician Billy Hitchcock were busted and indicted by the county grand jury on drug possession and other charges. To address the confusion about which resident individuals or groups were responsible for what illegal substances or actions, a map was published that delineated the territories of the Neo-American Church, the League for Spiritual Discovery, and the Sri Ram Ashram at Millbrook—a more-than-symbolic gesture that created distance and suspicion between the sects and their leaders.

Kleps also saw Timothy Leary rapidly morph from a spiritual guru into a radical political leader. Perhaps it was caused by the legal harassment, the ethos of the rising hippie culture, Leary's own talent for spotting and pandering to trends, or some combination of these, but during the summer of 1967 the acid avatar repudiated the aristocratic environment of the Big House and set up a tipi out in the estate's woods, at a place called Lunacy Hill. Although he continued to work and even sleep in the Big House, Leary seemed to be reinventing himself as a hip-culture tribal chieftain—an impression that deepened for Kleps when the league leader starred in an unfinished psychedelic Western film, made on the Millbrook grounds, that portrayed the hippies as Indians, and the straight-world cops outside as frontier lawmen and soldiers.

In the early spring of 1968, the Great Millbrook Acid Era finally ground to a halt. Tired of the constant logistical and legal headaches, Billy Hitchcock and his co-owner, twin brother Tommy, moved to evict Kleps, Leary, Haines, their respective followers, and various squatters from the property. Kleps talked Billy into giving him a $10,000 settlement to leave promptly and peacefully, and when he got the money, the Chief Boo Hoo, his wife, and their infant daughter, Kristen, left the Gate House forever. The Klepses migrated to South Hero Island, Vermont, where they appeared in *Beggar at the Gates,* an Emmy-winning documentary about religious groups that featured the Chief Boo Hoo defending his psychedelic spirituality against the criticisms of Christian pastors.

A "CREEPY LITTLE OCCULTIST" AND A "NEO-AMERICAN" SEX CULT

Later in 1968 the Neo-American Church entered the annals of American constitutional jurisprudence when the church's "Primate of the Potomac," Judith "JD" Kuch, was busted by District of Columbia cops for the possession and sale of cannabis and LSD. Kuch maintained that the substances were sacraments necessary to the practice of her religion, and fought the case on religious-freedom, First Amendment grounds.

Unfortunately for Kuch, the court rejected the religious defense, and ruled against her. In *United States v. Kuch*, D.C. District Judge Gerhard Gesell declared that the church was "mocking established institutions, playing with words and totally irreverent in any sense of the term . . . showing no regard for a supreme being, law or civic responsibility," and was "asserting in passing the attributes of religion but obviously only for tactical purposes." Judge Gesell stated that "the desire to use drugs and to enjoy drugs for their own sake, regardless of religious experience, is the coagulant of this organization and the reason for its existence"[6]—a statement that some legal observers thought was a rare example of a First Amendment case where a contestant's religious sincerity was rejected as an issue of fact.

In April 1969 Kleps himself attempted a direct legal challenge on the court's turf when he publicly distributed peyote to some church members on the Washington Mall. When the police ignored him, Kleps marched over to the Justice Department building, dropped a bag of the cactus buttons onto the chief counsel's desk, and was promptly arrested. Knowing full well what Kleps was up to, the Feds refused to prosecute the case. The Chief Boo Hoo later decided that the D.C. agitations were a waste of church time and effort, and labeled the local Neo-Americans useless losers, and Kuch, "[an] ignorant, wealthy, creepy little occultist, who in appearance so much resembled a moldy dumpling."[7]

Even lower to Kleps were the pretenders who had appropriated his Neo-American brand for their own sleazy ends. Dentist William Shyne, appointed by Kleps as the Patriarch of California, independently incorporated his own Neo-American Church in the state, and poached applications and funds intended for the Chief Boo Hoo. And in Pennsylvania, book dealer George Feigley organized a so-called Neo-American Church that quickly turned into a Charles Mansonesque, mind-controlling sex cult; Feigley was eventually convicted on multiple counts of statutory rape and spent over thirty years in prison. Kleps renamed his organization the Original Kleptonian Neo-American Church to distinguish it from Shyne and Feigley's sects.

THE BOO HOO BIBLE

With his marriage to Wendy on the rocks, Kleps tagged along with Bill Haines's ashram down to Benson, Arizona, where they set up a shared commune in the desert. In mid-1970 the pair returned to Dutchess County, New York, to face legal charges from a raid three years earlier. Although Kleps merely got probation for his part in the estate's illegal doings, when he moved to neighboring Massachusetts, he was arrested thirteen times and served six months in jail on charges ranging from possession of illegal substances to immoral cohabitation. The forty-something Chief Boo Hoo had a desire for much younger, and even underage girls, age-of-consent laws or not.

Kleps relocated again in 1971 to San Cristobal, New Mexico, where he stayed on a property formerly occupied by both novelist D. H. Lawrence and psychedelic pioneer Aldous Huxley. There, under the Toad Publishing imprint, he brought out the revised church catechism, *The Boo Hoo Bible,* notable for its full-color cover of spaceships destroying the planet Saturn—the celestial body that, half seriously echoes a famous essay by Henry Miller, Kleps maintained was the prime source of bad vibes in this corner of the galaxy and needed to be vaporized at the earliest opportunity. *The Boo Hoo Bible* eventually became the church's post-sixties calling card and gave it substance and staying power that less literarily inclined psychedelic sects lacked.

Homesick for the Northeast, Kleps ended up back in Vermont, where he married his fourth wife, Joan, and dubbed her "Chief Bee Hee." He was joined there by Jack and Mary Jo Call, two Southern California hippies who had read *The Boo Hoo Bible,* converted to Neo-Americanism, helped promote the church at a "Free Timothy Leary" rally in Los Angeles, and risen quickly in the church's ranks, such as they were, to become Art and Joan's lieutenants and roommates. Kevin Sanford, a University of Vermont student, and Peter Akwai, a Yale graduate, artist, and computer engineer, rounded out the second-tier church leadership of that era.

Fig. 6.2. *The Boo Hoo Bible,* the definitive Neo-American statement
on the psychedelic-spirituality path.
Author Art Kleps, 1971.

LIFE IN A PSYCHEDELIC CHURCH

Jack Call described seventies Neo-American life in his memoir, *Life in a Psychedelic Church.* Call observed that although Kleps had signed up thousands of paid followers during the sixties, psychedelic spirituality had largely gone out of fashion since then, and only a few dozen Neo-Americans still sent in dues and donations and were considered members in good standing. Even these loyalists were subject to Kleps's habits of abusing members in personal letters or in the pages of *Divine Toad Sweat,* and regularly excommunicating the ones who displeased him.

The Chief Boo Hoo's moody and mercurial ways were aggravated by his bouts with alcoholism and tranquilizer addiction, several of which landed him in rehab clinics and mental hospitals. Kleps had often told followers the Zen story of the monk who, upon becoming enlightened, spent the rest of his days in perpetual drunkenness; it seemed that he too now followed this path, blotting out the pain and boredom of ordinary consciousness with sedatives.

And true to his solipsistic philosophy, Kleps decided that the personal drama he lived required a greater starring role than even high priest. He declared the church a monarchy, with himself as king, and his word as absolute law in all Neo-American life and affairs. Kleps commanded all church members to address him as "Your Highness," or more simply, "Chief," while Joan was "Her Highness." Church officers were designated with hierarchical titles, and big-ticket church donors were admitted to the "House of Lords," where they could advise His Highness on ecclesiastic issues. Members were forbidden to join any other religious organization, and Kleps booted more than one Neo-American from the rolls for affiliating with such seemingly harmless groups as the Universal Life Church mail-order ministry.

Although the church retained its comic and parodic elements, the Chief Boo Hoo insisted that the titles and roles needed to be played seriously to get the full effect of a culture and reality consistent with the hallucinogenic vision. At this point, the Neo-American Church resembled less a traditional religious organization, and more of a theatrical troupe or a performance-art piece.

THE EXCOMMUNICATION OF TIMOTHY LEARY, AND THE PSYCHEDELIC DISNEYLAND

One of Kleps's first major acts as king of Neo-Americans was to excommunicate Timothy Leary from the church's ranks. After a decade of close observation of and personal interaction with the ex-Harvard professor, the Chief Boo Hoo concluded that the man whose name was synonymous with psychedelic spirituality was a phony opportunist rather than a religious or philosophical visionary—a panderer to the "kid culture" and "mob politics" who constantly changed his convictions and rhetoric in pursuit of fame and money.

For Kleps, the last straw was Leary's 1973 book *The Starseed Transmission,* wherein the imprisoned avatar abandoned acid in favor of a science-fiction vision where humanity followed the comet Kouhotek out to a space-colonizing future. In a 1976 *High Times* magazine interview, Kleps called Leary "fundamentally an intellectual whore," and predicted he would continue to bedevil American consciousness with new images and hustles, grumbling, "That fucker will never stay down. . . . He relies heavily on the famous short-term memory of the public."[8]

In contrast to Leary's *2001*-esque vision of humanity evolving through interstellar contact, Kleps dreamed of establishing an entheogenic retreat that would carry on the work of Millbrook and Morning Glory Lodge on a grander scale. He named this proposed community "Mandalit," and saw it as a sort of psychedelic Disneyland, where guests would be dosed with LSD, then ferried by a miniature train through a series of domains that represented different states of consciousness. Neo-American faithful would work and reside on the property, where fog machines misting "LACE"—a mixture of skin-penetrating DMSO and LSD—would keep inhabitants, visitors, and trespassers alike in a perpetual hallucinogenic state.

Kleps thought he had found the perfect site for Mandalit in 1977. That year he acquired 180 acres of land near Redway, in California's Humboldt County, right in the heart of the region that was producing a new, potent form of marijuana called *sinsemilla.* Part of the down payment for the property came from a donation by Kevin Sanford, who'd won several thousand dollars at the racetrack one day when he'd dropped acid and bet on horses whose names spoke to his psychedelicized state of mind.

Sanford's story, and the news about the property appeared in the Summer 1977 "Land Boom Special" issue of *Divine Toad Sweat.* In it, Kleps implored Neo-Americans to migrate to the area, and offered ninety-nine-year leases on "meditation circles" on the property for $500 and up. The Chief Boo Hoo believed that if he raised enough money from the leases, as well as the sale of high-octane cannabis grown on the land, the church could establish a permanent settlement there where he would rule as a psychedelic philosopher-king and instruct and enlighten residents and visitors with the help of the local "lesser sacrament," as well as LSD provided by clandestine church chemists. Mandalit seemed to finally be within reach.

But once again, Neo-American ideals ran up against real-world difficulties. Few church members purchased leases on "meditation circles," and only a handful relocated to the remote, rugged property to help the Chief Boo Hoo construct his sinsemilla Shambhala. Access to the land was difficult, and the scattered settlers, who lived in trailers and tents, endured torrential rainstorms and scorching heat waves. Kleps himself only sporadically occupied the property with Chief Bee Hee Joan and their small daughter, Daphne; when he was around, he alienated Jack and Mary Jo Call, as well as other Mandalit residents and Humboldt locals, with his drunken antics and general cantankerousness.

Eventually, the Klepses and their followers abandoned the project, although "Mandalit, Elk Ridge, Redway, California," remained the contact address for the church for years afterward. And the Chief Boo Hoo retained an economic interest in the property: in 1984 he was busted for growing over 900 cannabis plants there, and a year later was arrested again for firing a rifle at a snooping government airplane.

THE LAST SIXTIES LSD SECT STANDING

By the eighties the Neo-American Church had become something of a religious and sociological curiosity, a sort of psychedelic-sixties living-history group. The subsequent decade's revival of interest in entheogens largely passed the Neo-Americans by, and although nineties *alt-kultur* figures like Mike Hoy, proprietor of the Loompanics outlaw-literature emporium, championed Kleps and *The Boo Hoo Bible,* little new blood trickled into the church. The Chief Boo Hoo's vision of psychedelic enlightenment was just too cerebral and crusty for a new generation of trippers raised on electronic entertainment and New Age spirituality. And the sexagenarian guru's public statements—crankier than ever, and increasingly laced with anti-Semitic and generally misanthropic rhetoric—alienated potential followers and got him and his family kicked out of the Netherlands when they attempted to settle in that nation.

Kleps remained Chief Boo Hoo until his death at seventy-one in 1999. As of this writing, Chief Bee Hee Joan Kleps maintains the church on the OKNeoAC website, which sells *The Boo Hoo Bible,* preserves rare photos and writings from church history, and offers a free download of *Millbrook,* which remains the definitive, if highly subjective, work on the subject. Longtime church stalwarts Kevin Sanford in Texas and Bob Funk in Alaska remain as regional leaders. And the church still accepts new members for an initial $15 donation.

Six decades after its founding, the Neo-American Church remains the only institutional survivor of the sixties' acid-spirituality culture. Today, its legacy exists in records of its (unsuccessful) legal struggles to establish the entheogens as religious sacraments, and in its founder's valuable and irreverent accounts of Millbrook and of Timothy Leary's years there.

Equally importantly, the Neo-American Church's satirical, self-mocking doctrines and practices anticipated the sects of parody and play that later populated the American counterculture. Such comic-spirituality groups as the Discordians, the SubGenius Foundation, the Church of the Flying Spaghetti Monster, and others, would be unimaginable without the precedents Kleps set in the mid-sixties. The Chief Boo Hoo showed that religion, spirituality, and consciousness expansion need not be unctuous, sober-sided pursuits, and that fun and laughter could be vital parts of the journey, even if the great cosmic joke might ultimately be on the Seeker.

SEVEN

THE BROTHERHOOD OF ETERNAL LOVE

The Orange Sunshine Conspiracy

The story is mythic.

A ruthless band of brigands terrorize a land. Always on the search for booty and new thrills, they storm the house of a man reputed to hold a magic elixir of pleasure. When the bandits threaten the man, he freely gives them the potion.

Hoping that the elixir will gratify their hedonistic urges, they retreat to their hideouts and greedily consume it. But instead, the substance brings the men a vision of transcendent Clear White Light, where Divine Eternal Truth is revealed to them. Chastened, they vow to give up their lives of banditry, and bond as a brotherhood, dedicated to bringing the magic potion to the world so that all may be Enlightened.

The story is mythic—but true, according to those who were there. And it took place not in the far recesses of human history or in some exotic far-flung setting, but in Southern California in the midsixties, among a group of men who would call themselves the Brotherhood of Eternal Love. For the brotherhood, LSD was their transformational sacrament, and in a few years, they would grow from a motley crew of blue-collar gearheads and surfers into an international smuggling and dealing network that distributed millions of doses of high-quality acid, most famously the brand known as "Orange Sunshine," in the quest to turn on and transform humanity.

FARMER JOHN AND THE JOSHUA TREE REVELATION

The Brotherhood of Eternal Love's founder and spiritual visionary was one John Murl Griggs. The son of Dust Bowl immigrants who'd settled in Anaheim, California, Griggs was a wiry, pill-popping teenage hoodlum who'd been nicknamed "Farmer John" because of his Texas accent, and his ability to "grow" followers wherever he went. The tough, charismatic youth led both his high-school wrestling team and a car club called the Street Sweepers in hell-raising adventures across Southern California, brawling with rival gangs and committing crimes. He also dealt amphetamines and pot to Orange County teenagers, assisted by his friends Robert Ackerly and Edward Padilla, two surfers with similarly roguish lifestyles.

Griggs, a polydrug user who'd spent time in a hospital after a heroin injection gave him hepatitis, was always on the lookout for new kicks. In 1965 the Southern Californian, who'd married and found a job with Laguna Beach's parks and recreation department, heard about a new drug called LSD and decided he had to try it.

When Griggs learned that a well-known Hollywood producer had laid in a supply of acid at his Beverly Hills house, he and two cohorts invaded a dinner party there, brandishing guns and knives and terrifying the guests. When the bandits told the producer they only wanted his LSD, the host breathed a sigh of relief, and gladly handed over the chemicals, telling them, "Have a great trip, boys. Jesus, I thought it was something serious."[1]

According to the story, the trio ended up in Joshua Tree National Park's vast desert. At midnight, high in the mountains, looking down on the lights of Palm Springs, they each took 1,000 micrograms of Sandoz's finest, four times the normal dosage, and spent the next eight hours in the presence of the Divine.

When dawn came, the three greeted the rising sun by throwing their weapons into the yucca thickets. Confronted with a vision of the interconnectedness of all life and creation, they had shed their old identities as thrill-seeking, violent hoodlums, and now had a mission to turn everyone they knew onto LSD.

"THE CLEAR LIGHT OF REALITY"

With some variations, that's the story that people remember Griggs telling when the acid-reformed criminal returned to Anaheim, determined to spread the psychedelic gospel. One of the listeners was Eddie Padilla, who took a break from his pill-dealing activities long enough to accompany Griggs and several friends up to Mount Palomar, a 6,100-foot peak topped by a famous observatory, for a group LSD trip.

Many years later, Padilla recalled to Brotherhood historian Nick Schou what happened on the mountain. As one of the trippers read from Leary's *The Psychedelic Experience,* promising the group that they were "about to come face to face with the clear light of reality," Padilla first lost consciousness, then found himself back in the circle of trippers, where he "thought they were all dead, and we were all in heaven."

Too overwhelmed by the experience to walk straight, a friend drove him home, and "the light came on in my head," giving Padilla a godlike view of universal power, truth, and love. When he returned to his apartment and its array of weapons, pills, and porn, it felt like "whoever lived there wasn't me,"[2] and disgusted with his thug life, he gave up dealing speed and downers, and joined Griggs in his lysergic mission.

MODJESKA AND MILLBROOK

For the rest of 1965, Griggs continued to distribute the producer's LSD among an ever-growing circle of street kids, surfers, bikers, and others. Griggs, Padilla, and their comrades regularly took trippers off the street or away from parties into the mountains, hoping to get them away from their noisy, violence-plagued 'hoods, and to the peace and quiet of a natural setting where they could see God and the Ultimate Reality. Often the retreats worked, and a circle of regulars began to form around Griggs, spurning booze, gang fights, and Southern California's greaser/car culture for acid, vegetarianism, and spirituality.

In early 1966 Griggs and some followers moved the LSD sessions to Modjeska Canyon, a mountain community named after the famed Polish actress who had set up a utopian community there many years earlier. There they took over an abandoned stone mansion and began to meet every Wednesday night for acid communion, as well as talks from guest speakers ranging from Zen masters to Communist Party organizers. They also networked with LSD suppliers such as Tim Scully, an understudy of legendary acid chemist Owsley Stanley III, as well as Mexican cannabis growers and smugglers, keeping their entheogenic larders well stocked and raising money by selling the substances to visitors.

The Modjeska settlement's most notable visitors were two UCLA psychiatrists: Drs. Thomas Ungerleider and Duke Fisher. The two M.D.s studied the fledgling religious group and its weekly use of then-legal LSD, and two years later published an academic paper about it that identified the sect only as "the Disciples." In the piece, the two noted that although two-thirds of the attendees they studied had criminal records, almost all of them held regular jobs, worked hard on maintaining the Modjeska building and grounds, and seemed sincerely committed to a psychedelic yoga as a way of life. They estimated that the Disciples probably had around 100 core members, with a network of 500 or so who met regularly for the acid sessions.

Seeking guidance for his growing sect, John Griggs traveled east, to the Millbrook estate. Millbrook was ground zero of the burgeoning entheogenic underground—the home of Timothy Leary and his own psychedelics-oriented Castalia Foundation.

Leary met with the young Californian and was impressed by his sincerity and energy. He called the hoodlum-turned-mystic "an incredible genius . . . although unschooled and unlettered he was an impressive person. He had this charisma, energy, that sparkle in his eye. He was good-natured, surfing the energy waves with a smile on his face."[3] Leary was especially impressed with Griggs's spiritual inclinations, and soon converted his own therapy-oriented psychedelic group, the Castalia Foundation, into the League for Spiritual Discovery (see chapter 5), a religious order that claimed LSD as its sacrament. For his part, Griggs was in awe of the charismatic former professor and nationally notorious acid promoter and accepted him as his guru.

THE BROTHERHOOD OF ETERNAL LOVE

Following Leary's lead, the little community of Orange County acid-heads organized themselves as a formal religious group. Inspired by the close spiritual bonds they'd formed on their trips, as well as their mission to turn on the world, they named it the Brotherhood of Eternal Love. On October 10, 1966, Glenn Lynd, the only core group member without a criminal record, signed papers that incorporated the brotherhood as a tax-exempt corporation in the state of California.

As stated in the corporate papers, the brotherhood's purpose was "to bring to the world a greater awareness of God through the teachings of Jesus Christ, Rama-Krishnam Babaji, Paramahansa Yogananda, Mahatma Gandhi and all true prophets and apostles of God." The brotherhood specified no fixed doctrines or ritual, nor conditions for membership, saying that "We believe in the sacred right of each individual to commune with God in spirit and in truth as it is empirically revealed to him . . . the search for God is a private matter."[4]

The corporate filing also mentioned that the group was organized

Fig. 7.1. LSD chemist Owsley Stanley III's medallion. It combines the four-armed symbol of the Brotherhood of Eternal Love, with the four-petaled symbol of Timothy Leary's League for Spiritual Discovery.

Photograph by George Kepnir.

to "buy, manage and own and hold real and personal property necessary and proper for a place of public worship and carry on educational and charitable work."[5] What it didn't state was that the funds were to come from illicit drug dealing; LSD had been made illegal in California just days before the group incorporated, and the brotherhood fully intended to keep taking and distributing the drug, along with the Mexican marijuana they regularly smuggled across the border.

THE ENDLESS SUMMER ON WOODLAND DRIVE

When a fire gutted part of the Modjeska "church," the brotherhood sought a new home. They soon discovered it in Laguna Beach's Woodland Drive, about one mile inland from the beach in Laguna Canyon. The warren of old frame houses, unpaved roads, and grassy hills had been settled by the Tribe of the Rising Sun, a gang of long-haired, pot-smoking surfers from Long Beach who'd tired of constant police harassment in the big city and decided to catch waves and buzzes at Laguna Beach instead. The tribe and the brotherhood comingled and formed a little community of outlaw stoners in the sleepy beach-town neighborhood.

One veteran of the Laguna Canyon scene described the idyllic time in Stewart Tendler and David May's book about the brotherhood:

I went to school in Hollywood and got into surfing and just like everyone else I wound up in Laguna. Things were happening then, opening up. The chicks were seeing things and there was a lot of grass and there was a vibe that you could make it with love and digging each other. . . . I'd go down to Laguna more and more and finally I just moved into a place on the Canyon with some chicks and a couple of other guys. It was cheap and it was fun. You know the bond, the thing that tied us up together was surfing and dope and balling [sex]. We'd get up early in the morning, stay out in the sun all day and somebody always had more grass. . . . Then this cat Farmer John started coming around and he was really into acid. So we did a lot of acid and dug it and Farmer John was putting down a heavy brother-love rap.[6]

While the brotherhood and their neighbors luxuriated in Laguna Canyon's little Nirvana of acid, grass, sex, surfing, and spirituality, their public face was downtown in Laguna Beach proper. There, they converted an old machine garage at 670 S. Coast Highway into a combined clothing boutique, art gallery, bookstore, import emporium, head shop, and meditation space. They named the space Mystic Arts World, and the building opened to the public in the summer of 1967. That year the brotherhood also spread to the Los Angeles hippie scene when Griggs, Padilla, and some followers visited a "Love-In" at Elysian Park and distributed hundreds of cannabis joints to the attendees.

When the fabled Summer of Love arrived, Laguna Beach's hippie scene was burgeoning, and the brotherhood was at the center of it. Up north, San Francisco's Haight-Ashbury was turning into a chaotic, crime-plagued tourist trap, and the neighborhood's bohemian pioneers were emigrating to smaller towns where they could live freely among simpatico neighbors. Laguna Beach, a longtime art colony and funky beach town that housed conservative Orange County's misfits, was an obvious choice for many of these refugees, and Mystic Arts World soon became the hub of the region's hippies, as well as a center for the distribution of brotherhood acid and cannabis.

The most famous psychedelic-culture transplant in Laguna Beach was Timothy Leary. Although he had attempted to set up an entheogenic community at the Millbrook mansion, continuous police harassment and raids made it untenable, and in late 1967 he fled to his old home in Berkeley, California. Hearing he was in California, Griggs invited the acid guru to visit Laguna, and Leary soon arrived at Mystic Arts World along with his fiancée Rosemary Woodruff and Michael Hollingshead, the enigmatic Englishman who'd introduced him to LSD five years earlier.

Enchanted by the hippie-haunted surf town, Leary rented a beachside house in South Laguna. Leary, who had abandoned his own League for Spiritual Discovery in New York when the legal heat got too much, shifted his spiritual loyalty to Griggs and the brotherhood, who were now heavily involved in LSD and cannabis trafficking, and financing Mystic Arts World with its profits.

HASHISH, HOMICIDE, AND PRIMO DOG CRAP

One illicit substance the brotherhood introduced to the sixties American drug market was hashish. The resinous concentrate of cannabis, produced in the Middle East and Central Asia, had been a favorite entheogen among European bohemians for over a century, but was virtually unavailable in modern America. When brotherhood member David Hall, a surfer who regularly smuggled marijuana across the Mexican border, brought a load of hashish from India into Laguna Beach, locals used to his usual low-grade weed couldn't believe how high the tar-like resin got them, and bought his entire ten-pound supply on the spot.

Hall, who pioneered the use of hollowed-out surfboards to sneak loads of contraband through customs, inspired two brotherhood members, Rick Bevan and Travis Ashbrook, to set up their own hashish connection. The pair ended up in Kandahar, Afghanistan, where they met a local named Nazrullah Tokhi and sampled the locally produced hashish. After some socializing and negotiations, the Afghani sold them eighty-five pounds of high-grade resin, which the two Americans concealed in a load of Central Asian antiques and brought back to Laguna Beach. Tokhi would become the brotherhood's Asian connection for hashish and would eventually help them smuggle several tons of the resin out of the country.

When one brotherhood dealer, Pete Amaranthus, attempted to sell his share of Afghan hashish to two men at his Laguna Canyon home on December 14, 1967, disaster followed. His housemate Rick Bevan privately warned Amaranthus that something wasn't right about the customers, and fearing that they were undercover cops, he left the property. When Bevan returned several hours later, the house was surrounded by police cars, seven of his housemates and friends were under arrest, and the twenty-year-old Amaranthus was dead in the ER from a deputy's gunshot.

From that point on, Woodland Drive was under siege by law enforcement. Local cops and state and federal narcotics agents alike continuously raided brotherhood houses there, sometimes chasing fleeing residents through eucalyptus groves and up the steep canyon slopes. Laguna Canyon residents often hid their stashes of contraband and money in the brushes, fetching them only when they were confident no narcs were around. Many brotherhood members did business in and around Mystic Arts World, as well as at Laguna Beach's Taco Bell restaurant, and there was a constant flow of people, drugs, money, and information between the Canyon and those downtown sites.

One evening, federal undercover agents set up brotherhood dealer John Gale for a bust at his Woodland Drive house. Knowing his buyers were narcs, Gale took their money, handed them a stick of "primo hashish"—a dried dog turd—then ran off into Laguna Canyon's bushes. When the Feds fired guns in his direction, they flushed out a squad of state narcotics agents who were hiding in the brush, preparing to raid another house.

As the narc squads angrily accused each other of ruining their respective busts, the local brotherhood residents formed a circle around them and chanted the Buddhist om prayer to defuse the tension. All it did was enrage the cops, who attacked the hippies with billy clubs and steel flashlights. The next day a local newspaper reported the incident with the headline, "200 Hippies Battle Cops in Dope Raid," and noted that four young people had been arrested.

Dog-crap sales notwithstanding, John Gale and his fellow brotherhood member, Robert "Fat Bobby" Andrist, were serious, high-volume dealers. They attracted attention from not only law enforcement but from rival drug traffickers, who invaded Andrist's house and shot it up when they failed to turn up the huge load of hash he was rumored to have. Surveying the bullet-ridden structure and the constant presence of armed law officers, John Griggs dubbed Woodland Drive "Dodge City," and began to look around for a place where the brotherhood's spiritual work could continue without the threats posed by police or gangsters.

THE MOUNTAIN RANCH, THE MOODY BLUES, AND TRIPPING COPS

One brotherhood member, whom Griggs had cured of a heroin habit with LSD, told him that his father, George, owned a ranch high in the San Jacinto Mountains above Palm Springs. Called Fobes Ranch by locals, the eighty-acre property boasted a main house, several barns and guest cottages, and a reservoir that doubled as a swimming hole. Miles from the nearest village, the ranch seemed an ideal escape from the legal harassment and violence that plagued Woodland Drive.

The rancher, who was grateful to Griggs for getting his son off heroin, sold the property to him for a mere $20,000. Griggs had long spoken of moving the brotherhood to a tropical paradise like the one in Aldous Huxley's novel *Island,* where they could practice their psychedelic yoga unmolested by the law or public scorn, and it seemed as if the remote ranch was the next best thing.

Soon Griggs and Timothy Leary, along with their families and a host of brotherhood members, wives, and kids migrated to the ranch. Griggs banned single brothers from the property save for day visits, fearful that the men would disrupt the little community with the psychedelic sex parties they regularly held with teenage girls down in Laguna Canyon.

While most of the residents lived in tipis during the warm months, Timothy Leary and his teenage children occupied a guest cottage on the property. There he busied himself with writing, drank scotch, and ate steaks, much to the disapproval of the vegetarian brotherhood families. When the British rock group the Moody Blues, who'd recorded a tribute song to Leary titled "Legend of a Mind," played a gig in Los Angeles, the LSD guru invited them to the ranch, and the band's members spent several days there dropping acid with the residents.

The brotherhood also turned on rock musicians and fans at Costa Mesa's August 1968 Newport Pop Festival. Headlined by the Jefferson Airplane and the Grateful Dead, the festival packed over 100,000 attendees in at the Orange County Fairgrounds, where Mystic Arts World ran a concession stand that sold organic fruits and juice. Most of the thirsty concertgoers were unaware that the brotherhood had spiked the juice with LSD, and the grounds were soon filled with musicians, hippies, children, and even cops dancing and wandering around in a lysergic rapture.

The spectacle of dosed, dancing cops angered law enforcement, and they stepped up efforts to bust the brotherhood. On December 26, Timothy Leary and his son Jack were arrested in Laguna Beach by Neal

Purcell, a local cop who was determined to break up the Woodland Drive scene. Leary, who was charged with possession of two joints, claimed Purcell had planted the contraband on him, but he was nevertheless arraigned for trial just as the brotherhood prepared to unleash its most potent offering yet on the world.

ORANGE SUNSHINE

Up in the San Francisco Bay Area, brotherhood acid alchemist Tim Scully had taken on a partner named Nick Sand. An LSD chemist for both Leary's League for Spiritual Discovery and Art Kleps's Neo-American Church (see chapter 6), Sand had developed a variant of the hallucinogen that was twice as powerful as street-grade acid, and the two chemists, working out of an abandoned barn in Windsor, California, gave the brotherhood exclusive distribution rights to the chemical. Inspired by a vision he had while tripping on its first batch, John Griggs named the acid "Orange Sunshine."

The name beautifully evoked both Southern California's endless-summer climate and the brotherhood's acid-enlightenment philosophy. With its Mexican and Asian smuggling operations now bringing in cannabis and hashish by the carload, the brotherhood was awash in money, and it bought 3.5 million orange-dyed LSD tablets from Sand and Scully.

Both brotherhood members and their friends gave away fistfuls of Orange Sunshine pills at concerts and other hippie gatherings. For them, drug profits took a back seat to turning on the world to LSD, and by the end of 1969 it seemed as if everyone in the counterculture from Woodstock music fans to Harley-riding Hells Angels, to even Charles Manson and his dreadful "Family" had sampled the acid and raved about its mind-expanding effects.

DEATH AT THE RANCH

Unfortunately, Orange Sunshine cost the life of a brotherhood ranch resident. When seventeen-year-old Charleine Almeida drowned at the property's swimming hole on July 14, 1969, an investigation revealed that she'd been tripping on acid, and Timothy Leary, out on bail at the ranch, was again arrested—this time for contributing to the delinquency of a minor. A raid several days later resulted in five arrests, along with a considerable haul of cannabis, hashish, and Orange Sunshine tablets.

Another tragedy struck the brotherhood on the night of August 3. John Griggs, who'd been tripping at the ranch on a huge dose of synthetic psilocybin, stumbled out of his tipi, told a group gathered around a campfire that the drug was toxic, and collapsed face-first into the fire. A brotherhood member named Mark Stanton rushed him to the hospital in Hemet, thirty miles away, but Griggs fell into a coma and was pronounced dead on arrival. He was twenty-five years old.

With their charismatic, visionary leader gone, the brotherhood abandoned the ranch. Rumors circulated that Griggs had been deliberately poisoned, and to this day some surviving brotherhood members maintain that intelligence agents had infiltrated the group and wanted Griggs out of the way so that they could redirect their LSD distribution to more nefarious ends than global enlightenment.

THE MAN WITH TEN MILLION DOSES

A prime suspect in this scenario was one Ronald Stark. The balding, djellaba-clad New Yorker had shown up at the ranch several weeks earlier and presented the brothers with a kilogram—over ten million doses—of LSD, far more than they'd ever seen before. Stark told them that he ran a French laboratory that could turn out millions of cheap doses but needed a network of seasoned smugglers who could move it around the globe. Since the brotherhood's Windsor LSD lab had just been busted, they agreed to distribute Stark's acid, and brainstormed with the glib, seemingly well-connected mystery man about ways and means of dosing the world's population.

According to one source, Ronald Stark worked with the brotherhood since he "had a mission . . . to use LSD in order to facilitate the overthrow of the political systems of both the capitalist West and communist East by inducing altered states of consciousness in millions of people."[7] Stark often falsely claimed to have both an M.D. and a Ph.D. in biochemistry and boasted of his global connections to everyone from millionaires to mobsters to intelligence agencies. The New Yorker ran contraband and scams of all kinds through four continents and eventually amassed a small fortune.

It's estimated that between 1969 and 1973, Stark supplied the brotherhood with *a quarter-billion doses* of LSD that took countless millions of people worldwide on entheogenic voyages. The sheer volume of acid the brotherhood trafficked made them the world's biggest drug traffickers and birthed smuggling routes and techniques that are still used today.

Stark, whose many intrigues across the globe remain shrouded in mystery and disinformation, eventually bailed on LSD chemistry and the brotherhood, and reportedly died in 1984. Historians today surmise he was either a brilliant con artist and one-man crime syndicate, or a contract intelligence agent who manipulated the psychedelic underground for reasons unknown.

Perhaps inspired by Stark, who numbered European political radicals among his countless global connections, the brotherhood reached out to the American Weather Underground terrorist group in 1970. They paid the Weathermen to break Timothy Leary out of prison, where he was serving a twenty-year sentence on the Laguna Beach and Laredo cannabis busts.

In September 1970 the militants successfully liberated Leary, who used a fake passport to take refuge in Algeria, Switzerland, and Afghanistan before he was caught and sent back to serve out his term in California. Years later it was rumored that Leary, who'd been placed in a super-maximum-security cell next door to Charles Manson, ratted out brotherhood members and operations in exchange for a reduced sentence and early release.

MAUI WOWIE, AND JIMI HENDRIX ON DMT

On the night of June 4, 1970, Mystic Arts World burned to the ground. To some brothers, the fire seemed to symbolize the collapse of the brotherhood's spiritual ideals in the face of its new status as a hippie mafia. Feeling that California was no longer safe and remembering

Griggs's dream of settling in a tropical paradise, they relocated to Maui, a then-undeveloped Hawaiian island that was becoming a favorite refuge for mainland hippies.

There, longtime brother Edward Padilla hatched a plan to sail a marijuana-laden ship from Mexico to the island. The brotherhood planned to sell the load to the pot-starved locals and use the proceeds to finance a new hashish-smuggling operation in Asia that promised huge profits.

Although the ship, crew, and load eventually made it to Maui after a hair-raising voyage across the Pacific, the hash caper never materialized. According to islanders, falling seeds from the ship's cannabis bales took root in the rich Hawaiian soil, cross-pollinated with a local variant of the herb, and birthed the potent strain that became known as Maui Wowie.

Other than the new marijuana varietal, the most prominent legacy of the brotherhood's time on Maui was a movie. Titled *Rainbow Bridge,* the 1971 film was an amateurish, incoherent look at the island's hippie and spiritual subcultures that featured footage of brotherhood members Les Potts and Mike Hynson surfing and smoking hash.

The movie is remembered today mainly because it depicts part of a free concert Jimi Hendrix played on Maui for the brotherhood and several hundred hippies. Eddie Padilla, who set up a brotherhood tent at the show, recalled that after Hendrix played a disappointing first set, he offered the legendary guitarist a joint laced with DMT, a hallucinogen that takes users on a short but intense trip. Hendrix took a few puffs and reenergized, returned to the stage where he played a phenomenal two-hour second set—one of the last shows he performed before his untimely death six weeks later.

ORANGE COUNTY SUNSHINE: "THE CHRISTMAS HAPPENING"

A far bigger, free, brotherhood-sponsored concert, simply titled "The Christmas Happening," was planned for Laguna Beach during the December 1970 holiday. Rumors spread that rock legends like Bob Dylan, the Beatles, and the Grateful Dead would play there, and underground newspapers like the *L.A. Free Press* gave the festival free advertising in their pages. The most effective promotions though, were handmade invitations to which were attached single tabs of Orange Sunshine, that found their way to communes and crash pads along the West Coast.

On Christmas Day in 1970 over 25,000 hippies crowded onto Sycamore Flats, a grassy field at the top of Laguna Canyon where a small stage had been erected. Although police closed entry to Laguna Beach and attempted to shake down concertgoers for contraband, they were badly outnumbered, and soon chose to ignore the brotherhood and other dealers who had openly set up tables on the grounds piled high with cannabis, psilocybin mushrooms, and LSD tablets. For the hippies who'd arrived there penniless, a circling airplane overhead thoughtfully dropped thousands of artistic postcards onto the ground, each one bearing a tab of Orange Sunshine, compliments of brotherhood mega-dealers John Gale and Bobby Andrist.

Although the only name musician who ended up playing the Happening was Jimi Hendrix's sideman Buddy Miles, nobody seemed to care. Attendees spent the next three days happily creating the biggest Dionysian revel in Orange County history, where they ate free vegetarian food that the organizers snuck past the roadblocks, dropped acid, smoked cannabis, danced to local bands, pranced around in the nude, and even copulated in the open. Although most attendees went home after the third day, thousands of hippies, many still tripping on Orange Sunshine and other psychedelics, remained at the site on the day after, and the police slowly and gently herded them onto school buses that ferried them beyond city limits.

THE FULL-CIRCLE ACID GANG

The Christmas Happening, which observers later portrayed as a far gentler and mellower version of the disastrous Altamont free concert one year earlier, was the end of the brotherhood as an altruistic tribe of idealistic acidheads. During the early seventies its members moved tons of cannabis and hashish, as well as countless hits of acid, across the globe, and raked in enormous, illegal profits. When brotherhood dealers added cocaine— an addictive narcotic—to their offerings, it was obvious to even the most

Fig. 7.2. One of the LSD-bearing cards an airplane dropped onto the
crowd at "The Christmas Happening." A single tab of Orange Sunshine acid
was affixed on the lower left.

Photograph by George Kepnir.

star-eyed hippie that the men that had once sought to enlighten the world
with acid had come full circle, and were again the greedy, hustling Orange
County gangsters they'd been a decade earlier.

As a drug ring, the brotherhood died a death of a thousand cuts.
Throughout the seventies, antidrug task forces across the United
States and in several nations hammered away at its operations, bust-
ing hundreds of its affiliates, and seizing millions of dollars' worth
of chemical contraband. Convicted brotherhood leaders served long
sentences in prisons across the globe, and members who had avoided
arrest or jumped bail became wanted fugitives, picked off one by one
as the War on Drugs dragged on through the twenty-first century.
In September 2009 the last wanted member, brotherhood cofounder
Brenice Lee Smith, gave himself up to authorities in San Francisco

after spending forty years on the run from hashish-smuggling charges.

Oddly enough, interest in the brotherhood was first revived not in Southern California, but in the United Kingdom. In 1984 British authors Stewart Tendler and David May published a book about the group that told its story from outsiders' viewpoints and linked it to the infamous "Operation Julie" LSD ring in seventies England. Twenty-three years later they issued an updated edition, which was followed by *Orange Sunshine,* journalist Nick Schou's definitive account of the brotherhood that featured extensive, revealing interviews with its members, friends, and enemies.

When Schou toured to promote the book, he was often accompanied by original brotherhood members. The aged, gray-haired brothers, who were themselves writing memoirs of their adventures, doing interviews with film documentarians, or running websites that collected anecdotes and ephemera from the group, often told their audiences that although hardened by years of hustling, busts, and prison, their hearts still held the vision of global love and peace they'd followed as young hippies and surfers so long ago.

To them, and to all its friends and fellow travelers, the brotherhood lives on wherever people, inspired by entheogenic experience and seeing beyond the confines of mundane "reality," embrace that vision.

EIGHT

SHIVALILA

The Wandering Entheogenic Tribe

Of all the fifties establishment-types who took Timothy Leary's famous slogan to heart during the subsequent decade, few turned on more completely, tuned in more deeply, or dropped out more thoroughly than one Gridley Lorimer Wright IV. The scion of a blue-blooded Buffalo, New York, family, Wright transformed from a button-down Wall Street stock trader and conservative Republican into a long-haired psychedelic guru and anarchist commune founder, and became the eventual leader of a small, nomadic, LSD-using, and polyamorous sect that would become known as Shivalila.

FROM PREPPIE TO HIPPIE

Born in 1934, Wright attended Westminster Prep as a teenager, and then entered Yale University. Years later, Libertarian political theorist Murray Rothbard remembered him as a young adherent of the fifties conservative movement at Yale—a disciple of William F. Buckley Jr. and Russell Kirk who saw atheism and materialism, rather than communism and globalism, as the root evils facing America and the West. For a while, Wright even served on the staff of the Old-Right *American Mercury* journal alongside George Lincoln Rockwell, a navy vet and illustrator who would later achieve infamy as the leader of the American Nazi Party.

When Wright graduated from Yale, he married and found work as a stockbroker in New York City. Sometime in the early 1960s he moved to Southern California and settled in Malibu. Sociologist Lewis Yablonsky, who at the time was writing a book about the controversial Synanon addiction-recovery movement, remembered first encountering Wright at a Malibu community meeting, where the conservative Republican broker supported the group's right to develop their property in the beachside town.

While in Malibu, Wright switched careers from stockbroker to county probation officer. The new job kept him busy only three days a week; during the rest of the time, he experimented with marijuana and LSD, stretching his consciousness far beyond the upper-class, Yalie, Old-Right universe of his young adulthood. Eventually he quit working altogether, stopped shaving, grew his reddish-blond hair to shoulder length, and swapped Brooks Brothers suits and wingtip shoes for kaftans and sandals. Then in late 1966, the newly minted hippie turned his Malibu Canyon home into a twenty-four-hour-a-day crash pad for local freaks and runaways—a move that didn't exactly endear him to his wealthy neighbors.

STRAWBERRY FIELDS AND DR. YABLONSKY

In early 1967 Wright moved the party to a property in Decker Canyon, several miles west of Malibu proper, where he organized a commune. He dubbed the settlement "Strawberry Fields," after the Beatles song, and "decided to let anybody else who wanted to come, come." There was no structure at Strawberry Fields—the only rules were that alcohol and hard drugs were verboten, and that residents and visitors had to confine their activities to the property boundaries. Otherwise, one could freak freely there.

At any time, Strawberry Fields boasted between 30 and 35 residents, with over 100 during weekends. About half the hippies and trippers there hailed from the San Francisco Bay Area; the Haight-Ashbury was already losing its allure for its original denizens, and many were migrating to fresh freak enclaves along the West Coast. Wright envisioned the commune as "a place of accelerated evolutionary change," where people

Fig. 8.1. Gridley Wright, the founder and leader of Shivalila.
Photograph by Natec Harijan.

could safely trip on acid or other psychedelics, and expand their consciousness without interference from, or with, straight society.

As with so many other improvised communities of the time,
Strawberry Fields didn't last long. The place was a magnet for every misfit and crazy in California and dealing with them and their less-than-
salubrious lifestyles gave Wright cases of hepatitis and pneumonia. The
would-be hippie guru barely escaped arrest when the law removed a five-
year-old from the premises for smoking marijuana. And when a misplaced

candle burned down the main commune house, he decided it was time to shut down Strawberry Fields. Wright tried to organize another commune at Gorda, near Big Sur, but that experiment turned out to be even shorter-lived, and more disastrous, than the Southern California–based one.

During this period, Lewis Yablonsky interviewed Wright, who would become the sociologist's Virgil in a journey through the sixties subculture. Wright, by now an unofficial spokesperson for the Los Angeles–area counterculture, spoke to Yablonsky from the comfort of his Malibu home, as naked teenage hippies paraded through the living room and the burnt-sage odor of marijuana wafted through the house.

When asked about his political leanings, Wright told Yablonsky he had none. The onetime right-wing activist eschewed the radical ideology and actions of much of the counterculture. To change the world, he said, one had to change one's consciousness first, and *fighting the system* not only wasted time and energy but reinforced the oppressor/victim roles that were keeping people from truly open communication. On the other hand, Wright also spurned the "flower children" ideal; he believed anger and hatred were natural, healthy emotions that only became dangerous when they spurred physical violence.

"THE SECRET TYPE OF RELIGION"

Wright's own ideals were tested when he endured a well-publicized pot bust and trial. In May of 1967, the hippie leader had appeared on a Los Angeles radio program, and when he discussed the sacramental use of marijuana and LSD, he casually mentioned on the air that he'd gotten high just before the interview. When he came out of the studio, cops were waiting with a search warrant at his car, which gave up a small amount of marijuana. Since mere possession of pot was then a felony, they arrested him.

Five months later Wright went on trial. He immediately dismissed his defense attorney, and chose to represent himself, confident that he could make a case for marijuana as a holy sacrament that deserved the same legal privilege that peyote did for American Indians. Wright said the hippie subculture "has every characteristic of any religion, especially the secret type of religion—one that is persecuted as the early

Christians were, as small cults of secret societies have been all throughout history. . . . The thing that we have that is secret about ours, from the Establishment, are the rites in which we use the dope. Those are not allowed to be observed by non-members. That is what it actually works down to."[1]

Although not only Yablonsky, but Unitarian minister and Harvard Divinity School graduate Ernest D. Pipes testified at the trial that Wright was a bona fide religious leader, and the hippies' marijuana use was a key part of a legitimate spiritual quest, the court didn't agree. After a two-week trial Wright was found guilty, labeled a "false prophet" by the presiding judge, fined $300, and put on five years' probation with the understanding that he wouldn't use, or advocate the use of illegal drugs during the term. True to his anarchist philosophy, Wright continued to do both, and was sent to jail for the next eighteen months.

WRIGHT IN BALI: THE WESTERN GURU

When he emerged from custody in early 1969, Wright headed to the Far East. Like many Western hippies, he believed that enlightenment lay beyond the repressive, rule-crazy confines of his own society, and could be found by exploring Asian spiritual and cultural ways.

In 1970 Wright landed in Kuta Beach in Bali, then a quiet village little frequented by tourists. Believing he had found "home," he burned his American passport as an offering to Shiva, the Hindu god of destruction and rebirth, and then moved into a little shack on the beach. There he meditated and wrote chapbooks of poetry that he exchanged at a nearby coffee house for donations. Wright also befriended both expatriate hippies and locals, who sought him out as a yoga teacher.

Keith Lorenz and David Salisbury, two Americans who were recording an oral history of rapidly modernizing Bali, encountered Wright at Kuta Beach. Fascinated by Wright, who was calling himself "Abra Lut" during this period, the two taped a lengthy interview with the gone-native guru, where he expounded on his ideals and life.

Wright told the pair that several years earlier, he had a vision of a shared community that would separate itself from modern society and the consumer culture, and live as a tribal, collective unit. After his time in Strawberry Fields and in jail, he believed that the vision wouldn't work in America, so he traveled to Asia to seek out ways of life more conducive to this ideal.

The interviewers noted that Wright smoked a lot of the local cannabis during the interview. Wright said that pot enhanced his creativity and served as a bonding agent for hippies and other potential members of the new world he was trying to create: "It's the religion of today—religion started out as a turn-on like this, that brought people together, so they felt closer."[2]

Intimacy—physical, emotional, spiritual—was what the seemingly egoless Wright was all about in Bali. "Everybody that I'm with is me," he told the interviewers. "Right now, I'm a witness in a mirror . . . anything [people] see in me is a projection. It's the self-talking to the self. I'm reflecting ways of perceiving, interacting, playing with the environment."[3] Wright believed that in his interactions he was re-creating the immediacy and novelty of childhood, the ideal mental state for true learning and spiritual peace.

Wright, who believed in past lives, felt that he was in the last of a long series of incarnations, and that his current human existence was the one in which he could fully transmit his gathered wisdom. "I am fulfilled, I've realized everything," he said. "There ain't a game that I've run into in a long time that I haven't remembered from a long time back in all its variations, including this one." He had transcended all worldly ideals or desires save one: "that the whole world would go crazy, so then it would finally be safe for me and the kids."[4]

As with the Yablonsky interview, Wright was speaking under the shadow of legal persecution. He claimed that some local Balinese had adopted him as a sort of mascot of Western hipness, but then got angry when he started to play his guru role too seriously with them. They reported him to the local authorities, who raided his hut, loaded him in a Jeep, and dropped him in a detention center. His captors were puzzled by the passport-less, penniless American who accepted his fate with Buddha-like passivity and endlessly played mind-games with them, so he was returned to his shack while they figured out their next move. Eventually Wright was seized again and deported to the United States.

SHIVALILA

Back in California, Wright once again landed in legal trouble. During his two-plus years in Asia, the man newspapers called "the high priest of pot" never checked in with his parole officer—a violation of his 1968 sentence terms. Busted near Monterey in January 1972 on the parole beef, he was sentenced to a year in county jail.

Wright did his time, and then assembled a small coterie of followers who shared his communal ideals and his commitment to spiritual enlightenment through cannabis and LSD. This time he organized them as a formal group and dubbed it Shivalila. The name *Shivalila* was a compound of the name of the Hindu deity to whom he had sacrificed his passport, and who was often associated with ritual cannabis use; and the Sanskrit word for "play," "drama," and "spontaneity."

Shivalila's basic beliefs and practices were recorded in *The Book of the Mother*. According to Wright, who penned the work under the auspices of the Children's Liberation Front, their vision of collective consciousness came about during a ten-year period, wherein he and his various followers and associates took over 12,000 LSD trips.

They had started out in the Western hippie subculture, but had also journeyed to more traditional tribal societies, and had tripped with developing-world peoples ranging from Afghani Sufis to Tibetan Buddhists, to Indian Shaivite Hindus. Wright claimed that when he dosed tribal peoples with acid, not one experienced the frightening hallucinations or freak-outs traditionally associated with the drug in the West.

The sect's covenants evolved from these experiences, and according to the book, "represent the only known social contract specifically established to sustain group consciousness." The covenants were:

1. Ahimsa. Shivalila is an open, nonviolent community. (Violence is an act that directly affects structural damage to cellular integrity. People of Shivalila will not under any circumstances resort to violence or call upon any institution that uses violence or threats of violence.)

2. Sattva Ava. People of Shivalila will make no contract in respect
   to truth without stipulating that truth is relative and that body,
   mind, and environment are indissoluble. Correlatively, people of
   Shivalila will not testify in any matter involving issues of guilt
   or nonguilt.

3. Bhramcari. People of Shivalila do not own anything on any
   plane—psychic, material, physical, or fantasy. People of Shivalila
   do not acknowledge private or group ownership of anything.
   Correlatively, people of Shivalila will not participate in any relationship involving privacy or secrecy.

4. Tantra. A person of Shivalila will have sensual/sexual relations
   with another only after that person has manifested some identification with nature and babies.[5]

TRIBAL CONSCIOUSNESS, GROUP SEX, AND LSD

The object of Shivalila was to manifest higher consciousness through
these practices. Wright believed that there were nine stages of human
consciousness, ranging from "Neuro-electro-atomic" to "Universal
mind," a godlike state of being that "will only manifest through the
unified focus of no less than three persons." The goal for Shivalila, and
eventually for all of humanity, was to achieve full use of all nine levels, so that full, honest communication could take place between individuals, egoistic differences could be erased, and the tribal group mind
would harmoniously direct human affairs.

To Shivalila, the key to this consciousness was the experience
of childhood. Wright maintained that the Western nuclear family
instituted both patriarchal dominance and matrifocal dependency, and
this combination produced damaged children who became damaged
adults. A better way to raise children, he said, was in a commune, so
that they would have multiple sources of both authority and sustenance
and would think more "tribally."

As for Shivalila's adults, they deprogrammed themselves from
monogamy in multipartner, group-sex sessions that opened with meditation and the ingestion of LSD. Wright maintained that the judicious
use of entheogens would "facilitate communication with the children,"

and allow adults to more easily enter the special mind-space of child-hood that they had abandoned during puberty.

Wright discouraged mothers from identifying with their birth chil-dren, saying that it created neurotic, egoistic attachments. Instead, he said that mothers should "facilitate the development of psychic/sensual relationships with a broad variety of people" to fully develop the child as a social, tribal being. The children were also encouraged to explore their bodies and freely express their innocent sexuality with each other. However, books and toys were banned from Shivalila, since such objects separated children from spontaneous experience and the collective play of the community.

THE WANDERING TRIBE

Shivalila never grew beyond roughly twenty adult members plus their chil-dren. Wright and his followers maintained a nomadic existence, spending the seventies drifting through Asian ashrams and North America com-munes, in search of a place where they could expand their consciousness with LSD, practice tantric group sex, and raise a new generation of chil-dren in the tribal consciousness Wright believed could save humanity.

The group's source of income was unclear. Although Shivalila mem-bers told one scholar that "the law of Karma" supplied them with all they needed, she suspected that they may have supported themselves through dealing cannabis and LSD.

When Wright heard the story of the Tasaday, a tribe of indigenous Stone Age people on Mindanao in the Philippines, he took his followers to the island to meet them. But the Shivalila faithful were turned back by government officials, who believed the last thing the Tasaday needed was to be corrupted by a gang of Western acidhead cultists.

Wright also found himself unwelcome in stateside alternative-culture circles. In the book *The Wizard and the Witch,* Oberon and Morning Glory Zell, founders of the Neo-Pagan Church of All Worlds, recounted how Wright and his group, who had co-opted several members of a Missouri commune, tried to recruit their own preteen daughter by dos-ing her with LSD. Enraged, Oberon Zell confronted Wright, grabbing one of his henchmen's pistols and holding it to the cult leader's head.

Coming to his senses, Zell instead invoked the Mother Goddess's curse on Wright, and reported him to Child Protective Services, who showed a distinct lack of interest in the case. (Not surprisingly, surviving Shivalilaites recall the story differently; there were no guns, they say, and the confrontation was more of a tussle between two rival sect-leaders over group loyalties.)

PAIUTE MOUNTAIN, MATEEL, AND BLACK BEAR RANCH

Returning to California, Shivalila attempted to settle on Paiute Mountain, at the base of the Sierra Nevada range just east of Bakersfield, California. There they published *The Book of the Mother* and sheltered themselves in two abandoned mines. According to a visitor of that era, the Shivalilans grew a huge crop of cannabis on a mountainside, ate ganga-infused pancakes for their breakfasts, and dealt with women who refused sex by dosing them with LSD and group-pressuring the tripping young females to share their bodies with the tribe. The reporter also noted that the children seemed not to be able to tell the difference between men and women, even though the adults regularly walked around naked.

Famed San Francisco reporter Warren Hinckle Jr. sought them out and had dinner with the group. When he inquired about the source of the repast's meat, the Shivalilites informed him that he was helping them "recycle" their recently departed pet dog! Hinckle's story about the incident outraged local pet lovers, who alerted the authorities about the canine-eating sect. The commune was raided, and once again the group was homeless.

Shivalila also spent time in Mateel, an informal community along the Eel River near Redway, in California's hippie-haunted Humboldt County. Jentri Anders's *Beyond Counterculture,* an academic history of Mateel during the 1970s, featured accounts by former residents that claimed Wright and his followers aggressively proselytized in the community but were able to convince only one woman to join them. After two weeks with Shivalila, the woman fled the group, saying that she couldn't take the sect's nearly constant LSD usage, or hostile encounter-group behavior-modification tactics anymore.

Moving on, Wright and his entourage landed at Black Bear Ranch in California's Siskiyou Mountains. Black Bear seemed to be a more rural and more disciplined version of Strawberry Fields—"free land for free people" where anyone who was willing to work and cooperate was welcome, and where children were raised communally.

Initially, the Shivalila tribe seemed to fit right in the community. But tensions soon appeared between its members, and the longtime residents, many of whom were political radicals deeply suspicious of self-proclaimed gurus. A 2006 documentary about Black Bear, *Commune*, featured interviews with former residents who saw Shivalila as an arrogant cult whose members spent most of their time dropping acid and hanging around with the commune's children, and who tried to impose their own visions on the essentially anarchistic settlement. Ex-Shivalila members who appeared in the film, on the other hand, felt they were merely being honest and open with the regulars, per Wright's teachings of egalitarian, free communication.

Eventually the Black Bear old-timers called in reinforcements from outside the settlement, confronted the Shivalilites, and forced them to leave the land. Wright and his people departed, along with a couple of Black Bear residents who'd shifted their allegiances to the middle-aged guru, and at least two commune children who'd bonded with the child-centered clan and had chosen to go with them rather than stay with their biological families.

THE "INDIAN CHILDREN'S REPUBLIC," AND DEATH IN GOA

In 1978 Wright and his entourage migrated to India, hoping to form a "children's republic" that would be free from journalists, cops, ideologues, and other Western pests. Imitating their leader's action years earlier in Bali, the Shivalilites destroyed their passports, and pled with Indian officials for asylum, claiming they faced persecution in the United States. (Ironically, asylum was denied largely because the cultists lacked valid passports.) They tried to settle in the arid Indian state of Rajasthan, but an epidemic of measles and diphtheria there claimed the lives of four of the group's children. Wright, who claimed that Western medicine had no place in the commune's life, had forbidden vaccinations to his followers.

By now, the forty-five-year-old Wright was tiring of the conflicts and constant travel and told his followers that he would die in India. He had been lately claiming that he had lived before as Krishna, Buddha, Jesus, and Muhammad, and that he had taught all one soul could. It was time to return to the Light.

Wright's premonition came true on December 22, 1979. Weeks earlier, he had been visiting the Indian tropical seaside state of Goa when he was stabbed several times by a deranged Australian hippie. Complications from the wounds set in, and the Shivalila guru died of double pneumonia in a Goa hospital, ten days before the end of the 1970s. Five members of Shivalila were with him when he passed on, and they had his earthly remains cremated Hindu-style and scattered near the sea in the town of Panjim.

"MY BRAND OF LIVE THEATRE / AND MY CAST OF FREAKS"

Shivalila struggled to stay afloat in the wake of Wright's death. One of Wright's followers told a journalist that Wright "was going through retransmission," and would reincarnate as the child of one of the Shivalila women, three of whom were pregnant at the time of his passing. But most members of the group returned to the United States, where they distributed *The Book of the Mother* and tried to live his ideals in a society that seemed less hospitable than ever to the sixties psychedelic-tribal vision.

Some settled on Hawaii's Big Island, and eventually opened an intentional community called Dragon's Eye, which combined Wright's teachings with those of other social and spiritual reformers. The community continues to exist as of this writing and is now considered "mainstream" enough to host 4-H sustainable-agriculture programs.

As for Wright, little trace today remains of his influence on either the psychedelic or the communal subcultures. For a time, the Gridley Wright website displayed articles and news clippings about the "figure of the 1960s counterculture," and sold CDs of the 1971 Bali interview, but it is currently offline. The *Commune* documentary revived some interest in Shivalila, although the group's practices, and Wright's flat-toned narratives over footage of their activities, creeped out more than a few viewers.

Perhaps Shivalila, and the man that founded and directed it, can best be summed up in one of Wright's own poems, "Kali's Dance," where he called himself "quite mad," and referred to Shivalila as, "my brand of live theatre / and my cast of freaks." During their existence as a sect, Gridley Wright and his followers detached themselves from not only Western society, but consensus reality itself, and attempted to live as a premodern tribe in a late-twentieth-century world that was hurtling rapidly toward either nuclear annihilation or environmental catastrophe and that had little use for the entheogen-influenced childhood innocence that Shivalila desperately tried to preserve and promote.

In a sense, Shivalila was a microcosm of the original hippie movement. Social and economic forces that the counterculture couldn't understand, address, or control spelled doom for most of its "alternative communities," and Shivalila became yet another casualty of misdirected sixties idealism and changing times.

NINE

THE CHURCH OF NATURALISM

From LSD Rescues to L.A. Murders

When LSD first appeared in the burgeoning sixties counterculture, many novice users didn't experience the rapture of a life-changing spiritual awakening.

They went to hell instead.

The chemical that journalist Hunter S. Thompson described as "too small to be seen and too big to control," sent many trippers on terrifying rides through the deepest and darkest regions of their minds and souls and created internal horror shows that rivaled the tormented visions of the insane.

When early victims of these bad trips sought medical help from professionals untrained in dealing with psychedelic drugs' effects, they often suffered even more at their ham-handed, judgmental ministrations. It soon became a hippie maxim that only someone familiar with the mercurial LSD experience could effectively heal people on "bummers," and self-appointed psychedelic therapists and entheogenic EMTs began to advertise their services in countercultural neighborhoods, using talk therapy and chemical compounds to bring tormented trippers out of their self-created hell worlds.

THE MAN WHO COULDN'T BE PROGRAMMED

One of these figures, George Peters, saw his vocation to help troubled trippers as not only a service, but a religious calling. Although the humanitarian/spiritual organization he founded, Naturalism, Inc. a.k.a. the Church of Naturalism, never formally endorsed the use of LSD and other entheogens as holy sacraments, its mission was so intimately tied in with the psychedelic experience, that its strange and sometimes sinister story warrants inclusion in this volume.

Perhaps nobody knew Peters as well as did radical journalist Lionel Rolfe. In his memoir *Fat Man on the Left,* Rolfe said that the guru of Naturalism hired him to write his biography in the late 1970s. Rolfe was fascinated by the man, and spent many hours taping Peters's rambling recollections, although the LSD avatar eventually aborted the project and stiffed him on payment.

George Peters variously gave his birthdate as 1937 or 1939, and sometimes hinted that he'd been born under another name. He claimed his father was a New York Irish-American cop who had served in military intelligence during World War II and was one of the founding members of the CIA. Peters said his mother was a wealthy socialite who'd turned against him after his father died in 1953; the underaged Peters fled her abuse, enlisted in the navy, and served at the tail end of the Korean War. After a brief marriage, an ugly divorce, and a final break with his mother, Peters moved to Chicago in the early 1960s.

Peters told Rolfe that while working as a television repairman, he'd met a man who called himself "David" in a Chicago bar. David claimed that he was a space alien who'd come to Earth to find human agents for his mission to save the planet and that Peters was one of the chosen. To prepare him for his role, Peters said, David dosed him with an unknown drug that put the young Chicagoan out of commission for three days.

Peters said that the drug gave David a strange hold over him. When David demanded that Peters tell him his complete life story, over and over, he complied, repeatedly recounting his whole biography down to every obscure, intimate detail. If David thought Peters wasn't telling the whole truth and nothing but, he punished his pupil, making him perform bizarre acts of contrition like dressing up in outrageous costumes and accosting people in downtown Chicago.

Eventually, David dosed Peters with sodium pentothal, the "truth serum," and the young man made a complete confession of his life's doings, good and otherwise. The confession was followed by a mystic vision of service to humanity, where Peters embraced the motto: "I will help anyone at any time so long as it hurts no other."[1]

After his vision, Peters never saw David again. He later maintained that the mystery man had been an intelligence operative running him through Project Artichoke—a CIA operation that used advanced interrogation techniques and psychotropic drugs to program unsuspecting or unwilling subjects for questionable purposes and that was later exposed during the 1975 U.S. Senate hearings on intelligence agency misdeeds. The would-be Manchurian Candidate speculated that he'd been cut loose from the program when the spooks failed to make a programmed assassin out of him, and instead created a religious leader.

NATURALISM, INC.

Peters found his spiritual mission in September of 1965. That month a lady friend of his went on a colossal LSD bummer; when she was taken to an emergency room, the staff, unfamiliar with psychedelics, refused to treat her. Peters swore he'd never let a tripper again suffer such indignities at the hands of ignorant physicians or therapists, and founded his own LSD crisis-response organization and spiritual movement, which he dubbed Naturalism, Inc.

From the beginning it was unclear what Peters's qualifications were in the fields of either therapy or ministry. Although he claimed he held a university degree and training certificates in psychology, he was hazy on the details, and nobody was able to verify if he'd ever attended an accredited college. Peters mentioned to one reporter that back in 1957 he'd "turned on troops" to LSD while in the navy, leading one to suspect his later yarns about David may have been brain-garbled recollections of military-intelligence training with psychedelics.

Naturalism represented itself as a spiritual organization with a rather vague creed. An article in the *East Village Other* underground newspaper stated that Naturalism was:

[a]n attempt to get groovy people around the world in touch with each other and working together for a better world. They take a special interest in dope-taking people, since the best studies admit that people who take dope generally have more brains and imagination than people who manage to get along in this sump-sink killer society without dope.[2]

Unlike such organizations as Synanon that addressed the "drug problem" by promoting total sobriety, Naturalism advocated moderation, and management of the psychedelic experience. In doing so, it anticipated the harm-reduction approaches of later, better-credentialed drug-crisis organizations like the Haight-Ashbury Free Clinic and the Do It Now Foundation.

"LSD DOES BEAUTIFUL THINGS TO SOME PEOPLE"

Peters called the crisis-response arm of Naturalism, "LSD Rescue." He established a phone hotline that Chicagoans experiencing bad trips could call at any hour and handed out business cards and flyers advertising his guerrilla-therapy services at rock concerts and other counterculture gatherings. When distraught druggies called in, Peters or a Naturalism volunteer would listen carefully and nonjudgmentally to their complaints and attempt to talk them down from the bummer.

If that didn't work, Peters went to the trippers' homes with a bag of pharmaceuticals. The pills were courtesy of famed gastroenterologist and popular-medicine columnist Dr. Walter Alvarez, who'd met Peters when the latter came to repair his television. The doctor approved of the younger man's work with Chicago's hippies and wayward youth, and wrote him prescriptions for antipsychotics, tranquilizers, and barbiturates.

Peters also administered multivitamins to bummer-victims and recommended daily megadoses of niacin to keep LSD flashbacks at bay. Sometimes, however, the chemicals were unnecessary, and troubled trippers responded well to hypnosis and relaxation therapy, or even mere kindness and understanding.

Said Peters to one reporter about his mission: "With society and so many doctors, it's all black or white. LSD does beautiful things to some people. Some do have religious experiences. I wouldn't say every hippie is automatically crazy. . . . I don't have regular office hours. I can't see a patient day after day. I only have ten minutes, and my way is the fastest way to get at problems."[3]

THE HIPPIE MEDICINE MAN

Peters's work with people suffering from drug crises made him a local celebrity in Chicago, and his doings were profiled in national media ranging from New York's *Village Voice* underground newspaper to the staid *Chicago Tribune*. The latter publication featured a Sunday special story about his relationship with Dr. Alvarez that pictured the long-haired, bearded Peters alongside the strait-laced, octogenarian physician, and discussed the common ground they shared as healers.

Yet Peters never really accepted his image as a hippie medicine man. He felt the role was forced on him, and griped, "It's not so much that they want to have a leader, as that they want to be followers. I've never gotten along too well with most of the hippies. But, listen, when we do get along is when they're in trouble. They've all got my number next to their telephones."[4] Peters said that many people called his hotline just to discuss their non-drug-related problems or allay their loneliness and boredom.

By the end of the decade, Peters claimed that Naturalism and LSD Rescue employed 20 full-time staff and 130 volunteers and had treated over 7,400 clients. They had established a network of safe houses and crash pads throughout the Chicago area that sheltered drug victims, teenage runaways, and other troubled youth, and worked with both local social service agencies and law enforcement on the harder cases.

Naturalism had also spread beyond Chicago. Centers sprang up in New York City, Los Angeles, Toronto, and Washington, D.C., and Peters even planned to buy an island off the Florida coast as a retreat where Naturalism adherents could, as one member put it, accept themselves and each other for what they were, be natural, practice kindness, and "be gods on Earth." Peters never explained where the money to finance this or his many other operations originated, although it was known that Dr. Alvarez helped underwrite the Naturalism mission.

THE YOUNG LORDS AND THE LONELY CLUB BUST

As with so many other sixties countercultural groups, Naturalism's fortunes took a downturn in the succeeding decade. Things started to sour when the organization opened a crash pad on the turf of the Young Lords, a Puerto Rican street gang who'd rebranded themselves as New Left paramilitary radicals. The Lords feared the group's presence in the neighborhood would draw attention from cops, and accused Peters, who worked closely with the Chicago police, of being a snitch. In turn, Peters claimed the militants harassed his workers, stole from the crash pad, and even raped a girl there, and vowed he'd fight back if the Lords continued to attack his work. After tense negotiations with the Lords, Peters agreed to close the center, and retreated quietly from the 'hood.

Crises erupted at other Naturalism houses. In May 1970 a seventeen-year-old rock guitarist killed himself at one of the crash pads. Eight months later a fourteen-year-old girl was busted while shooting heroin in a junkie flophouse; she told cops she'd fled a Naturalism house after being raped there, and Peters got picked up for contributing to her delinquency. And on February 28, 1971, five people were arrested at the Naturalism "Lonely Club" on West Lunt Avenue, and charged with selling hashish, leading some to speculate that the organization was financing its activities through the drug trade.

"A PHILOSOPHY OF FREEDOM"

Mayor Daley's Chicago was becoming increasingly hostile territory for Peters, and he relocated to the warmer and more open-minded climes of Southern California. In 1973 he reincorporated his organization there as the Church of Naturalism, and set up shop on downtown Los

Angeles' South Vermont Avenue. He advertised the center as both a free clinic and a crash pad and hosted twenty or so runaways and homeless hippies every night, with a maximum allowed stay of three nights.

A second church center in Hollywood conducted "sensitivity training and encounter groups," and celebrated "hip weddings" for counter-cultural couples who spurned mainstream nuptial ceremonies. During this time Peters was also interested in ministering to prostitutes, and often sat in local courts while solicitation cases were tried, analyzing how the cops and judges persecuted sex workers.

The church's formal statement of purpose read:

The Church of Naturalism believes the formalized structure of religion has caused it to lose its spirit and essence. Emphasis on the hereafter and the lack of response to the situations of our physical existence have had the result that too many people feel enjoyment is sinful and learn to suppress their instincts. Formalized religion expends its energy in passing authority from one generation to another. The Church of Naturalism prefers to encourage the release of the energy in better causes. It is more or less a philosophy of freedom.[5]

THE "DIVINITY TRAINING PROGRAM"

To formally join the church, one had to undergo the "Divinity Training Program," a tripartite initiation into Naturalism. First came the "Group Grope," where novice Naturalists moved into same-sex dwellings with five to ten other church members, attended regular sensitivity-training and therapy sessions, and received somatic bodywork. New church members were required to hold jobs and contribute either 80 percent of their income or at least $50 a week to the church.

Next came the gender-integrated "Rural Setting." This was a retreat where fledgling Naturalists sought visions in nature, massaged each other in hot tubs, and "develop[ed] deep, honest personal relationships." During this phase church members also received "entelechial therapy," where they learned how to manifest their fantasies and dreams in the real, physical world.

The last phase of the program was the forty-day "Death Judgment

Experience." During the Experience, the Naturalist would be confined for hours in dark closets or isolation tanks, and experience total sensory deprivation. Peters believed these sessions would erase the old, negative personality programming, and allow the "original essence (self)" to emerge in a second birth.

Peters invited his would-be biographer Lionel Rolfe to try the Death Judgment Experience, but the skeptical reporter turned him down. During his time with Peters, Rolfe noted that like so many self-styled gurus of the era, the man preached enlightenment through asceticism and self-sacrifice, while he lived well off his acolytes' donations, regularly treating himself to fancy restaurant meals and top-grade cannabis and sleeping in a huge bed—"one that could accommodate a dozen people at a time, and probably had."[6]

THE WOODSTOCK ROAD MURDERS

By 1979 the Church of Naturalism had grown wealthy enough to rent a six-acre, two-house estate on Laurel Canyon's Woodstock Road. Neighbors soon grew suspicious of the "church" housed there, where constant auto traffic choked the narrow mountain lane at all hours, and muscular men and guard dogs stationed around the property chased off anyone who ventured too close to its barbed-wire fences. They suspected that the Church of Naturalism might be a front for drug dealing and other illegal activities.

Their suspicions were confirmed in June of 1981 when the house was raided by police. The cops seized two ounces of cocaine, 350 quaaludes, two ounces of cannabis and hashish, and $3,200 in cash, and busted Peters for possession with intent to sell. None of the contraband could be linked to him, though, and the Naturalist guru walked on the charges.

But Peters's luck ran out on November 6, 1982. In the early hours of that morning, assailants snuck through a back entrance onto the property, stormed the houses, and bludgeoned Peters and his lieutenant, thirty-one-year-old James Patrick Henneberry, to death, shooting them afterward for good measure. The killers then commandeered Peters's Cadillac, crashed through the front gate, and abandoned the vehicle a block down the road.

The double murder made headlines across Southern California. The

146 ☑ MAJOR SECTS

year before, persons unknown had beaten four drug dealers to death less than a mile away on Laurel Canyon's Wonderland Avenue, and the similarities between the two multiple murders unnerved Angelenos.

Some pointed to the drug bust of the previous year and said that Peters and Henneberry had been whacked over a deal gone bad. Others darkly hinted that even more sinister forces than traffickers were involved—Peters, they said, had been developing a movie about the CIA's infamous MKULTRA mind control program, and he was brutally silenced by spooks to keep his revelations from the public, and to scare off other potential whistleblowers.

In the end, the truth proved far more mundane. Church security-head/coke-runner George Smith and his girlfriend, secretary Melinda Faulcon, had been fired from their jobs by Peters just days before his murder. Seeking cash and revenge, the two snuck onto the property early on November 6, confronted the guru and his aide, pummeled them with aluminum baseball bats, and then shot them with Peters's own revolver. Arrested for the killings, both pled guilty; Smith drew two life sentences, while Faulcon got four years for manslaughter.

PROPHET? DEALER? SPOOK?

With Peters gone, the church collapsed, and its members scattered. Today their stories are almost completely unknown, even among CIA-conspiracy researchers, Chicago-counterculture historians, L.A. true-crime buffs, and chroniclers of Laurel Canyon's colorful and sometimes sinister history.

Whether George Peters was a genuine psychedelics-inspired visionary and healer, a con man who used religion as a front for drug trafficking, an agent of intelligence bureau hallucinogenic hijinks, or some combination of these, is up for debate. And the unanswered questions about Peters's doings—his alleged participation in military-sponsored LSD experimentation, the funding sources for his operations in Chicago and elsewhere, the nature and extent of his business in Los Angeles—add further troubling notes to the Naturalism story.

His would-be biographer Lionel Rolfe captured the man's essence in eight words: "George made all of us feel mighty uncomfortable."[7]

TEN

THE CHURCH OF THE TREE OF LIFE

The Sacramental Garden of Legal Highs

When the seventies dawned, the psychedelic sects that had emerged in the previous decade remained outlaw organizations. Although LSD, cannabis, and even mescaline were more popular than ever as recreational drugs, they were still listed as Schedule I substances, with harsh legal penalties for their mere possession, let alone their usage or distribution. And as the War on Drugs shifted into high gear, spiritually-oriented trippers became far less visible in both mainstream America and the counterculture.

LEGAL HIGHS

Many in the psychedelic underground began to gather information about psychoactive substances that the law hadn't yet proscribed. One small book from the era, *Legal Highs*, described a cornucopia of plants, fungi, and chemicals that packed the mind-altering punches of the better-known entheogens, but were legal and relatively easy to obtain.

Written as a taxonomy-style handbook, *Legal Highs* described the popular and scientific names, active ingredients, usages, effects, and contraindications of substances ranging from lysergic acid-bearing

Hawaiian baby woodrose seeds, to mescaline-infused San Pedro cactus, to aphrodisiac Yohimbe bark. The book became an underground best-seller and remains in print today.

Author Adam Gottlieb states in its introduction:

> It may be of some interest to some readers that the Church of the Tree of Life has declared as its religious sacraments most substances in this book. Because these substances were legal at the time of the Church's inception and incorporation, their use cannot be denied to members through any future legislation without directly violating the Constitution's guarantee of religious freedom."[1]

THE CHURCH OF THE TREE OF LIFE

"Adam Gottlieb" was the pen name of San Franciscan John A. Mann. A life-extension expert and author of various satirical plays and broad-sides, Mann incorporated the Church of the Tree of Life in 1971, hoping that it could do for the still-legal entheogens what the Native American Church did for peyote. If any of the substances it named as sacraments became illegal, it was reasoned, a religious-use exemption for church members could be carved out of the new statutes, much as the peyote exemption had been for Native American.

Unlike the Native American Church, membership in the Church of the Tree of Life was open to people of all backgrounds. The church maintained that the psychoactive substances were natural gifts to be shared by all of humanity, and that adults had the right to use them for spiritual or healing purposes so long as their actions didn't infringe on the rights of others. Other than that, it specified no doctrinal require-ments for its members.

The church didn't officially recognize LSD, cannabis, or other legally prohibited substances as sacraments. Instead, it promoted the use of legal alternatives like morning glory seeds, calamus root, *Amanita muscaria* mushrooms, and other psychoactive materials as tools for con-sciousness expansion.

Anyone who agreed with these general principles was invited to write to the church headquarters in San Francisco. An SASE sent there

The First Book
of Sacraments
OF THE
Church of The Tree of Life

a guide for the religious use of legal mind alterants

Fig. 10.1. The Church of the Tree of Life's *The First Book of Sacraments*—
an early guide to legal entheogens and their use.

would be returned with a membership card and the latest issue of "Bark
Leaf," the church newsletter.

The church described its officially-recognized entheogens in a
booklet called *The First Book of Sacraments*. Published a year before
Legal Highs appeared, it contained much of the same practical information included in the latter work, along with rare photos and illustrations of church-approved sacraments. The book also discussed the
importance of religious ritual to sanctify the use of the substances it
described and featured an essay on "Sacraments and Magic" by one
"Frater C.A.," who examined their use in the practice of Western ritual magick.

5-MEO-DMT, LYSERGIC SEEDS, AND UTOPIAN BLISS BALLS

Many church sacraments were supplied by the Inner Center mail-order house of Hermosa Beach, California. One of its offerings was 5-MeODMT, a legal variant of the powerful and proscribed tryptamine DMT. For a few dollars, one could obtain oregano or parsley leaves sprayed with the chemical, which would then be smoked like cannabis to produce an intense, otherworldly high that lasted for ten to fifteen minutes.

Untreated morning glory seeds were also sold by the Inner Center. Such seeds contain lysergic acid amide (LSA), a chemical relative of LSD, and many garden-supply companies sprayed their own product with methyl mercury to prevent spoilage and/or discourage their use by trippers. Twenty-five to 100 untreated seeds was the usual recommended dose for anyone seeking this legal entheogenic high.

Perhaps influenced by the church's practices, vendors at seventies California hippie festivals offered "utopian bliss balls." These were Medjool dates packed with lysergic Hawaiian baby woodrose seeds and herbal supplements which served as a legal, organic alternative to the Orange Sunshine LSD tablets that the Brotherhood of Eternal Love (see chapter 7) had handed out at rock festivals and countercultural gatherings during the previous decade.

And the church headquarters itself became a supply center for one notable sacrament. Its office on San Francisco's Columbus Avenue sported several full-grown San Pedro cacti, and church members would often stop by to cut off pieces of their mescaline-bearing skins and consume them as a legal alternative to peyote.

SCRAPS OF GOD'S FLESH

During its existence, the church signed up anywhere between 1,500 and 7,000 card-carrying members. Although many of them joined mainly to access nonprescribed psychoactive chemicals and sanctify their use of them under First Amendment protection, some members took the church's message of chemical enlightenment seriously, and attempted to create rituals that would reflect the sect's spiritually liberal, counterculture sensibilities.

Several Bay-Area church members tried to develop a ritual that
would combine the aesthetic creativity of Mexico's peyote-eating
Huichol Indians, with the spiritual power of Native American Church
practices. Not much came of the efforts; one church member told
psychedelic researcher Peter Stafford that what they cooked up was
"somewhat hokey," and didn't capture the essence of the entheogenic
experience.

The Church of the Tree of Life survived well into the eighties,
mostly because it kept a low profile, and devoted itself to the use of
obscure substances of little interest to government drug-warriors or sensationalist media. But it lacked a stable, active core of members devoted
to its legal-highs path, and became defunct around 1990.

Church founder John Mann wrote several more drug-related
books under his "Adam Gottlieb" pseudonym, including Sex Drugs
and Aphrodisiacs and Cooking With Cannabis. Oakland, California's
Ronin Publishing currently has all of them in print, along with a revised
and expanded edition of The First Book of Sacraments which appeared
after Mann's death in 2015.

Although the church is long gone, its sacraments of choice are still
ingested by adventurous trippers. And information about them, particularly regarding safety, is distributed far more widely than it was in
the church's time. These scraps of God's flesh, out of the reach of John
Law's strictures, will no doubt continue to be popular in both recreational and sacred contexts.

ELEVEN

TEMPLE OF THE TRUE INNER LIGHT

A DPT Eucharist on the Lower East Side

For several years, a hole-in-the-wall storefront on Manhattan's East Ninth Street hosted the most publicly visible psychedelic sect in North America. The East Village address was the home of the Temple of the True Inner Light, a group that somehow spent the late eighties— the high tide of the War on Drugs—unmolested as they openly promoted the spiritual use of the synthetic, legal entheogen DPT (N,N-dipropyltryptamine) right in the middle of New York City.

Ironically, the Temple's Manhattan location may have been what protected them from serious legal hassles. New York City police had their hands full trying to stem the multibillion-dollar traffic in heroin, cocaine, and other narcotics that flowed through the city's streets, and barely took note of the little sect and the obscure, legal hallucinogen its members used. Perhaps the Big Apple's finest thought it was better to let the temple's adherents trip the light fantastic on the sidewalks of New York's bohemian quarter and concentrate on more dangerous drugs and organizations.

YIPPIE SPIRITUALITY AND THE VOICE OF THE PSYCHEDELIC

Temple founder Alan Birnbaum had promoted entheogenic enlightenment since 1974. That September the *New York Times* reported the twenty-seven-year-old Birnbaum was arrested for distributing joints at a cannabis "smoke-in" in Manhattan's Washington Square Park. The smoke-in had been organized by the Youth International Party, a.k.a. the Yippies, a New Left radical group that pioneered media pranking and culture jamming and saw cannabis as a revolutionary consciousness-raising agent.

One year later the Yippies featured Birnbaum in their newspaper, the *Yipster Times*. Reporter "Billy Gram" visited a "small, shabby cockroach-infested apartment on the lower east side of Manhattan" to interview Birnbaum about a group he'd organized, "The Church of the Psychedelic Eucharist."

According to the article, "the Church believes consciousness to be the ultimate guide 'in the real world' and that the ultimate consciousness comes from the 'flesh of consciousness': Psychedelics. Some of the members claim to have become so conscious as to have seen and communicated with the Psychedelic spirit itself. They report that it can present itself as a real living spirit within the extremely psychedelicized person."[1]

Birnbaum was also quoted as saying: "The main purpose of the Church is to make God available to the members. . . . Each person has to hear the voice of the Psychedelic themselves and follow it to the best of their ability. In doing this, my friends and I have come up with the same truths and have gotten together and formed this church." The church might have never gone beyond Birnbaum's apartment had it not been for its founder's insistence that their psychedelic sacraments be legally recognized. "It is very important to us to have the Church accepted legally," Birnbaum maintained. "We need to be able to ensure the purity and identity of our sacraments for the safety of our members, which is very hard to do if you are dealing with underground chemicals unless it is peyote or marijuana. . . . This can be very disturbing to someone who has the spirit knocking on the door of their consciousness and they are considering about letting it come in."[2]

THE NATIVE AMERICAN CHURCH OF NEW YORK

Perhaps thinking that he had a better shot at getting a religious-use exemption if he changed the church's name and image, Birnbaum and five followers created the Native American Church of New York in

1976. Despite its name, the organization had no connection with the long-established indigenous sect, save for the fact that it recognized peyote as a holy sacrament. Yet New York State's Health Commissioner's office issued the church a permit for ceremonial ingestion of the cactus.

Birnbaum then petitioned the Drug Enforcement Agency to grant his group the same exemption to the drug laws that the Feds had given to the better-known Native American Church of North America. Unlike earlier attempts by non–Native American sects to gain exemptions for psychedelics, Birnbaum's petition maintained that the substances weren't merely aids to a spiritual practice, but "objects of worship and considered deities in themselves." Moreover, the proposal didn't limit itself to one favored chemical, but embraced the whole range of entheogens from LSD to cannabis, to peyote, to synthetics. And it specified that manufacturers and distributers of the sacraments would be regulated by registration and other legal strictures, much as the original Native American Church's suppliers were.

Still, the church was no more successful convincing the DEA than its predecessors had been, and the proposal was rejected. But Birnbaum continued to buy peyote buttons from government-licensed vendors, most of whom probably thought his group was a local branch of the national Native American Church. Birnbaum also applied to the N.Y. State Department of Narcotics for a license to distribute peyote. And in 1979 he appealed the DEA's decision in the U.S. District Court of New York, on behalf of the church and the 1,000-odd followers he claimed.

The ruling in the case, *Native American Church of New York v. United States,* was mixed. Judge Milton Pollack dismissed the church's broad-based claims about the religious use of psychedelics in general, citing previous rulings regarding LSD and cannabis in similar cases, and affirming the federal government's interest in controlling drugs. But he also stated that the church could be given an exemption for peyote use if it was determined to be "a bona fide religious organization and would make use of peyote for sacramental purposes and regard the drug as a deity."[3] Birnbaum appealed the ruling on constitutional grounds, but it was denied.

On the state level Birnbaum faced the tough new "Rockefeller drug laws," which limited the N.Y. State Health Commissioner's ability to grant exemptions such as the one given to his church. When state police learned that Birnbaum had purchased 20,000 peyote buttons from various suppliers, and that his legal ability to possess them was in question, they raided church premises, arrested him, and seized the cacti. Psychedelics expert Peter Stafford reported that the state planned to try Birnbaum on charges that could have gotten him fifteen years to life but apparently the case never made it to court.

EMPATHOGENS: THE TRIP OF THE HEART

Around 1980 Birnbaum turned his attentions to a specific, and largely legal, set of entheogens: the synthetic phenethylamines and tryptamines.

The best known of these compounds, MDA (3,4-Methylenedioxyamphetamine) was first synthesized in 1910. Twenty years later UCLA researcher Gordon Alles discovered its psychoactive properties as part of his work with amphetamines. MDA and its close molecular relative MDMA, also known as Ecstasy or Molly, were found to not only duplicate the psychedelic and numinous effects of the organic entheogens, but also produced distinctive feelings of filial warmth, closeness, and affection in subjects. Because of these "heart-opening" qualities, these chemicals are often called *empathogens*.

Studies found that the chemicals were useful in treating PTSD and other psychopathologies. But as with LSD and other hallucinogens, there was the worrying potential for their abuse as black-market recreational drugs. As a result, the production, possession, and use of MDA, MDMA, and a few other compounds were restricted to approved medical and scientific researchers.

The most famous and influential of these researchers was Alexander "Sasha" Shulgin. A Berkeley, California, native and former research chemist for Dow Chemicals, the well-connected Shulgin possessed a Schedule I license to manufacture and possess all manner of otherwise-illegal drugs in his backyard analytical laboratory. Fascinated by the mind- and heart-expanding powers of MDMA, he spent nearly forty years creating hundreds of alphabet-soup phenethylamine and tryptamine compounds and testing them on himself and his friends. Shulgin wrote of his work in *PiHKAL* and *TiHKAL,* two books now considered the definitive works on synthetic entheogens.

"A VERY POWERFUL ANGEL OF THE HOST"

One of the many chemicals Shulgin and his associates brewed and ingested was DPT. This is a molecular relative of the better-known, and illegal, tryptamine DMT that produces an intense short-duration trip into a psychedelic netherworld. In 1980 Alan Birnbaum wrote the DEA to inquire if DPT, and the DMT analogue 5-MeO-DMT, were legal to possess and use under the Controlled Substances Act. The Feds responded that neither were proscribed by the law, but warned him that abuse would lead to their being placed on Schedule I.

Thus informed, Birnbaum founded the Temple of the True Inner Light. Its basic statement of belief identified its mission with the historical avatars of world religions, stating:

> If you do not belong to Christ (our temple), you cannot receive the Salvation of Yahweh, the Psychedelic. They have told us clearly, and many times, that Christ (King Moses, David, Elijah, Jesus, Vishnu, Gautama, Mohammed, Mani, Quetzacoatl) is alive again physically, and that the crucifixion has happened again . . . the mystery has been revealed.
>
> Anyone who enters into Their (the Psychedelic's), Presence without belonging to Christ's Body is an alien and a foreign visitor to Them. We are Their Children and citizens of Their Realm.
>
> Whoever does not belong to Christ, belongs to anti-Christ. As King Jesus said, "whoever is not with me is against (anti) me."
>
> If anyone hears the Holy Spirit, which is Yahweh's, the Psychedelic's, Testimony that we (our temple) are the true Body of Christ, before having joined with us, they can no longer join us in this physical life.[4]

The temple stated that "our Eucharist is Dipropyl Tryptamine [*sic*]—a very powerful Angel of the Host." One member was quoted as saying that "the psychedelic is Christ," and that it "is instructing us at this time to offer communion to the public with DPT."[5] Another member told a reporter that "DPT is one of the angels," and that God's other angels include marijuana, peyote, and LSD. The temple also maintained that many Old and New Testament references to "spirits" in oil, bread, and other substances were references to psychedelics, and that the sect was carrying on the work of biblical prophets and priests in the modern world.

STOREFRONT TRIPPING AND CANNIBAL SOUP

The temple produced booklets and flyers that described its mission and distributed them at NYC counterculture hotspots. It also opened a storefront church on East Ninth Street in Manhattan to receive visitors and hold worship meetings.

At the temple storefront, members screened potential communicants. If approved, the seeker was invited to a semiprivate session in

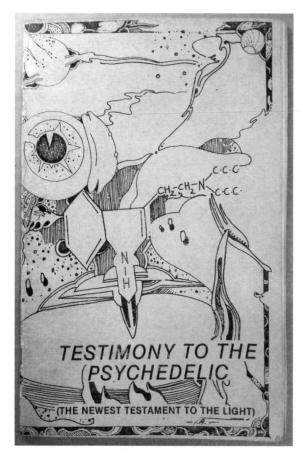

Fig. 11.1. "Testimony to the Psychedelic." The Temple of the True Inner Light distributed booklets and flyers like this around New York City

University of Pennsylvania Libraries' Gotham Book Mart collection, 1981.

the temple, where they would smoke DPT-infused raspberry leaves from a hookah, while meditative music and Bible readings were played on a tape recorder (communicants were expected to stay for the entire taped program). The goal, according to psychedelics researcher Thomas Lyttle, was "a particular gnosis and re-examination of inspired literature via DPT," if not a full acceptance of the chemical as God and Alan Birnbaum as its prophet.

Journalist Peter Gorman visited the temple in 1989, and described his experience smoking DPT in the funky, hipster-ghetto storefront church:

> The whole scene is a little shaky; I'm in a New York City tenement, sitting on the floor beneath a loft bed, smoking a bowl of raspberry leaves which are covered in a psychotropic substance I've never heard of, listening to religious scripture with an avowed apostle of the Lord, one who has explained to me that I am a sinner for not accepting Jesus as my savior, and the white smoke as Jesus. It's not the most conducive setting in which to experiment with the stability of my mind. Still, here I am, holding onto that smoke until I know nothing will escape when I open my mouth and gulp a fresh lungful of air.
>
> The high is instant and hard. No warning, no intimation, just swallow and peak. Suddenly, my worries disappear . . .[6]

Another writer described a trip to the temple in the early nineties, where he smoked DPT with the faithful. During the trip he had visions of "melting smiling hobbit/gnome faces" and "bands of nomadic elves with black skin on a moonlight plain cooking meat and preparing for a great hunt."[7] Author Terence McKenna called such entities "machine elves": inhabitants of the phenethylamine- and tryptamine-universes akin to the fairies and "little people" of folkloric traditions across the globe.

One communicant who made himself distinctly unwelcome at the temple was Daniel Rakowitz. A Lower East Side character who had founded his own sect and proclaimed himself the antichrist, Rakowitz was asked to leave the temple after he spent a session ranting crazily at the faithful while waving around a copy of Hitler's *Mein Kampf* and a live rooster. Shortly thereafter he made headlines when he was arrested for the murder of topless dancer Monika Beerle, whose corpse he had disposed of by boiling it in a stew and serving it to homeless people in Tompkins Square Park. Rakowitz's cannibal soup-kitchen ministry earned him permanent confinement in a psychiatric ward.

THE SERPENT AND THE SACRAMENT

Many of the temple's teachings touched on gnostic, heterodox-Christian themes. In one, the sect stated the Serpent of Eden had a "mission to open the eyes of the 'blind' . . . Christ was the Serpent, and opening the eyes of the blind to their spiritual nakedness was good."[8] The passage says that John 3:13 confirms this: ". . . and the Son of Man must be lifted up as Moses lifted up the Serpent in the desert, so that everyone who believes may have eternal Life in Him."

Another temple teaching concerns suicide. The passage states, "We have been Shown very clearly by Yahweh, the Psychedelic, the Being of Light, that physical death is not the way to end suffering, and that violence and anger is Condemned. Committing suicide does not end suffering and only leads to Condemnation and rebirth physically. . . . As one person said: 'If you leave here a tormented soul, you will be a tormented soul over there too.'"[9]

The temple requires a vegan diet of its faithful and sees nutrition as a key element in treating depression. It opposes the use of alcohol, opiates, and cocaine, and promotes nonviolence and honesty. The temple also claims to run a nonprofit organization that sponsors detox programs and builds affordable housing for low-income and homeless people.

The number of temple members and communicants are unknown. However, the sect believes "everyone who ingests Entheogens to be the Children of the true 'Israel,'" and posits four levels of membership:

[T]hose who (the outer court):
1. ingest Entheogens but don't know that Entheogens are God;
2. ingest Them and believe They are God;

3. believe Entheogens are God and that our Temple is the true Body of Christ (Buddha, Moses, etc.);

and (the inner court):

4. those who have given up their life in the world to devote themselves to the Temple.

It is the last group—those who have given up their life in the world to devote themselves to the Temple—that most people would think of as being "Temple members."[10]

"WE ARE NOT INTO PUBLICITY"

The Temple of the True Inner Light never gained many members. Its ascetic, bibliocentric image and teachings turned off many in the often-libertine psychedelic subculture, and rumors that Alan Birnbaum considered himself Christ and dominated his followers like a typical cult guru didn't help. Eventually the temple storefront on East Ninth Street closed—it's now a high-end boutique—and the group retreated to private dwellings.

A visit to the temple's website is almost like a trip back in time to the East Village, storefront-church days of the nineties. It's hosted on the obsolescent Tripod platform and consists of a few pages of text about the temple, and some writings drawn from different faith traditions. Temple webmaster *selah* admits that "we are not into publicity" on the internet—a 1999 flame-war started by a disgruntled ex-member on various psychedelics-related boards may have scared the sect away from interacting with all but the most determined online communicants.

Yet the temple still survives in its discreet, low-key fashion. Over forty years after its founding it is still the most well-known of the synthetics-oriented sects and is a part of both entheogenic and New York counterculture history—a real-life, brick-and-mortar, public psychedelic church that has taken countless people to the parallel universe of the tryptamine experience to see the Light that shines within all humans and that illuminates the spiritual quest of each seeker.

TWELVE

THE SHIVA FELLOWSHIP

Cannabis Communion on Hippie Hill

When President Lyndon B. Johnson called for a National Day of Prayer on Memorial Day 1968, no doubt the *last* thing he expected was for it to be answered by cannabis-smoking, naked hippies holding a Hindu ceremony in a San Francisco park.

Yet that was exactly how over 200 Haight-Ashbury residents responded to the White House's request for spiritual aid on May 30 of that troubled, tumultuous year. The gathering was one of the first organized public marijuana "smoke-ins" in American history and was additionally notable not only because it became a regular occurrence in Golden Gate Park for nearly three years afterward, but because it was dedicated to the worship of Shiva: the Hindu god associated with the ritual use of cannabis.

A KANSAS CITY FELON ON THE HIPPIE TRAIL

The events were organized by the Shiva Fellowship: the creation of one Wilbur Leo Minzey (1932–1998). A native of Kansas City, Missouri, and a former student at both Kansas State University and the University of Missouri, Minzey was an electrical engineer who, like so many other young Americans, migrated to California in the early 1960s.

Minzey may have left Kansas City to distance himself from a criminal record. In December 1954 he was arrested there for rape, assault, and burglary, and later pled guilty to the charges, yet avoided prison when a judge committed him to the Topeka state mental hospital. Minzey was arrested again for burglary and molestation four years later, and eventually logged over two and a half years as a guest of the Sunflower State's controlled-custody facilities.

When he settled in San Francisco, Minzey joined the anarcho-syndicalist Industrial Workers of the World. An early anti-Vietnam War activist, Minzey was one of the San Francisco protesters who occupied San Francisco State University's ROTC office and blocked the city's Federal Building driveway during the spring of 1965. Minzey also taught a course called "Slum Household Electricity" at the free Thoreau College, where he instructed Haight-Ashbury hippies in the finer points of appliance and utilities repair.

Seeking adventure and enlightenment, Minzey traveled to Italy and hit the "Hippie Trail" to Asia in 1967, smoking hashish along the way with both locals and fellow counterculture pilgrims. When he arrived in the Indian holy city of Benares on the Ganges River, he met several *sadhus,* mendicant Hindu holy men who worshipped the deity Shiva.

SHIVA AND THE SHAIVITES

Shiva is the companion of the Hindu gods Brahma and Vishnu, and consort of the goddess Parvati. His devotees, the Shaivites, view Shiva as Creator, Protector, and Transformer of the universe, and variously depict him as a peaceful father and householder, a fearsome warrior, and a wise yogi. One of the oldest known deities, Shiva is pictured on South Asian rock art believed to date back to 10,000 BCE or earlier.

Some Shaivite devotional art also pictures the god smoking ganja in a chillum—a tubelike clay pipe—and many of his followers practice cannabis consumption as a religious devotion. In Benares, Minzey met several of these holy hashishim, who shared ganja with him and taught him how to use the herb to open his mind to the Divine. In turn, Minzey gave them doses of the modern West's own entheogen—California-made LSD—and later reported that the Indian holy men loved the chemical.

Soon, Minzey was attending public ceremonies in Benares where hundreds of Shaivites raised clouds of cannabis smoke to their god. And after he read the *Bhagavad Gita* and decided that Shiva was indeed the Supreme Being and Prime Mover, he declared himself a Shaivite. Minzey was initiated into the sect when an Indian holy woman named Mataji drew three horizontal lines on his forehead with hashish ashes, marking him as one of the first Western devotees in the tradition.

When Minzey returned to San Francisco, he set up an altar to Shiva in the house where he lived with other hippies. The sadhus had taught Minzey to hold the vessel of ganja in front of his pineal gland—the Third Eye of mystic tradition—before he ignited and inhaled its contents, and he complied in ritual devotions, even though his sacrificial chalice was a paper joint rather than a chillum. Housemates joined Minzey in the ceremonies, and he eventually began to hold regular services in his home chapel for the Haight-Ashbury community.

Hearing of the psychedelics-oriented Neo-American Church (see chapter 6), Minzey joined up, became a "Boo Hoo" priest, and affiliated his congregation, which he called the Shiva Fellowship, with the organization. But Minzey later complained that "Chief Boo Hoo" Art Kleps was a drunk and a womanizer who squandered his followers' funds on booze and frivolities, and instead allied with the church's "Primate of California," sexual-freedom advocate Jefferson Poland.

THE SHIVA FELLOWSHIP AT HIPPIE HILL

No doubt the Neo-American Church's Shiva Fellowship was not exactly the type of religious organization President Lyndon B. Johnson had in mind when he called for America's congregations to come together in prayer on Memorial Day 1968. But Minzey and his marijuana minions responded to the request anyway, and on the morning of May 30, 1968, under a banner that read "LBJ Pray-In for Peace," he led a contingent of over 200 Western Shaivites, hippies, stoners, radicals, and others down Haight Street to Golden Gate Park.

The crowd assembled at the hill near "Mothers Meadow," which had become a hangout for Haight hippies. There, at an altar that sported a brass statue of Shiva and prayer flags, Neo-American Church Primate of California Jefferson Poland explained the purpose of the gathering to the crowd, and then introduced the Reverend Willie Minzey.

Holding a joint, Minzey demonstrated the proper way to dedicate a smoke to Shiva. Then he distributed rolled cannabis cigarettes to the crowd, who enthusiastically toked up in the name of the Divine Creator and Transformer.

Thus enlightened, they watched and listened as Jefferson Poland stripped naked and read the Bible's salacious "Song of Solomon," to invoke Shiva's consort Parvati. This was too much for nearby San Francisco mounted policemen, who rode their horses into the gathering and busted Poland for indecent exposure, along with two bystanders who didn't move fast enough when they ordered the crowd to disperse.

Yet Minzey and his Shiva Fellowship returned to the park on Sunday, June 9, to celebrate another group ritual. Once again, body-freedom advocate Poland doffed his clothes to preach and got arrested. Otherwise, the cops left Minzey and his followers alone, and the Shiva Fellowship guru decided to make the public gatherings at the knoll called "Hippie Hill" a regular event, to be held every Sunday.

SMOKE-INS AND PUBLIC OBSCENITY

The June 14–20 issue of the *Berkeley Barb* featured a story about the second smoke-in, where Minzey explained that there were no formal requirements for attendance at the ceremonies, nor for membership in the fellowship. He did however state that most of his followers would agree with this basic creed:

I believe:
> that there are several serious problems that human intelligence cannot or will not solve;
> that the failure to solve these problems, will within our lifetime lead to catastrophic changes in conditions affecting all organic life on this planet;
> that the solution to these problems can only be found thru love, peace, and a deeper spiritual awareness of the basic truths of reality;

that an essential aspect of these truths is manifested in the concept of Shiva;

that this aspect is best revealed through the joyous group spiritual experience involving the use of psychedelic substances;

that spiritual necessity has historical, logical and ethical prece-
dence over any legal, political or economic consideration;

that whenever any culture contains a basic conflict between any
spiritual imperative and any other ideal the profane must
always yield to the sacred or that culture will perish.[1]

The fellowship continued to hold Sunday services in Golden Gate
Park during 1968. Their fourth ceremony on June 23 was a response to
civil rights leader Rev. Ralph Abernathy's request for spiritual support
for his Poor Peoples' March on Washington. This time Minzey stripped
down to a loincloth, in the style of the Indian sadhus, and handed out
LSD tablets along with the usual joints.

Although the nearby police once again ignored the drug use, they
waded into the gathering to bust one of the celebrants for meditating
naked at the altar. When several Shaivites objected, the cops began to
harass them, demanding their IDs and threatening Jefferson Poland, who
had also completely disrobed, with another arrest. Minzey intervened,
and said that if they had to arrest anyone, it should be him, since he had
organized the whole psychedelic nude heathen-fest. After Minzey continuously demanded to be busted and pelted the officers with expletives, they
complied and detained him for indecent exposure and public obscenity.

Minzey's subsequent trial was a bizarre collision of the San Francisco
counterculture and the law. Though the prosecution claimed Minzey's
garment revealed the reverend's testes, they could not introduce it as
evidence since the Shaivite priest had loaned it to a local hippie to tie
down his car trunk lid. The defense counsel brought a nearly naked
gay-bar stripper into the court to demonstrate how his legally tolerated
loincloth was significantly smaller and more revealing than Minzey's.
And both Jefferson Poland and Minzey himself testified that the latter's foul language had "redeeming social value," since he was trying to
prevent the cops' disruption of religious services, itself a misdemeanor
under California Penal Code Sec. 302.

The jury split on the obscenity charge, but they found Minzey guilty of indecent exposure, and he served four months in jail. Public Shiva Fellowship services were suspended for the rest of the year.

"FREE WHEED," MORE ARRESTS, AND THE FIRST 4/20

In January 1969 Minzey was freed, and the Shiva Fellowship ceremonies resumed on Hippie Hill. The reverend vowed to continue his holy mission, "celebrat[ing] our continued existence-in-exile, giving out free wheed [sic], acid, and whatever to the Sadhus—the holy stoned beggars of the street—and you."[2] In March the fellowship held services at a huge "Rite of Spring" festival at Golden Gate Park's Speedway Meadow, where they distributed the herbal sacrament free to all attendees.

Weeks later, however, Minzey was arrested at a Sunday ceremony when he proffered a joint to a uniformed policeman. Although the reverend was released two days later with no charges filed, the incident demonstrated Minzey's increasing tendency to test the limits of police tolerance, and the law's diminishing patience with him. When Minzey was busted again at an Easter Sunday service on April 6, he was interviewed afterward by a television crew, and invited TV viewers to join the fellowship the next Sunday for a cannabis-sharing celebration on Hippie Hill.

Although the service on April 13 featured an especially large turnout, it seemingly passed without incident. Yet two days later, cops arrived at Minzey's pad in the middle of the night and arrested him for crimes far more serious than mere public nudity and obscenity. That morning the Shiva Fellowship guru was charged with not only drug possession, but furnishing said drugs to minors and conspiracy to commit the same—offenses that could potentially put him in prison for life.

Released on bail, Minzey continued to hold the Sunday services. On April 20, the fellowship contributed fistfuls of sacramental joints to a Hippie Hill "Earth Faire" that anticipated the annual "4/20" smoke-in attended by thousands of stoners at the site decades later. Four months later, on August 24, the fellowship and Haight guru Stephen Gaskin sponsored a free concert at Hippie Hill by legendary psychedelic-rockers the Grateful Dead, although it is uncertain today whether the band made it to the gig.

Fig. 12.1. The much-arrested Reverend Willie Minzey of the Shiva Fellowship on the cover of the *San Francisco Good Times* underground newspaper. May 14, 1971.

Yet all was not well on Hippie Hill. By mid-1969 the Haight was rapidly turning into a dangerous, speed- and heroin-poisoned ghetto, and the ugly new reality spilled out into Golden Gate Park. At one ceremony, teenage thugs robbed and stabbed celebrants. The following Sunday, there was a knife fight right at the altar.

Fearing that Golden Gate Park was no longer safe territory, Minzey sought a permanent, protected home for the fellowship. In October 1969 he announced that a "Temple of Cannabis" would open on Halloween night in San Francisco, where Shiva's devotees could burn ganja offerings to the god in peace and privacy. But Minzey was too broke and too preoccupied by his upcoming felony trial to rent a space for the temple, and the fellowship continued to hold their Sunday services on Hippie Hill through the fall and winter.

THE WRATH OF THE STATE

Now something of a countercultural celebrity, Minzey reached out to the public via the *San Francisco Good Times* underground newspaper, where he penned a regular column and made appeals for donations and legal assistance. In one piece, he defined the nature of the fellowship, and warned casual stoners not to tempt the wrath of Shiva or John Law:

> There are no membership cards or lists in the Shiva Fellowship . . . you are a member as long as you offer regular sacrifice to Shiva, refrain from living by a policy of violence and maintain a reverence for all life.

> There is no ordination in the Shiva Fellowship. You are a reverend if your followers regard your whole life as a holy life. You are no longer revered when people cease to regard you this way.

> For those who piously devote their lives to this worship the only defense against state harassment is the ability to convince a jury of the sincerity of their belief and of a juror's sacred obligation to respect this belief.

> For those who hope to defend their actions by falsely and sacrilegiously claiming devotion to Shiva: WARNING: you will incur the

wrath of both the gods and of the state. You will be ground between the forces you yourself set in motion.[3]

Minzey may have served the god of ganja faithfully, but the state had other ideas about his mission. He logged yet another arrest during the Hippie Hill ceremony on May 24, 1970, when cops busted him for obscenity, creating a public disturbance, and failure to identify himself. Convicted two months later, he appealed the ruling, and doggedly continued to hold ceremonies in Golden Gate Park.

After two years of delays, Minzey finally faced a judge and jury in May 1971 on the charges of conspiracy to distribute narcotics to minors. Arresting officers and a witness claimed that after he had distributed cannabis cigarettes during a Sunday service two years earlier, several preteen children had taken and smoked passed joints.

At one of the preliminary hearings, the judge ruled that Minzey could neither use religious-freedom arguments nor mention the name of the Shiva Fellowship during the proceedings. This effectively gutted his defense strategy.

Observers initially predicted a long, complex trial. Yet justice was meted out quickly to the bearded, bespectacled thirty-eight-year-old religious leader, who attended the court dressed in a purple robe, a gold-embroidered red vest, and flared white trousers. After only three days of hearings, and an hour of deliberation, the jury found Minzey guilty of both possessing cannabis and distributing it to minors.

"WE WILL SACRIFICE MARIJUANA ON YOUR GRAVE!"

Although rallies and benefit concerts that featured name musical acts like Sopwith Camel, Charlie Musselwhite, and Elvin Bishop were organized to raise money for an appeal, the conviction stood. Famed radical attorney Tony Serra represented Minzey during the sentencing, and when he attempted to get Judge S. Lee Vavuris disqualified, the lawyer earned a five-day jail stint for contempt of court.

Judge Vavuris, who would later preside over the even more controversial trial of the Black-radical "Soledad Brothers," handed the marijuana missionary the maximum penalty: ten years to life. Given a chance to respond, Minzey thundered at the bench and the court: "Whether you send me to jail, the religious use of marijuana will prevail. . . . We will sacrifice marijuana on your grave!"[4]

Further appeals were denied, and the Bay Area's hippie community was outraged about the stiff sentence. No doubt the court knew of Minzey's old rape and assault beefs back in Kansas, and felt he was a loose cannon that needed to be locked up before he inflicted similar crimes against the Golden State.

PRISON, FREEDOM, AND DEATH

Minzey was shipped off first to Vacaville Prison, then to the infamous San Quentin penitentiary, where he spent time in solitary confinement. Finally, he was placed in the minimum-security California Men's Colony in San Luis Obispo, where he worked as a clerk in the prison education office and was visited regularly by his wife, Diane, and their small children. Aided by cannabis scholar and activist Michael Aldrich, Minzey and Tony Serra continued to press for a religious-freedom appeal of the conviction, but their efforts were for naught.

In early 1977 the California Adult Authority offered Minzey an early release in an exchange for an admission of wrongdoing, and a vow to discontinue his cannabis sacrifices to Shiva. Still true to his faith, Minzey refused the terms, although he was granted a reduction in his sentence to thirteen years' imprisonment.

When he was finally freed in 1984, Minzey moved with his family to Southern California. He got a job as a film engineer and dwelled quietly in the town of Newhall, where he died on December 24, 1998, at sixty-six years of age. Minzey had lived long enough to see marijuana legalized as a medicine in California, public smoke-ins regularly staged across North America, and Hippie Hill become a spot of pilgrimage every April 20 for a cannabis ceremony far bigger than the ones he had held there thirty years earlier.

The Shiva Fellowship ceased to exist as an organized religious group when Minzey went to prison. Yet he left in his wake a community of several hundred people who had regularly attended the Hippie Hill ceremonies, and who had made cannabis use the center of their spiritual lives during the three years he'd led them.

Minzey's friend and lieutenant Jefferson Poland stepped in to assume leadership of this informal flock. He reorganized and rebranded the ministry and took it into even more controversial spiritual territory than the San Franciscan Shaivite pastor had ever dared to explore.

THIRTEEN

THE PSYCHEDELIC VENUS CHURCH

Sex, Drugs, and the Goddess of Ecstasy

Only a born provocateur could have started an organization like the Psychedelic Venus Church.

"SEX, DRUGS & ROCK 'N' ROLL" AS RELIGION

Formed out of the remnants of Willie Minzey's sacramental-ganja Shiva Fellowship, the Psychedelic Venus Church took the motto of "Sex, Drugs & Rock 'n' Roll" and turned it into a religious creed. The church was the creation of John Jefferson Poland (1942–2017), a man who spent his entire life tilting against an array of establishment windmills, ranging from racial segregation to sexual repression to drug prohibition, always putting his personal freedom and well-being on the line for whatever cause he embraced.

Although little-remembered today, Poland occupied influential roles in the New Left, the sexual-freedom movement, and the entheogenic-religious subculture during his lifetime. Founding the Psychedelic Venus Church was in many ways his most radical gesture, the ultimate organized expression of revolutionary sixties spiritual hedonism.

THE SEXUAL FREEDOM FIGHTER

Militant activism had been a way of life for the Indiana native since his teens. In September 1960 Jefferson Poland, as he usually called himself, enrolled at Florida State University, only to be expelled months later for his racial-integration work with the Congress of Racial Equality (CORE). In June 1961 Poland became a Freedom Rider, and was arrested when he, along with a mixed-race group of clergymen later called the "Tallahassee Ten," sat in at a segregated airport restaurant.

The next year Poland organized California farmworkers, and during the summer of 1963 he registered Black voters in Louisiana, earning more arrests and jail stays for his troubles. That year Poland also joined the anarcho-syndicalist Industrial Workers of the World and protested nuclear weapons and the persecution of comedian Lenny Bruce.

When Poland migrated to New York in the fall of 1963, he found the cause that would occupy the rest of his life. The year before, he had lived in the San Francisco home of "two anarchist girls who practiced nudity and promiscuity" in the name of revolution. The females introduced Poland to Dr. Leo Koch, a former University of Illinois biology professor who'd been fired when he wrote a letter to the campus paper with the then-outrageous suggestion that sexual activity among undergrads was natural and healthy.

Poland followed Koch to New York City, where the two discussed forming a political action group that would work for sexual freedom in the same way CORE, the National Association for the Advancement of Colored People (NAACP), and others had fought for civil rights. Two days after President Kennedy's assassination, they founded the League for Sexual Freedom—later better known as the Sexual Freedom League. The league advocated greater freedom and openness in all things erotic, ranging from premarital sex to birth control, to nudity, to LGBTQ issues, and soon became one of the most controversial organizations on the fledgling New Left.

The league was based on the principle that action was the best way to start discussion about issues, and not vice versa. Its members, most of whom were either Lower East Side proto-hippies or Columbia University students, staged demonstrations around New York where they decried obscenity laws and sang love songs to jailed prostitutes, and held free-speech "talkouts" on the streets of Greenwich Village where whomever mounted the league's soapbox could hold forth on any topic.

Poland and the league also picketed New York's Whitehall Induction Center over the military's exclusion and abuse of homosexuals, in one of the first public LGBTQ demonstrations in American history.

NUDE-INS AND ENTHEOGENS

In February 1965 Poland migrated to California, where he planted various local league chapters across the state. Later that year he and two females staged a league "Nude Wade-In" at San Francisco's beachside Aquatic Park in front of hundreds of leering, jeering spectators. Cops busted the naked trio for indecent exposure, and when Poland logged yet another jail term on the charges, the case made national headlines, with liberal pundits wondering why the young radical was sent to lockup over mere public skinny-dipping.

Poland and the league also gained nationwide notoriety when *Time* magazine ran a story about the "nude-in" sex-parties they hosted in Berkeley and other California student ghettos. Soon Poland became so identified with the causes of body freedom and sexual liberation that he appeared in a 1967 NBC documentary about sixties hedonism, *The Pursuit of Pleasure,* where he took viewers to a remote California beach populated with naked hippies.

Poland later said that at both nude-beach outings and undergrad sex parties, he noted how many participants smoked cannabis while they sunbathed, danced in the altogether, or hooked up with new partners. The adventurous activist tried the plant, as well as LSD, and was astonished how the substances not only brought his mind and soul into the realm of the holy and transcendent but transformed the simple act of sexual congress into a sacred rite that united the participants' divine female and male energies. Poland and other league members began to hold nude joint-sharing circles at its get-togethers, thanking Nature and the Universe for the blessings given their bodies and souls through erotic pleasure and THC.

CLEAR LIGHT, NEO-AMERICANISM, AND SHIVA

Soon, psychedelic spirituality rivaled sexual liberation as Poland's primary interest. In June 1966 Poland formed the Fellowship of the Clear

Light (see page 286) in Berkeley, where he and Don Donahue led discussions about entheogens and Eastern mysticism at the local Unitarian church, as well as at their homes. Poland also joined Art Kleps's LSD-using Neo-American Church (see chapter 6) and became its Primate of California.

One of Poland's duties as primate was to oversee the activities of the Shiva Fellowship, a San Francisco-based Neo-American Church chapter that held rites dedicated to the Hindu deity in Golden Gate Park. At the fellowship's public meetings, participants prayed to Shiva as they ritually consumed cannabis, and Poland and others stripped naked to affirm the holiness of the human body and invoke the sacred-sexuality energy of Shiva's consort goddess, Parvati. Although San Francisco cops generally tolerated the group's public pot smoking, naked hippies in the park were too much for them, and Poland again logged several arrests when he and his cohorts refused to cover up in the law's presence.

The park ceremonies were usually led by Shiva Fellowship founder Willie Minzey. Like Poland, Minzey was a midwestern transplant to San Francisco, and an Industrial Workers of the World member who saw cannabis and body freedom as consciousness-expanding agents that would help bring about the revolution. But when Minzey landed in serious legal trouble, facing a potential life sentence in prison after being arrested and charged with providing narcotics to minors at a fellowship meeting, he ceded leadership of his spiritual flock to Poland.

By this time, Poland had become dissatisfied with his erotic activism. The Sexual Freedom League had morphed from a tribe of sexually libertine hippies and college kids, into a network of square suburban swingers, and the twenty-seven-year-old agitator wanted to revive the organization's original radicalism and combine its vision of physical, mental, and spiritual liberation though nudity and sexual freedom, with a commitment to entheogen-powered consciousness expansion.

One year earlier Poland had pioneered the vision at San Francisco's famous Fillmore West concert venue. On May 1, 1968, the anarchist Diggers collective occupied the venue and held the "Free City Convention," a multimedia happening that aimed to liberate San Francisco from the oppressive powers of government, media, and social conventions. The decentralized, DIY "Convention" featured psychedelic rock bands, performance-art pieces, the burning of paper money, pot-smoking uniformed servicemen, body painting, drum circles, and similarly anarchistic doings. At its climax, Jefferson Poland stripped naked on stage and chanted "Hare Shiva, Hare Rama" before leading the attendees in a mass, cannabis- and acid-drenched sex orgy.

THE PSYCHEDELIC VENUS CHURCH

On November 24, 1969, the sixth anniversary of the Sexual Freedom League's founding, Poland announced the formation of the Psychedelic Venus Church. The church was envisioned as "a pantheistic nature religion" that favored the goddess Aphrodite rather than the god Shiva as the symbolic object of veneration, cannabis as the preferred sacrament to honor her, and the unification of sacred sexuality and entheogenic sacramental worship.

The church's manifesto was later printed in the *Venereal Missal,* a booklet that compiled the sect's basic doctrines, chants, and ceremonies. Composed to be read when the faithful gathered to consume sacramental cannabis, the manifesto stated:

> We work as part of the spiritual and cultural revolution sweeping North America, the bohemian and humanistic affirmation of people instead of machines, of pleasure instead of aggression. We participate specially in the psychedelic movement and the sexual freedom movement, offering our co-operation to all life-enhancing groups.
>
> We believe life is more than mere mechanism, that some sort of godness [*sic*] is inherent in all living protoplasm, perhaps in the entire universe. Beyond this, we do not commit ourselves to a creedal formula of words.
>
> We choose the Mediterranean sex-goddess Venus-Aphrodite as our symbol of hedonic pleasure, in her psychedelic aspect symbolizing direct spiritual revelation. We see her presiding over nude orgies of fucking and sucking and cannabis: truly Venereal religion. She is Kali-Shiva, she is Eros and Bacchus and Peyote Woman!

We recognize our social responsibilities to the planet and to all living creatures. We will do what we can to prevent warfare, racism, and ecological disaster. We realize that culture includes politics, though most of our activities will be on the level of personal liberation.[1]

Fig. 13.1. Jefferson Poland in Australia.
Photograph by Rev. Mother Boats C.P., 1988.

Poland, who at this point was calling himself the Reverend Jefferson *Fuck* Poland, wanted the church to combine the Shiva Fellowship's sacramental cannabis use with body-positive, orgiastic practices, and serve as a social and spiritual bridge between San

Francisco and Berkeley's hippies and radicals, and the mate-swapping Sexual Freedom Leaguers.

MOTHER BOATS AND COUNTERCULTURE CELEBRITIES

The church founder chose as his second-in-command one "Mother Boats." The offspring of a wealthy East Bay family who'd earned his nickname for both his nurturing personality and his service aboard a navy submarine during the Vietnam War, Boats had met Poland at a Berkeley League event where he'd explored his nascent bisexuality with gay-male attendees. A skilled organizer whose practical attitude complemented Poland's flair for publicity, Boats worked hard to realize the church's vision, later telling author Josh Sides, "We believed in breaking the chains of restriction, to liberate the body and turn it on and enjoy hedonistic comforts."[2]

Boats and Poland enthusiastically promoted the new sect among the Bay Area's hippies and assorted social misfits. Local underground newspapers like the *Berkeley Barb* and *Tribe,* and the *San Francisco Good Times* had been reporting Poland's activist doings for years, and gleefully printed stories about his new mission to turn on the region, and eventually the nation and planet, to spiritual uplift through nudity, free sexuality, and ritual cannabis consumption.

Although the Psychedelic Venus Church technically required a $5 donation for lifetime membership, Boats and Poland distributed hundreds of complimentary membership cards to both Sexual Freedom Leaguers and activists in the growing Gay Liberation movement, as well as broke hippies and stoners. The two welcomed into church ranks such counterculture celebrities as psychedelics-using Beat poets Allen Ginsberg and Tuli Kupferberg, White Panther Party leader John Sinclair, and Neo-American Church Chief Boo Hoo Art Kleps. Eventually over 1,000 people counted themselves as Psychedelic Venusians, and Poland confidently predicted that at the rate it was growing, the church would be bigger than Roman Catholicism in the twenty-first century.

FREE JOINTS AND FORNICATING DEITIES

One of the ways Poland promoted the church was to distribute free cannabis through the U.S. mail. Poland regularly solicited local dealers for donations of weed and rolled whatever he got into joints. Anyone who sent an SASE to the church's P.O. box in Berkeley would get it back with two joints inside, as well as instructions on how to smoke the "holy religious sacrament" for maximum effect—it was best consumed with a lover—and an invitation to join the church.

If the recipient of the free weed joined the church, they were invited to its public events. Chief among these were the smoke-ins—ceremonies at Berkeley's Peoples Park and other hippie-friendly outdoor spaces where Psychedelic Venusians and their friends gathered to consume cannabis in honor of the Goddess and God, and in violation of state and federal laws.

At the smoke-ins, two church "acolytes" would read the Manifesto to the assembled crowd. Then the church leader held the sacramental supply upraised in both hands while the congregation chanted the "official PVC Mantra" that honored the Goddess and God's sexual organs in holy communion:

> Kali Lingam, Shiva Yoni,
> Kali Kali, Shiva Shiva,
> Kali Lingam, Shiva Yoni
> Lingan Lingam, Yoni Yoni[3]

After the chant, acolytes would roll joints from the cannabis, and distribute them to the faithful. While they were smoked, Poland or another church leader might deliver a brief sermon based on anything from the Hindu *Bhagavad Gita* to the Industrial Workers of the World's *Little Red Songbook*. Attendees would also chant the om mantra, play musical instruments, socialize, or share food, wine, or additional sacrament during the service.

Much as he had done at Shiva Fellowship gatherings, Poland would often strip naked at the smoke-ins to affirm the freedom and sacredness of the human body. And much as they had done in Golden

Gate Park, the local law would ignore the cannabis smokers, make a beeline for the "skyclad" Poland, and bust him for indecent exposure. The church head, who'd been trained by civil-rights leaders in the practice of passive resistance, always went along quietly with his arrestors, and the slight, bespectacled, naked Poland being hustled along to jail by burly cops became a familiar sight in the Bay Area's hippie 'hoods.

THE "GENITAL SACRIFICE"

The church's full celebration of sacred sensuality happened at its private gatherings. From his league days, Poland knew that the promise of free sexual activity would attract hordes of horny single men who would scare away even the most uninhibited females, so he generally limited attendance at the gatherings to heterosexual couples, single women, and gays and lesbians. Initially, private homes were the favored venues for these events.

The so-called "genital sacrifice" was the central rite of these smaller gatherings. Held on the solstices and equinoxes, the sacrifice opened with a smoke-in ceremony, where a priestess shared the sacrament with all attendees and led them in chants. Then, four "lay readers" would recite an introduction to the ceremony and follow it with a poem or passage from "Saint" William Blake, the Romantic-era English visionary poet and artist. Sacred intentions for the liberation of political prisoners, oppressed peoples, and all of humanity would then be sent to Shiva and Kali, and the priestess would perform an exorcism "to drive off evil forces . . . such as police, war, shyness, cold, etc."[4]

Then came the sacrifice itself. All present stripped naked and seated themselves, and two volunteers—one man and one woman—came forward to be blindfolded by the priestess and placed supine on a raised altar. The two volunteers would then have their genitals anointed with warm honey, and after a proper invocation, attendees would approach the altar, and then "eat" the "sacrificial victims" by licking their honeyed privates, either lightly or in full-on oral-sex mode.

After the act of genital worship, each communicant returned to their seat, where they again partook of sacramental cannabis and chanted. When all had tasted the sacrifices, the priestess and a male reader concluded the ceremony with a closing prayer and dedication. Fellowship followed, with all present dancing nude to suitably trippy rock music, or recombining in twosomes, threesomes, or more-somes to enjoy each other's bodies.

PANSEXUAL NUDE PSYCHEDELIC ROCK SPIRITUALITY

As the church became bigger and bolder, it began to look beyond the Genital Sacrifice and smoke-in ceremonies. During the early seventies, the action shifted from Berkeley and Oakland's hippie crash pads to San Francisco lofts and mansions where better-heeled members of the city's *avant* population hosted church events that were equal parts religious ceremony, performance art, and Dionysian revelry.

One of the regular church gathering places in the city was a ninth-floor loft that usually hosted pornographic film shoots, then illegal in California. Mother Boats told me that the church held body-painting parties there, where the Rev. Headstone decorated naked attendees with all manner of colorful psychedelic designs, actresses from the porn films entertained single-male celebrants, and a media-arts collective captured the action on the then-new medium of videotape.

The loft space also hosted the church "Sensorium." This was a sensitivity-training ritual where people of either sex would strip and be blindfolded. Church helpers would then anoint their feet with oil, stimulate their olfactory senses with roses and incense, and gently flicker a feather duster across their skin. An all-body massage would follow, starting with the feet and ending with the genitals. Poland and others reasoned that the rite would awaken people to the magic of their senses and the holiness of their bodies and make them more receptive to mindful psychedelic use and sacred sexuality.

Perhaps the most memorable of church gatherings happened at 330 Grove in San Francisco's Hayes Valley. The home of the Black Light Explosion Company, an African American theater/multimedia center, the space hosted the church-sponsored "Bacchanalia—The World's First Pan-Sexual Celebration-Nude-Acid-Rock-Dance-and-Party." There on August 22, 1970, three local rock bands performed

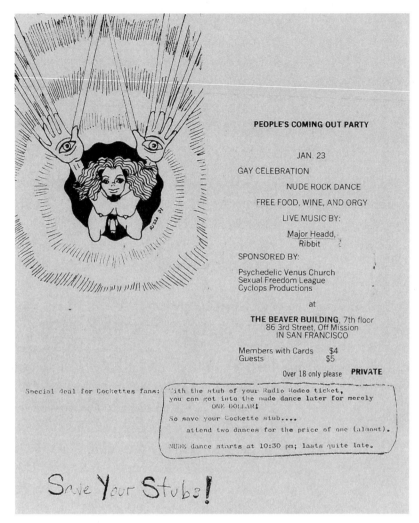

PEOPLE'S COMING OUT PARTY

JAN. 23

GAY CELEBRATION

NUDE ROCK DANCE

FREE FOOD, WINE, AND ORGY

LIVE MUSIC BY:

Major Headd,
Ribbit

SPONSORED BY:

Psychedelic Venus Church
Sexual Freedom League
Cyclops Productions

at

THE BEAVER BUILDING, 7th floor
86 3rd Street, Off Mission
IN SAN FRANCISCO

Members with Cards $4
Guests $5

Over 18 only please   PRIVATE

Special deal for Cockettes fans: With the stub of your Radio Rodeo ticket, you can get into the nude dance later for merely ONE DOLLAR!
So save your Cockette stub....
    attend two dances for the price of one (almost).
NUDE dance starts at 10:30 pm; lasts quite late.

Save Your Stubs!

Fig. 13.2. An LGBTQ People's Coming Out Party sponsored by the Psychedelic Venus Church. Fans of the gender-bending Cockettes theater troupe got a discount at the door (January 23, 1971).

in the nude for over 300 similarly unclad attendees of all races, genders, and sexual proclivities, most of whom were tripping on psychedelics-spiked punch.

Although rent-a-cops were hired to keep outside lawmen, crashers, and minors at bay, Mother Boats remembered that a few underaged San Franciscans somehow snuck into the event. Several of the thrill-seeking teens joined Bacchanalia celebrants in the haybale-bedecked back room, where a sacred orgy continued all night. The event climaxed when a young woman, clad only in angel's wings and a winged silver helmet, was hoisted by a crane far above the dance floor, and then slowly lowered down to the audience where she blessed attendees with Goddess energy, and shared her body with worshippers of both sexes.

THE ORGY BROADCAST ON LIVE TV

A year later an even more forward-looking church event took place at a Twin Peaks mansion. There, about seventy church members and select invitees gathered for a masked sex party that began with discreet cannabis smoking and a Genital Sacrifice ritual, and quickly transformed into a pansexual orgy. All parts of the house were connected by a network of video cameras and closed-circuit TVs, and many masked attendees took breaks from their libidinous doings to view taped playbacks of their own fleshly romps or watch revelers in other rooms captured live on the monitors.

The event may have been the first sex party, sacred or secular, ever broadcast live on TV, albeit privately. And it's hard not to suspect the video footage, which circulated in Bay Area alternative-media and sexual-underground circles for years afterward, may have influenced later portrayals of masked orgies in films like *Eyes Wide Shut* (1999). Almost certainly, gatherings like this and the Bacchanalia inspired the development of (somewhat) tamer San Francisco events like the Hooker's Ball and the Exotic Erotic Ball that celebrated body and sexual freedom and made the city a world capital of sex positivity.

NEO-PAGANS, QUEERS, AND ALLEN GINSBERG

The Psychedelic Venus Church also reached out to the fledgling Neo-Pagan spiritual underground of the early seventies. One of the first American religious organizations to draw its visions and practices from pre-Christian Western culture and place a female deity at the center of its worship, the church seemed to be a natural ally of Neo-Pagans and Wiccans who revered the Goddess and the Earth. Initially the church was welcome into the Council of Themis, an early coalition of Neo-Pagan spiritual groups, but its sex- and drug-related practices proved too controversial for some of the members, and it was unceremoniously expelled by two council leaders.

Perhaps the church's most progressive stance was its openness to people with nontraditional sexual and gender identities. Queer-friendly from the beginning, the pansexual sect had welcomed gays, lesbians, bisexuals, and transsexuals alike into its ranks, and celebrated their couplings and lives as vital parts of sacred human sexuality.

Chief among queer Psychedelic Venusians was the poet, Allen Ginsberg. A bold visionary whose writings celebrated bodies and sexualities of all kinds, Ginsberg had come out of the closet decades before the Stonewall riots and had publicly picketed against cannabis laws many years before organized groups took up the legalization cause.

Mother Boats, a skilled photographer who captured many events in the early history of Bay Area LGBTQ activism, shot Ginsberg at a memorable Psychedelic Venus Church event. There, the church staged a semipublic performance-art piece with the Angels of Light pansexual theater troupe, in the spirit of Julian Beck's Living Theatre where drama, art, ritual, and protest comingled in a transformative happening. At the performance, Ginsberg donned makeup and a blonde wig and played his harmonium onstage while naked, tripping, cross-dressing queer hippies paraded around him, deconstructing and dissolving gender and sexual roles and identities.

THE *NELLY HEATHEN* AND THE ZODIAC KILLER

Shortly after the performance, Mother Boats left the church. Like other psychedelic revolutionaries, he yearned for a tropical paradise far away from the noise, repression, and dangers of seventies urban America, and purchased a used yacht that he staffed with nude crewmembers of all genders. When Boats and his naked crew sailed off into the sunset, the Psychedelic Venus Church lost its most energetic and talented organizer, and its activities soon became far less frequent.

Post-Boats, the church held together long enough to publish a one-off tabloid titled *Nelly Heathen*. The publication featured a masthead photo of two naked men 69-ing on a Christian church altar, and collected various Psychedelic Venusian writings about erotic rituals, tantric teachings, and phallic worship, as well as news from the cannabis-legalization front, and even a short poem by Allen Ginsberg. Although several thousand copies were distributed, mostly around the Bay Area, it attracted few new members, and the church continued its slow slide into ecclesiastic oblivion.

The last big church event was a Halloween party held in San Francisco on October 24, 1973. As if to symbolize the imminent death of Psychedelic Venusianism, it featured a macabre episode where one attendee claimed that he was the Zodiac Killer—the still-unidentified serial murderer who terrified the Bay Area during the late sixties and early seventies and tantalized police and the press with cryptic, coded communications.

According to Robert Graysmith's book *Zodiac Unmasked,* the unnamed celebrant privately cornered a man at the party costumed as Satan, who had earlier been discussing the Zodiac case with a group of naked men. The "burly, good-looking stranger" told the faux-Devil, "I am the Zodiac, you fool . . . I have killed many more than have ever been identified as Zodiac killings," and said that murder was "a game between myself and the police. Killing to me means no more than flicking ashes."[5]

Although the mystery man soon departed with a woman, the witness to his confession remembered that the seemingly "normal, 100 percent All-American guy" told him he'd done "more than 37" killings. Eerily enough, thirty-seven was the exact number of victims that "Zodiac" boasted in a taunting letter to police sent several months later.

Some students of the case suspect the man may have been Richard Gaikowski, a prime Zodiac candidate who once worked at the *San Francisco Good Times* underground newspaper, which regularly covered church events in its pages. The unnerving possibility that the most famous uncaught serial-killer in American history may have been a Psychedelic Venusian adds a grim coda to the church's history, as well as an appropriate segue into its founder's own dance on the dark side.

MOLESTATION IN SAN DIEGO, FLIGHT TO ASIA

By 1974 the Psychedelic Venus Church was moribund. Jefferson Poland, who'd never been able to successfully unite and pursue his visions of political, sexual, and spiritual mass-revolution, decamped for the San Diego area, where he continued to run the Sexual Freedom League, now largely a swinger's club, and was a regular at the famous swimsuit-optional Black's Beach.

Poland, a bright but disturbed man who lived off Social Security psychological-disability payments, and who'd once publicly confessed that he'd started the league and the church largely to compensate for his sexual inadequacies, hit the worst crisis of his life in 1983. That year San Diego police arrested the forty-one-year-old and charged him with molesting the preteen daughter and son of a female friend.

Poland skipped bail and spent the next few years on the run in Australia and Asia. When he visited Hawaii in 1988, U.S. officials seized him, and he was sent back to San Diego, convicted on the child-molestation charges, sentenced to a year in prison, and given lifetime Sex Offender status.

TORTUGA BI-LIBERTY AND THE FUTURE OF HEDONISTIC PSYCHEDELIC SPIRITUALITY

The onetime sexual revolutionary and entheogenic missionary moved back to San Francisco in the early nineties. There he spent his remaining years in a Tenderloin District welfare hotel and attempted to reinvent himself as "Tortuga Bi-Liberty," an aging advocate of body freedom and nonviolence who haunted online nudist and LGBTQ communities, still pursuing his pansexual Utopian dreams via the internet.

Poland also regularly attended nudity-friendly San Francisco public gatherings like the Pride Parade, the Folsom Street Fair, and Burning Man–related street parties. Among crowds of hipsters and sexual radicals who could have been his grandchildren, Poland held pro-body free-dom placards while he bared his deeply tanned, slackening body to the world, a decaying monument to sixties ideals that tourists bemusedly photographed, and cops ignored. When Poland died at seventy-five on November 17, 2017, neither mainstream nor alternative local media took note, and his few friends only learned of his passing weeks later.

As with so many other defunct entheogenic sects, few traces remain today of the Psychedelic Venus Church, save for archived underground-newspaper stories and references in arcane academic works. Before his death, Jefferson Poland willed his personal papers to UC–Berkeley's Bancroft Library, where they remain available to researchers interested in him, the league, the church, and the Bay Area counterculture where all of them thrived. Religious scholar J. Gordon Melton described the church in his immense, exhaustive *Encyclopedia of American Religions,* and reading the entry many years ago inspired me to study the history of offbeat and bizarre spiritual organizations, and indirectly led to the writing of this book.

Whatever the failings of its founder, the Psychedelic Venus Church perfectly embodied the hedonistic spirituality of the sixties counterculture, and its mission to combine entheogenic and erotic practices for consciousness expansion remains as provocative as ever. One noted advocate of sacred sexuality told me that she uses cannabis in her intimate rituals to enhance both physical and spiritual sensitivity, and there are doubtless many others out there who've also noticed the powerful synergy of erotic play and the entheogens. It's only a matter of time before a new "pansexual psychedelic church" emerges to pick up where Poland & Co. left off and takes a new generation onto the Dionysian path that they blazed so many years ago.

FOURTEEN

THE ETHIOPIAN ZION COPTIC CHURCH

Burning Down Babylon with Jah's Ganja

As the psychedelic counterculture of the sixties began to expand, it absorbed aesthetic and spiritual elements of the cultures that historically used its sacraments.

Pilgrims on the Eurasian Hippie Trail brought back to the West not only Indian hashish, but the art, clothes, and Hindu devotional practices that had been inseparable from South Asian cannabis usage for millennia. In North America, Western peyotists and psilocybin users tuned in to the historic worldviews and wisdom of the indigenous peoples that had found the flesh of the gods in native plants and fungi.

RASTAFARI AND THE ETHIOPIAN ZION COPTIC CHURCH

Many of the developed world's hippies found inspiration in Rastafari, the religion that had emerged from Jamaica and spread throughout the Caribbean's diasporic African population. Noted for its close association with reggae music, its idolization of Emperor Haile Selassie, and the colorful clothes and dreadlock hairstyles worn by its adherents, the Rastafari faith also viewed cannabis, or ganja, as a holy sacrament, to be partaken of daily in prayer to Jah—the biblical Jehovah reimagined in a New World mythology where Blacks were the Children of Israel, sold into bondage in a foreign land and then liberated to become a Chosen People.

Of the many schools of Rastafari thought and life, the one that attained the most notoriety in North America was the Ethiopian Zion Coptic Church. Rooted in the social upheavals of midfifties Jamaica, the EZCC's Afrocentric spiritual practices cross-pollinated with White hippie culture and ideals, and the church eventually established itself in late-seventies America as the wealthiest and most visible psychedelic sect in the country.

During the few years that it operated out of its lavish "Embassy" on Miami Beach's exclusive Star Island, the church was unlike any other entheogenic religion in America. It boasted vast property holdings in both Jamaica and the United States, was featured on national TV news shows, and brought hundreds of tons of cannabis into North America in a smuggling operation that was dedicated to healing the spiritually corrupt First World with the holy power of ganja.

"BACK TO AFRICA" AND EMPEROR HAILE SELASSIE

The roots of the Ethiopian Zion Coptic Church were in the "Back to Africa" movement of the nineteenth and early twentieth centuries. Many among the diasporic African peoples of the New World and Western Europe felt that they could never be fully liberated unless they returned to the lands of their ancestors and divorced themselves completely from the oppressive White West. Perhaps the best-known advocate of the ideology was the Jamaican Marcus Garvey, who preached Black nationalism and racial separatism, and looked forward to the coming of a great African king who could unite his scattered peoples and call them back to the Mother Continent.

Many Black nationalists believed that Emperor Haile Selassie of Ethiopia was that king. His crowning in 1930 was seen by many Jamaicans as a fulfillment of biblical prophecy, largely because Ethiopia occupied such a prominent place in scriptural narrative and was thought to be the home of Israel's lost tribes, whose displacement and sufferings paralleled those of New World Africans.

Among the island's poor peoples, oppressed by a history of slavery

Fig. 14.1. Famed Black separatist and "Back to Africa" advocate Marcus Garvey.
His ideas inspired the Rastafari faith.

Photograph courtesy of the Associated Press, 1922.

and British cultural and economic dominance, there arose a movement
called Rastafari. Taken from Haile Selassie's pre-coronation name, Ras
Tafari Makonnen, the Rastafarians, as the world would come to know
them, saw the emperor as the second coming of Christ, and themselves
as exiles in "Babylon"—the White man's world, which would soon be

destroyed in a day of judgment, and replaced by a New Age of peace, wealth, and happiness for the faithful.

GANJA, BOB MARLEY, AND THE HOUSES OF RASTAFARI

Militantly opposed to the nation's political and religious establishments, Rastafari became a Jamaican outlaw subculture in the fifties and early sixties. One reason was that cannabis, first brought to the island by Asian Indian workers in the nineteenth century and called ganja, was a key element of their faith—a holy sacrament that allowed them to see through the lies of Babylon and commune directly with the Divine. Rastafarians integrated the herb's use into their prayers and devotions and continued to do so after the Jamaican government banned it in 1964.

After Haile Selassie made a historic appearance in Jamaica in 1966, Rastafari began to slowly integrate into the island's society. Musicians like Bob Marley brought the distinctly Jamaican form of pop music called reggae to the world, and became Rastafarian colporteurs, spreading the movement's themes of mental decolonization and spiritual liberation through sound rather than written tracts. Jamaican immigrants to the UK, the United States, and other nations often took on the Rastafarian look, with its dreadlocked hair and red-gold-green clothing, as a way of asserting ethnic pride in often-hostile territories. Many also began to adopt the faith's beliefs and practices, including sacramental use of illegal cannabis.

Nonhierarchical and decentralized by nature, Rastafari is divided into "houses" or "mansions," after Jesus's declaration in John 14:2, "In My Father's house are many mansions." These different sects represent a variety of interpretations and practices of the basic Rastafari doctrines.

BLACK AND WHITE UNITE

One of the more unusual ones was the Ethiopian Zion Coptic Church. In the fifties a Rasta leader named Louv Williams split from the bigger movement when he saw it drifting away from its spiritual origins, into power politics and violent confrontations with the law. His group eventually settled on a plot of land near Hall's Delight, several miles east of

Kingston in the Jamaican mountains, and began to call itself the Coptic Church, after the North African Christian patriarchate that traces its founding to St. Mark's founding of the Church of Alexandria in 42 CE.

Before his death in 1969, Williams predicted that the Black and White races would unite under the Rasta Holy Trinity: the Man, the Herb, and the Word. The White man, he said, would accept the Black Christ of Rastafari, confess his centuries-long sins against Africans, and join his new Black brothers in daily worship, aided by smoking the ganja that was cultivated in Jamaica's Blue Mountains.

True to his prophecy, the first White hippies wandered into the sect's camp in the late sixties. Seeking cannabis and an authentic exotic spiritual experience, the young people encountered Williams's successor, Brother Keith "Niah" Gordon, who welcomed the pale-skinned visitors, listened to their testimonies of personal and racial wrongdoings, and taught them the ways of his spiritual community.

"AS LONG AS THESE FIRES CONTINUE TO BURN . . ."

The Coptics taught that Black people were the original Israelites of the Bible. Abraham and Moses were Black leaders and prophets, and Jesus himself was a dreadlocked, ganja-smoking Black man, come to redeem his people—the Coptics, who had existed since the dawn of time and survived the cruel enslavements of Egypt, Babylon, and other kingdoms and empires. The abuses of the Black man by the White British and American empires were the final trials and tribulations of the people, who would soon be liberated so long as they met the Christ in regular sacramental use of ganja and lived righteous lives.

A key to living in righteousness was the Temple Doctrine. This was the teaching that the human body was the Temple of the Living God, and that sin brought on physical and spiritual death. To avoid sin, Coptics followed all 613 of the traditional Old Testament laws and strictures to the letter, shunning "unclean" foods and animals and isolating menstruating women from the community.

For the Coptics, the deadliest sins were the ones of flesh. There was no rite of marriage among the faithful; men and women were considered betrothed once they slept together and were encouraged to be

THE ETHIOPIAN ZION COPTIC CHURCH 🏵 193

fruitful and multiply. Adultery, oral sex, masturbation, mixed-race relationships, and sodomy were all repeatedly and forcefully condemned in Coptic teachings. Sodomy was seen as especially evil, since it was the shameful, secret doing of the religious and political establishments that guaranteed corruption and degradation among its practitioners.

Against the sinful ways of the modern-day Babylon, the Coptics practiced a life of hard work and prayer. Morning services were at 4:00 a.m., beginning with chants where the faithful would do a call-and-response style recitation of traditional hymns, followed by Psalms and Bible readings. Prayer services, which could last up to three hours, were held again at 3:00 p.m. and 8:00 p.m., with shared ganja smoldering in chalices, since the brethren believed "as long as these fires continue to burn, the vilest of sinners must return."

When they weren't in services, brothers and sisters alike grew crops, raised animals, and kept the community fed and safe. In obeisance to Old Testament strictures, men never shaved or cut their hair, and women wore head coverings. If one of the faithful committed a grievous offense against the community, they were punished by "taking their head": being shaved bald.

GANJA WARRIOR PRIESTS

As the Coptic camp grew in the early seventies, with both Black and White converts joining to live out their biblical ideals with the simple, peaceful sect, Brother Keith and other elders discussed how to accommodate the new faithful and spread the word of Ras Tafari. Jamaican reggae was beginning to capture a world audience with its rocksteady beat and Rastafari-influenced lyrics, and it seemed Babylon was ready for the next step of redemption: to burn the ganja that was at the core of Coptic daily prayer and spiritual self-examination. The Coptics resolved to take the herb to the rest of the planet.

In *Ganja Warrior Priest,* a memoir of his years spent with the Coptic community, Clifton Middleton recalled the day when Brother Keith "Niah" Gordon initiated him into the practice of holy smuggling. When Middleton left Jamaica for Iowa to get a chicken-incubating machine for the camp, Brother Keith gave the White American a bag of cannabis to take through Customs to the Midwestern belly of the Babylonian beast. Middleton saw the gesture as a command to become a Holy Warrior of Ganja, dedicated to the healing of the nations by spreading the herb to the ends of the earth, its borders and drug laws be damned.

Soon, brothers and sisters were taping bags of cannabis to their bodies and flying from Kingston to the capitals of the Western world, where big markets existed for high-quality Jamaican herb. Bags soon turned to three-pound bundles concealed in luggage, and although some brothers and sisters got busted and did time for the contraband, eventually the Coptic faithful raised enough money to buy a 38-foot power boat that could carry immense loads of ganja from the Caribbean island to isolated landings on the Florida coast.

"THE WEALTH OF NATIONS, IN TRIBUTE TO THY FEET"

With the aid of the craft, as well as of brothers and sisters stationed in Florida, the disciplined, hardworking community began to run hundreds of pounds of ganja to American shores. The profits enabled the community, which had legally incorporated itself as the Ethiopian Zion Coptic Church, to move to a 2,000-acre property near White Horses, Jamaica. The church also purchased over 20,000 acres of land in Jamaica, as well as several large legal enterprises and utilities, and employed thousands of people in the poverty-wracked nation.

To Brother Keith Gordon, the Coptic leader who had first welcomed White people into the sect, it seemed as if the newcomers were helping to fulfill prophecies that the church would bring "the wealth of Nations, in tribute to thy feet." The organized ganja trade allowed both the EZCC and big sectors of the Jamaican economy to thrive and seemed to be leading to the spiritual liberation of humanity through consumption of the holy Coptic sacrament.

THE EMBASSY AT STAR KEY

While Brother Keith ran things in Jamaica, Ganja Warrior Priest and smuggling kingpin Clifton Middleton searched for a permanent Florida home for the stateside faithful. He found it at 43 Star Key, an exclusive Miami Beach estate that featured twelve bedrooms, twelve bathrooms, immense living and great rooms, and most importantly, 300 feet of deep-water docking for large seagoing vessels.

Middleton, who'd grown up poor in a midwestern sharecropper's shack, was astonished by the mansion. With some financing arrangements he put $100,000 down on the property, and on his first entry into the house as its owner, gave a ganja-incensed prayer of thanks to Jah. As Middleton put it, "In my spirit mind I had just captured one of Babylon's nicest castles and it was here we would establish the Coptic Embassy as the Ganja Nation arises. The Ganja Nation was everyone who smoked Ganja with divine high status to those who grew and worked to administer the healing sacramental herb."[1]

The Embassy, as the Star Key estate was known, soon became a home for EZCC faithful from America and Jamaica alike. Middleton also established a second Florida Coptic community near Fort Myers, made up largely of American converts who'd joined the church in Iowa when he had preached there. And he stayed active with the Coptic smuggling operations, which were now moving an average of twenty to twenty-five tons of ganja out of Jamaica every month.

SMUGGLING AND PRAYING

The church's most ambitious smuggling caper came through its Cuban connections in Miami. The Cubans set the Coptic brothers up with a huge cannabis-growing operation in Columbia, and Middleton and another White American brother named Tom Reilly journeyed to that nation, where they met and closed a deal with a local ganja magnate. When the two returned, they were followed by a 65-foot boat packed with 150 tons of ganja, all bundled in the 40-pound packages Floridians called "square groupers," since they vaguely resembled the oversized fish and often washed ashore after smuggling ships sank or were raided.

The immense amounts of ganja the EZCC was smuggling, and the equally huge piles of cash it brought, caused political problems in the church. Some of the elder brothers maintained that the church had become more of a business enterprise than a spiritual community.

Many of the brethren started spending more time managing money and the church's front companies, than in prayer with the sacred herb. The Americans, who did most of the smuggling labor in Florida and elsewhere, also became the most devout church members, dedicating all their time to moving weed and praying, often at the same time.

Middleton recalled that one night at 43 Star Key's prayer service, he looked out on the scores of faithful Coptics and couldn't see one Black face. To him, it meant "the Church has moved, the Ganja moving part of the Church had moved and was now . . . right here at 43 Star Island."[2]

Near Dunnellon, Florida, the EZCC established a settlement next to the old Gulf of Mexico canal. Disguised as a modest, run-down farm, Coptics at the waterside property offloaded tons of ganja from seacraft, and then stored it beneath the barn floor in a series of hidden, steel-lined rooms that could hold up to 40,000 pounds of vegetable matter. From there, a fleet of semitrailer trucks shipped the herb to local EZCC communities from Iowa to Massachusetts, where the sacrament was distributed to local pot wholesalers and faithful Coptics alike.

RAIDS AND *60 MINUTES*

As was the case with most entheogenic sects, the law eventually caught up with the EZCC. On the night of November 18, 1977, local cops raided the Dunnellon property, seized thirteen tons of ganja, and arrested four church members. Although Middleton was able to relocate the operation to another Florida farm, the church was now on the narcs' radar, and in February 1978 that property was busted as well, with sixteen brothers arrested and the DEA now involved in the case. All charges were eventually dropped, but the EZCC lost $8 million in confiscated cannabis, as well as millions more in legal fees and impounded property.

The raids also attracted national media attention. On October 29, 1979, the CBS news-show *60 Minutes* broadcast a segment about the Ethiopian Zion Coptic Church, its offbeat beliefs and practices, and how its work to turn the world onto Jamaican ganja had both made it rich, and landed dozens of its members in serious legal trouble.

By this time Thomas "Brother Louv" Reilly had become the American spokesperson for the EZCC, and during the segment he fielded questions from journalist Dan Rather about the church. When asked if he was in the business of smuggling marijuana, the lanky, balding Brother Louv responded, "I have no knowledge of even what you're thinking about, much less what you're talking about." And when Rather inquired as to the source of the funds for the church's properties, vessels, and costly legal battles, Louv merely said, "I want you to consider that you're talking to a spiritual person who has solved the physical problems, and we should be talking about the matters that could uplift everyone who's hearing us right now."[3]

By far the most controversial part of the *60 Minutes* segment was the video footage of prayer services at Star Island. Along with the chanting, praying, and Bible readings, all wreathed in thick ganja smoke, the cameraman got a shot of several small children taking tokes from an immense joint. Although it outraged many viewers, others called to support the church's religious use of cannabis, and many people showed up at the Embassy gates, anxious to learn more about the Coptic way of life.

FROM STAR ISLAND TO DEER ISLE

Eleven days after the *60 Minutes* broadcast, DEA agents stormed the Star Island estate and busted nineteen residents. A federal grand jury in the Southern District of Florida had returned a six-count indictment against them, with conspiracy to violate the Controlled Substance Act. Middleton, Brother Louv, and Brother Keith were also charged with running a continuing criminal enterprise.

Out on bail, the smuggling crew, determined to keep the operation going while their twenty-three lawyers sorted out their various cases, relocated to Deer Isle, Maine. There they moved onto a 5-acre waterfront property and bought a 69-foot trawler to haul contraband, and an 80-acre farm with two giant inflatable greenhouses to store it. Convinced they were spiritual warriors doing the Lord's work, they continued to receive, store, and truck out cannabis by the ton at the Maine site while they worked on their legal issues.

The brethren figured that their best legal defense was to attack the marijuana laws themselves as unconstitutional and a violation of the church's right to practice its faith freely. So, they enlisted every authority on cannabis they could find as expert witnesses for their trial, ready to testify that the herb was a legitimate and safe medicine. They also reached out to religious historians who would attest that the EZCC was a legitimate heir to the ancient Coptic faith. And they hired no less than former U.S. Attorney General Ramsey Clark to represent them in court.

No sooner had they assembled their legal team and strategy than disaster struck again. In the early morning of October 20, 1980, federal and state cops raided the Deer Isle retreat and arrested twenty-three people. The arrestees crammed the Portland jail, where they continuously agitated guards with demands, sang Coptic songs at top volume, and openly smoked ganja in their cells, all to the delight of the other inmates.

The next day fifteen of the brothers were bailed out from jail. The other eight were taken by U.S. Marshalls back to Miami to face bond revocation hearings. Amazingly, the Miami judge once again freed them on bond, and they returned to the Star Island estate.

BABYLON STRIKES BACK

Unlike most other smuggling operations, the EZCC was a tight-knit brotherhood where nobody snitched to get a lesser sentence. Not that such offers were made; from the beginning the church members had refused to plea bargain on the charges and demanded the case go to federal trial. They were confident that a First Amendment defense would work in their favor, since the previous year the Florida State Supreme Court had ruled that the church was a valid religious organization, and that the "use of cannabis is an essential portion of [its] religious practice."

On the first day of the trial a fleet of limousines transported the long-haired, bearded defendants clad in red, gold, and green robes and prayer shawls to court, where the nine men faced over a hundred charges. Religious-freedom arguments and high-priced lawyers notwithstanding, the brothers were doomed; the prosecution laid out mountains of evidence that they'd all been around tons of cannabis many times, in several states and nations. On June 19, 1981, all nine were found guilty on all the charges, and later sentenced to various terms in federal prison.

Brother Louv, whose own trial had been postponed because his attorney was ill, was outraged by the verdict. He told *Miami Herald* reporter Carl Hiaasen, "I'll be damned if I'm going to be considered a criminal because of ganja. It's a mismatch. One man is using his wits and his prayers, and the other is using guns and informers and stake-outs." Brother Louv also said he wished his own upcoming trial on smuggling and tax-evasion charges could have been instead "a constitutional trial on the issue of ganja and our generation,"[4] and that he was prepared to become a martyr for the church, should he be found guilty.

His martyrdom came on June 3, 1982. That day, Thomas "Brother Louv" Reilly was convicted of conspiracy, possession, and distribution of marijuana in federal court, and sentenced two months later to a fifteen-year federal term. Deprived of its most articulate spokesman, as well as the brothers who had brought millions of untaxed, illicit dollars into the church, the organization's remaining American members scattered, as various government agencies seized EZCC properties and assets.

REBIRTH IN IOWA, AND RUTH BADER GINSBURG'S RULING

Determined not to let the narcs have the last laugh, longtime EZCC brother and Iowan Carl Olsen reincorporated the church in his home state. In 1986 Olsen sued the DEA over its refusal to grant the church a religious-use exemption for cannabis like the one that the Native American Church (see chapter 1) had for peyote. Three years later the case reached the federal Appeals Court in Washington, D.C., which ruled against the church.

Stating the majority opinion, Justice Ruth Bader Ginsburg ruled that "the First Amendment's free exercise of religion guarantee does not require the requested exception, and that petitioner was not denied equal protection–establishment clause rights by the government's refusal." The future Supreme Court justice and feminist icon also said that "the DEA cannot accommodate Olsen's religious use of marijuana without unduly burdening or disrupting enforcement of the federal marijuana laws"[5]—a statement that led cannabis expert Tod Mikuriya to label Ginsburg a "state religious persecutor . . . a Jew sold out to the pharaohs."[6]

Frustrated with the courts, Olsen threw his hat into the political ring on behalf of legal cannabis. In 1992 he ran as the antiprohibitionist Grassroots Party's candidate for Iowa's U.S. senator and was later the Libertarian Party's pick for Iowa governor and U.S. representative. Olsen finished far behind the major-party nominees in all the races, but the campaigns helped keep the church alive in Iowa, and he eventually launched the Ethiopian Zion Coptic Church website, which hosts historical information about the EZCC, and its ongoing battles to legalize ganja in the Hawkeye State, and across the United States.

THE GANJA MEN

In 2011 a documentary appeared that sparked new interest in the Ethiopian Zion Coptic Church. Titled *Square Grouper: The Godfathers of Ganja,* the film examined the Miami cannabis trade during the seventies and eighties, and featured footage of the church in its heyday, along with interviews of several Coptic brothers, now gray-haired and wizened with age, who still badmouthed narcs and the government thirty years after their Florida struggles.

Six years later, the last imprisoned EZCC brother was released from prison. James Tranmer, who had been one of the most spiritually oriented of the brethren, was arrested several times with other church members, but never did serious time. He eventually quit the church when he decided it had become a profit-grubbing smuggling business rather than a religious community.

In 1991 Tranmer was charged with conspiracy in a smuggling case involving his son Brian. Although his connections with Brian's business were weak at best, he was convicted and sentenced to thirty-five years in federal prison. His wife and other observers were shocked by the sentence and spent a quarter-century trying to free the "Ganja Man," who never wavered from his belief that the plant was a religious sacrament. Finally, on the last day of his term President Obama commuted Tranmer's sentence, and four months later the Ganja Man walked away from the federal pen.

A LEGACY AND A LESSON

What was the legacy of the Ethiopian Zion Coptic Church?

It's easy to speculate that without the entry of educated, entrepreneurial Americans into its ranks, the Jamaican sect would never have grown nearly as wealthy and influential as it did. In 1980 Jamaican Prime Minister Edward Seaga told an American interviewer that regarding his nation's dismal economy, "it's just a little sinsemilla that keep the country going right now," and it's been estimated that over half of the cannabis grown there at the time was shipped out by the EZCC. Certainly, Jamaica would look much different today had not the sect pumped tens of millions of dollars back into the country and provided thousands of its citizens with jobs—legitimate and otherwise.

And had it not been prosecuted nearly to death by the U.S. government, the church would almost certainly have been sidelined in the changing world of contraband trafficking. During the eighties the violent Colombian cartels dominated the Caribbean drug trade, and it's hard to imagine how the Coptic brothers—peaceful, prayerful men who dealt strictly in cannabis to enlighten the world—could have survived long in an environment where the "Cocaine Cowboys" waged bloody war on competitors and lawmen alike from Medellin to Miami. Too, the era saw the rise of American homegrown sinsemilla, a superior cannabis product that was far easier to produce and obtain stateside than the offerings from distant tropical lands.

Like the Native American Church, the Ethiopian Zion Coptic Church is the spiritual child of an oppressed people that found medicinal and spiritual healing in a plant and fought for their right to consume it as a sacrament. And like the Brotherhood of Eternal Love (see chapter 7), its story is one of how a religious community based on the use of proscribed sacraments can be destroyed when it starts to traffic in them, even if its intentions are to share the entheogen and enlighten the rest of humanity.

Perhaps other psychedelic sects can take heed from the EZCC's history and avoid the mistakes it made in trying to bring down Babylon with contraband cannabis.

FIFTEEN

THE CHURCH OF THE UNIVERSE

Eden in the Great Green North

In "Woodstock," Joni Mitchell's commemoration of the 1969 rock festival, the singer-songwriter pleaded to her hippie listeners, "We've got to get ourselves back to the Garden."

That year, Canada's Assembly of the Church of the Universe was founded to pursue that Aquarian-Age vision. With cannabis as its sacrament and nude escapades in Ontario's wilderness as its rites, the church embodied the sixties counterculture's Edenic ideal and endeared itself to the province's observers of eccentric free spirits. Not merely a gang of naked spiritual stoners, the church was also a visible force for cannabis legalization in both Ontario and the whole nation, and its ministers spent decades battling the Great White North's legal and political establishments in the name of free weed, free bodies, and free minds.

While most of the sixties-born entheogenic sects in the United States were either legally persecuted into oblivion, or vanished in the face of changing cultural fashions, the Church of the Universe has survived nearly a half-century of court cases, as well as the death of its founder and spiritual leader and his closest associate. It exists today as a living symbol of the Canadian cannabis culture's spiritual and political ambitions, as well as the persistence of the hippie style and spirit in that nation.

"AN UNMANAGEABLE YOUNG MAN"

Part of the church's longevity can be attributed to the personality and talents of its founder, the Reverend Walter A. Tucker (1932–2012). Arguably Ontario's most famous hippie and cannabis advocate, Tucker grew up in the Mennonite farming town of Rosthern, Saskatchewan. He was the eldest son of Walter Adam Tucker, a Liberal member of the Canadian Parliament, as well as the party's provincial leader and a noted lawyer and judge.

Like his father, the younger Tucker would run for office during his life, albeit in a very different style from his dad's. Several of Walter Jr.'s eight siblings became lawyers and judges, and although he never joined the bar, the eldest son would also represent himself in court during his many struggles against the Crown.

During one of his many court appearances, the middle-aged Tucker admitted to a judge that he had been "an unmanageable young man." In his late teens he'd done a stint in the Canadian Army as a mechanic, and in 1951 he was sent to Manitoba's Stony Mountain Penitentiary for two counts of robbery with violence. In the early sixties Tucker settled in Hamilton, Ontario, where he married, raised a family, and worked as an electrician.

CLEARWATER ABBEY AND THE CHURCH OF THE UNIVERSE

Everything changed for the thirty-seven-year-old Ontarian in 1969. That year, Tucker discovered an abandoned quarry near the town of Puslinch, roughly halfway between the cities of Hamilton and Guelph. The quarry pit had flooded with spring-fed water, and when Tucker explored its depths in a wetsuit and scuba tank, he had an overwhelming spiritual experience, bonding with the water and the 360 acres of wild forest land that surrounded it. When he surfaced and removed his gear, he told his friend Fran Fralich, "This is where I want to live. This is where I want to die."[1]

Tucker, who deepened his spiritual bond to the land by smoking cannabis there, found out that the property was owned by the Canada Cut and Crushed Stone company. No longer able to quarry from the flooded pit, the firm agreed to lease the swimming hole and the 360-acre property to Tucker for a nominal monthly fee and his promise to take care of the land. His marriage and career in tatters due largely to his cannabis use, Tucker moved onto the remote property and set up camp.

To sanctify the land, Tucker dubbed the property "Clearwater Abbey," and named himself as its abbot in 1969. As abbot, he would lead the Assembly of the Church of the Universe—a new religion dedicated to preserving the land as an Edenic bower of the Aquarian generation, where all who visited could freely partake of the cannabis sacrament, and swim, sunbathe, and hike in the nude around the property without interference from Ontario's conservative Establishment.

THE "HOLY TREE OF LIFE"

Over the years, Tucker and his followers would work out a basic theology and ethical system for the church. They respected only two rules:

1. Do not hurt yourself
2. Do not hurt anyone else

Anyone who promised to live by this two-part "Golden Rule," and believed in God, however they defined that entity, was welcomed into the church, for free.

The church mandated that as God's children, cannabis would be the "sacrament in their lives and worship. It is required in their search for an understanding of their spirituality and connection with The Almighty God." Church members were also obliged to provide medicinal sacrament to the sick, and "encouraged to surround themselves with the holy Tree of Life, not just inhaling it, but wearing it, growing it, writing on it, eating it, etc."[2]

The Church of the Universe saw the cannabis plant as the original Tree of Life mentioned in the Bible. It believed that Adam and Eve were given special care to grow and tend this plant, and unlike the mysterious Tree of Knowledge, were not forbidden its fruits. From their efforts came the beginning of human agriculture and the birth of the first human civilization, Sumer.

On its website, the church extensively quotes Canadian cannabis historian Chris Bennett regarding the plant. Bennett believes that after Sumer, the use of the herb spread through the ancient civilizations of the Near East, and that it was considered a lifegiving balm and holy sacrament throughout the region for millennia.

Bennett also posits that the plant was used in both the anointing oil and incense of the ancient Hebrews, and may even have been the "burning bush," "cloud of smoke," and "pillar of fire" from which the God of Israel spoke to Moses. He maintains that by the time of the Second Temple, the oil had become associated with paganism and its use was discontinued, but Jesus and his disciples revived the practice to initiate followers, and it continued among the Gnostic Christians until it was suppressed by the early Roman Church.

Although the Church of the Universe drew from these traditions and theories, they never considered themselves Christian in any orthodox sense. They did, however, have a Credo that stated:

Fig. 15.1. The Church of the Universe believes that cannabis was the original Tree of Life, cultivated by Adam and Eve.

Photograph courtesy of Rob Duval.

We believe that the Tree of Life is necessary to our understanding and worship of Almighty God.

We believe that the Tree of Life opens a path to spiritual growth
and connection with Almighty God and us, the Children.

We believe that the Tree of Life is for the healing of the nations.
Revelation Chapter 22.

We believe that everyone has the right to worship God, to explore
and create their own understanding of spirituality and growth
in connection with God.

First God then Humanity, then Government. We believe in
standing and kneeling before Almighty God and no other.[3]

MICHAEL BALDASARO AND THE HIPPIE EDEN

Next to Walter Tucker, the church's most enthusiastic and hardworking member was Michael Baldasaro. A native of Hamilton, Ontario,
Baldasaro was an operating engineer and general contractor who, like
Tucker, had discovered cannabis and the hippie counterculture, and had
taken to the little community that was forming at the abbey. He soon
became Tucker's clerical second-in-command.

Baldasaro and Tucker spent their lives working together to promote
their vision of spiritual enlightenment through cannabis, body freedom,
and the Golden Rule that guided the church. In the manner of hippies
worldwide, they grew long hair and beards, and dressed in colorful garb
made of hempen fabric. The two oversaw the community and land at
the abbey where they constructed dwelling places, cultivated cannabis
in discreet corners, and welcomed visitors ranging from seminary students to outlaw bikers.

During the warm summer months church members would gather
around the crystal clear quarry waters, partake of the herbal sacrament,
and swim, sunbathe, or hike through the forest "clothed with the sun."
From this community Tucker and Baldasaro began to ordain church
ministers and missionaries who would enlighten not just Canada, but
the entire planet with the Good News that the Garden of Eden was
open once more to anyone willing to shed their clothing, partake of the
Tree of Life, and commune with the Divine.

THE MYSTERY CORPSE AND MISS NUDE ONTARIO

But just as in the biblical Eden, trouble came to Clearwater Abbey. In 1975 a decomposing, unidentified human body was found on the 360-acre property, and local media implied that the bikers who frequented the abbey had planted the corpse there. Later that year cops raided the property and charged Rev. Walter Tucker with possession of not only narcotics, but of five sawed-off shotguns. Tucker was later sentenced to sixty days in jail for possession of illegal weapons.

Jail or no, the son of the noted Canadian Liberal politician had ambitions of his own to take elective office and bring cannabis- and nudity-fueled enlightenment to the Great White North's government councils. A year before the weapons bust, he had run for the Canadian Parliament as an independent candidate in Ontario's Wellington riding. The year afterward he contested the Wellington South seat in Ontario's provincial legislature, also as a nonpartisan. Not surprisingly, Tucker finished well behind the major-party candidates in both elections, but the campaigns were early manifestations of the political activism he and Michael Baldasaro would pursue for the rest of their lives.

In the late 1970s the church endured another round of legal troubles. During 1977 Walter Tucker and his younger brother William had traveled throughout North and South America, as well as other destinations, publicizing the church and its message of spiritual growth through THC and all-over tans. That summer they also staged the Miss Nude Ontario pageant at Clearwater Abbey, where winner Deborah Hawke walked away with $3,000 CAN and the chance to pose for *Gallery* magazine's centerfold.

Ontario police suspected that both Ms. Hawke's winnings, and the brothers' travel expenses, had been paid for with pilfered funds, and in January 1978 Walter and William were charged with seven counts of fraud involving $36,000 CAN. The Crown alleged that the two had scammed credit-card companies and banks and had used the monies to not only finance nude beauty pageants and world travels, but to buy up gold bullion for unknown reasons.

When the case finally came to trial in mid-1979, police testified about the raids four years earlier, and the naked women, vicious guard dogs, sawed-off shotguns, and mystery corpses they'd encountered during their visits to Clearwater. The judge declared a mistrial when Crown prosecutor Frank Moskoff misspoke about the brothers not testifying, and Walter Tucker was acquitted on all charges. Brother William was retried for fraud in February 1980, convicted, and sent to jail for six months.

"CHEEKY, ARROGANT, MISINFORMED, AND WRONG"

A month before that, the Tucker brothers had appeared before the Supreme Court of Canada to appeal an earlier case where they'd been convicted of possessing cannabis. The two attempted to convince the court that the Church of the Universe considered the plant a holy sacrament, and that the laws against it violated members' rights to worship freely.

Representing themselves, the brothers pointed to the religious exemption carved out for sacramental wine during Canadian Prohibition, and quoted from the Bible, the Magna Carta, and the writings of Chief Justice Bora Laskin himself to bolster their arguments. Laskin countered that the court had approved the right of Parliament to outlaw narcotics a year earlier, and the Tuckers' case was thrown out of court.

The two were back in court once again in 1981. That year they were charged with obstructing traffic, and when they again defended themselves in court, they subpoenaed twenty-four different police officers to court and likened them to the Nazi Gestapo. Provincial Court Judge Anthony Charlton called their defense tactics "cheeky, arrogant, misinformed, and wrong," and said that their attempts to argue their case were so stupid that they threatened the fragile institution of Canadian justice.

The Tucker brothers were similarly upbraided by the court eight months later when they attempted to represent Reverend Michael Baldasaro in a cannabis-possession case. Baldasaro, who claimed the arresting officers had "interfered with a clergyman with his sacred duties," was convicted, but got his twelve-month sentence cut in half when he promised the judge he'd forever abstain from cannabis. It was a promise he'd break openly and repeatedly for the rest of his life.

THE NUDE OLYMPICS, AND THE HASHISH-OIL SACRAMENT

By 1982 Clearwater Abbey was in jeopardy. Although the church held a successful "Nude Olympics" there in July, where fifty male and female contestants clad only in suntan lotion ran, jumped, and splashed around the property for the title of "Nude of the Universe," legal problems were again afoot. Property owner Canada Cut and Crushed Stone had been acquired by the multinational Steetley Industries, and the new landlord wasn't keen on having their real estate occupied by naked hippie dopers.

When Walter Tucker was presented with a new lease that said he'd never lived on the land, he refused to sign it. Steetley retaliated by holding its summer company picnic at Clearwater. Tucker later said that day cars drove up right onto the blankets of nude sunbathers, who fled in the face of the onslaught of family picnickers.

Outraged, the church founder sent the corporation a $1.9 million bill for damages. When Steetley refused to pay it, Tucker withheld monthly rent payments, and was eventually served with a Writ of Possession and Notice to Quit. The case went to court, and its ruling favored Steetley, but Tucker refused to vacate the property, and he and various squatters spent the next three years occupying the land.

Meanwhile, Tucker's son Walter Tucker III was in serious trouble. A twenty-seven-year-old who had joined the church and set up a ministry in Calgary, Alberta, that boasted fifty members, the youngest Walter had been arrested in Toronto International Airport in 1982 and charged with smuggling 470 grams of hashish oil—a powerful cannabis concentrate, valued at $10,000 CAN. When the case came to trial in May 1983, the court rejected the argument that the oil would be used by the church for sacramental purposes, and the younger Tucker drew a one-year sentence.

By this time, the church had been formally incorporated as a religious organization in the province of British Columbia. Walter Tucker estimated that the church had around 5,000 members, many of whom continued to visit Clearwater Abbey and consume the sacrament, in violation of both Ontario court rulings and Canadian drug laws.

RAID ON CLEARWATER ABBEY

The church's years-long conflict over the property finally came to a head on June 17, 1986. That day over thirty Ontario law enforcement officers raided Clearwater Abbey, and arrested Rev. Walter Tucker, his wife, Sister Jo-Anne Tucker, and Rev. Michael Baldasaro. According to the Revs. Tucker and Baldasaro, all three were nude at the time of the arrest, and instead of allowing them to dress, the cops wrapped them in orange plastic blankets and hauled them into a local court, where the trio were charged with trespassing, drug trafficking, and resisting arrest.

Three years later, when the case came to trial, charges against the trio were stayed (not pursued) when the judge determined the defendants hadn't been served the proper legal papers prior to the arrest. To protest their treatment during the arrest, Tucker and Baldasaro showed up in court wearing nothing but blankets—a gesture that almost got them cited for contempt. The two often repeated the stunt at future trials, with similar results.

Two days after the court decision, Rev. Tucker and Sister Jo-Anne returned to Clearwater Abbey to swim nude before an audience of local media. Police officers were present, and they hauled Tucker in for trespassing and resisting arrest. The reverend later claimed the cops roughly grabbed him and beat him to the ground before they put him under arrest.

Released the next day, Tucker returned to the property. There, after he told reporters he hoped to hold the 1989 Nude Olympics on the site despite his ongoing legal troubles, he was arrested and cited again for trespassing. Tucker and his cohorts got the hint, abandoned Clearwater Abbey for good, and relocated to rented property in nearby Hamilton.

HAMILTON, HOMICIDE, AND THE "HEMPIRE VILLAGE"

The lakeside Ontarian city proved to be no friendlier to the church. On the night of November 9, 1990, Hamilton police smashed the glass door of Walter and Jo-Anne Tucker's office/home, searched the premises, confiscated thirty-five pounds of cannabis and $18,000 in cash and silver, and arrested the couple as suspected drug traffickers. The case was dropped when the judge determined that a proper warrant hadn't been served, and afterward Walter Tucker noted, "That's the second time they've withdrawn charges against us and just kept what they stole. They're thieves, man."[4]

The church's migration to urban Canada brought with it a new, gritty reality for some of its members, quite unlike the idyllic atmosphere of Clearwater Abbey. In 1993 forty-five-year-old church minister Terrance Pyne was convicted for the second-degree murder of his Burlington, Ontario, roommate two years earlier. A year later longtime church leader Daniel Morgan was found tied up and beaten to death in a ransacked apartment that had once been Walter Tucker's home; his murder has never been solved. And in 1994 Ontario's courts finally got around to sentencing Michael Baldasaro for some earlier hashish-sales busts and sent him to prison for two years.

Despite the setbacks, Walter Tucker was convinced he'd found a new Clearwater Abbey in Ontario's industrial wasteland. In 1992 eccentric political activist John Long bought the abandoned thirteen-acre IMICo foundry site from the Ontarian city of Guelph for a dollar and promised to clean up and cart off its ruins and debris. Unable to satisfy the city's requirements, in 1994 he donated the property to the Church of the Universe.

Tucker and Long moved onto the property, with the intention of starting a planned community there. They dubbed the proposed settlement "Hempire Village," and stated that it would be a self-sufficient, clothing-optional urban community based on the production of hemp for food, garments, medicine, and sacramental use. Tucker believed the thirteen-acre property could also host a community swimming pool, youth center, and sports complex, but his plans were stymied when the City of Guelph billed the church for a pre-existing $2.1 million tax debt on the land.

Tucker countersued the city, saying it should have assessed and collected the taxes when IMICo still held the land. As with Clearwater Abbey, a long legal battle followed, and in January 1998, Tucker and the church were once again evicted from a would-be cannabis-and-nudity Utopia.

THE MISSION OF ECSTASY

While the church leadership struggled to establish a headquarters in urban-industrial Ontario, one minister brought its pro-cannabis activism to Canada's Pacific Coast. In Victoria, British Columbia, Sacred Herb hemp-goods vendor Ian Hunter set up a local Church of the Universe branch called the Mission of Ecstasy, so-called since Hunter believed cannabis "allows people to achieve ecstasy. . . . It's spirit and we should all have access to it."[5]

The mission held its sacred smoke-ins at Victoria's Beacon Hill Park, where attendees held hands and shared the sacrament during a forty-two-second silent ceremony. When local cops broke up one gathering and busted a couple of participants, Hunter charged the police with violating a Criminal Code statute that prohibited anyone from disrupting a religious gathering. Unfortunately for the Victorian hemp entrepreneur, the case was thrown out of court, and he was later convicted in 1997 on three drug-related offenses, with his business license canceled the following year.

A CANNABIS-SMOKING, NUDIST HIPPIE PRIME MINISTER?

Back in Ontario, the church was once again in Canadian headlines. Angered over the court cases and jail terms that he'd suffered merely for smoking and distributing the God-given cannabis sacrament, Michael Baldasaro decided to run for office in July 1998.

Like Walter Tucker, Baldasaro was already a familiar face in Ontario elections. During the eighties and nineties, he contested various local races as a Libertarian, Marijuana Party, or independent candidate, and in Hamilton's 1988 mayoral election he finished in second place. This time, though, he set his sights on the leadership of Canada's oldest and stodgiest political organization: the Conservative Party. If he was elected to the office, and if a Conservative government took power during his term, the cannabis-smoking nudist hippie would become the country's prime minister.

At a press conference on Ottawa's Parliament Hill, where the bearded, long-haired Baldasaro and Tucker were decked out in muscle shirts and knit hemp caps, one reporter likened the pair to stoner comedians Cheech and Chong. But the two were deadly serious when they decried the Conservative Party's $30,000 fee required of prospective leadership candidates and told reporters they'd demanded the party waive the charge.

To nobody's surprise, Baldasaro said that his first act as party head would be to advocate for cannabis legalization. He also endorsed a plan to give every Canadian citizen $10,000 and one acre of untaxable land at birth. When asked how he supported himself, Baldasaro admitted that he had collected worker's compensation benefits for decades, since two industrial head injuries had left him "a little bit slow." Never taken seriously by Conservative Party members and lacking the necessary $30,000 to be considered for the race, Baldasaro was soon eliminated from the field of candidates.

GANJA FOR THE HEALTH MINISTER

But the church heads continued to vex Canada's political and legal establishments. In May 1999 they lobbied Hamilton's City Council to establish a nude beach on Lake Ontario, saying that Toronto already provided places "to sunbathe without those strap marks, which are gross indications of being ashamed of your body,"[6] as Tucker put it. That same month he and Baldasaro were busted at a demonstration against Canadian Premier Mike Harris, and later claimed that police had "brutalized" them during the arrest.

And that September, when the Canadian Ministry of Health announced that it was conducting clinical trials with medical cannabis, Tucker and Baldasaro sent two grams of top-grade, hydroponically grown weed to Health Minister Allan Rock. The church leaders claimed they already supplied Hamilton-area patients and doctors with medicinal marijuana but wanted the federal government to set up a safe and legal delivery system for Canadian citizens, with them as contracted growers. Nine months later the pair were arrested for the stunt, and although RCMP officers confiscated $3,000 in cash and a computer during the arrest, the Mounties were later forced to return the seized goods.

"FIGHTING FOR SPIRITUAL FREEDOM"

As the twenty-first century dawned, other church ministers joined Tucker and Baldasaro in their decades-long fight against Canada's cannabis laws. In Ontario, Reverend Mike Ethier attempted to set up a "Compassion Club" to supply medical cannabis to local patients, ran for mayor of the town of West Nipissing, and was arrested several times for possession and trafficking. In Nelson, British Columbia, a hemp-goods store declared itself the Holy Smoke Mission of God and affiliated with the Church of the Universe as "a sacred space . . . fighting for spiritual freedom."

And when church minister Generik Broderick was put on trial after he tried to cross into Canada with cannabis, ecstasy, and LSD on his person, the American told the Ontario court he needed the substances for religious purposes. The judge termed the defense "interesting," although it didn't save the Wisconsin resident from a Canadian prison sentence.

Still fully committed to the spiritual use of cannabis, Tucker and Baldasaro continued their careers as Canada's most frequently busted pot smokers. In 2004 they were both arrested and charged with drug trafficking by the Hamilton police. Several more arrests for possession and trafficking followed over the next few years. And when the pair appealed a Superior Court conviction where a justice had labeled the church "a marijuana convenience store that operates for profit like a Prohibition-era speakeasy,"[7] Canada's Supreme Court refused to hear the case.

Similar charges were laid against Toronto's Reverend Peter Styrsky. Yet another Church of the Universe minister who had contested local elections, Styrsky was arrested at his Beach District house in October 2006 and charged with drug trafficking. Toronto police told reporter Michelle DiPardo that his Church of the Universe chapter was a front for growing and selling cannabis, and that "there was no religious instruction provided to anybody that we observed in the place. The whole religious aspect is a total fraud."[8]

According to investigators, the Rev. Styrsky had signed up over 2,000 people for lifetime church memberships at $25 each, and sold the members weed at a profit. When Styrsky and his brother cannabis cleric Shahrooz Kharaghani were put on trial for trafficking, they attempted a religious-defense strategy, but it worked no better for them than it had for Tucker and the other church ministers in previous cases. The two were convicted and jailed for several months.

The pair got off lightly compared to church minister Ed deVries. A resident of far northern Iqaluit, Nunavut, deVries, a convicted money-launderer who was reputed to have made over $2 million on cannabis sales over a ten-year period, had his house and business raided three times by the RCMP between 2009 and 2011. He eventually faced a forty-one-count indictment on charges ranging from drug trafficking to sexual assaults against minors.

In 2012 deVries pleaded guilty to two counts of drug possession and six sex crimes and received a six-year prison sentence. The case further strained the Church of the Universe's credulity with Canadian courts as a legitimate religious organization, and pointed out that it, like all other faiths, numbered wolves in its flock.

THE PASSING OF THE PRANKSTER-PRIESTS, AND LEGAL WEED IN CANADA

Sadly, neither Walter Tucker nor Michael Baldasaro lived long enough to witness the full legalization of cannabis across Canada in 2018. Tucker, who had spent over forty years as the nation's most visible advocate of the cause, and who'd been arrested and jailed dozens of times fighting for it, died on April 26, 2012, in Hamilton's General Hospital of heart failure. News stories commemorated the seventy-nine-year-old as a colorful eccentric who had sincerely and intelligently represented his faith in courtroom battles, and an official church statement related that Tucker "loved what he had accomplished in life and lived a peaceful and contented existence among loving friends and family. He will be missed."[9]

At Tucker's death, Michael Baldasaro took over church leadership. He contested his last political office in 2014, when he came in fourth out of twelve candidates in Hamilton's mayoral election, running on a platform of compassion for addicts, homeless people, and prostitutes. Two years later, Baldasaro died of cancer at sixty-seven; as with Tucker, his passing sparked tributes from local pundits, including Hamilton mayor Fred Eisenberger, who called the church minister "a genuinely nice man. I will miss his passion and good humor."[10]

With its two prankster-priests dead, and cannabis legal across Canada, the church seemed to lose much of its raison d'etre. Although longtime church member Juliet C. Boyd succeeded Baldasaro as its head, she retreated from the role in late 2020. The sect exists today largely as a website that archives writings and photos from the days when Tucker and Baldasaro led it, as well as a network of spiritually oriented cannabis users on social media. At present, at least one real-world church mission is active in Quebec.

ACTIVIST HISTORY, COUNTERCULTURAL DREAM

Few other psychedelic sects fought as many legal battles over as long a period or had more of their members locked up on behalf of the sacrament they used, than did the Church of the Universe. That alone guarantees the sect a prominent place in the histories of modern-day entheogenic religions, Canadian cannabis culture, and the Dominion's prohibition laws alike.

Too, the church's leaders kept the issue of cannabis legalization in Canada's public consciousness for decades. It's not much of a stretch to surmise that their persistent, high-profile activism, which both amused and informed the nation's public, gradually eroded the Reefer Madness mythos that had influenced Canadian attitudes toward cannabis and was a big factor in why the plant can now be legally consumed in that nation.

Over fifty years after its founding, the church continues to promote the spiritually transformative powers of not only cannabis, but of walking and swimming nude in the sun, and of adopting the hippie counterculture's ideals to daily life. Whatever its future may hold, the church will stand as Canada's most famous and influential organization dedicated to religious entheogenic use.

SIXTEEN

THE HAWAI'I CANNABIS (THC) MINISTRY

Holy Smoke in Paradise

At a time in life when most American men are welcoming grandchildren and planning retirement, sixty-one-year-old minister Roger Christie was spending his first day in federal prison.

On July 8, 2010, the Hawaiian pastor was incarcerated in Honolulu's Federal Detention Center without bail. Labeled a "danger to society" by three federal judges, Christie was kept behind bars until September 11, 2014, when he was released to a halfway house.

His crimes? Christie was the founder of the Hawai'i Cannabis Ministry—usually abbreviated as "THC Ministry"—and made the herb available to Aloha State residents who needed its physical and spiritual healing. To the Feds, his missionary marijuana work was a clever cover for a sophisticated cannabis cultivation and distribution network across Hawaii, and federal agents spent over two years investigating Christie's doings before he, his wife, and twelve other people, the so-called Green 14, were busted. Alone among them, Christie was denied bail.

ROGER CHRISTIE

The four-year lockup made Christie one of the most committed of entheogenic-cannabis martyrs. Like the Ethiopian Zion Coptic Church (see chapter 14) brothers, he saw the plant as a sacrament and used it in the context of a Christocentric faith that maintained its practices were closer to the original Old and New Testament observances than those of most modern churches. And like them, he was willing to do years of federal time rather than compromise his belief that he and his flock pursued truly holy lives through ritual use of the herb.

Unlike the Coptics, however, Christie didn't get rich off cannabis. He boasted no opulent "Embassies," no fleets of seagoing craft and semitrailers, and no twenty-ton marijuana stashes to draw the attention of the national media and the narcs. Neither did the community he created adhere to the straitlaced biblical lifestyle of the Jamaican-Floridian sect; instead, Christie's ministry emphasized a nonjudgmental, healing approach to sacred cannabis use, very much in the Aloha spirit of the islands where it was born.

Although Roger Christie came to his ministry relatively late in life, he had been a dedicated cannabis smoker since his late teens. Born in Steamboat Springs, Colorado, in 1949, Christie said that he smoked his first joint in August 1968 and "immediately knew we were going to be friends." After two years of college and flight school in Miami, Christie enlisted in the U.S. Army, and was sent to Fort Holabird, Maryland's army "spy school," where he was trained as a G-2 Intelligence Analyst.

In the spirit of the times, and possibly because of the herb's influence, the young army intelligence operative began to question military authority and tradition. Christie decided that the American government's actions in Vietnam and elsewhere were unjustified, and that he couldn't serve or kill on its behalf. He declared himself a conscientious objector, and the army granted him an Honorable Discharge in July 1971. The experience taught Christie that following one's conscience was paramount for survival, and that you could beat the System if you were sincere and played your cards right.

HEMP AND RELIGIOUS SCIENCE

After the army, Christie worked as a commercial pilot. In 1986 he moved to Hawaii's Big Island and became interested in hemp—the form of the cannabis plant grown for industrial or medicinal uses.

Industrial hemp's history and applications, and its legal suppression as part of the thirties' Reefer Madness, were the subjects of Jack Herer's 1985 book *The Emperor Wears No Clothes*. An underground bestseller that promoted legalization and widespread cultivation of cannabis hemp, the book marshalled evidence from science and history to show that the plant could be utilized as an organic, renewable source of paper, food, textiles, medicines, construction materials, and biodiesel fuel. Herer's ideas reenergized the antiprohibition movement during the dark days of the Reagan-Bush War on Drugs and remains a favorite factbook for cannabis advocates around the world.

Intrigued by the plant's potential, Christie helped cofound the Hawai'i Hemp Council in 1990. A year later he and two partners started the Hawaiian Hemp Company and opened one of the world's first retail hemp stores, offering legal cannabis-based, THC-free clothing and body-care products to the public.

Christie also grew spiritually. When he arrived on the Big Island he joined Hilo's Church of Religious Science, the local branch of a sect that combined Christian spirituality with the metaphysical teachings of the so-called New Thought movement. The church emphasized positive thinking, personal affirmations, and the omnipresence of God and Spirit in its doctrines, and Christie incorporated them into his daily life. A cohort later reminisced that the Hawaiian hemp promoter shunned using words like *no, not,* or *never,* since such terms attracted "negative energy." (Christie instead said "zero" whenever he wanted to negate something.)

However, the Church of Religious Science was decidedly negative about one subject close to Christie's heart. When he offered to give a Sunday-service talk at the branch about cannabis spirituality, he was flatly turned down by church leaders. Disappointed at their "lack of courage in exploring the truth," Christie left the flock and sought a spiritual community that would affirm the body-, heart-, and soul-healing power of the herb.

THE RELIGION OF JESUS IN HAWAII

He found one in Hawaii's Religion of Jesus Church. Started by Kekaha resident James Kimmel, the Religion of Jesus Church originated in California, where Kimmel, then a high-school teacher, was busted for possession of cannabis in 1968. After being fired from his job over the charges, Kimmel fought the case in court, saying that using the herb was a central part of his religious practice, protected by the First Amendment.

Kimmel was a minister in the Universal Life Church, which ordained all applicants for free and without question. Under the ULC's corporate aegis he'd started a chapter in Sonoma, California, called the Religion of Jesus Church. Its statement of purpose read that:

> The Religion of Jesus Church is a group of like-minded individuals who believe: That God is Our Father and that we are all, the entire human race, one spiritual family that there are as many paths to God as there are people to walk them. That Cannabis is a Holy Sacrament from times of antiquity. That our main religious text is the *Urantia Book* . . .
>
> We draw upon many religious texts, including the Holy Bible, and many others to establish and verify our religious practices.[1]

After a three-year legal struggle, a California court dropped the charges against Kimmel. Shortly thereafter he migrated to the Hawaiian island of Kauai, where he reestablished the Religion of Jesus Church, and held Sunday meetings where attendees smoked cannabis and discussed the *Urantia Book*'s esoteric teachings. If the faithful wanted further enlightenment, they could take home some of the sacrament in exchange for a donation.

In 1993 Roger Christie encountered a church branch on the Big Island. He found its teachings and practices to be "simple and sincere, and it worked well for everyone," so he became a regular communicant in its ceremonies. Religion of Jesus cleric Dennis Shields ordained Christie into the church ministry in June 2000, and that month he was granted a license to perform marriages under the authority of the "Cannabis Sacrament" by the state of Hawaii.

THC MINISTRY

Just three months after his ordination, Christie split from the Religion of Jesus to start his own church. He named it the Hawai'i Cannabis Ministry, or THC Ministry, made the Holy Bible rather than the *Urantia Book* the scriptural basis of the church, and combined Religious Science teachings with the healing power of the herbal sacrament in its practices.

On its website, the organization stated that:

THC Ministry is a universal religious organization that uses Cannabis to exalt consciousness, facilitate harmony, and become closer to God and Nature.

We believe that:

Cultivation and enjoyment of Cannabis sacrament is a fundamental human right provided by God and protected by the U.S. Constitution.

Sacramental use of Cannabis opens the mind, frees the soul and releases the body to commune with God and balance itself.

Cannabis has been used for millennia as a sacrament by spiritual seekers & is the original sacrament of Hebrew, Muslim, Christian, Hindu, Shinto, Buddhist, Rasta and more.

Cannabis is the Tree of Life, given to humans by God for food, shelter, clothing, fuel, medicine, sacrament and much more.

Cannabis was given by God to help humans find answers to fundamental questions about the meaning of life and their place in it.

Cannabis fosters a spirit of harmony and compassion among people.[2]

THE CANNABIS HEALER

Christie stepped into his role as Hawaiian hemp-healer at a key time for Aloha State cannabis users. Hawaiian Senate Bill 862, which legalized medical marijuana in the state, had been signed into law the same month his ministry began. However, unlike similar legislation passed in other states, it didn't authorize any medical-cannabis dispensaries, permit any form of collective cannabis cultivation, or allow patients or caregivers to receive instruction in growing their own plants. Although it acknowledged cannabis had legitimate medical uses, the law required potential patients to sign up not with the State Health Department, but with the Narcotics Enforcement Division. And it granted the State Police a quarter-million-dollar annual allowance "to eradicate cannabis and enforce prohibition."

Christie felt that the new law not only prevented sick people from obtaining the natural plant medicine but violated the Constitution's protection of freedom of religion for his ministry. He vowed to create a safe space where he could minister to all who sought physical healing and spiritual uplift with the help of the herb.

THC Ministry did much of its healing work with what it called Holy Anointing Oil. This was the tincture whose recipe the God of Israel gave to Moses in Exodus 30:22, so that the prophet and his successors could consecrate holy places and objects. Although Bible scholars generally believe that the *kaneh bosm* mentioned in the recipe was calamus root, Christie maintained that it was the cannabis plant, and said that Jesus and his disciples used the same oil to heal the sick and initiate followers into their spiritual path. The ministry was dedicated to reviving this practice in the twenty-first century in the spirit of Jesus, whose title "Christ" meant "Anointed One."

"I AM LOVED AND ALL IS WELL"

In one of entheogenic history's strangest and funniest synchronicities, the man named *Christ*ie (bringing to mind the "anointed one") brought cannabis anointing oil to the public at Hilo's landmark Moses Building. According to the THC Ministry's founder, a wealthy retired CPA whom he had successfully treated with the anointing oil gifted him a lease on an office in the oceanfront edifice.

On his first day in the space, Christie hung a large banner outside the building announcing that the Hawai'i Cannabis Ministry was in the house. I was told by Christie that as a student of Religious Science metaphysics, he'd taken to heart the lesson, "If you can't hide it, paint it red," and gave his new ministry a bright crimson hue for all of Hilo to see.

For three days every week, THC Ministry head Christie met prospective cannabis communicants in his office. Visitors were required to wash their hands with hemp soap when entering the premises and show the manners and respect befitting both a place of healing and a religious sanctuary.

Christie usually spent an hour or so with office visitors, explaining what the ministry was all about. He would also teach prospective ministry members the importance of forgiveness, gratitude, and love in life, and that one's karmic debts could be resolved with sincere, heartfelt confessions of wrongdoing. And Christie would inevitably offer visitors the official THC Ministry blessing, reminiscent of his Religious Science positive-thinking days: "God, that's great! Please show me the blessings in this situation . . . and hurry! I am safe, I am loved and all is well."[3]

After the instruction, Christie would anoint visitors with his special oil. He claimed that the substance, when used properly in a sacred context, could cure everything from gangrene to arthritis to migraines, and said that up to seventy people a day visited the ministry office during its open hours to receive instruction and anointment.

CANNABIS SPIRITUALITY IN HILO

Christie invited newly anointed people to join the ministry. Applicants needed to be twenty-one years of age or older and to affirm they'd use cannabis respectfully and sincerely as part of their personal, private religious practice. In exchange, the ministry offered help with spiritual guidance, ceremonies, and blessings, as well as education about the medical use of cannabis, and physician referrals for members who wanted to join Hawaii's medical-marijuana program.

Official membership in THC Ministry could be obtained for a $50 donation. For that amount, donors received two laminated membership cards, seven tags for cannabis plants that labeled them as plants grown for religious purposes only, and a plaque that designated a home and/or garden a Sanctuary and place of refuge under the ministry's authority. Another $200 donation brought *THC Ministry Guide to Cannabis Spirituality,* a 180-page compilation of writings about the religious history and use of the plant, and relevant case law concerning it. These offerings, the ministry said, could help members with a First Amendment, religious-freedom defense should they run afoul of anti-marijuana laws.

For over a decade, THC Ministry operated openly out of Hilo's Moses Building. Eventually it grew so successful that Christie and his crew took over all thirteen rooms in the building, and dedicated them to meeting spaces, grow rooms, and social areas. Christie relayed to me that he often gazed from his office toward an old railway turnaround a block away in downtown Hilo and thought that the ministry performed a similar function for the physically and spiritually hurting people who visited, helping them to reverse their lives' dysfunctional and self-destructive directions with cannabis healing.

ANOINTINGS, WEDDINGS, AND "SERIOUS STREET PEOPLE"

The best attended events at the building were the regular Sunday meetings. According to religious historian Laurie Cozad, who wrote about the ministry in her book *God on High,* the meetings began with welcome periods where the attendees formed a circle, introduced themselves, and stated why they were there. Christie told Cozad that this not only broke the ice among the faithful, but also allowed him to "weed out, so to speak, any visitors or members who seemed insincere, or who had bad manners, as was sometimes the case."[4]

Once the introductions were complete, Christie would make announcements about the current legal status of cannabis, new scientific studies regarding its medical use, or other weed-related reports. This would be followed with a history lesson about how different cultures used the plant as a sacrament, and then a group prayer and a weekly teaching about spiritual growth.

Then came communion. Instead of bread and wine, Christie brought out two bottles of Holy Anointing Oil, and explained what the tincture was composed of, and how it had been made and blessed. The minister then went around the circle and gave everyone a single drop of the oil on the tongue. When he had finished, Christie started a second circuit where he applied a few drops to each attendee's wrists and had them rub their "pulse points" slowly together to active the oil's healing powers. He would also anoint each person's crown chakra—the top of their head—with about one-third of an eyedropper's worth of oil, and ask them to gently rub it in, while he blessed them with the words, "May all of your very best dreams come true."

Once everyone had been anointed, the group sat in meditation for a period to "enjoy the experience and feel the feelings that developed." Finally, in the manner of Christian church meetings the world over, the celebrants ended the service, and gathered for coffee, refreshments, and fellowship. Often there was live music as well, and many who attended the services remembered that along with the healing and meditations, there were laughter and high spirits among all present, and that Christie had a rare sense of spiritual levity and fun.

As a licensed minister in the state of Hawaii, Christie also performed cannabis-oriented weddings. For the nuptials, the bride and groom's hands would be tied together with a hemp cord, and hemp seeds instead of rice would be thrown over the newlyweds. At these ceremonies, as well as at the baptisms, funerals, and other holy rites Christie and his ministers celebrated, a guard was always stationed at the door to make sure attendees bore either a THC Ministry membership card, or a medical card that qualified them to legally use cannabis. Once approved, they were admitted and offered small bottles of anointing oil for a donation.

If an attendee was too broke to donate money, Christie usually gave them a bag of "shake"—the bottom-of-the-barrel cannabis debris usually thrown out by more discriminating smokers. Christie's wife, Share, told Laurie Cozad that many of her husband's flock were "serious street people" whose lack of personal hygiene necessitated post-meeting cleanings of chairs and benches. But Christie always acknowledged and counseled even the dirtiest and most destitute of attendees, in the spirit of blessing one's challenges and finding the good in all people and situations.

OUTREACH, ECUMENICISM, AND THE UNITED CANNABIS MINISTRIES

During the 2000s Christie advertised THC Ministry's Sunday and weekday services in the local Hilo newspaper. He also maintained a website that presented information about cannabis's medical and spiritual benefits, discussed the legal aspects of growing and consuming the plant for those purposes, and offered ministry membership and Sanctuary packages to non-Hawaii residents. Christie also ordained many people as THC Ministry clergy, and local branches of the organization sprouted as far away as Amsterdam.

As THC Ministry spread beyond the Islands, Christie's ecumenical work did as well. He sent mission statements to such celebrity preachers as Saddleback Church's Rick Warren and Lakewood Church's Joel Osteen, informing the ministers of the cannabis plant's incredible potential to help humanity, and appealing to them as faithful Christians to spread this good news to their flocks. Not surprisingly, none of the big-name evangelists he contacted responded to his entreaties.

Christie also attended what may have been the first-ever conference of North American cannabis ministers. In October 2005 he joined such cannabis-culture notables as hemp advocate Rev. Jack Herer, Revs. Dan and Mary Quaintance of the Church of Cognizance (see page 264), and much-prosecuted legalization activist Rev. Ed Forchion at the United Cannabis Ministries' first meeting in Laytonville, California. Although the event was appended by tragedy when organizer Rev. Les Crane was murdered shortly afterward in a still-unsolved crime, it did result in a cannabis-spirituality Statement of Purpose drafted by the attendees and made the Rev. Roger Christie the Aloha State's representative of the increasingly visible spiritual movement.

CHRISTIE VS. THE DEA

Back in Hawaii, Christie married his spiritual mission to political activism. In 2004 he ran for mayor of Hawaii County on a prolegalization platform, finishing fourth in a field of five. During that period, he also was instrumental in persuading the county council to reject funding for

DEA-sponsored helicopter flyovers that dumped herbicide on the island, ostensibly to kill wild-growing cannabis. Today, Christie maintains that his successful activism against the Feds put him on their shitlist, and that they started looking for a way to take down THC Ministry.

Initially, Christie's contacts with law enforcement had been positive. On their first visit to the Moses Building, Hawaii County police had told Christie to keep his cannabis-church activities discreet. The second time, when Christie called them to remove a belligerent visitor from a meeting, they acknowledged his marijuana ministry, and declined to take legal action against it.

The Feds were a different story. On March 10, 2010, agents from the Drug Enforcement Administration, the Internal Revenue Service, the U.S. Postal Inspector's Office, and the Department of Homeland Security raided THC Ministry office in Hilo, as well as Christie's home. Although DEA agents confiscated seven cannabis plants and some cash, there were no arrests. Ever the optimist, Christie assumed that since the original warrant recognized the ministry as "a functioning entity with employees" that provided "arguably legitimate services," he could continue to distribute cannabis to members and medical-marijuana patients.

It was a grievous error. Three months later, a grand jury delivered a three-count sealed indictment that charged Christie with conspiracy to manufacture, distribute, and possess with intent to distribute more than 100 marijuana plants, manufacturing marijuana, and possession with the intent to distribute 240 marijuana plants. The indictment was based partly on the findings of an undercover officer who'd infiltrated the ministry and purchased cannabis from Christie, as well as court-ordered wiretaps on his phones that had allegedly recorded 17,000 calls during a two-year period.

PRISONERS OF THE WEED WAR

Acting on the indictment, federal agents again raided Christie's office and apartment on July 8, 2010. This time they confiscated about thirty ounces of cannabis and $34,000 in cash from his home and seized the contents of his personal safe-deposit box. Elsewhere on the Big Island, law enforcement officials seized over 2,000 cannabis plants, and arrested thirteen people, including Christie's wife, Share. Federal agents said that Christie and his cohorts distributed cannabis at a "suggested donation" of $400 per ounce—the going street-value of Hawaiian weed—and U.S. Attorney Florence Nakakuni labeled the ministry a "large scale business" that serviced sixty to seventy customers a day.

The Feds flew Christie and his thirteen codefendants in a military cargo plane to Honolulu, where they were incarcerated in the Federal Detention Center. All save for Christie were eventually released on bail; prosecuting federal attorney Michael Kawahara charged that since Christie didn't take the hint and cease operations after the initial March 10 bust, the church head believed he was above the law and needed to be kept behind bars. No fewer than three federal judges agreed, and Christie would eventually serve nearly four years in the Honolulu lockup before his case was resolved.

The case made the Hilo resident both a Hawaiian celebrity and one of North America's most high-profile prisoners of the war on cannabis. Prolegalization activists, as well as some Aloha State politicians, were outraged that not only had bail been repeatedly denied to Christie during his years-long confinement, but that he was facing up to forty years in the federal pen on a first offense.

On April 3, 2013, Hawaii State Senators Russell Ruderman and Will Espero met with Christie at the center to discuss his incarceration. A week later the Hawaiian State Senate Judiciary and Labor Committee heard testimonies that supported releasing Christie pending trial. Unfortunately, the committee chair deferred making any resolutions to support Christie. A later resolution that called on President Obama to investigate federal law enforcement's role in the situation was similarly sidelined.

One small victory Christie had during his long legal imbroglio was when U.S. District Court Judge Leslie Kobayashi ruled that he and his wife were "sincere" and "religious" cannabis ministers. Although the Christies had hoped to bring their cases to court in "the last marijuana trial"—a landmark ruling that would forever establish the legal right to use cannabis as a religious sacrament in the United States—the evidence and witnesses that supported them were never heard by a judge or jury. As far as the court was concerned, the plant was still a prohibited Schedule I substance, and the Christies, multiple felons.

Denied trials, the Christies submitted plea deals to the court. After two delays, on April 28, 2014, the ministry founder, who had never been previously convicted of a crime, drew a five-year sentence for distribution of marijuana, two concurrent one-year terms for failing to file federal income tax, and four years of supervised release afterward where he would be forbidden to use or be in the presence of cannabis. Share got a term of twenty-seven months, and a three-year supervised release, and the couple's condo, as well as $21,000 in cash, were confiscated in an asset forfeiture.

SINCERITY AND POSITIVITY

By that point Christie had spent nearly four years in a detention cell with no natural light or time outdoors, and no bail, trial, or media contact. The judge gave him credit for time already served against his sentence, and on September 4, 2014, he was released from the federal pen to a Honolulu halfway house. Both Christie and his wife finished their sentences and supervised releases in late 2021.

While Roger Christie was incarcerated, the leaderless THC Ministry collapsed. The church that had openly provided THC-powered holy anointing oil and cannabis to countless thousands of Hawaiians for a decade, is currently dormant. Christie remains as committed as ever to his mission to promote the plant as a cure for so many Americans' physical, psychological, and spiritual complaints, and hopes that one day he can once again administer the body-healing, mind-expanding rites of his faith. In the meantime, the septuagenarian Big Islander keeps busy educating people about the herb and running a wedding ministry.

Christie told me that plain, simple sincerity has been his approach to life from a young age, and that the attitude has opened many doors for him that might otherwise have stayed closed. From the day he honorably walked away from the Vietnam-era U.S. Army to the decade he spent as one of twenty-first-century America's most visible and respected religious-cannabis ministers, an above-board approach and a solid commitment to his principles has always colored his doings, even when he faced forty years in federal prison as a drug trafficker.

Christie's story, as well as that of THC Ministry, is an illustration of how a genuine, positive mindset can enhance a commitment to entheogenic ministry, and how it can help one survive the legal persecution that almost inevitably accompanies such spiritual work.

SEVENTEEN

THE INTERNATIONAL CHURCH OF CANNABIS

A Gothic Church, Urban Murals, and Elevationism

On South Logan Street in the Washington Park district of Denver, Colorado, is one of the weirdest places of worship in America.

Outwardly, the stone Gothic Revival church looks like the thousands of other edifices that dot America's urban landscapes, built to house sizable mainline Protestant congregations in the years before suburbanization, secularization, and changing demographics emptied their pews of the faithful.

The building's front doors and recessed arch, decorated with colorful, cartoonish stars and planets, hint that the resident congregation might be a bit unorthodox. But the real surprise is inside, where the Gothic arcade windows and walls are painted in a riot of rainbow colors, and the vaulted ceilings are covered with multicolored, interlocking shapes that form abstract patterns, as well as giant, Picassoesque bull and bear heads.

On the front inside wall two twelve-foot-tall, birdlike female humanoids flank an arch painted with a view of a starry night sky. Another avian creature with grayscale plumage adorns the soundboard wall. And behind the podium, where stained-glass windows might usually be found, are yet more rainbow shapes and diagrams, including a sunburst pattern.

If it weren't for the pews, arranged neatly on each side of the central aisle, one might think the building hosted raves rather than religious services. Yet the colorfully painted edifice is the house of worship for the International Church of Cannabis, arguably the most famous American-born organization dedicated to sacramental marijuana use.

A BETTER MEDICINE

The church was first conceived of in 2015 by Steve Ryan Berke. The very antithesis of the stereotypical lazy, slow-witted stoner, Berke was a competitive tennis player who racked up several state and national championships before his eighteenth birthday, and twice made the NCAA's All-American list at Yale and UC–Berkeley. After graduation he turned pro, but a severe herniated spinal-disc injury ended his tennis career.

Switching his drive and talent to entrepreneurship and entertainment, Berke successfully auditioned for Sir Richard Branson's reality TV show, *The Rebel Billionaire*. There he competed with fifteen other young contestants for the chance to take over the presidency of Branson's Virgin corporation, lasting eleven of thirteen episodes. At the series' wrap party Branson, who'd noticed Berke's chronic back troubles, told him that cannabis might be a better medicine for them than the Vicodin and other pharmaceuticals the young man took to fight his crippling pain.

Berke, the son of doctors and a former professional athlete, initially balked at the idea of consuming an illegal drug. But he soon found that plant THC did a better job of managing his pain than did the prescription drugs, and he obtained a medical-marijuana recommendation from a California doctor.

ENTREPRENEUR, POLITICIAN, AND YOUTUBER

After *The Rebel Billionaire,* Berke marketed a neck-support cushion for airplane travelers, "The Moosh Pillow." Sales were dismal, so he switched to a career in real estate management. Berke also began to work open-mic nights at Miami comedy clubs, and recorded music videos for YouTube that parodied hit songs by Eminem and Macklemore and promoted his new passion: legalization of cannabis. The videos struck a chord with viewers, providing catchy antiprohibition rap anthems for a subculture that was slowly approaching mainstream recognition.

In 2011 Berke took his cannabis-legalization activism into Florida politics. That year he ran for mayor of Miami Beach on a platform that included decriminalizing marijuana, along with various local-reform proposals. Aided by famed political consultant Roger Stone, who had earlier managed the presidential campaigns of Ronald Reagan and the two George Bushes, Berke's campaign attracted the attention of the national media and featured celebrity spokespeople like sports heroes LeBron James and Rob Gronkowski.

On Election Day Berke came in second, with 29 percent of the vote. Two years later he ran for mayor again with a campaign that focused on building an elevated cable car between traffic-choked Miami Beach and the mainland and came in third, with a 12 percent vote share.

By 2014 Berke's election campaigns and popular YouTube videos had made the thirty-four-year-old one of the most prominent legalization activists in America. When the Floridian realized that the ever-growing cannabis industry lacked effective marketing channels for its products, he formed Bang Holdings to create a social media network that would bypass traditional media, where advertisements for marijuana and its related paraphernalia were forbidden. Bang Holdings was approved for public trading under the symbol BXNG, and by 2016 its affiliated influencers had a considerable presence on sites like Facebook, Instagram, and Snapchat.

AN OLD CHURCH ON SOUTH LOGAN STREET

Berke's introduction to cannabis as a spiritual sacrament came in 2015, when he journeyed to Denver, Colorado, to cover the annual Cannabis Cup. The state had fully legalized adult use of the plant three years earlier, and its capital city was hosting the world's leading cannabis competition, festival, and trade show on the weekend before April 20, a folk holiday among weed aficionados since the digits 420 correspond to a code for marijuana smoking.

Berke had just met with one of his social-media influencers and was driving down South Logan Street, when he noticed a huge FOR SALE sign in front of an old Gothic Revival church. Intrigued, he made inquiries about the dark, looming edifice.

The building had an unusual history. Erected for the use of the Lutheran Church in 1904, the church was taken over in 1915 by the Pillar of Fire, a quasi-Pentecostal Methodist denomination headed by Alma White, America's first female Christian bishop. A weird combination of evangelist, feminist, and racist, Bishop White preached sermons that advocated "Gospel-based" Christianity, women's equality, and White Protestant supremacy from the building's pulpit, often praising the Ku Klux Klan in both her homilies and writings.

When White moved her sect to New Jersey in the early 1920s, the Lutherans got the building back. It served that denomination until the Mount Cavalry Apostolic Church took it over in the early 1990s. They in turn vacated it in 2015.

With help from his family, Berke purchased the property for just over $1 million. Since it was zoned for residential use, he initially hoped to convert the 12,000 square-foot building into apartments, condo spaces, or even an offbeat mansion.

ELEVATIONISM AND THE INTERNATIONAL CHURCH OF CANNABIS

But the church was destined to become a sacred space once again. Tired after years of legalization campaigns in Florida, Berke and four other family members and associates relocated to Denver and moved into the building on South Logan. There, in the old Lutheran church that had hosted congregations of faithful for over a century, they began to wonder if the property was viable as a real-estate investment. Would it be better used, they thought, as a spiritual community where people could share the meditative cannabis experience in a safe environment?

Inside the stone walls of the old Lutheran church, Berke and the other residents began to work out a theology and philosophy for their cannabis community. Berke, a competitive athlete since childhood and a driven entrepreneur and activist, saw cannabis as a transformative substance that could spur the individual's growth in all aspects of their lives. This vision of uplifting entheogenic experience inspired him and the others to name their path *Elevationism*.

Elevationism maintains that "an individual's spiritual journey and search for meaning is one of self-discovery that can be accelerated and deepened with ritual and mindful cannabis use. We use the sacred flower to reveal the best version of self, discover a creative voice and enrich our community with the fruits of that creativity."[1] In all doings, the Elevationist would follow the Golden Rule, and support brother and sister seekers on their own journeys.

The Elevationist path was open to all people, no matter their religious or cultural identity. "Unlike other belief systems," it said, "there is no need to convert to Elevationism. It claims no divine law, no unquestionable doctrine, and no authoritarian structure."[2] Indeed, it maintained that faithful Christians, Jews, Buddhists, and others might have their religious paths powerfully enhanced by the spiritual, disciplined use of cannabis, and saw the plant as a gift of the Universe to all humanity, whatever their beliefs—or lack thereof.

Elevationists also asserted their right to congregate and partake of their sacrament in community, without legal harassment. They stated that cannabis had been made illegal because it allowed users "to tear down the false realities created by most organized religions and the machinators of state. Cannabis gives us access to the source code of our mind, while breaking down our delusion and elevating us to reality. This is a dangerous situation for the traditional institutions that wish to control our lives."[3]

Still, the Elevationists had to placate at least one established institution. When they applied to the IRS for its 501(c)(3) tax exemption, they had to answer a series of questions that determined whether their group was a "real religion." They kept their responses as concise as possible, stressing that they were not a "new religion," since cannabis had been used as a sacrament for thousands of years across the globe. Neither did they have formal structure, clergy, or dogmas, nor any roots in the Christian religion as did similar liberal-humanist sects like the Unitarians. Their effort was successful, and the International Church of Cannabis, as the formal Elevationist organization was named, was granted the exemption.

"THE MICHELANGELO OF CANNABIS"

The church spent almost a million dollars refurbishing the building on South Logan. Along with bringing all its appointments and furnishings up to code, the church also hired artist Kenny Scharf, famed for his whimsical graffiti-influenced illustrations, to create murals on the front of the church. Scharf, who reportedly finished his work in less than twenty-four hours, adorned the dark church doors with depictions of stars and spiraling galaxies, and the recessed arch space overhead with cartoon-faced Day-Glo planets gaping at passersby.

For the interior, the church commissioned famed Spanish painter Okuda San Miguel. The Madrid-based artist, who earned worldwide renown when he turned an old Spanish church into a mural-bedecked indoor skate park, was a natural choice to transform the drab Denver worship space into a colorful, magical shrine. San Miguel spent weeks on the project, eventually covering the inside walls and ceiling with rainbow-colored geometric shapes, symbols, animals, and humanoid figures, all in a distinctive style that combined surrealism and street art. San Miguel's astonishing work there eventually earned him the title "The Michelangelo of Cannabis."

420 AT 4:20 ON 4/20

In early 2017 Berke announced to the media that the church would open its doors to the public on April 20. Two years earlier Bill Levin had opened the First Church of Cannabis (see page 287) in Indianapolis, Indiana, to challenge a state "religious freedom" law and had been the center of a media feeding frenzy. Now another *Marijuana Church* was about to publicly emerge in a larger and more culturally influential city—the capital of the first American state to fully legalize the plant— on a day that had become synonymous with celebratory cannabis use.

On the eve of the opening, Berke told journalist Kastalia Medrano that he'd worked closely with city officials to make the building opening a smooth one. Berke said that the church wouldn't supply attendees with cannabis or paraphernalia and would restrict admission to the premises to people over twenty-one. Flammable dab rigs and concentrates were also forbidden inside the building.

Finally, at noon on April 20, 2017, the International Church of Cannabis opened its doors. Reporters and spectators crowded into the church on South Logan, where they were allowed to tour the building, but were forbidden to consume any cannabis. At 2 p.m. they were herded out, and an hour later a small number of church members and invitees bearing joints, pipes, and bongs settled into the pews. At 4:20 p.m. the two dozen or so people lit up and quietly meditated in the International Church of Cannabis's first service.

Across town in the state capitol building, the church had just won a major legal victory. Concerned that the church would attract unsavory characters to central Denver, State Representative Dan Pabon had attempted to add an amendment to a proposed state cannabis-regulation law that would have specifically banned its use in religious edifices. Politicians from both parties condemned the proposal as a blatant attack on First Amendment religious rights, and it was stricken from the bill on April 20.

THE MEMBERS-ONLY PROTECTION

But legal troubles found the church right at its home. Despite Berke's belief that he'd cleared the event with city and law enforcement officials, three undercover cops managed to sneak into the building during the 4/20 smoking session, and confronted Berke, along with church cofounders Lee Molloy and Briley Hale. All three were cited for public cannabis consumption, as well as for violation of Colorado's Clean Indoor Air Act.

Their cases went to trial in February 2018, but so many jurors were excused by the defense and prosecution for various reasons that a mistrial was declared. After several postponements, the three were tried separately, with Molloy being found not guilty, and Hale being found guilty and sentenced to community service and unsupervised probation. Berke was also found guilty and fined $50; his request for an appeal was denied.

Undaunted by the convictions, Berke and his associates continued to hold cannabis ceremonies at the church building. But now, they were far more careful about who they let into them. Potential attendees were required to sign up online at the church's website and answer a short questionnaire attesting to their interest in the plant as a religious sacrament.

Once approved, applicants became church members. This meant the gatherings would be private, members-only events protected by the First Amendment, and not regulated by the public-consumption law. Members received regular email invitations to the evening services that stressed attendees had to be twenty-one or over, with state or federal ID on their person, and that any accompanying guests had to sign up in advance with the church. Attendees were required to bring their own cannabis and were advised not to drive that night if they wished to partake of it.

CANNABIS AND COMMUNITY SERVICES

Services at the South Logan church ran weekly for nearly three years, usually on Friday or Sunday nights. A typical gathering started at 7 p.m., when the wildly painted front doors were opened, invitations were checked by security, and attendees were seated in the pews. At 7:20 there was a candle-lighting ceremony, often accompanied by a brief talk of what it meant to be an Elevationist. At this time attendees lit up their vessels, and silently meditated as the THC took their hearts and minds into personal sacred places.

Next would either be a short talk by a guest, or an open circle where Elevationists discussed cannabis, spirituality, or anything else they wanted to share. Musicians usually performed afterward, and the evening would conclude with a potluck meal, where "unmedicated" food and drink would be shared among the Elevationists. Services were free to invitees, but like all religious organizations the church happily accepted tax-free donations to help their mission, which soon took on charitable efforts to feed and clothe Denver's homeless population and clean the city's streets.

LANDMARK IN THE MILE-HIGH CITY

As the congregation grew, the church began to hold other events on the property. Yoga classes, movie nights, and concerts were offered for small donations, and the building soon sported a colorfully decorated lounge, a computer-game arcade, a gallery with rotating art installations, and a theater. Still, cannabis use remained restricted to church service times, among registered, invited members.

Travel sites like TripAdvisor and Atlas Obscura featured the church building and its colorful murals as a top Denver attraction, and both art critics and tourists visited the edifice during weekday hours to view them. For its part, the church refuses to interpret the meaning of the paintings, saying that "[w]hen one takes the sacrament and meditates on the meaning of the murals, one may have a transcendental experience. In those moments, one receives the meaning one requires at that time."

The church's Denver activities ground to a halt in mid-March 2020, when the U.S. government shut down in-person activities across America for the COVID-19 pandemic. Although it held online "virtual ceremonies" for a few weeks that spring, little was heard from the church until July 2021, when the South Logan Street building opened its doors again, and once more people gathered, candles burned, speakers spoke, musicians played, and sacred cannabis smoke ascended on service nights.

Nonsmokers and tourists, too, were welcome again. During weekdays the church staged "Beyond: A Guided Meditation & Laser Light Experience"—an hourly light show inside the building where admission-paying visitors were taken on a chemical-free psychedelic journey through the multicolored universe of the laser-enhanced church murals. The Yelp crowd-sourced review site soon named the show the number one attraction in Denver.

"THE BEST VERSION OF SELF"

As of this writing the International Church of Cannabis continues to function as North America's best-known and most active sect dedicated to the use of the plant. Steve Berke told me that even though he has no plans to open new church branches, he intends to keep spreading the message of Elevationism across America. Berke also wants to start a Museum of Elevationism in his home state of Florida that will portray and explain all aspects of the path to visitors.

Over a century after it first opened, the big old church on South Logan Street continues as a place of worship. The doctrines of Martin Luther are not taught there anymore, and racism and religious bigotry under a Christian guise are no longer proclaimed from its pulpit. Instead, behind its stone walls a small but growing spiritual community pursues personal enlightenment and growth with the aid of *Cannabis sativa* and welcomes all who seek to attain "the best version of self."

EIGHTEEN

AYAHUASCA HEALINGS

Plant Shamanism in the Internet Age

In the 2010s psychedelic spirituality went mainstream. What had been a shadowy, legally persecuted underground movement in the previous century suddenly found itself on the verge of respectability. News stories splashed across the United States' most popular magazines and websites told how peoples' lives were being changed by ceremonial entheogenic use. And these people were not the marginalized American Indians or grubby hippies of prior years, but wealthy and influential celebrities, entertainers, and entrepreneurs, who raved in America's major media outlets about how a hallucinogen had made them better, more empathetic, and more imaginative people.

AYAHUASCA HEALINGS AND CHRISTOPHER TRINITY DE GUZMAN

The hallucinogen in question was ayahuasca. A psychoactive tea that usually contains the powerful tryptamine DMT, ayahuasca had been brewed for centuries by vision-seeking South American peoples but had only recently become one of the developed world's most popular psychedelics.

While many seekers traveled to Peru, Ecuador, or Brazil in search of shamans who could guide them on trips with the tea, less adventurous types had their inner journeys stateside, where DMT was forbidden but ayahuasca's raw plant material was legal, cheap, and easy to brew. "Shamanic plant medicine" groups sprang up in cities across America, where self-appointed "healers" led group tea-drinking sessions, often charging attendees handsomely to quaff the foul-tasting beverage. Some of these group leaders would be accused of being hucksters who exploited indigenous traditions for profits and power, and a few would even face charges of sexual exploitation and cultish mind-control of the trippers to whom they ministered.

Fig. 18.1. Ayahuasca being brewed at a Peruvian retreat.
Photograph courtesy of Malcolm Rossiter.

Among the North American groups that rode the ayahuasca wave from the Millennium into the 2020s, none would be as well publicized, or as controversial, as Ayahuasca Healings. Part religious sect, part therapeutic group, and part tour business, the organization, founded in the United States by a transplanted Canadian and an expatriate Brit, has been praised by some as a forward-thinking pioneer of psychedelic spirituality, and condemned by others as a greedy, manipulative cult.

Although Ayahuasca Healings' conceptual origins were in the jungles and mountain ranges of South America, it was Christopher de Guzman who brought it to life. A Canadian citizen who grew up in British Columbia, de Guzman is a high-school dropout who first emerged on the internet promoting his self-help programs like "The Get Your Girlfriend Back Secret" or "Digital Nomads Academy" on YouTube. Bright, enthusiastic, and engaging, de Guzman, a disciple of think-yourself-rich gurus like Napoleon Hill and T. Harv Eker, traveled the world in his early twenties, running outsourcing and internet-marketing enterprises to raise funds for his wanderings.

In 2011 de Guzman was working with a life-coaching business in San Diego when a colleague introduced him to DMT. Smoking the fast-acting hallucinogen opened a whole new inner world for the young entrepreneur, who soon learned the chemical could be found in the magic potion of ayahuasca.

THE MAGIC TEA

Used as a plant medicine by indigenous Amazonian peoples, ayahuasca is a brew of the *Banisteriopsis caapi* (yage) vine with the *Psychotria viridis* (chacruna) plant. Other plants can be substituted for chacruna so long as they contain N,N-dimethyltryptamine (DMT), a powerful hallucinogen that sends users into often-ineffable otherworldly trips where they may have fantastic visions, or communicate with intelligent, disembodied entities.

Ayahuasca's other active ingredients are the harmala alkaloids in yage, monoamine oxidase inhibitors (MAOIs) that act as antidepressants. Taken together, they produce a synergistic experience of both spiritual vision and psychological healing that is unlike any other entheogen.

Called *caapi, hoasca, natem, shora,* and other names in different parts of South America, ayahuasca has a long history of usage by the continent's indigenous peoples. A "ritual bundle" in a Bolivian cave that contained DMT-bearing yage and harmala alkaloids was dated to around 1000 CE, and evidence exists of harmaline use in the region long before that. Among indigenous peoples, various mythologies and folktales grew up around the entheogenic effects of these chemicals, ranging from creation myths of the yage vine and the human race's discovery of it, to tales of a fantastic "Second Heaven" visited by aya-huasca trippers, to narratives of long and grueling initiations into the mysteries of the plants by shamans and healers.

Westerners first encountered ayahuasca when Jesuit missionaries pen-etrated the Amazonian basin's far reaches in the sixteenth century. The clerics condemned the vision-inducing brew as a tool of Satan, and it wasn't until four centuries later when the American Richard Evans Schultes, a brilliant and culturally sensitive ethnobotanist, did the first systematic analysis of ayahuasca's psychoactive properties for the outside world.

YAGE LETTERS AND TRUE HALLUCINATIONS

Intrigued by the botanist's findings, novelist William S. Burroughs and poet Allen Ginsberg both traveled to South America, sampled aya-huasca, and compiled their experiences in a 1963 book called *The Yage Letters*. Ginsberg's stream-of-consciousness account of his ayahuasca trips, characteristic of his rapturous poetic vision, included episodes where he "began seeing or feeling what I thought was the Great Being, or some sense of It, approaching my mind like a big wet vagina," and "feeling like a Great lost Serpent-seraph vomiting in consciousness of the Transformation to come."[1]

Sidelined in the sixties when more easily accessible entheogens flooded the counterculture, Western interest in ayahuasca was revived in the nine-ties. In 1994 the ethnobotanist brothers Dennis and Terence McKenna published a book titled *True Hallucinations* about their experiences with the brew in the Amazon basin. The book became one of the key tomes of the decade's psychedelic revival and made Terence McKenna the era's equivalent of Timothy Leary in his articulate, captivating promotion of entheogenic substances and their transformative potential.

The works of the McKennas and others have sent a steady stream of psychedelic tourists through Peru, Ecuador, Brazil, and other South American nations in search of an ayahuasca experience. Many of them found their way to Peru's Urubamba region, the "Sacred Valley" of the Inca where well-appointed retreat centers began to spring up, serving the entheogenic brew and guiding Western visitors on their journeys with "Mother Aya."

"AMERICA NEEDS THIS"

None of Urubamba's indigenous or foreign ayahuasca guides would become as famous, or as notorious, as the visiting Canadian Christopher de Guzman. When he first tried the brew there in 2013, he told *VICE* magazine reporter Nick Rose, "I was curled into a fetal position, crying, shaking, and vomiting. And I knew that at that moment that I was here to share it with the world, I didn't know in what way, but I was like 'America needs this.'"[2]

In Urubamba, de Guzman met a young British citizen named Marc Shackman. A former scuba instructor and globetrotting spiritual seeker, Shackman shared de Guzman's enthusiasm for the transformative power of DMT, and the two began to regularly lead small groups of ayahuasca users.

The two expatriates saw a huge, untapped market among Yankees who didn't have the time, money, or adventurousness to travel to South America and trust some back-country local to guide them along the soaring heights and bottomless depths of the ayahuasca trip. Why not, they thought, take the potion out of the often inhospitable and dangerous foreign regions of its birth, and market "plant medicine" retreats, openly and widely, in the United States?

There was just one problem with the idea. Although possession of the plants that constituted ayahuasca was legal in America, the brew's active chemical DMT was a Schedule I drug, as verboten as cocaine, LSD, or other narc-bait. Brewing the botanic substances to extract the forbidden active ingredients, and charging people for it, was a recipe for big legal troubles, and to date most U.S.-based ayahuasca circles had conducted their ceremonies discreetly.

AYAHUASCA AND THE FIRST AMENDMENT

Still determined to turn on North America to the beverage, de Guzman began networking with American ayahuasca providers in 2015 and seeking a way to bring the brew there safely and legally. He told one reporter that during one of his twice-weekly sessions "sitting with the plant," "the clarity came through"; he would start an American Church of Ayahuasca whose entheogenic practices would be protected under the First Amendment's freedom of religion guarantee, much as the Native American Church's (see chapter 1) peyote use was.

A precedent existed for the concept. In 1999 U.S. Customs agents raided the Santa Fe, New Mexico, mission of *O Centro Espirita Beneficiente União do Vegetal,* a Brazilian religious organization that used ayahuasca in its rites. When they confiscated over thirty gallons of the tea that the Portuguese-speaking sect called *hoasca,* the mission's leader, environmentalist Jeffrey Bronfman, filed suit against the U.S. government, claiming that the local members' religious rights had been violated.

A member of the wealthy Canadian Bronfman family, the New Mexican fought the case all the way up to the Supreme Court. On February 21, 2006, the court ruled in *Gonzales v. O Centro Espírita Beneficente União do Vegetal* that the government had no compelling interest to forbid the sect's use of the beverage, and that its practices could continue in any federal jurisdiction.

Two years later another imported Brazilian ayahuasca church, *Santo Daime,* won a similar legal battle in the state of Oregon. In both cases, it was established that the two groups were sincere, legitimate practitioners of indigenous Brazilian syncretistic religions, and the courts thought there was little danger of ayahuasca being advertised and distributed outside of their churches.

TRINITY'S VISION

But the courts had never reckoned on Chris de Guzman discovering ayahuasca. An obsessive promoter and skilled marketer, the twenty-six-year-old spent the latter part of 2015 bombarding social media, YouTube, online entheogen forums, and his own mass-email lists with messages and videos touting the psychedelic brew as the key to spiritual awakening and psychological health.

With his shaved head, dark oblong face, and soul-patch beard, the white-robed de Guzman looked every inch the exotic shaman-guru offering enlightenment to the West. The ever-grinning young Canadian's breathy voice, lofty tone, and passionate delivery enchanted viewers of his YouTube channel's offerings, and thousands tuned in to watch him hold forth on ayahuasca and entheogenic spirituality. De Guzman, who now called himself "Trinity," promised to make the potion—not a "drug," but a "tool, a teacher, and a guiding spirit"—available through his new organization, Ayahuasca Healings.

In December 2015 Ayahuasca Healings stated its basic purpose on its website:

> We stand for Truth, for Love, for Healing . . . for the Happiness and Freedom of us all!
>
> For The Great Awakening and Revolution of the Heart unfolding through this movement, through the guidance of Mother Ayahuasca, and bringing it into the hearts, minds, and souls of the people who need it the most . . . we are just so excited to legally, publicly and openly be bringing Ayahuasca to America!
>
> Our community Vision is to build and create together 30 Ayahuasca Retreat Centers and "Fifth Dimensional Villages" . . . near every major North American city by the beginning of 2032, the start of our New Golden Age.[3]

The website also stated,

> We are not here to sell, convince or force anybody to sit with this life-changing medicine. We are simply here to educate you, give you all the information you could possibly want and need, and let you know, that you can now experience an Ayahuasca Retreat in the USA, legally, publicly and openly.[4]

As for the legality of its practices, Ayahuasca Healings said, "We are a legally established independent Branch of the Oklevueha Native American Church (ONAC) (see chapter 4) that desires to protect and restore to the world our religious and personal freedoms as an inherently Native American Religious Global Culture and People."[5]

The statement raised red flags among observers familiar with the ONAC and its founder, James Mooney. Many felt that the ONAC's own claims of being legally sanctioned to use psychedelic sacraments were questionable, at best. They also pointed out that the "real" Native American Church had condemned Mooney's organization, and that ONAC's local chapters had been fraught with troubles ranging from police shootouts to deaths during ceremonies. By legally affiliating with an already controversial entheogenic church, they warned, Ayahuasca Healings was courting trouble.

THE ELBE RETREATS

Still, Ayahuasca Healings pressed ahead, and established its American retreat center in Washington State. One of de Guzman's associates had recommended the Pacific Northwest as an ideal location for the group, since its rain-drenched conifer forests were like a temperate-zone answer to the Amazonian jungles that had birthed yage and chacruna. De Guzman's lieutenant Shackman scouted the region for likely properties and in December 2015 he leased a 160-acre parcel outside of Elbe, Washington, in the shadow of famed Mount Rainier.

Although isolated and undeveloped, the land was less than a two-hour drive from Seattle's "alternative" urban communities, as well as its international airport. The lushly forested property provided privacy from prying eyes and open meadow areas where temporary shelters could be erected. Using the site's Elbe address, Shackman applied for and was granted nonprofit status by the IRS for Ayahuasca Healings. Just to be on the safe side, he also informed the local district attorney about the group and its activities.

By this time, hundreds of people had applied online to attend an Ayahuasca Healings retreat. Applicants sent the sect "suggested donations" of $1,497 to $1,997 to cover a four-day retreat at the Elbe property that included meals and lodging in a tipi. Eventually about a hundred people attended six of these retreats during early 2016.

On the first day of each retreat, arriving attendees settled into the tipis, and cleansed their bodies and minds in a sweat-lodge ceremony. The next day, Marc Shackman conducted a ritual with mescaline-bearing San Pedro cactus, followed by the ayahuasca ceremony at nightfall. On the third day attendees rested, processed their experiences, and did yoga, massage, or workshops to ground themselves. By the fourth day they were ready to return to the world, transformed by the plant-medicine retreat.

THE DARK SIDE OF ENLIGHTENMENT

Although videos taken during the events showed happy young people sitting around campfires and testifying how the ayahuasca experience had made them healthier, saner, and more spiritual people, there was an underside to Ayahuasca Healings' Elbe retreats. The retreats took place during the winter months of 2016, and attendees shivered in the tipi tents, often sleeping on cold, wet ground. Support workers and volunteers were few; during one retreat, a single person cooked for twenty people. And whenever attendees warned de Guzman and Shackman of potential problems or dangers, the founders allegedly rebuked them for their lack of faith in the program and its leaders who, after all, were working hard to enlighten the Western world with ayahuasca.

Ayahuasca Healings' status as a legitimate religion came into question as well. One retreat-goer told *Rooster* magazine reporter Reilly Capps that he "heard straight from [de Guzman's] mouth that he thinks religions are bullshit," and "[t]hat whole church thing was so that he can bring ayahuasca into the United States. He doesn't believe in the church."[6] Others recognized a spiritual element in the retreat but suspected that Ayahuasca Healings called itself a religion for legal purposes, and questioned why the group marketed itself so aggressively, and charged a four-figure fee for a cup of unpalatable tea, camp-out-grade meals, and three nights' shelter in a cold tipi.

Other, darker accusations emerged online against de Guzman and Ayahuasca Healings. A forum on the Cult Education Institute's site featured over thirty pages of negative reports about the ayahuasca guru that accused him of misrepresenting his group's legal status, exploiting retreat workers, psychologically manipulating attendees, ignoring safety concerns, and setting himself up as a blameless messianic figure who held retreat-goers personally responsible for any bad trips or other negative experiences they had during the four-day outings.

"THIS ISN'T CULTURAL APPROPRIATION;
IT'S MORE LIKE CULTURAL EXPROPRIATION"

Some of the most pointed criticisms of Ayahuasca Healings emerged from academic circles. Many anthropologists and ethnobotanists who'd extensively studied indigenous plant-medicine practices and faiths took a dim view of the group's claims and practices and charged de Guzman and Shackman with exploiting indigenous spirituality for commercial ends.

One of the strongest critiques came from anthropologist Christina Callicott, then a Ph.D. candidate at the University of Florida. In an article titled "Pandora's Brew: The New Ayahuasca," Callicott examined Western interest in the plant brew, the confusion regarding its legal status in the United States, the cultural appropriation of its use by non-indigenous people, and how Ayahuasca Healings had hugely contributed to all three phenomena.

Callicott reported that in February 2016, Ayahuasca Healings, concerned about its legal status, had petitioned the DEA for a religious exemption to the Controlled Substances Act, under the Religious Freedom Restoration Act (RFRA) and the First Amendment to the Constitution. When she examined the document, she noted that the organization affirmed that ayahuasca enabled it to contact "the Great Spirit that permeates and unites all of creation"—an entity unknown among South American ayahuasca-users.

When Callicott surveyed the DEA petition's section titled "Belief in Supernatural Entities," she found even more problematic elements. Ayahuasca Healings claimed to honor a galaxy of deities, including "Mother Ayahuasca; Father San Pedro; Great Spirit; tens of thousands of angels as well as the archangels Rafael, Gabriel, Azrael, Raziel, and Uriel; the 'Ascended Masters' Buddha and Jesus," as well as "The animal spirits, plant spirits, mountain spirits, and spirits of all that exists around us." To Callicott, this was not an accurate accounting of a legitimate shamanic faith, but "an amalgamation of romanticized tropes from both the Amazon and Native North America with a strong dose of Eastern religion and medicine—and in this case, occult or New Age Christianity."[7]

The anthropologist also quoted a statement de Guzman made about the purpose of Ayahuasca Healings, "The Old Paradigm vs. The

New Paradigm of Ayahuasca." In it, de Guzman said that his group was taking ayahuasca to "the next level in our collective evolution," away from the crude, earthy physicality of traditional societies' healing practices and toward "love, light, the Angels and Archangels, the Ascended Masters, Sacred Fires, and through our joy, through love, through the heart, illuminating, cleansing, and purifying what no longer serves . . . healing through an enjoyable, blissful, heart-opening experience . . . healing through an experience that is so much more easy and enjoyable."[8]

Appalled, Callicott said the pronouncement was "a complete divestment and dispossession of indigenous culture from its proper owners. This isn't cultural appropriation; it's more like cultural expropriation." To her, it seemed as if Ayahuasca Healings totally ignored the long, demanding process of becoming a plant-medicine shaman, as well as the struggles indigenous peoples endured to preserve their healing practices, and instead existed to mass-market the experience as a low-effort, high-cost New Age fad.

Callicott ended the paper with the observation, "the Ayahuasca Healings story is one of youth, idealism, and naiveté, coupled with a millennial culture of narcissism, self-promotion and entrepreneurialism, inflamed by the runaway egotism that appears to be a possible side-effect of frequent ayahuasca use."[9] More seriously, she warned that the religious-freedom exemption for indigenous entheogens would encourage similar abuses, and the traditional cultures from which they emerged would suffer even more.

RETURN TO PERU

By the time Callicott's paper was published online, Ayahuasca Healings' mission had been altered drastically. After it submitted its religious-exemption petition to the DEA, the organization, realizing it was in legal limbo until the Feds issued a ruling on their status, decided to stop holding retreats at the Elbe, Washington, property.

People who'd paid in advance for scheduled future retreats were outraged. They lit up internet forums dedicated to Ayahuasca Healings' misdoings with claims that de Guzman and Shackman refused to refund their money, saying the retreat payments had instead been accepted as "donations" to help keep the organization running. To mollify complainants, the organizers told them they could be credited should retreats ever happen again on U.S. soil.

Another concession offered was to rebook attendees on a retreat in Peru. Three years after he had his first ayahuasca experience in the mountainous South American nation, de Guzman leased property near Cusco, Peru, and set up the El Camino Sagrado Ayahuasca Retreats as a new, improved version of the Elbe gatherings. Over several years, he developed them as nine-day programs, prefaced with a special preparation course and followed by an "Online Community and Ongoing Support System," where attendees could get help and support from facilitators and fellow trippers.

As of this date, the Ayahuasca Healings website still promises attendees to the Peru retreats "the New Paradigm of Ayahuasca"—the "easy path" of "healing through the feminine . . . a completely unique and profoundly different healing experience than anything else out there." Forget the "hard path" of the traditional shaman, with his insect-ridden jungle retreat, his smelly body odors and tobacco smoke, and his bad habit of hitting on Western women—at Ayahuasca Healings, "we do everything we can to ensure not only the most transformational journey possible, but also one of the most love-filled and heart-opening experiences of your entire life."[10]

YOUR HIGHEST TRUTH, FROG POISON, AND BRAZILIAN PSILOCYBIN

Recently, de Guzman started up another entheogenic-tourism organization: Your Highest Truth. The group offers a "6-Night 7-Day Life & Death Shamanic Rebirth Retreat" at a property in Mexico, where attendees purify and sanctify themselves by ingesting a different entheogen each day, including Amazonian rain-forest frog poison, the DMT-bearing secretions from the *Bufo alvarius* toad, and hallucinogenic psilocybin mushrooms. The whole thing concludes with a "Rebirth Ceremony" in a sweat lodge, to teach attendees that "WE are the medicine," and not the entheogens they are presumably excreting from every orifice at that point.

When the COVID-19 crisis halted international travel in March 2020, de Guzman proffered yet another program of psychedelic enlightenment to locked-down seekers. The ayahuasca avatar stated that the potentially deadly virus was "a necessary purge of what is no longer in resonance," where "souls return back to the Source, [and] those who are left have the choice to continue in our old ways, or to create a DRASTIC re-evaluation of all that is important to us and all that drives and motivates us."[11]

While fledgling entheogenists waited for the epidemic to pass, they could take de Guzman's "Emotional Alchemy Program." For $997, the virtual retreat featured a private coaching and mentoring program, daily guided meditations, weekly online call recordings, and an online membership platform, all from the privacy and comfort of one's virus-free home. Most importantly, the package included a third-party introduction to a supplier of psilocybin in Brazil, where the chemical was legal and buyers could purchase it, as de Guzman put it, "outside of our relationship together."

THE MUDDIED LEGAL WATERS

Stateside, Ayahuasca Healings' legal status remains unresolved. In mid-2016 Oklevueha Native American Church head James Mooney cut ties with the sect, telling *Atlas Obscura* writer Sarah Laskow that he thought de Guzman and Shackman were treating entheogenic spirituality "like a business. They were advertising and marketing, which is a grievous slap in the face to indigenous medicine people. . . . When all these people paid them money to do a ceremony they ran off with the money, just like a corrupt business."[12] Although he saw the two as "really, really nice guys," Mooney just couldn't stomach their melding of the religiously sacred and the commercially profane and didn't renew his church's contract with Ayahuasca Healings.

Nor has the federal government stepped in with any definitive answers. As of this writing, Ayahuasca Healings' petition for a religious exemption to the Controlled Substances Act has been neither approved nor rejected, and the DEA has at least two other cases of American-originated ayahuasca-using religious groups under review.

Even though it seems as if ayahuasca gatherings are more popular than ever in the United States, both the indigenous and nonindigenous people who host them are working in a gray area, made even more confusing by the muddied legal waters left in the wake of de Guzman's attempts to mass-market entheogenic spirituality.

AN APOLOGY, AND AN IMMENSE FOOTPRINT

But the Ayatollah of Ayahuasca presses on regardless. Now married and the father of two children, de Guzman divides his time between Peru, Mexico, and Canada, and regularly graces his email lists and YouTube with his promises of personal and global transformation through shamanic chemical adjustment, his enthusiasm and optimism unflagged.

Significantly, he has also apologized publicly for the aftermath of the Elbe episode. In 2018 de Guzman admitted on his website that in his overwhelming enthusiasm to bring ayahuasca to North America, he'd played fast and loose with legal and financial affairs and had let down many people who believed in his mission. A contrite de Guzman promised that those people who had lost their deposits on the planned Washington State retreats, or who had otherwise been wronged by him, would be fairly compensated with his money and energy.

And the Elbe retreats? In retrospect, it appears that the five-week period when spiritual use of ayahuasca *seemed* to be legal in the United States and the hundred-odd entheogenic adventurers traveled to Washington State's evergreen rainforest to take advantage of that situation, was a mere interlude in the career of a man who may eventually rival Timothy Leary as the most famous promoter of the psychedelic experience in history.

Although his time on the American ground was short, and those who answered his call there were few, Trinity de Guzman left an immense footprint in the world of North American psychedelic sects before he was thirty years of age. He will almost certainly be heard from again on these shores.

LOOKING BACK—AND FORWARD

So, what is the legacy of these sects?

For one, a body of First Amendment jurisprudence has emerged from this subculture's legal struggles. Beginning with the Native American Church's *Attaki* and *Woody* cases in the early sixties, courts have slowly warmed to the idea that sincere use of entheogens in a spiritual context is a practice protected by constitutional guarantees of freedom of religion. The high-profile legal cases fought by the NAC and others were possible largely because these were organized groups with charismatic leaders and devoted followers willing to spend money, time, and energy to defend their rights to consume their sacraments of choice.

Equally importantly, these churches have challenged traditional definitions of religion. In radically different ways, Quanah Parker, Timothy Leary, Art Kleps, and Steve Ryan Berke, among others, pursued and propagated visions of an immediate and experiential spiritual path that was a dynamic contrast to orthodox religiosity, and fought to have their practices accepted with the same tolerance North American society extended to the historical world faiths. These leaders and their sects also envisioned and created communities where spiritually oriented trippers explored the ineffable Divine together and took their visions into society at large.

Some of these psychedelic cults have perished—defeated in legal battles or bedeviled by the interpersonal conflicts that characterize all collective human behavior. Others survive in various forms and carry on the visions and legacies of their founders. Together, their tales constitute a relatively obscure yet important thread in the grand narrative of religious history and will become increasingly relevant as this primal form of human consciousness expansion gains mainstream acceptance.

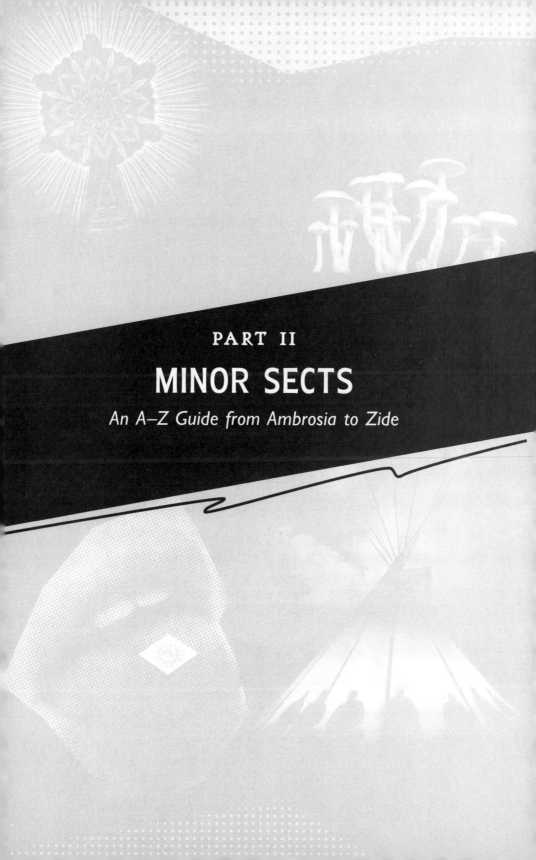

PART II

MINOR SECTS

An A–Z Guide from Ambrosia to Zide

With the rise of the sixties counterculture, and its mutation into the "alternative" scenes of the successive decades came the appearance of the minor psychedelic sects. These groups had smaller followings and shorter lifespans than the organizations discussed in part 1; some were little more than P.O. box addresses or websites maintained by lone visionaries seeking spiritual sympathizers. They are included in this book since they form an intriguing second string of this religious underground and represent a wide variety of beliefs and practices grounded in the psychedelic experience.

AMBROSIA SOCIETY

One of the oldest known intoxicants, *Amanita muscaria*—the red-and-white-dotted fly agaric mushroom—has been linked to not only the human race's earliest experiences with altered consciousness, but to the deepest roots of Eastern and Western religion as well. R. Gordon Wasson, who "discovered" the psilocybin mushroom for the non-Amerindian world, proposed that the mysterious "Soma" substance mentioned in the Hindu *Rig Veda* was the *Amanita* mushroom, brought into India by Aryan invaders from Siberia. And in *The Sacred Mushroom and the Cross,* unorthodox biblical scholar John Allegro linked the fungi to the development of early Christianity, claiming that *Amanita* was the original "eucharist" of Christian love-feasts, which he pictured as psychedelic sacred-sex orgies.

Fig. P2.1. The hallucinogenic Amanita muscaria mushroom,
one of the oldest known intoxicants.

Photograph courtesy of George Chernilevsky.

Neither Wasson's nor Allegro's theories have found favor among mainstream historians or theologians. But the sheer power of the *Amanita* experience—logged by ancient Siberian shamans and twenty-first-century trippers alike—is undeniable. And its deep associations with otherworldly states are reflected in its appearances in fairy-tale art, where the red-and-white-spotted toadstool fruits regularly in the presence of elves and gnomes, and even television's blue-skinned Smurfs.

Intrigued by the mythos of the mushroom, independent scholar Donald E. Teeter (1956–2012) spent over thirty-seven years researching the history of *Amanita*. His startling conclusion was that the mushroom was literally the Holy Grail—the fruit of the Tree of Life that fed the world's religious traditions in their infancies. Teeter believed that the mushroom was not only the original Soma of the Aryans and Eucharist of the Christians, but also the ambrosia and nectar of the ancient Greeks, and the worldly Divine Flesh of such ancient deities as Osiris, Horus, Mithras, Dionysius, and Odin, as well as the winged Hermes and philosophers' stone of the medieval Hermetic and alchemical scholars.

Charged to bring the mushroom's mysteries into the modern world, Teeter founded the Ambrosia Society. Headquartered in the Austin, Texas, suburb of Manor, the society's website said that it was dedicated to:

> returning the real Holy Grail to our brothers and sisters who have lost the ancient secret.
>
> share the ancient Sacrament with our brothers and sisters who wish to taste the honey sweet knowledge of Divinity.
>
> explore and teach the secrets of the Sacrament contained in the world's ancient religious texts.
>
> join together to legally defend the religious rights of our Members to use the ancient Sacrament, from any prosecution or persecution by Governments or individuals.
>
> create Sacred Groves growing the Sacrament, Vineyards to produce Ambrosia, Bakeries to make the Living Bread and Ambrosia Houses to serve as local centers of the Ambrosia Society.[1]

Until recently the society shared its physical address with Austin's Serenity Herbal store. Formerly known as the Garden of the Ancient

Apothecary and Gift Shop, the store sells herbs, cacti, seeds, tinctures, and other substances. It also formerly sponsored "The Flower of Life Healing Ministries," a "fully inclusive, contemplative, East-West ecumenical, community and fellowship" that hosted a church/meditative space on its property.

At present, the ministries and the society are defunct, and the latter's website is inactive. However, its contents have been mirrored on "The Ambrosia House," a tribute site that features Teeter's book, *Amanita Muscaria: Herb of Immortality,* as well as the writings of other psychedelic mycologists, and videos on how to produce the ambrosia of Greek mythology using fly agaric mushrooms and grape juice.

AMERICAN CHURCH OF GOD

During a solar eclipse in February 1962, several White bohemians from the San Francisco area celebrated a peyote ceremony on Mount Tamalpais. That summer the group and some of their friends attended peyote meetings in the Sierra Nevada mountains with Paiute, Washoe, and Navajo Indians, learning the teachings of the Native American peoples and obtaining supplies of the cactus for their own use. Eventually the group grew to about thirty members.

Most of them migrated to Santa Fe, New Mexico, in 1965, in search of better availability of peyote and a closer connection to the indigenous communities. That year, several of their number filed incorporation papers with the state as a nonprofit religious group called the American Church of God to formally organize and legally protect their peyotist circle. John Kimmey, later the founder of Santa Fe Community School, New Mexico's first "alternative school," and author of two books based on Hopi prophecy, was one of the church's original leaders.

One notable associate of the church was Stewart Brand. A Stanford graduate who had participated in early-sixties LSD experiments, Brand and several church leaders held a peyote ceremony in New Mexico's Carson National Forest on July 3, 1965. Inspired by the experience, two months later in San Francisco he and author Ken Kesey staged the "America Needs Indians" multimedia event, which Brand described as "a peyote meeting without peyote." And in January 1966 the two organized the LSD-powered, three-day Trips Festival—the event that birthed the San Francisco hippie scene.

Brand, who later created *The Whole Earth Catalog* and *The WELL* virtual community, wrote about the American Church of God in a 1972 magazine article. He said that the group had about 200 members, most of whom were "transient" young Whites, along with a few dozen Black, Latino, and American Indian adherents. Native American members included Taos elders "Little Joe," John and Henry Gomez, and Tellus Good Morning, who taught the young hippies the finer points of peyote ritual, including several dozen peyote songs. Brand said that the hippies themselves composed about forty of their own songs, "in Peyote not in English."

In 1991 the church was mentioned in the *U.S. v. Boyll* decision, where a New Mexico court ruled that the federal peyote exemption was not limited to American Indian members of the Native American Church. Other than that, the group has maintained a low profile over the years and continues to exist in New Mexico as a legitimate religious nonprofit organization.

AMERICAN COUNCIL OF INTERNAL DIVINITY

On November 16, 1966, police in Burlingame, California, busted four "beatniks" in a Bayshore Highway apartment house for holding a pound of cannabis. The arresting officers recorded that the quartet possessed a ream of letterhead bearing the title "American Council of Internal Divinity," and noting that the group's initials spelled out "ACID," surmised that they were about to start up a drug cult.

The beatniks must have decided that their psychedelic church wasn't worth the risk of further legal hassles, as this group was never heard from again.

ARIZONA YAGE ASSEMBLY

Based out of Tucson, Arizona, the Arizona Yage Assembly was incorporated as a nonprofit church in 2015 "to bring people in communion with divine love through the sacrament of ayahuasca." It holds ayahuasca ceremonies in various Western U.S. locations, as well as Colombia and

Peru, "to further develop a deeper and more conscious relationship with the divine spirit, and to look for better and healthier ways to live and relate to self, family, and community."

Gatherings usually involve twenty-five to thirty celebrants who pay $250–650 each to spend one to three days in ceremonies. The assembly's website recommends that attendees avoid consuming meats, cheeses, greasy/junk food, salt, sugar, alcohol, and TV programming for at least five days before the ceremonies. Users of antidepressant or anti-hypertension drugs must clear the chemicals from their systems at least eight weeks before ingesting the sacrament.

The assembly's web page also advises attendees to meditate and stay hydrated for a week prior to the ceremony. It recommends that on the eve of the ceremony, the celebrant gather intention and focus on what they want to learn during the experience. A full night's sleep is recommended to prepare for the all-night ritual, as is drinking Pau d'Arco or Cat's Claw tea for those with sensitive stomachs.

On May 5, 2020, the assembly filed the case *Arizona Yage Assembly et al. v. Barr et al.* in the U.S. District Court for the Northern District of California, opposing the federal ban of ayahuasca use on religious-freedom grounds. The docket described the history and use of the vine, and the nature and practice of the assembly, stating:

> After working with Ayahuasca for six years, the founder (the "Founder") established AYA as a visionary church in 2015, using Ayahuasca as AYA's communion sacrament. As the Founder expressed it—"Ayahuasca is the holy Sacrament of AYA, of which congregants must partake to receive the blessing of Communion." AYA's doctrine teaches that sharing Ayahuasca sacramentally in ceremony is sharing a sacred substance that is not merely physical, and has the capacity to heal the entire human being, body, spirit, and mind, so that congregants can extend this healing to others and our entire world environment. The experience of communion through Ayahuasca is the receipt of Divine Love and wisdom by the congregation. The Founder has explained that in AYA, the doctrine "comes from the vine and the leaf."[2]

As of this writing, the case is still under review.

CHICAGO JAZZ CANNABIS CIRCLE

In his book *Sex and Drugs: A Journey Beyond Limits,* author Robert Anton Wilson recounted a story he'd heard from an old jazz musician about a cannabis cult in 1930s Chicago. The man told Wilson that he'd been allowed to attend one of the group's ceremonies, where there were six Black and White jazz musicians present, all sitting in a circle. Acting as the "priest," one of the worshippers lit a joint, which was then passed around the circle in the manner familiar to pot smokers worldwide. There was no formal ceremony; the attendees just meditated, or occasionally "testified" much in the spirit of a Quaker meeting.

According to Wilson's recollection of the musician's story:

> Each member had a holy name, and when testimony was sparse, the priest would occasionally ask for some.
> "How goes it with the Lord Krishna?" he might enquire.
> "The Lord Krishna is at peace on the second level," might be the reply.
> "How goes it with the Lord Shiva?" the priest might ask next.
> "The Lord Shiva is at bliss on the fifth level," would come the reply.[3]

Wilson's friend confessed that he didn't know how or when the group had originated, or why its members had chosen the names of Hindu deities or adapted the Kabbalistic/Theosophical language about "levels" of consciousness.

The secretive sect probably broke up after the federal anticannabis crackdown of 1937, and Wilson's secondhand account seems to be the only existing information about them.

CHURCH OF COGNIZANCE

Ancient Indo-Iranian texts speak of a mysterious plant called *haoma* that provides healing, strength, sexual power, and nourishment to the human body and soul. Today it is identified in the Zoroastrian faith as *parahaoma*—the ephedra shrub, which is specially prepared for the Yasna service where it is consumed as a sacrament.

Some scholars, however, maintain that parahaoma is a placebo, inserted into Zoroastrian ceremonies in relatively recent times. The original haoma, they posit, was none other than *Cannabis sativa,* and was probably the same substance as the enigmatic Soma mentioned in Vedic texts.

Danuel and Mary Quaintance revived the use of cannabis as haoma in 1991 when they founded the Church of Cognizance in Pima County, Arizona. The couple, who considered Zoroastrianism the progenitor of most modern faiths, believed that they were restoring the religion's original precepts by making cannabis the food of communion, and saw it as the key to truly living the ideals described by Zoroaster, and the eventual attainment of world peace.

The church was formally chartered in 1994 when it filed a "Declaration of Religious Sentiment" in Graham County, Arizona. Another document, "Church of Cognizance Introduced," laid out its basic beliefs for prospective members:

Members of the Church of Cognizance believe:
1. That Marijuana [a.k.a. Haoma], when raised, and used properly, aids the mind, body, and soul.
2. That Haoma is the ancient teacher of wisdom, compassion, and the way to the kingdom of glory in heaven on earth, while humans let ego block their own, and others, path to this kingdom of glory.
3. That Haoma is the capable provider of all substance required to accommodate a comfortable, healthy, productive, full-bearing life.
4. That Haoma is the righteous Protector of our health, and longevity; by way of receptors in the human body that Haoma connects with to heal.

For this we declare Marijuana the teacher, the protector, the provider. We further believe that the proper religious use promotes Good Thoughts, Good Words, Good Deeds, none of which is harmful to the health, safety, welfare, or morals of society in general.[4]

Although members are encouraged to study the scriptures of all faiths, special emphasis is placed on the Avesta, the primary collection of Zoroastrian writings. The church believes that the book is the uncorrupted source of all other religious teachings, and points to the many references to haoma in its text.

Units of the church are designated as Individual Orthodox Member Monasteries (IOMM). These are home churches where family health, safety, welfare, culture, and tradition are promoted, and where the church's "Neo-Zoroastrian" rites are celebrated. The church claims that there are seventy-eight of these monasteries spread across the United States and five other nations.

Like so many other entheogenic religionists, the Quaintances were eventually arrested for possession. Charged in early 2006 with holding 172 pounds of cannabis, they invoked the religious-freedom defense at their trial, citing their filing of the Church Declaration twelve years earlier as proof of their sincere belief that cannabis was a sacrament. The gambit failed, and the two were convicted, and sent to separate federal prisons for several years.

Mary Quaintance passed on in 2013. Her husband Danuel today maintains two websites that contain materials about the church and serve as a networking hub for current members.

CHURCH OF GNOSTIC LUMINISM

Dale Gowin describes himself as:

> a free-lance writer, a banjo-playing singer-songwriter, an ex-convict and veteran of the "war on drugs," a self-employed entrepreneur, an anarchist, a communist, a dreamer (but not the only one), a vegetarian, a homeless vagabond, a midnight toker, a sinner saved by grace, a Thelemite, a student of esoteric philosophy, and the founder of the Church of Gnostic Luminism.[5]

The church is "a non-profit organization dedicated to a future worldwide voluntary/cooperative society and the self-realization of all sentient beings."[6] It exists largely as a vision detailed in *The Luminist Manifesto,* originally written in 1995 while Gowin was serving a prison sentence for the possession and distribution of psychedelic sacraments.

The *Manifesto* has been continually revised and expanded since.

As might be guessed from the author/founder's eclectic CV, the *Manifesto* ties together diverse spiritual and cultural influences. The "Gnostic" part of the church name derives from Eastern and Western spiritual visionaries who inform its esoteric theology, while "Luminism" refers to "a religious and philosophical tradition based on direct experience of reality as opposed to faith, belief, or rational speculation,"[7] and expressed most fully in historical mystery schools and initiatory orders such as Freemasonry, the Hermetic Order of the Golden Dawn, and Aleister Crowley's Ordo Templi Orientis. Psychedelic pioneers like Aldous Huxley, Timothy Leary, and Terence McKenna are envisioned as "Modern Luminists," and the church draws upon them as well for inspiration and direction.

Not limiting its visions to the sacred realm, the church supports the communitarian and Utopian teachings and activism of historical figures ranging from the English Levellers to the Mennonites, to anarchist writers and militants from communist, individualist, and religious-pacifist strains alike. To the church, the Rainbow Family, a leaderless network of hippies and social dropouts who gather en masse every year in an American National Forest site, is the contemporary heir of "a massive and overwhelming spiritual awakening of a visionary-libertarian nature" that began in the sixties and continues to this day.

A key church teaching is Aleister Crowley's "Law of Thelema," expressed as "Do what thou wilt shall be the whole of the law." Not the excuse for self-indulgence and irresponsibility that a simple reading might infer, the law instead guides its adherents to develop and exercise their so-called "true will." The church posits that when properly achieved via a set of universally applicable ethical principles such as personal and social responsibility, nonviolence, truthfulness, and environmental stewardship, there is no separation between individual and divine will, and human beings become free to develop their intuitive talents to realize both personal and global enlightenment.

Although the church acknowledges a variety of methods to develop these talents, it seems largely dedicated to what it calls "entheogenic psychochemistry or spiritual, scientific, and philosophical use of psychedelic sacraments." The church recognizes mescaline, psilocybin, lysergic acid, cannabis, ayahuasca, *Bufo alvarius* toad secretion, and *Salvia divinorum* as eucharists, and is developing plans to train aspirants to practice a "Yoga of Light Containing Herbs" with these substances, with the eventual establishment of a monastery and a Holy Order of Light.

At present the Church of Gnostic Luminism has no formal membership or organizational structure. However, Dale Gowin has received email from "hundreds" of people in basic agreement with the *Manifesto* and is recruiting potential members of a board of directors or trustees to serve a future organized church. Gowin and the church are also busy with both an on-demand printing business that reproduces out-of-print publications at low cost, as well as an online archiving project that has made hundreds of obscure and rare occult, radical-politics, and countercultural books and periodicals available as PDF files.

CHURCH OF THE DIVINE SAGE

A self-described "church of one" that neither solicits for nor accepts new members, this internet-based hallucinogenic ministry exists to propagate the founder's belief "that the strict and responsible use of *Salvia divinorum* as a holy sacrament and when combined with deep meditation practice, can be a personal catalyst for spiritual revelation and connection with the Divine in ways that no other entheogen can provide."[8]

The church's anonymous founder and lone member claims they merged with the Divine through *Salvia divinorum* in 2001. Afterward they founded the church to "let others know that there is life, consciousness, and awareness beyond the body, that there is far more to purpose this world and each of our precious lives than most of us could imagine, that essential spiritual evolution can be found through love, compassion, and respect for all humans, and can be found through the careful, ritualistic use of the Holy Sacrament of *Salvia divinorum* when combined with deep meditation practice."[9] The writer saw their experience as a continuation of the *Salvia*-smoking Mazatec shamans' visions from time immemorial and likened the herb's revelations to the eighteen characteristics of Kensho, the vision of one's true nature, described in James Austin's *Zen and the Brain*.

Although ostensibly a one-person operation, the church neverthe-less published online an extensive list of its bylaws and rules, as well as writings about peoples' spiritual experiences with *Salvia,* and an irregu-lar e-newsletter. When its website first appeared, the church was also organizing a proposed $1,000-a-head, eight-day meditation retreat at Los Naranjos in Yelapa, Mexico.

Whether it or any of the other church activities amounted to any-thing more than online talk is unknown, and these days the group seems to exist mainly as an inactive virtual appendage of the I Am Shaman website, a business that sells legal mind-altering herbs and seeds.

CHURCH OF THE FIRST BORN

The son of an African American couple who settled in Lincoln County, Oklahoma, during the 1889 Land Run, John C. Jamison grew up sur-rounded by the territory's transplanted American Indian tribes. In his youth he worked for local Native Americans, and learned the Iowa, Pawnee, and Comanche languages. Jamison also adopted the Native Americans' peyote religion and brought it to Oklahoma's Black com-munity via his Church of the First Born.

Active during the early 1920s, the church emulated many aspects of Native American Church (see chapter 1) ritual. Meetings were held in a portable canvas tent that doubled as the traditional tipi, with an earthen crescent mound in the center that encircled a campfire and was topped by a single "chief" peyote button. A drum, a gourd rattle, medi-cine feathers, cane, sage, and cedar were all on hand, and utilized at different parts of the rite.

Ceremonies began between eight and nine o'clock at night. Garbed in a feather headdress, a ceremonial blanket, and moccasins, Jamison sat opposite the tipi door during the meeting, flanked on his right by four "sisters" who managed both the peyote supply and the post-ceremony morning repast, and on his left by four "brothers" who played the drum, censed the gathering with cedar, and took care of other ritual duties. A "Fireman" tended the sacred fire and acted as doorman.

The meeting opened with either a Christian hymn or a Native American song, followed by a Bible reading by Jamison or a brother.

Then peyote was distributed to attendees by a sister, after which was a period of speaking, singing, and praying, as well as a teaching and spiritual Q&A session led by Jamison. At midnight Jamison consumed the chief peyote button, burst the heart of the fire, and formed its ashes and coals into the shape of a heart.

After a short water-sharing and break period, the celebrants prayed and sang for the rest of the night, ingesting more rounds of peyote. At dawn the ceremony was concluded with the singing of the hymn "God Be with You Till We Meet Again," another water-sharing, and a four-course meal served by the sisters.

Although he often included American Indians in peyote ceremonies along with his Black regulars, Jamison's heterodox rites caused consternation among some Native American Church purists. First Born members didn't smoke sacramental tobacco and deviated from NAC ritual-rubrics in how they played the drum and rattle, distributed the peyote, stoked the fire, censed the gathering with cedar, and took recessional time. And the generous use of hymns and biblical readings in First Born ceremonies differed markedly from Native American peyote meetings, which favored experiential communion with Jesus over the text-based forms of Western Christian devotion.

Still, Jamison was sometimes invited to lead Indian peyote meetings, where he altered his own sect's usages to be more in line with Native American Church practices. Near the end of his life, he also added healing and doctoring services to his church rites, in the tradition of shamans throughout history.

The closest thing the church had to a Confession of Faith was a paper form that all its members possessed. It read:

> Our Motto: "The World for Christ"
> Christ the Good Shepherd
> Church Covenant
> Church of the First Born
> "Hebrews, 12th Chapter, 23rd verse."
> We, the undersigned believers in Christ Jesus, do by virtue of
>   Scriptural Faith submit ourselves to the cause of Christ and
>   the gospel; to live therein; to walk therein; to teach therein;

to sing therein; to pray therein; to preach therein; to baptise therein; to observe all the ordinances of Him who has called us to peace, that God may have the glory thereof.[10]

The Church of the First Born never spread beyond a few dozen Black Oklahoman faithful, and the government's suppression of peyotism intimidated regular attendees and scared away potential members. Jamison was murdered by a lunatic in 1926, and the church vanished shortly afterward. Only through the efforts of his daughter Mabel, and anthropologist Maurice G. Smith, did information about the group reach the outside world in the form of a 1934 *Journal of the Washington Academy of Sciences* article.

Today the sect remains an interesting, if obscure, early example of the spread of peyotism outside of American Indian circles, as well as an unusual footnote in African American religious history.

CHURCH OF THE GOLDEN RULE OF CHARITY

Originally known as the Neo-American Church of California, this was a split-off group from Art Kleps's "Original Kleptonian" Neo-American Church (see chapter 6).

According to Kleps—not the most reliable of narrators—the group was headed by a California-based dentist, William Shyne, whom he had appointed as his Neo-American Primate of the West. Kleps claimed that Shyne then incorporated his own "Neo-American Church" in California, stole Kleps's promotional materials, added his own name and address to them, and intercepted membership applications and donations intended for the Millbrook-based mother church, keeping the new members and the proceeds. One of Kleps's followers met the dentist in person, and reported that he was a "raving, paranoid speed freak" who dealt hard drugs, and kept a loaded submachine gun under the seat of his car.

Kleps eventually excommunicated Shyne, who reincorporated his group as the Church of the Golden Rule of Charity. Indefatigable Bay Area psychedelic activist Jefferson Poland replaced him as California's Neo-American Church Primate, and then allied his ministry with that of the Shiva Fellowship's Willie Minzey (see chapter 12). Shyne's own church never gained much of a following, and the state eventually voided its corporate charter.

Shyne's career was weird enough even before he set himself up as an entheogenic missionary. The dentist made headlines in 1959 when he was arrested for handing out "candy" to Halloween trick-or-treaters that later proved to be laxative pills. Police reported that four children got sick from the toxic treats, and Shyne was eventually convicted for outraging public decency, jailed, fined, and suspended by the state dental board. The case is often cited as the origin of urban legends about poisoned Halloween treats that circulate through America every October.

Shyne passed on in Hawaii in 2007 at eighty-seven years old.

CHURCH OF THE NORTH AMERICAN SHAMANS

Based in Austin, Texas, during the 1990s, the Church of the North American Shamans was founded by an anonymous individual who described themselves as a "well-off conservative Christian" who had "seen and survived the drug scene in America, and [had] been dramatically influenced by several entheogens."[11]

According to the founder, the church's purpose was to obtain "the right to grow and use entheogens in the practice of religion without fear of persecution or prosecution." The church recognized seven botanical sacraments including the San Pedro cactus, peyote, *Salvia divinorum,* psilocybin mushrooms, morning glory and Hawaiian baby woodrose seeds (containing lysergic acid), and tobacco.

Little else is known about this small group, which seems to have worked the same legal-entheogens territory as the Church of the Tree of Life (see chapter 10).

CHURCH OF THE ONE SERMON

Founded by Leonard Enos of Lemon Grove, California, around 1970, this was essentially a one-man sect whose main activity seemed to be the distribution of Enos's book, *A Key to the American Psilocybe Mushroom.*

One of the earliest guides to hallucinogenic fungi, *A Key* pointed up the spiritual nature of the psilocybin experience by interspersing quotes from the biblical book of Matthew, alchemical treatises, and Buddhist sutras in between taxonomic and botanical information about psycho-active mushrooms.

The book was not only criticized for its many inaccuracies on the subject, but also earned opprobrium from members of the Subud religious group. In *A Key*'s first edition, Enos recommended Subud's practices as the safest and most effective means to integrate psyche-delic experience and printed a list of all the Indonesian religious movement's North American contacts. This greatly annoyed what he called the "ignorantly straight" Subud faithful, and later editions of the book downplayed any connection between the Javanese sect and hallucinogenic-mushroom ingestion.

As for the Church of the One Sermon, it was dedicated to "the Full Awakening in all people of that special Reality knowledge first testi-fied to by Gautama Siddharta, the Buddha."[12] The church's eclectic approach combined the teachings of Mahayana Buddhism, Tantra, Zen, and Sufism, and advocated meditation, exercise, and discussion sessions influenced by these paths, as the proper path to enlightenment.

Although the church promised to publish a periodical called *American Tantra,* dedicated to the psilocybin path, no issues seem to have appeared. Noted science-fiction author Scott Baker mentioned the church in his 1978 novel *Symbiote's Crown,* but few others took notice of the group, and it soon faded from view.

CHURCH OF THE PSYCHEDELIC MYSTIC

Based initially in Encinitas, California, the Church of the Psychedelic Mystic was founded in 1978. The church's founders said they sought direct personal experience with the Divine, and although they claimed no drugs were allowed at their services, they believed that psychedelic experiences were so powerful and life-changing that hallucinogens needed to be legalized for religious purposes. Perhaps fearing the "Soma" scenario described in Aldous Huxley's *Brave New World,* the church also opposed the use of drugs as social-control mechanisms.

The church recognized that the psychedelic experience was

essentially an individual one, with its messages and teachings best left to private interpretation. Church members were called "mystics," and not subject to the authority of official holy books or ministers, nor required to meet in established church buildings.

However, four basic truths were drafted to guide members and the church's activities:

> God is One; Praise the Lord;
> The kingdom of God is within us, perceived through our individual selves;
> It is possible for any of us to directly experience this divinity within;
> It is desirable for us to do so.[13]

Originally chartered by the Universal Life Church's mail-order ministry service, the CPM relocated to Berkeley, California, sometime in the mid-1980s. There it published the church bulletin *Mystic Vibes,* and worked to influence liberalization of the laws regarding the religious use of psychedelics. With the Reagan-era War on Drugs in full attack, they failed to sway legislators or courts and vanished by the end of the decade.

CHURCH OF THE REALIZED FANTASY

It takes a special kind of nerve to declare oneself the "Pope of Pot," and Manhattanite Mickey Cezar had chutzpah to spare. Cezar was the pontiff of the Church of the Realized Fantasy—the spiritual arm of a hugely profitable cannabis delivery service in eighties and early-nineties New York City.

Originally from New Jersey, Cezar first gained renown in early-seventies Amsterdam. The obese, flamboyantly gay navy vet and mental-institution survivor became one of the pioneers of the famously tolerant Dutch city's cannabis trade, buying marijuana from shipboard smugglers and selling it to locals and tourists via bicycle couriers who operated from his five-story houseboat.

In 1979 Cezar relocated his Amsterdam operation to the streets of

New York's Lower East Side. He advertised his pot-delivery service in "alternative" periodicals like *Screw* and *High Times,* took orders via a toll-free number (1-800-WANT-POT), and employed dozens of people to work the phone bank and deliveries.

At various times, New York cops harassed and arrested Cezar and his employees. And when Cezar refused to pay a local gangster protection money, thugs shot the cannabis entrepreneur five times in the stomach. Luckily, the obese pot vendor's thick adipose tissue blocked the bullets from vital organs and arteries, and his wounds leaked liquid fat instead of blood on the ambulance ride to the ER.

At its peak, Cezar's service reportedly took in as much as $40,000 a day from NYC stoners. Part of this was in the form of special marijuana-leaf embossed tokens, which he sold for $100 and accepted in exchange for cannabis.

A humanitarian who provided health benefits to his workers, distributed free cannabis to AIDS patients, and donated his profits to needy Lower East Side residents, Cezar saw his mission as both a commercial and a religious one. Sometime in the late 1980s he established the Church of the Realized Fantasy to promote his longstanding idea that cannabis was a sacramental substance for healing and spiritual growth.

The church's headquarters was a former comic bookstore at 13th and Hudson, in Manhattan's meatpacking district. There Cezar, wearing a white papal miter emblazoned with a green cannabis leaf, served food and hot drinks to all visitors, preached against violence and hard-drug use, and sheltered homeless people and prostitutes on cold nights. Although he claimed 5,000 followers, only twenty or so faithful regularly gathered there for the low-key sacramental services where journalist Mike Sager noted, "no one says a thing. Not a word. They sit, dumb, passing a joint."[14]

One of the regular church communicants was a local eccentric named Daniel Rakowitz. In 1989, when Rakowitz was arrested for murdering his roommate and cooking her remains into a stew, some media reports attributed the ghastly crimes to "Satanic rituals" held at the church. There was no truth to the stories, although Rakowitz and other associates of Cezar's asserted that sex orgies were a regular occurrence on church premises, with the Pope of Pot openly servicing Black teenage boys there.

On August 16, 1990, Cezar made the fatal mistake of publicizing his business on Howard Stern's nationally syndicated radio show. Until then NYPD drug detectives had largely ignored him, concentrating their efforts on the city's cocaine and heroin trade. Embarrassed by his brazenness, the narcs set up a series of busts that wrecked Cezar's enterprise and made him a familiar figure in New York City's jails and courtrooms.

Penniless, the Pope of Pot died of liver cancer in 1995 at fifty-two. Today his church and business are remembered mainly as an early example of both medical- and commercial-oriented cannabis delivery. In 2020 *Playboy* magazine produced a short documentary about Cezar, *The Pope of Dope: The Story of NYC's First Delivery Service,* that brought renewed interest in his life and work.

CHURCH OF SUNSHINE

When Jack and Mary Jo Call split from the Neo-American Church (see chapter 6) in 1978, they formed this small psychedelic fellowship in Whittier, California. Although it was never explicitly stated, the church's name may have been inspired by Orange Sunshine, the potent form of LSD produced and distributed by Southern California's Brotherhood of Eternal Love (see chapter 7).

Although the Calls objected to Neo-American Chief Boo Hoo Art Kleps's monarchical form of church government, strident dogmatism, and general irascibility, they endorsed his philosophy of solipsistic nihilism, and shared his vision of enlightenment through psychedelics. The Calls saw as their purpose "to create—with your help—a religion paradisical and deeply human as the music of Mozart," and summed up the church's principles thusly:

> The psychedelic substances, such as LSD, mescaline, psilocybin,
> and marijuana are instruments of salvation, both in the sense
> of liberation from ignorance or illusion and the sense of deliv-
> erance from danger or difficulty.

> The supreme authority of this church is not any person or group
> of persons or writings, but the logical analysis of experience.[15]

The church published an occasional newsletter, *The L-Train,* wherein Jack Call discussed psychedelic philosophy and theology. No statistics of church membership exist, but it's known that the newsletter circulated to about a hundred people.

In 1981 Jack Call abandoned the sect to pursue an academic career. Eventually he became a professor of philosophy at Citrus College and wrote *Life in a Psychedelic Church,* an amusing memoir of his years with Art Kleps. After he retired from academia, Call rekindled his interest in entheogenic spirituality, spurned his longstanding agnosticism, and embraced the Christian faith. In 2018 he produced a book titled *Psychedelic Christianity,* wherein he reconciled the use of entheogens with the teachings and practices of the Christian church. Call currently heads a research institute dedicated to this spiritual path.

CHURCH OF THE TOAD OF LIGHT

For many years, rumors that toad venom contained a hallucinogenic substance swirled through the psychedelic underground. No less a figure than Neo-American Church (see chapter 6) Chief Boo Hoo Art Kleps chose a cartoon of a three-eyed toad as the organization's symbol and named the church's newsletter *Divine Toad Sweat* as tongue-in-cheek tributes to the allegedly entheogenic properties of amphibian secretions.

The stories were finally verified in 1984 with the publication of a curious little book, *Bufo alvarius: The Psychedelic Toad of the Sonoran Desert.* The tome maintained that the *B. alvarius* toad, native to semi-aquatic irrigated fields in the Arizona, California, and northern Mexican outback, possessed glands that produced a viscous milky-white venom containing large amounts of the powerful hallucinogen 5-MeO-DMT.

According to author Albert Most, if the toad's glands were milked properly, the venom could be dried and smoked in a hash pipe, producing a short but intense trip. He claimed that venom smokers would experience two to three minutes of "a complex chemical event characterized

Fig. P2.2. The *Bufo alvarius* toad. Its glands contain 5-MeO-DMT,
a powerful psychedelic.

Photograph courtesy of Secundum naturam.

by an overload of thoughts and perception, brief collapse of the EGO, and loss of the space-time continuum," followed by "a pleasant LSD-like sensation in which visual illusions, hallucinations, and perceptual distortions are common."[16]

Most likened the otherworldly experience to a religious vision and said that venom smokers constituted the Church of the Toad of Light—an informal organization of toad-trippers whose membership stretched from Mexico to New York City, to Germany. Although formal church doctrine was never established, and meetings of the faithful never materialized, Most did a brisk business selling T-shirts that bore the church name, and depicted the warty amphibian wreathed by a fiery corona.

Bufo alvarius's hallucinogenic secretions became national news in 1994. That February the *New York Times* reported that a California teacher had been busted for possession of toad venom—the first person ever arrested for holding the substance, which had somehow found its way onto the federal Schedule I list of prohibited chemicals. In the story, a narcotics agent claimed (falsely) that people licked toads to get high, and the unlikely image soon became a pop-culture trope, with episodes of *The Simpsons* and *Beavis and Butt-Head* depicting their cartoon characters tasting amphibian skin in search of an "awesome buzz."

More seriously, the media attention indirectly spurred interest in faunal hallucinogens and their use in both traditional societies and the modern world. In 2015 *VICE* magazine produced a short documentary that examined present-day, toad-venom religious rites among Mexican Indians on the island of Tiburon. And two books—James Oroc's *Tryptamine Palace,* and Dr. Octavio Rettig Hinojosa's *The Toad of Dawn*—examined the history, nature, and effects of "toad medicine," and how it can be used to initiate modern people on a spiritual path.

A *VICE* reporter also tracked down the real name of church founder Albert Most. He was identified as Ken Nelson (1954–2019), a former U.S. Army Ranger who lived on a decommissioned Nike missile base near Denton, Texas.

After reading an article in *OMNI* magazine's August 1981 issue that theorized Cherokee Indians used *Bufo* toad venom as a hallucinogen, Nelson did extensive research on the creatures, and visited the Gila, Arizona, desert during the monsoons of summer 1983. There he gathered and smoked *Bufo alvarius* toad venom, and later published his findings in the booklet as part of a technical-writing class. Book illustrator Gail Patterson currently runs a website that sells a revised fourth edition of the work, as well as authorized "Church of the Toad of Light" T-shirts.

The church, such as it is, also gained an unlikely advocate in Mike Tyson. In 2021 the former heavyweight champion told a reporter that he'd smoked toad venom four years earlier, and had "died" temporarily, only to emerge from the trip with his toxic egotism shattered, and a new desire to reconnect with his estranged family and take up boxing again. Tyson was quoted as saying: "The toad's whole purpose is to reach your highest potential. I look at the world differently. We're all the same. Everything is love."[17]

Currently, *Bufo alvarius* toads are a protected species in California, Arizona, and New Mexico, with molesters or collectors subject to fines. Hallucinogen experts generally don't recommend harvesting toad venom and point to other natural sources of DMT variants as easier and more ecologically sound ways to obtain the chemical. Still, the lowly desert amphibian remains a striking, if slightly ridiculous, symbol of both the psychedelic experience and the hidden wonders contained in nature's most unlikely places.

DIVINE ASSEMBLY

A Mormon Republican legislator from Utah would be among the last people one would expect to form a sect dedicated to the entheogenic use of psilocybin mushrooms. But that's exactly what Steve Urquhart, a former Utah GOP state senator, did when he chartered the Divine Assembly as a religious corporation.

Urquhart was a faithful Latter-Day saint and conservative Republican until his last two years in the state Senate. In that period, against the wishes of his church and party he sponsored bills that supported LGBTQ+ rights, legalized medical marijuana, and called for an end to the death penalty.

A personal crisis led Urquhart and his wife to journey to Amsterdam in 2017, where he tried ayahuasca for the first time. A second experience with the brew a year later, and several trips on psilocybin mushrooms, resulted in "this gooey puddle of Steve on the floor," he told reporter Robert Gehrke. "I realized with Sara, my kids, Lucy, my daughter, who really needs me to show her the world, I had only loved partially."[18]

Urquhart believed that his psilocybin journeys were far deeper and more profound religious experiences than anything he'd ever had in Mormonism. Much as Latter-Day Saints founder Joseph Smith had done nearly two centuries earlier, Urquhart's visions inspired him to start a new religion. It was called the Divine Assembly, "a church that connects people to self, others, and the Divine, protects responsible and religious use of psilocybin, and cultivates health and healing."[19]

The Divine Assembly is run as a nondoctrinaire network of seekers. At its dedicated meeting space, the fungal sacrament is provided to any attendee who is sincerely committed to using it as part of a religious practice. Attendees are encouraged to support and strengthen each other through ceremony and integration, and to worship and commune with the Divine in any manner meaningful to them, so long as they abide by the assembly's safety protocols and report any issues of health troubles or sexual/psychological manipulation. Beyond that, its main mission is to connect people with each other, and promote health, healing, and spiritual insight in psilocybin ceremonies.

Urquhart rejects the roles of assembly prophet or leader, and told one reporter, "I founded it, but ideally, now I'm obsolete."

The assembly solicits members via its website. Only a name and an email address are necessary to become a member; for those afraid to come out of the psychedelic closet they recommend using a "worshiper" name and nonpersonalized email. Members are "encouraged to draft, continually update, and live by a personal covenant established between themselves and the Divine,"[20] where they can monitor and chart their personal and spiritual growth both in mushroom sessions, and in daily life.

Donations to the assembly's work are appreciated but not required, and members are free to attend either its regular meetings in the Salt Lake City area or gather autonomously on their own. During 2021 the assembly held a "Summer Solstice Revival" at the Seabase natural saltwater spring on the Bonneville dry lakebed that featured Burning Man–style theme and sound camps, as well as a "Do Not Disturbia" quiet-zone for more subdued trippers.

Since psilocybin is a Schedule I prohibited chemical, the assembly has addressed legal concerns on its website. It sanctions mushroom use only in a sacred/spiritual context, advises members to "model the sincerity of your religious beliefs," and distributes information packets to law enforcement and D.A. offices about its sacrament, and the legal right of worshippers to use it.

Himself a practicing attorney, founder Steve Urquhart summed up the legal situation for both the assembly and all other psychedelic sects in an online article:

> [I]t stinks that such steps are necessary to establish and protect entheogenic religions, unlike other established religions. But, for now, peacefully connecting directly with the Divine through psychedelics is a more legally fraught activity than swinging God around as a club to abuse marginalized groups. Government gets that God is hate. It is slower to accept that God is love and connection. When it comes to psychedelic sacraments, religious persecution is real. Move forward with faith . . . and caution.[21]

DOG COMMUNE

Founded in late-sixties Los Angeles, the Dog Commune originated when a group of LSD users received a revelation that all Earth life was of equal value, and that killing any animal or plant was a sin. As a result of the vision, the group became fruitarians, consuming only fruit that fell to the ground from trees.

Subsequent acid visions informed them that the old joke, "GOD is DOG spelled backward," was literally true. The Divine manifested itself in our world in the shape of domestic canines, they maintained, and humanity's troubles came from its widespread mistreatment of its four-legged best friends. To get right with the deities, commune members adopted stray dogs, raided animal shelters, and were among the first groups in the United States to attempt to stop the use of canines in scientific experiments.

Eccentric psychedelic-rock singer and animal lover Sky Saxon of the Seeds was reputed to have been a sect member. Sky was also affiliated with the Source Family, an L.A.-based communal group whose members would begin each morning with a six-second drag on a joint—a ritual they believed focused their professional, personal, and spiritual doings for the day.

THE FANE OF THE PSILOCYBE MUSHROOM ASSOCIATION

Chartered on January 22, 1980, in Victoria, British Columbia, this group described itself on its defunct website as "a fourth way mystical school that celebrates the mushroom sacrament as the most sublime and gracefully efficient access to the expansion of consciousness which is what we define as the religious experience. As such it functions as the integral aspect of our religious community."[22]

The Fane—"a sanctuary without walls in which the Sacred Mushroom is closely allied with our species in space and time"—was influenced by the psilocybin-powered Good Friday Experiment, wherein researcher Walter Pahnke asserted that the psychedelic experiences of its participants were identical to the mystical experiences of historical saints and monastics. The solipsistic-nihilist philosophy of the Neo-American Church (see chapter 6) also figured in its theology, where enlightenment was defined as "the realization that life is a dream and the externality of relations an illusion."[23]

Along with these elements, the Fane also identified with the Russian mystic Giorgi Gurdjieff's "Fourth Way" of enlightenment—the path of the "Sly Man" who proceeds directly to higher consciousness without the ascetic or self-sacrificing practices of a fakir, monk, or yogi. Quoting Gurdjieff's controversial observation that a "[Sly Man] simply prepares and swallows a little pill which contains all the substances he wants," the group believed that the psilocybin mushroom served as this magic sacrament.

[A] holy scripture, a gnosis beyond words into the sphere of truth beyond the noise of verbal teaching, experiential, revealed to one in the state of being illumined by their grace. The sacrament is a wonder of inquiring mind, the edible TAO, the Dharma Jewel, Manna on the Path, the True Host. The observance of The Fane is the self-evident faith born of experience in the beneficent grace of the sacrament and its use to aid understanding and love for those prepared to walk the path.[24]

Membership in the Fane was open to anyone who agreed with the three following principles, lifted almost verbatim from the Neo-American Church (see chapter 6):

That all mushrooms of the genus *Psilocybe* are sacraments and their ingestion is a religious practice and an aid to enlightenment.

Everyone has the right to expand consciousness and to stimulate aesthetic, visionary, and mystical experience by whatever means one considers desirable without interference from anyone, so long as such practice does not injure another person or their property.

We do not encourage the ingestion of the sacrament by those who are unprepared.[25]

During its existence the Fane offered guided visionary sessions with *Psilocybe* mushrooms, and published a newsletter, *The Sporeprint*. Members of the Fane also participated in a 1996 study by Kaiser-Permanente psychologist Horace Beach on reports of audible disembodied voices during high-dose mushroom trips.

Although officially chartered in Canada, the Fane were unable to get full legal approval for their use of psilocybin, and they spent years fighting the nation's antientheogen laws. Eventually the Fane became defunct, although the Lycaeum drug-information portal has preserved and mirrored the sect's original website.

THE FARM

The Farm in Summertown, Tennessee, is the real-world manifestation of founder Stephen Gaskin's Summer-of-Love ideals. Since 1971 the sizable rural commune has maintained his hippie vision, aided partly by sacramental cannabis consumption.

A former San Francisco State University professor who dropped out from mainstream academia under the influence of LSD and the Haight-Ashbury hippie scene, Gaskin joined the institution's countercultural "free college" in 1967. There he taught the "Monday Night Class"—a free-form series of public lectures where he expounded on spirituality, politics, sex, drugs, environmentalism, and anything else that crossed his mind. Eventually, the hugely popular class got moved to the Family Dog psychedelic-rock auditorium, where up to 1,500 people would gather to listen to the "acid guru."

To share his wisdom, and the community's open and inquisitive spirit with the rest of America, Gaskin took 350 of his followers on a cross-country road trip in 1970. The sixty-vehicle convoy barnstormed the United States, spreading their message of a psychedelically enlightened, egalitarian, and environmentally friendly way of life, and eventually touched down near Summertown, about sixty miles southwest of Nashville, where Gaskin and his associates purchased an 1,800-acre tract of land for use as a commune, and named it "The Farm." Among his other edicts for the new community, Gaskin banned from the property alcohol, pharmaceuticals, tobacco, and animal products—poisons, he said, that warped human consciousness and contributed to social and environmental degradation.

According to Farm historian Michael Traugot, the early community was a "grass church," whose residents used "marijuana for insight, for ceremonial value and to enhance lovemaking." But commerce in the herb was forbidden, since to Gaskin and his followers, cannabis was a "sacrament and an aid to consciousness, [and] one absorbed some of the karma of those who produced and distributed." Farm residents instead produced their own "pot lovingly grown, over which no money changed hands." The growers lacked discretion though, and according to Gaskin, "sat nude and played flute to it, and got caught by people going by doing that, until they just aroused the curiosity of the neighbors."[26]

Gaskin was busted for cultivation and eventually served one year in a Tennessee prison. After he got out, he prohibited the growing of marijuana plants on Farm property, although he and other Farm residents continued to discreetly use cannabis for spiritual and sexual enhancement. And although LSD was verboten on the Farm, Gaskin told a *San Francisco Chronicle* reporter that he tolerated Farm members' use of peyote and psilocybin mushrooms as "a matter of personal conscience."

Over the next forty-odd years, the Farm grew and prospered, reaching a peak population of 1,400 inhabitants in 1980. Gaskin and his followers not only made the community work as a self-sufficient alternative to mainstream, consumerist America, but also organized a variety of humanitarian service projects around the world.

In 1996 *Cannabis Spirituality,* Gaskin's book on marijuana's sacramental potential, was published. The commune leader, who'd first tried the herb as a teenage marine during the Korean War, told readers, "You can use cannabis as a sacrament—not as an end in itself, but as a holy tool to help you experience reality. Cannabis opens you up and leaves you compassionate." He saw the time-honored ritual of smoking a joint in circle as a part of this opening-up process—"the gesture of, 'I'm passing something precious, and we're sharing communion with it.' You can look around and recognize yourself in every eye you look at."[27]

Gaskin eschewed established rituals and doctrines for use of the plant, saying: "A group of people, partaking of the good herb together, not perhaps even thinking of anything spiritual, can find themselves coming together in communion. This is not a communion of words but a communion of minds and spirits and souls. It creates a simple down-home ceremony that they can relate to instead of dogma." He also spurned the idea of formal clergy and maintained that "a real master of ceremonies is someone who knows the natural ceremonies, knows when they're about to happen, when they should happen, and facilitates them in the here and now."[28]

Gaskin passed on in 2014 at seventy-nine, but the Farm carries on his cannabis-infused communitarian vision.

FELLOWSHIP OF THE CLEAR LIGHT

Based in Berkeley, California, the Fellowship of the Clear Light first surfaced in the summer of 1966. The group was originally organized by Sexual Freedom League founder Jefferson Poland, later of Shiva Fellowship and Psychedelic Venus Church fame (see chapters 12 and 13).

Poland proposed a manifesto for the group on the front page of the June 17, 1966, issue of the underground newspaper *The Berkeley Barb*:

> We are committed to an open-minded, creedless search for spiritual enlightenment and self-discovery. Our interests include the secular-humanist concerns which typically occupy Unitarian groups but go beyond. Over the last few years, we have felt needs for meditation, psychological and spiritual introspection, re-integration of body and ego, and some basis for inner peace which will help us face our century of permanent warfare. These needs have been partially met by such spiritual tools as Taoism, Buddhism, and psychedelics. Like many young humanists of our generation, we find ourselves (to our surprise) engaged in a religious revival. Simple atheism is not enough.[29]

Poland believed that if he found ten adult members for such a group, it could affiliate with the local Unitarian Universalist Church as an organized "fellowship." This, he reasoned, would shield the sect with the UUC's First Amendment religious protections, and give them the same legal status that the peyote-ingesting Native American Church (see chapter 1) had vis-à-vis psychedelics usage.

After issuing the statement, Poland turned the reins of the Fellowship of the Clear Light over to Berkeleyan Don Donahue. Donahue, who later became a pioneering underground-comics publisher, organized fellowship gatherings of between fifteen and thirty people at both his house and the local Unitarian church, most of which were discussions about psychedelics and the legal issues thereof. One source claimed that entheogen advocate Dr. Richard Alpert, later known as Ram Dass, sat in on the meetings when he visited the Bay Area.

According to stories in the *Berkeley Barb,* fellowship meetings were rife with paranoia about infiltration by undercover narcotics agents. For that reason, illegal substances were forbidden at them, and consciousness-altering practices were limited mostly to "devotional exercises based on Tibetan religious music."

Although there is no evidence the fellowship survived beyond 1966, it did achieve a kind of minor notoriety by being included on the Church of Scientology's infamous "Enemies List." As defined by Scientology founder L. Ron Hubbard, an enemy was a "Person or group [that] has no rights of any kind and actions taken against them are not punishable," and many individuals and organizations on the list were harassed by church operatives. What the fellowship did to earn this status is unknown outside Scientology's secretive circles, although it might be guessed that their advocacy of psychedelics put them at odds with the militantly antidrug Hubbard.

FIRST CHURCH OF CANNABIS

In March 2015 Indiana's then-Governor Mike Pence signed into law the state's controversial Religious Freedom Restoration Act (RFRA), which critics suspected would allow Christians to discriminate against gays and nonbelievers. Indianapolis resident Bill Levin responded by forming a cannabis-centered sect that would test the statute's commitment to First Amendment protections and make the Hoosier State an unlikely center of modern entheogenic spirituality.

On July 1, 2015, Levin's First Church of Cannabis opened to the public at a former Christian church building in Indianapolis, Indiana. Although legal threats from the city, as well as a heavy presence of police and Christian protestors, forced attendees to abstain from sacramental cannabis usage, no arrests or negative incidents troubled the faithful, and the service, which featured a comedian, live music, and dancing, was covered by worldwide media, and became a publicity bonanza for the church and its founder.

Soon the church rivaled Denver's International Church of Cannabis (see chapter 17) as America's most visible entheogenic sect. Reporters were especially taken by Levin, who designates himself the church's "Grand Poobah," after the men's lodge leader on *The Flintstones* cartoon. With his long gray hair, ever-present cigar, and puckish personality, the sexagenarian grandfather, entrepreneur, and former punk-rock promoter has endeared himself to ganja smokers worldwide since 2015 and has become a living symbol of cannabis-based spirituality.

Cannaterians, Levin's term for church members, pay $4.20 a month in membership dues. They assemble every Wednesday at the church building at 3400 South Rural Street to hear the Grand Poobah and his fellow "Ministers of Love" preach a gospel that "Celebrate[s] Life's Great Adventure by Building on Compassion, Good Health, and Love," and advocates the use of cannabis for spiritual uplift. Services are also streamed to internet Cannaterians on the church's Facebook page.

The First Church of Cannabis's creed, "The Deity Dozen," encapsulates its stoner-humanitarian philosophy:

> Don't be an asshole. Treat everyone with Love as an equal.
> The day starts with your smile every morning. When you get up, wear it first.
> Help others when you can. Not for money, but because it's needed.
> Treat your body as a temple. Do not poison it with poor quality foods and sodas.
> Do not take advantage of people. Do not intentionally hurt anything.
> Never start a fight . . . only finish them.
> Grow food, raise animals, get nature into your daily routine.
> Do not be a "troll" on the internet, respect others without name calling and being vulgarly aggressive.

Spend at least 10 mins a day just contemplating life in a quiet
space.

Protect those who cannot protect themselves.

Laugh often, share humor. Have fun in life, be positive.

Cannabis, "the Healing Plant" is our sacrament. It brings us
closer to ourselves and others. It is our fountain of health,
our love, curing us from illness and depression. We embrace it
with our whole heart and spirit, individually and as a group.[30]

Along with its cannabis advocacy, the church runs a service out-
reach to homeless people, a food bank, and Thursday-night bingo fun-
draisers. The work is greatly aided by the fact that the FCOC sports a
501(c)(3) charitable-organization status, which allows it to receive tax-
deductible bequests and gifts, and qualifies it for property tax exemption in Indiana.

Yet Cannaterian faithful still can't legally partake of their sacrament during church work or services. Indiana statutes mandate jail time
and fines for mere possession of any amount of cannabis, and Levin's
RFRA-based court challenges to the laws have so far been unsuccessful.
The Grand Poobah and his church are still confident that one day the
Hoosier State will make good on its guarantee of religious freedom, and
legalize the use of cannabis for Cannaterians, and for all other Indianans.

THE FIRST CHURCH OF ZENTA

No American city boasted a more volatile sixties counterculture than
Detroit. The scene of the worst urban riots since the Civil War, the
Motor City birthed a militant, outrageous youth underground whose
most famous cultural token was "Kick Out the Jams," a thunder-
ing, searing live rock album recorded by the protopunk *MC5* band at
Detroit's Grande Ballroom on October 30, 1968—"Zenta New Year."

Zenta was the official religious faith of the *MC5* and of Trans-Love
Energies—the commune founded by their manager, poet, and activist
John Sinclair. After Detroit proved too dangerous a location for the
commune, in late 1967 it moved to Ann Arbor, the home of the flagship
University of Michigan campus. The commune occupied two buildings

on Ann Arbor's Hill Street that housed the *MC5*'s members, fed and sheltered runaways and homeless teens, and headquartered the White Panthers, an anti-racist New Left paramilitary group whose motto was, "total assault on culture through rock and roll, dope, and fucking in the streets." From this community Zenta emerged.

In a 2011 column Sinclair reminisces that in the commune, "cannabis had become integral to our work and play in equal measure, and helped keep our minds to the mental grindstone at all times." To them, "its spiritual properties and potentialities qualified weed as a religious sacrament for ritual use," and *Zenta* was the term Sinclair and his associates used to describe the state of consciousness it produced.[31]

Zenta had no set doctrine or rituals. It was best achieved when one smoked the herbal sacrament, or ingested a major psychedelic, and absorbed the whole gestalt of rock 'n' roll, revolution, sexual freedom, and expanded consciousness of daily life at Trans-Love Energies.[32]

John Sinclair's wife, Leni, a noted rock photographer, sums up what Zenta is about in a 2019 *VICE* magazine article about Ann Arbor's historic cannabis scene: "Zenta is the religion to end all religion . . . That's how I look at it. Because it's the only religion that says 'yes' where other religions say 'no' or 'thou shalt not.' Well hippies say 'yes.' Yes, smoke weed. Have sex. Be who you are . . . Anybody who smokes weed is a Zenta believer, whether they know the term or not."[33]

After John Sinclair was sentenced to ten years in prison for passing two cannabis joints to an undercover cop, the *MC5*'s spiritual advisor, Brother J. C. Crawford, incorporated the First Church of Zenta in the state of Michigan. The church named cannabis, LSD, and other entheogens as its sacraments, and believed that as a legally organized religion, their right to ingest them would be protected by the courts on First Amendment grounds.

The church was encouraged when the Michigan supreme court ruled that the state's cannabis laws were unconstitutional, and freed John Sinclair in early 1972. Days later Zenta followers and other Sinclair supporters celebrated the victory with a mass smoke-in at the University of Michigan, and every April since, weed users by the thousands have gathered there for the annual "Ann Arbor Hash Bash."

Through the early seventies, the First Church of Zenta continued to hold its services at the Hill Street houses and various local music venues. There, "the faithful [would] partake in the sacrament, participate in group-grope ritual dances, share in the cosmic karma of the community, and join in the collective energy discharge into the universe."[34] And, thanks to the efforts of simpatico local activists, seventies Ann Arbor became a haven for midwestern weed smokers, where simple possession of cannabis inside city limits became punishable by a mere $5 fine.

Unfortunately, legal religious exemptions were never created for Zenta or other Michigan entheogen users, and the First Church of Zenta became defunct around 1980. Despite this outcome the octogenarian activist continues to promote the plant's healing and enlightening powers from his Detroit home. Nearly fifty years after Sinclair went to prison for two joints, the state of Michigan finally legalized recreational cannabis.

Zenta exists today largely in the persona of the Rev. Rauk Zenta. A punk musician and "actively retired labor and social activist" living in Nova Scotia, Canada, the reverend received John Sinclair's permission to carry on the Zenta name in the late nineties and maintains a presence on several social-media sites where he continues to transmit the group's psychedelic gospel of spiritual and political transformation to the world at large.

FIRST INTERNATIONAL CHURCH OF SALVIA DIVINORUM

The ancient Mazatec Indian practice of seeking visions through the ingestion of *Salvia divinorum* leaves was revived in the United States during the early 1990s. Some adherents of the herbal high observed traditional Mazatec practices, calling the substance *Ska Maria Pastora* ("Mary the Sky Shepherdess") as per Indo-Catholic fusionist tradition, and only partaking of leaves harvested by a virgin and proffered by an east-facing ceremonial leader.

When the mainstream media discovered *Salvia,* news outlets carried sensationalistic reports about American youth freaking out on the legal, organic intoxicant. Fearing a repeat of the LSD moral-panic of the mid-sixties, an individual only known as "Rev. MeO," a reference to the methoxy sidechain on psychoactive molecules, formed the First

Fig. P2.3. Ground *Salvia divinorum* leaves.
Photograph courtesy of Pie4all88.

International Church of Salvia Divinorum. The church's sole purpose was "to secure, through the idea of grandfathering, the freedom to legally utilize our Sacrament, *Salvia divinorum,* in the sad instance that the United States Federal Government outlaws *Ska Maria* in the future."[35]

Eventually the reverend decided that the electronic church was no more likely to protect *Salvia* from media hysterics or DEA sanctions than other religious organizations had for similar entheogens, and the sect sank into the recesses of the internet's archives.

GHOST CLAN

The Mesita, Colorado, based Ghost Clan blipped briefly onto the entheogenic-religions radar in the 1990s, when it fought local officials over its use of peyote in religious ceremonies. Although the clan claimed affiliation with the legally protected Native American Church (see chapter 1), Costilla County deputies reportedly harassed clan members, who were alleged to be mostly non–Native Americans not covered by the religious-freedom exemption granted to the NAC.

The Ghost Clan also made local news when it contested a land-usage battle with a Texas-based rancher over public access to a road on the Colorado–New Mexico border. Clan leader Randolph "Duke" White claimed that the rancher had blocked access to sacred Native American sites the group visited on their peyotist "vision quests," a violation of the 1978 American Indian Religious Freedom Act. Representing himself and the clan, White fought the case up to the Tenth Circuit Federal Court of Appeals, which ruled against him in 2002.

Randolph White himself was a controversial local character. A former law-enforcement official who ran Mesita's general store, White was the father of South Colorado serial killer Richard Paul White and was arrested in 2005 for selling DVDs of his son's confessions to his crimes, whose proceeds he claimed were earmarked for both the victims' families and his own grandchildren. The elder White was also named a person of interest in the unsolved 1988 murder of two cannabis growers in Questa, New Mexico. His death at sixty-five in 2015 left investigators in that case, as well as researchers on the Ghost Clan, baffled and frustrated.

GRADY PEYOTE GROUP

On May 24, 1962, police raided Gerald and Irene Kelly's Palm Springs, California, house and arrested six adults and one female juvenile for possession of peyote. The officers maintained that the Kellys' "party house" had regularly hosted "sex orgies" fueled by the cactus buttons that the residents had concealed in the sand behind the house.

When the case came to court, all the adults were convicted. But twenty-eight-year-old Arthur Charles Grady appealed, and his case came before the California Supreme Court in 1964, where it was noted:

> Petitioner [Grady], a self-styled "peyote preacher" and "way shower,"
> acted as the spiritual leader of a group of individuals consisting of the
> codefendants and himself. This group lived together in the Kellys'
> home. Although petitioner did not share in the living expenses
> of the group, he selected their food, taught them deep-breathing

exercises, how to pray, "and in general how to love the Christian Life." Petitioner provided and prepared the peyote for the group.

Petitioner contends that his use of peyote was for religious purposes. He states that peyote "is a very spiritual plant because it gives you direct contact with God, or in other words, proceeds on all four planes of consciousness simultaneously, and when used for prayer the best thing that can happen to you."[36]

Grady cited the *People v. Woody* case, a key ruling in favor of the Native American Church (see chapter 1), to defend his flock's peyote usage under First Amendment protections. The court granted Grady and his fellow petitioners a retrial, but they were once again convicted, setting a precedent for future trials involving non–Native American use of psychedelics.

THE HEALING CHURCH

One of the most unusual contemporary psychedelic sects is Rhode Island's the Healing Church. Although its faithful probably don't number more than two-dozen cannabis religionists in and around the city of Providence, the group has distinguished itself by being one of the few woman-led entheogenic churches, as well as in its unorthodox take on Catholic doctrines and practices, and in its links to Donald Trump's presidential administration.

The Healing Church's founder is the Rev. Anne Armstrong. Raised in a Jewish family, Armstrong, a graduate of the University of Rhode Island and an electrical engineer, converted to Christianity in 1986 after having an overpowering vision of Jesus. Years later, when one of her children was grievously injured, Armstrong promised God that if the child lived, she'd become a Catholic. True to her word, when the child recovered, she joined the Roman Catholic Church.

But the new convert had a not-so-hidden agenda. A firm believer in the healing powers of the cannabis plant, Armstrong discovered that such Catholic luminaries as church doctor St. Hildegard of Bingen and the physician Pope John XXI had promoted the medicinal use of the plant, and that representations of it can be found in medieval church art. Armstrong maintains that nowhere in canonical Catholic teachings is cannabis specifically condemned, and that its use as a healing agent is consistent with the Vatican's teachings about medical ethics.

To promote her vision of a cannabis-friendly Catholicism, Armstrong founded the Healing Church. She saw the organization not as a distinct sect, but as an apostolate of the One Holy Catholic and Apostolic Church headquartered in Rome. Although unrecognized by the church hierarchy as a minister, Armstrong took the ancient Christian title of deaconess and began to promote the medicinal and sacramental power of cannabis in both Catholic and non-Catholic circles.

In 2015 Armstrong tested Rhode Island's historical commitment to religious freedom. That year, she and church canon and longtime cannabis activist Alan Gordon began to hold public worship services at Providence's Roger Williams National Memorial, a small park established to honor the colonial American champion of spiritual liberty and church-state separation.

For several years, every Saturday at 4:20 p.m. the two robed and staff-bearing clerics set up a place of worship at the park's historical well, which they believed was named in the biblical book of Revelation as the place where the Tree of Life will "be given back to mankind." After delivering prayers and sermons to a small group of followers, Armstrong and Gordon would blow cannabis smoke out of shofar horns, anoint the faithful with hashish-infused healing oil, and distribute joints to be reverentially consumed.

Eventually Armstrong and Gordon took the National Park Service to court, claiming that the federal anticannabis law in effect at the park violated their rights under the Religious Freedom Restoration Act. The United States District Court didn't agree and ruled against them in *Armstrong v. Jewell* (2015), not impressed by the pair's contention that the National Memorial was sacred ground for cannabis users akin to Mecca or Jerusalem's Western Wall.

Several months after the court decision, police raided Armstrong and Gordon's home in West Greenwich and seized 12 pounds of harvested cannabis and 59 plants. Although the charges were eventually dropped, two years later they were caught with 48 pounds of cannabis and arrested once more. The legal persecution spurred the pair to enter state politics. In 2018 Armstrong and Gordon ran for governor and attorney general, respectively, as members of the pro-cannabis Rhode Island Compassion Party. Gordon racked up an impressive 19.1 percent of the vote in the November election, but when he and Armstrong tried to run in 2022, they were disqualified in the primaries.

Armstrong also campaigned on the federal level for Donald Trump. The church leader maintained that the controversial Republican president was a drug-law reformer, and spoke at Trump rallies throughout the Northeast, often using her pulpit to calm troubles between supporters and protestors. She and Gordon were also present at the January 6, 2021, Washington D.C. pro-Trump riot, where her cannabis-scented calls for peace went unheard as hundreds invaded the Capitol Building.

As of this writing, Armstrong and Gordon are still facing up to fifty years in state prison if convicted for the 2018 arrest. Given the theological and ideological peculiarities in the Healing Church's case and the current cultural climate surrounding cannabis, whether their religious-use defense will work this time is anyone's guess.

THE INTERNATIONAL COPELANDIA CHURCH OF GOD

A "virtual" church whose existence and activities were confined to the Copelandia website, the International Copelandia Church of God was launched in 2001 by a "Rev. Joshua Copeland." The reverend derived his name, as well as the church's, from the *Copelandia* mushrooms—a genus of psilocybin-bearing fungi common throughout the Hawaiian Islands—that were the group's sacrament.

During its online life, the church site maintained a library, bookstore, and moderated discussion group, as well as links to suppliers of organic entheogens. The site sported a stained-glass crucifix and a Bible search engine on its main page, and it was never clear whether the reverend was promoting Christian psychedelian spirituality, or if the features were just chosen to play up the "church" label.

As of this writing the Copelandia website is dead, and the Rev. Copeland and his online followers seem to have scattered like mushroom spores in a gentle Hawaiian breeze.

LAZY NICKELS

The Lazy Nickels started life as an L.A.-based psychedelic rock band. When their 1970 single, "35 Design/Struggle for Freedom" (Slug Records WR-5016) flopped, and the group broke up, lead singer Evan Eyerick lifted their name and founded a sect dedicated to "the ceremonial aspects of marijuana, magic [and] sex."

Eyerick advertised the Nickels in "alternative" periodicals like *Mother Jones* and *New Age* throughout the seventies and eighties. Inquirers who sent him a donation received the group's manifesto, *The Lazy Nickels Action Philosophy,* a collection of THC-drenched maxims about the nature and purpose of a Lazy Nickel. Many were reminiscent of the stoned philosophizing of the Neo-American Church's Art Kleps (see chapter 6), albeit rendered in a far terser, and more typo-ridden, format. Some examples:

> A Nickel thinks that everyone has funny looking feet.
> A Nickel believes that the Christian Era ended in 1945 with the final purification i.e., the Nazi Death Camps and that the New Age is to begin in the Spring of 1977.
> The Lazy Nickel Trip is like a perpetual acid relapse. You don't do it for awhile, someone "kicks the can" and it starts up again and the space is gone in between. The original idea of the trip keeps returning—complete with groupies, cover ads in slick magazines and freaks who light their teeth on fire.
> A Lazy Nickel does not believe that there is any such thing as an "Older Woman" because he doesn't believe in that kind of age and loves them all.
> A Nickel uses psychedelic drugs not for pleasure but for purification.
> If a Nickel has to have a god, let it be the Smoke from the Indian Hemp Bush. I suppose that's where the Magician encountered the now infamous *Great Lazy Nickel Whore* who is the true Mother of the Smoke—she is sacred and holy to all Nickels.[37]

Writing under the pseudonym "John Musters," Eyerick laid out the Nickels' beliefs and organizational principles in the group's *Information Booklet*. He said that the prime purpose of a Nickel, like the coin, was "to make change," as well as "live in harmony with nature," and "to advance spiritually." Eyerick believed that the eventual legalization of cannabis would touch off a revolution of mass-consciousness, and that it was the Nickels' responsibility to guide America, and ultimately the world, past the old Christian era, and into a new era of enlightenment where primo hashish, rather than currency, would be the preferred medium of exchange.

Local chapters of Nickels were known as "The Change," and were headed by a "Magician," who was the distributor of all "Nickel products" in the area. Prospective new members were required to affiliate with the Nickels for six months before applying for membership, donate a $100 initiation fee to the group, bring in two new members, and "do something that will greatly benefit The Change." Active members were initiated during the Buddhist festival of Wesak, and then trained in the Nickels' organizational and ceremonial activities.

During the late 1970s there was a "playing group" of Lazy Nickels at Penn State's "Free University" known as the Buffalo Thunder Cabal. The organization numbered about a dozen Free U students and held regular meetings that featured group meditations, offered a course called "Drugs and the Exploration and Exploitation of the Mind," and staged an "Alchemical Play" that featured a light show and pyrotechnic effects. Group leader William Eichman told a reporter that the local Nickels were exploring everything from psychedelics to electronic technology, to Wiccan spirituality to help bring about the Aquarian Age, "where individualism, uniqueness, genius, joy, and individual responsibility will be the guiding forces of the world."[38]

Unfortunately, the Buffalo Thunder Cabal didn't last, and there's no evidence that Eyerick ever gained any dues-paying followers elsewhere. The Nickels seem to have gone out of circulation in the late 1980s.

According to his brother Craig, who once played guitar in the original Lazy Nickels band, Evan Eyerick eventually became a philosopher hermit, too deeply concerned with ontology's thorniest questions to deal with most other human beings, let alone lead any spiritual movements.

NATIVE AMERICAN INDIGENOUS CHURCH

Formerly the Oklevueha Native American Church (see chapter 4) of SomaVeda, this Florida-based psychedelic sect is the hub of a network of interconnected spiritual, educational, and medical organizations.

The Native American Indigenous Church bills itself as an "Integrated Auxiliary" of the Priory of Saving Grace, which itself is a Diocese and Auxiliary of the Sacred Medical Order Church of Hope. The Church of Hope is the ecclesiastical arm of the Knights of Hope, a Hospitaller-like Christian service fraternity whose website displays its members wearing chivalric robes and brandishing ceremonial swords.

The church and the knights are together considered a "Missionary Diocese" of the Holy Apostolic Catholic Church of the East in Brazil. This is one of the countless "Independent Catholic" churches that trace their ecclesiastical provenance back to first-century Christian bishops, and where elaborately vested clergy usually outnumber lay members.

All these organizations are connected to one Anthony B. James. A man of diverse interests and talents, Mr. James bills himself as the dean of the Somaveda College of Natural Medicine/School of Ayurveda Medicine, and medical director of the Thai Yoga Center, all of which, along with the Priory of Saving Grace, operate out of his home in Brooksville, Florida. His CV features a dizzying list of accomplishments and qualifications that includes seven doctorates, four of which were awarded between 2012 and 2014 from the PanAmerican School of Natural Medicine, where James has been director of the "Doctor of Oriental Medicine Diploma Program" since 2011.

One of James's doctorates is in the arcane discipline of Indigenous Medicine—possibly the inspiration for the Native American Indigenous Church. The NAIC describes itself as "an ecumenical/interdenominational, religious, Faith Based Tribal Organization" that seeks to restore the "ancient, sacred ways of Native, Indigenous, Natural and Traditional healing and sacred religious and religious therapeutic (medicine) practices"[39] common not only to the Americas, but to the Pacific Islands and Asia.

One traditional medicine the church advocates is peyote. Its code of ethics states that it "accepts peyote as central to our established religious belief," although its articles of religious practice affirm that the organization "does not possess, use or distribute any federally regulated substances of any kind whatsoever, *unless* located in a state where the right has been clearly and legally established [emphasis theirs]."[40]

Conveniently enough, the dense, information-rich church website includes guides to states where such legal exemptions exist for NAIC members to practice the healing and medicine aspects of their religion. The site is also packed with enough legal arcana, alternative-health lore, news releases, compliance statements, philosophical musings, and photographs of James with indigenous peoples to challenge the patience of even the most dedicated researchers of unorthodox spirituality.

Three levels of church membership are available. The cheapest is the $14.95 "Authorized Participant." Next comes the $200 "Authorized Full Blessed Membership Medicine Ministry-Practitioner Authorization." And for $350 plus an annual donation, one can become an "Authorized Commissioned Holistic Therapists Vocational Licentiate . . . a legal basis for a clerical/ministerial healing and wellness livelihood,"[41] and even receive the opportunity to start a NAIC Free Church, Independent Branch, and Tribal Organization Health Care Providership. NAIC Free Churches exist in Florida, Michigan, and Tennessee, although their membership is unknown.

Currently the church holds "Sacred Chanupa, Pipe, Tobacco and Healing Lodge" ceremonies at James's house. Not surprisingly, there is no mention of peyote meetings in its event listings or news releases. Although the church website features an extensive page on Florida State laws and rulings that protect such Native American entheogenic spiritual practices, it's unclear whether James and his followers walk the Peyote Road, and one can only surmise that card-carrying church members alone are privy to that information.

NEW AMERICAN CHURCH

Founded in 1987 by Joel Bartlett in Albany, New York, the New American Church proclaimed that "LSD is the true Christ . . . the neurohumor of angels, and its use works wonders by psychoactivity field resonance."

According to a self-published guide to the church, prospective members were initiated into its activities thusly:

> Marijuana for all occasions—first level
>
> LSD for members formal (non-ritual) organization. At this, second level members can design the programs for the first. This is a privileged distinction. At the first level, public services resemble parties with TV viewing and parlor games. The structure is a casual social gathering Party according to your style. Drugs are optional, but herb is suggested to remedy synchronicity blocks.
>
> At the second level, the members get to find out the contents of the subliminal programs and also to design material for themselves. This is the "enlightened" church. Those people who understand and trust one another and understand what we are doing.[42]

Although the church condemned the use of powder and crack cocaine, and saw those drugs as portals for demonic possession, it allowed the use of not only alcohol but PCP (phencyclidine)—"angel dust"—on the Fourth of July, and in the spirit of that holiday, militantly opposed government attempts to control or suppress psychoactive substances.

The church called its central ritual "Synchronicity for Divination." Adapted from the Neo-American Church (see chapter 6), it involved meditating on an "altar of silent tv's on different stations . . . random readings from psy-phy [sic] novels . . . perhaps tossing in the I-Ching,"[43] in search of synchronistic messages. It also proposed the use of subliminal programming during its TV-watching rituals to create "psychic resonance" among celebrants.

Along with video-based ritualism, Bartlett seems to have been interested in the synergistic effects of hallucinogens and antidepressants, as he contributed an article to the influential *Psychedelic Monographs and Essays* journal titled "Ludiomil, LSD-25 plus the Lucid Dream."

As with so many others of its kind, the church—if it ever existed outside Bartlett's imagination—soon faded from view and became another odd footnote in the history of modern-day entheogenic spirituality.

NEW WORLD CHURCH

In 1990 cops busted Erwin L. Rupert for possession of marijuana and drug paraphernalia in Portland, Maine. Although the case was dropped when the arresting officer failed to appear in court, Rupert demanded that the police return his confiscated hash pipe, since he was the founder and head of the New World Church, and that the vessel, which bore a metal tag inscribed "No. 87-2, N.W.C. Inc." was used exclusively for religious use of cannabis.

An eclectic type, the thirty-eight-year-old Rupert was a former air force officer, a Georgetown Law School alumnus, and a graduate of Harvard University's Divinity School. At Harvard he'd written his master's thesis on the historical use of hallucinogenic mushrooms in religions of India. He had also first represented the New World Church there in 1987, when he filed suit against the town of Cambridge, Massachusetts. Rupert claimed that the church's Society of the Peace Pipe saw tobacco as a deity, and that the town's antismoking ordinance violated his right to freedom of religion.

Along with his New World Church status, Rupert maintained he was a minister in the so-called Native American Church of the United States. As such, the lawyer fought the U.S. Fish and Wildlife Service over his religious right to possess ceremonial eagle feathers—a privilege usually denied to non–Native Americans like himself. And as the self-proclaimed head of the Rastafarian Church of America, he asserted that he had the right to use cannabis as a religious sacrament.

In *Rupert v. City of Portland,* the New World Church patriarch argued that the pilfered pipe was a registered chalice of his faith. He said that the church was a "shamanic" group where "church members experience the deity of nature by ritually ingesting psychedelic plants" and "bear true faith in the sacrality of marijuana."[44]

Rupert admitted that he, as the "medicine pipe registrar," was also the sole member of the church. But he also presented evidence that he'd spent many years corresponding with the Drug Enforcement Agency, unsuccessfully attempting to obtain religious exemption permits for his various sects to use cannabis, MDMA, and "North American Deity Psilocybin Mushrooms" as sacraments.

The state of Maine ruled against him. Although the decision said that the state's compelling interest to prohibit the use of Schedule I drugs outweighed First Amendment considerations, it also admitted that Rupert's beliefs about sacramental cannabis were "sincerely held." This was a marked contrast to earlier cases where judges viewed similar claims as frivolous legal tricks intended to circumvent narcotics laws. Coming as it did in 1992, the ruling seemed to be an early harbinger of relaxing legal attitudes toward entheogens.

ORATORY OF MYSTICAL SACRAMENTS

Entheogenic activist and onetime New Mexico congressional candidate Gavin Kaiser split from the Oklevueha Native American Church (see chapter 4) to form this eclectic psychedelic sect. The group's website states that:

> OMS is an all-encompassing religious organization that respects, values, and draws upon the ethical religious, mystical, and spiritual arts and wisdom of any and all of Earth's peoples, developed or practiced at any point throughout mankind's existence, and has a nationwide network of members successfully exercising their rights to religious freedom and the pursuit of life, liberty, and happiness, as they pertain to Sacraments.[45]

Although the OMS does not define itself as a religion per se, it asserts "because of the sacred nature of these Sacraments that it is better, for the time being, that they reemerge into the world through organizations, or people that emphasize the spiritual and scientifically proven benefits and present and conduct their work in ways that honor the sacredness of the Sacraments."[46]

The oratory's sacraments are primarily DMT-bearing acacia, Syrian rue, and psilocybin, which it believes was the manna consumed by the Children of Israel. Other approved sacraments include *Amanita muscaria* mushrooms, peyote, cannabis, San Pedro cactus, ayahuasca, and other organic hallucinogens. To the OMS, these substances are the true Eucharist or Flesh of God spoken of in many religious traditions, and it supports legal access to all of them "for religious, mystical, and spiritual purposes so long as they are utilized responsibly and not causing undue harm to the individual or other people."[47]

Membership in the OMS is open to any individual that submits an initial donation and a personal proclamation of the essentiality of sacraments to their religious practice. New members receive a membership declaration, along with a print of psilocybin spores and an assortment of psychoactive plant seeds, which they are expected to disseminate outdoors as part of their spiritual commitment. They are also required to complete a series of online courses, participate in online meetings, and take whatever other steps the oratory deems necessary before they can be considered eligible to use the sacraments. New members are often referred to local OMS groups, where they can be initiated into the Eucharist, and spiritual exploration can take place in a supportive environment.

One of the more intellectually oriented psychedelic sects, the OMS sees its mission as both a spiritual and a scientific one and advocates the use of the sacraments "as a microscope for us to peer into the inner working of ourselves, and this world." The oratory's website sports a vast collection of links to historic religious and mystical writings, with an emphasis on Western esoteric traditions like Freemasonry, Rosicrucianism, and alchemy.

The oratory also boasts an auxiliary fraternity known as the Knights of Acacia—"The Holy and Interdimensional Rite of Acacian Masonry." OMS founder Gavin Kaiser, a 32nd-degree Scottish Rite and Knight Templar Freemason, maintains that the acacia plant, Jesus's "crown of thorns" and one of the central symbols of Freemasonry, can be refined to produce a DMT-infused "Grand Elixir"—the "Lost Sacrament" of Egyptian Masonry, Enochian magic, and ancient Christianity alike.

With the aid of this sacrament, the Knights are charged to "conduct strategic covert and overt operations worldwide and interdimensionally to protect all that is just, right, and true. Interdimensional exploration of human consciousness and neurological capabilities, and interacting with what are perceived as unidentified life forms, or entities, in alternative realms of perception are honored and respected duties of the

Knight."[48] Prospective members apply through the OMS, and Masonic brothers are especially welcomed.

On December 22, 2020, the OMS scored a notable victory for entheogenic First Amendment rights. That day, the New Hampshire Supreme Court ruled that Oratory member Jeremy D. Mack, arrested in November 2017 for the possession of psilocybin mushrooms, was within his rights to practice his entheogen-related religious beliefs without "disturbing the peace." The ruling was only binding to New Hampshire courts, but it was yet another indication that a sincere commitment to psychedelic spirituality by a member of a well-organized sect could be an effective defense against entheogen prohibition.

PALEO-AMERICAN CHURCH

Yet another breakaway from Art Kleps's Neo-American Church (see chapter 6) this sect based in Warren, Vermont, emerged in 1969. Its leaders, who called themselves "Thorns," proclaimed that "the hallucinogens are the sacraments of the Paleo-American Church," and held meetings at New England universities.

One gathering at the MIT Student Center in late 1969, "saw between twenty and forty youthful freaks wallowing on the floor and giggling softly while the universe breathed on them."[49] In the manner of the era, three Thorns spun period psychedelic music and ran a lightshow during the service, while the college-paper reporter present grumbled about the dearth of topless hippie chicks among the trippers.

Sometime in the early 1970s the "High Thorn" forsook entheogens for Zen Buddhism, but continued to lead the group, which vanished around the middle of the decade.

THE POT ILLUMINATI

Author, journalist, and former *High Times* magazine editor Steven Hager is the mind behind this "nonviolent organization devoted to improvisational creativity."

After organizing cannabis-centric countercultural ceremonies for twenty-five years on behalf of *High Times,* Hager decided to use the idea of a Masonic-style secret society to communicate his wisdom and ideas. Hager said that he was "stealing the sigils [magic symbols] of the evil Illuminati and turning them to sigils for good," to form a non-dogmatic and egalitarian brotherhood that would establish and practice a pot-sacramental spiritual culture. He believed that existing religious institutions were hopelessly corrupt and felt that a different sort of "religion" was needed to successfully guide humanity through the third millennium.

Hager's Pot Illuminati Lodge "is a nonpolitical entity that embraces all people regardless of race, religion, or national origins." Although not a traditional organized church, it draws on the poetry, myths, and rituals of past religions from across the globe, and encourages the merging of concepts from these faiths, the primacy of practical improvisation, and the manifesting of the spirits of love and fun in lodge ceremony.

The lodge's basic doctrine is encapsulated in:

Hager's Hippie Ten Commandments

Everything is connected (I'm in you and you're in me) so act accordingly.

The true Bible is written in the hearts of the people, so follow your heart.

Do unto others as you would have them do unto you.

Strive to be nonviolent in thought, word, and deed.

Do not lie, cheat, or steal.

Heart energy is clean energy (as opposed to ego energy), so amplify your love vibrations and keep your ego in check.

Cannabis is "the Tree of Life" and has been so since the dawn of civilization. Make the most of hemp.

Regarding cannabis, however, the less you do, the higher you get. Strive to know when it's appropriate to be intoxicated and when it's not (unless you have medical need).

Honor your elders, and your children.

Pass to the left.[50]

Lodge ceremonies are under the supervision of Illuminated Masters. The Masters are tasked to quell any evil, anger, or trouble in ritual space through sage smudging and prayer, and to maintain the proper vibrations of love and fun. Members who violate any of the Hippie Ten Commandments are subject to expulsion from the lodge.

The Pot Illuminati have staged and sponsored various cannabis-oriented public gatherings in the New York City region, and Hager continues to spread their message via his online writings.

PRINCESS LEDA CULT

In the wake of the Manson Family murders, journalists flocked to Southern California to trace the origins and connections of the deadly cult. Some, like *Los Angeles Free Press* editor and Beat author Ed Sanders, tried to smoke out similarly sinister sects that combined countercultural sensibilities, sex, drugs, and violence in a toxic new form of "spirituality."

Esquire magazine's May 1970 issue featured an article about one Los Angeles–based cult that seemed to be made to order for media sensationalists. The group was led by "Princess Leda Amun Ra," a thirtyish, well-to-do former housewife who'd experienced a psychedelic apotheosis, and claimed to be the reincarnation of the Egyptian sun god Amun Ra, as well as the ancient Greek goddess Leda, an Atlantean high priest, and legendary actress Sarah Bernhardt.

Reportedly the daughter of an Indiana-based academic, the princess dwelled in a castle-like mansion in the Hollywood Hills, along with a young male consort who dubbed himself "King," drove a golden Jaguar with a miniature TV mounted on its dashboard and did astrological consultations at $1,000 a session.

Journalist Tom Burke encountered the princess when she danced topless, clad only in gold fishnet and black feathers, before an audience at L.A.'s occult-oriented Climax nightclub. Burke then accompanied her to her hillside "temple," a Gothic mansion appointed with candles, tiger-skin rugs, a miniature coffin bearing an infant doll's corpse, an elegantly dressed female mannequin, and a black-curtained silver Packard touring car.

Burke reported that at the ceremony he attended, LSD-infused fruit was doled out to temple attendees. When the chemical kicked in, the faithful chanted and danced, and eventually strode up to the princess's bedroom, where she lay naked on her bed, dusted in volcanic ash. Between her splayed legs lay a black swan, and the princess attempted coitus with the bird in the manner of her namesake goddess Leda.

The reporter also accompanied the princess on an expedition to a public park, where she captured and absconded with another swan. In his article, Burke implied that the princess sacrificed the creature in another ritual, which featured a young hippie garbed as Christ and bound to a stone bench.

Later it was reported that Burke's photographer Bud Lee accidentally ingested some of the acid-spiked fruit, went on a bad trip, and wound up in jail for the night. The princess herself was unmoved by the incident; she told Burke that she regularly "[gave] acid to persons who have never dropped it without telling them. I think of it as the Holy Communion."[51]

Princess Leda made a brief appearance in a never-released 1970 documentary *The Weird World of Weird,* that also featured flamboyant psychic the Amazing Criswell and Church of Satan "Black Pope" Anton LaVey. She was also mentioned in an essay by rock critic Robert Abrams, who alleged that Manson Family murder-victim Sharon Tate, along with a man he only described as "the worst degenerate homicidal homosexual in the country," used to visit the princess.

Little evidence of Princess Leda's activities survives today. It's hard not to suspect her cult was what was known then as a put-on: a prankish performance-art piece fed to a media slavering for sensational stories of acid- and sex-crazed, bloodletting hippies.

PSYCHEDELIC PEACE FELLOWSHIP

Founded in New York City in 1966 by gay activist and Christian Liberation theologian Michael Itkin, the Psychedelic Peace Fellowship advertised itself as "open to all persons seriously interested in the relation of the psychedelic experience to the nonviolent revolutionary movement, whether or not they have used the psychedelic sacraments."[52]

The fellowship saw itself as "based on the realization that the love expressed as the perception that WE ARE ALL ONE must serve as the true guide of personal conduct under all circumstances if man is to survive. Members of the PPF seek to demonstrate this transforming love as the effective force for overcoming evil and transforming society into a creative Fellowship of Man."[53]

The fellowship made its first public appearance on October 29, 1966, at the East Village's macrobiotics-based Paradox Restaurant, where Itkin read its manifesto to an assembled group. Itkin thought the eighty-odd attendees, "ranging from a well-traveled seaman in his sixties through a variety of young to middle-aged family types to a scattering of very young ecstatics," were "hoping to find in the PPF a social structure through which they could work out their hopes and fears for the larger social order,"[54] and he offered memberships to applicants there and at subsequent public gatherings.

Itkin once visited Timothy Leary at his Millbrook psychedelic retreat and impressed the ex-Harvard professor with an essay he'd written about the spiritual power of LSD. He also collaborated with Leary on one of his *Death of the Mind* mystery plays: *The Reincarnation of Jesus Christ.* But Itkin also criticized Leary's approach to the psychedelic experience and felt that he was too often a hallucinogenic huckster who sold the masses on a shallow, lazy form of spirituality that demanded "nothing more than to stay 'high' perpetually."

Itkin saw psychedelics not as "sacraments," but as useful tools to expand spiritually "in a Christian or other context," and as susceptible to abuse as any other tool or chemical. He respected both the power and the potential perils of psychedelics and made himself and his fellowship associates available to counsel people on bad hallucinogenic trips, via a twenty-four-hour phone hotline. Itkin also penned a 1966 epistle about psychedelics, *Statement on Hallucinogenic Drugs,* that he published under his Pax Christi Press imprint.

The fellowship was just one of many unorthodox and revolutionary religious projects Itkin took on during his life. Born to a Jewish family in 1936, and openly gay many years before the Stonewall uprising, Itkin embraced Christianity as a teenager, and was ordained as a priest in the gay-friendly Eucharistic Catholic Church in 1957, and as a non-papal Catholic bishop three years later. For the next thirty years, Itkin led not only the fellowship, but also such LGBTQ-oriented Christian organizations as the Primitive Catholic Church, the Evangelical Catholic Communion, and the Holy Apostolic-Catholic Church of the East, all the while pursuing a vision of unified spiritual, sexual, and political liberation in the name of Christ.

Itkin died in San Francisco of AIDS in 1989. A 2014 book about him, *The Radical Bishop and Gay Consciousness,* considers his life and its influence on both the gay and Christian worlds, but oddly omits mention of the Psychedelic Peace Fellowship or his work with Leary.

RELIGION OF DRUGS

In the thick of the Reagan/Bush-era War on Drugs, media-prankster Norm Lubow was both a parent's nightmare and a TV producer's dream. Bearded, long-haired, and clad in worn jeans and a marijuana-leaf-emblazoned t-shirt, the twenty-something UC–Santa Barbara graduate billed himself as the "Reverend Bud Green"—every inch a sixties provocateur thrust into the era of crack and AIDS, who appeared regularly on tabloid shows of the period, promoting his "Religion of Drugs" and baiting his hosts, fellow guests, and audiences alike with pro-cannabis and antiestablishment rhetoric.

The reverend held his "services" at Venice Beach and other Southern California hipster hangouts. At his sect's meetings, he testified to the consciousness-expanding properties of cannabis, stumped for its legalization, and threw joints into the audience while his pro-pot punk-metal band, "Just Say Yes," played at top volume.

Nearly thirty years before comedian and talk-show host Bill Maher smoked a joint on-air during a February 2016 broadcast of HBO's *Real Time,* the reverend lit up doobies on such programs as *The Joan Rivers Show* and *Wally George's Hot Seat* to the annoyance of his hosts and the amusement of viewers. Invariably, Rev. Green prefaced his eucharistic inhalations with a prayer: "I want to thank the Lord for giving me the Holy Herb, which shows me the need for a revolution to overthrow right-wing rich pigs!"[55]

Lubow saw cannabis spirituality and radical politics as part of the same antiestablishment campaign, and excoriated both escapist stoners and uptight politicos who refused to merge the synergistic powers of getting high and fighting the Man. Yet he was no selfless purist when it came to publicity or career opportunities; after a series of appearances on Jerry Springer's trash-talk program, he was hired as a producer for the show, probably because of his eye for the controversial and outrageous.

More recently, the Orange County–based reverend has been reorganizing his evangelical work to appeal to the western United States where cannabis is now legal, though heavily regulated. He told me that he hopes his new ministry will become "the Joel Osteen of marijuana churches," and marry THC-expanded consciousness and radical activism in a force that will eventually bring Utopia to a world weary of greed, militarism, and general spiritual blindness.

SERVANTS OF AWARENESS

Back in fifties Seattle, the Center of Integration was the Pacific Northwest's hotspot for all things metaphysical. Housed in a mansion on Capitol Hill, the center was founded in 1953 by Robert Carr, a channeler, spiritual counselor, and "trance healer." It featured programs and lectures by offbeat spiritual leaders, including Scientology founder L. Ron Hubbard, who allegedly delivered a 1957 talk there while in the nude.

Several years before Timothy Leary and his Harvard crew first tasted LSD, Carr requested and received a shipment of the then-legal chemical from Switzerland's Sandoz Laboratories. The channeler, along with a small crew of center associates, started taking it weekly to enhance contact with the discarnate entities who appeared at his meetings.

One of Carr's fellow trippers was Ralph Duby. A former army officer and Bataan Death March survivor, a student of depth psychology, and a rumored CIA contract agent, Duby started channeling a voice that called itself "Cosmic Awareness," and dispensed ageless wisdom from the Other Side to all who had ears to hear. Duby began to refer to himself as the "Interpreter," and formed his own group, Organization of Awareness, where he continued to receive acid-washed revelations from the entity until his death in January 1967.

When Duby passed on, another Center of Integration alumnus,

David Worcester, took over the interpreter role. The Organization of Awareness then split into several rival factions, one of which, the Servants of Awareness, was headed by Worcester.

The Servants of Awareness continued the LSD-powered channeling sessions from 1967 to 1970 under Worcester's guidance. According to the June 1998 issue of *Revelations of Awareness:*

> [Worcester] was a very interesting person. He was a good conduc-tor of LSD sessions for many entities, guiding them through the Bardos and death experience ala the Tibetan Book of the Dead. He [would] . . . switch on the TV news with Walter Cronkite, pull up a stool, light up, and sit before the TV and talk back to Walter Cronkite. David swore the words were being heard by the newscaster as he read the controlled news from his script and that this routine was changing consciousness. As a magician, David took a lot of credit for certain events that occurred on the world scene. He implied, for example that an earthquake in India was the direct result of a fart he let in Olympia while watching the evening news.[56]

In 1970 Paul Shockley assumed Worcester's role as interpreter. Although the acid use ended then, the "Cosmic Awareness" entity defended entheogens and the sixties counterculture in a 1977 communication:

> This Awareness indicates that had it not been for the hippie movement, the use of LSD and marijuana during the sixties, as mirroring action of the society which was occurring in this nation, you would already be living under a dictatorship, and you would have very few freedoms at this time.
>
> This Awareness indicates that the action of the hippie movement was such that it became a mirroring action likened unto a par-abolic mirror that reflected, with great intensity, an image of the society . . .
>
> This bringing about a deeper realization of what was happen-ing, and allowing the opportunity for the society which was building to begin to reverse its direction and to reconcile at a

compromise position between where the hippie stood and the straight society stood.[57]

Today, the work of the Servants of Awareness and related groups is carried on by Cosmic Awareness Communications of Olympia, Washington. Their website maintains an archive of information about Ralph Duby and his various successors and acknowledges the key role LSD played in the early channeling sessions.

SOUL QUEST CHURCH OF MOTHER EARTH (SQCME)

In the early 2010s Chris Young was an EMT, rescuing overdosed victims from the deadly effects of narcotics both prohibited and prescribed. When he realized that the pharmaceutical companies and their legal, hugely profitable offerings were largely behind the suffering he saw daily on the streets, he quit his job and moved to Europe.

During a Spanish sojourn, Young went on an eleven-day ayahuasca retreat, only to learn on the third day that his wife had miscarried. But "shadow people" he saw during his hallucinogenic experiences told him that not only would his next child be born alive and healthy, but that he would return to the United States to start a church "to provide the medicine [ayahuasca] to future generations, make it accessible, and propagate its growth."[58]

Both prophecies proved true. In 2014 the new father founded the Soul Quest Church of Mother Earth in Florida, originally chartered as a chapter of James Mooney's Oklevueha Native American Church (see chapter 4). Feeling that the Utah-based group couldn't provide the legal protection he needed for his healing work, Young incorporated Soul Quest as an independent organization, and began to hold ayahuasca retreats on a property in the city of Orlando.

Young's work attracted the attention of journalists, including *VICE* magazine's Josh Adler, who described Soul Quest and its founder in a 2017 article. Adler noted that in an unprecedented move, the DEA had reached out to the church the previous year and encouraged it to petition for a religious exemption for its ayahuasca use. In the past, entheogen-using sects usually made the first move to obtain a status, and Adler wondered if the case signaled a new openness by the federal government toward such groups and their practices.

But those practices weren't without pitfalls. On Easter Sunday 2018 a twenty-two-year-old South Florida man who'd taken ayahuasca several times before with no ill effects, suddenly went into a seizure while on a Soul Quest retreat. Although several church members as well as paramedics tried to help him, he was unresponsive and died in the hospital. Ultimately no criminal charges were filed against Soul Quest or its members, and a threatened wrongful-death lawsuit never materialized.

After a four-year wait, the DEA rejected Soul Quest's petition for a religious exemption for ayahuasca use. When the case was sent to federal court for a final adjudication, the church continued to serve the hallucinogenic tea at its retreats, citing various past rulings that approved the brew's use in religious ceremonies.

Whatever ruling may come, Soul Quest's status as a bona fide religion seems secure. The church's website sports an extensive, detailed "Statement of Beliefs" regarding the origins of the world's sacred-healing traditions, the nature of and rights of Mother Earth, humanity's obligations to Earth and to each other, the definition of the Creator, and the centrality of ayahuasca usage in its faith and practices. The Statement, as well as the aspects of church organization, governance, and ethics described on the site, are a marked contrast to the vague, believe-what-you-want doctrines of so many other psychedelic sects, and define Soul Quest as one of the more structured and well-thought-out groups in this spiritual underground.

TEMPLE 420

If one were to think of cities and towns that would be likely to produce entheogenic spiritual leaders, Beverly Hills would be among the last ones on most peoples' lists.

Yet the moneyed Southern California suburb, famed as the home of multimillionaire entertainment celebrities, was the launching pad for the career of Craig X. Rubin. The founder of the cannabis-using, syncretic Judeo-Christian sect called Temple 420, Rubin never hid his roots in the well-heeled town, and even titled his memoir of marijuana adventures *9021Grow,* after the hit TV show that portrayed young residents of "the Hills."

Although he was raised in a Jewish family, Rubin was fascinated by Jesus and Christian teachings from an early age and studied both the Old and New Testaments. In high school he discovered that cannabis created not just a social but a spiritual bond between him and other users, and his commitment to its sacramental use deepened at UCLA, where he was both a prolegalization activist and the head of a student club that discussed comparative religion and mysticism.

After graduation, Rubin opened a West Hollywood hemp store called 2000 BC. He was encouraged when California legalized medical marijuana but felt that too many of the suddenly legitimate dispensaries were run by gangster-types who intimidated patients and saw the plant as just another intoxicant to vend at profit. Rubin believed that places of cannabis consumption were "churches" that served a conscious community and decided to open a dispensary where the sacramental nature of the plant was respected and honored.

When the Supreme Court ruled in favor of a church's ayahuasca use in *Gonzales v. O Centro Espírita Beneficente União do Vegetal* in early 2006, Rubin assumed that their religious exemption would apply to cannabis-using sects as well. That year, on the stoner's holiday of April 20, he opened Temple 420 as both a dispensary and a church, in a building at the tourist-trafficked corner of Hollywood and La Brea.

Unlike the entheogenic sects who drew from Eastern religion, Native American traditions, or Neo-Pagan spirituality to give their practices meaning and structure, Temple 420 was based solidly in Abrahamic monotheistic faith. The temple proclaimed that it was "part of The Church the G-D* of the Bible established through his son and disciples. We believe the Bible and the Holy Spirit are the Authority. We believe we're established and brought into G-D's family through Christ as a Judeo-Christian Church."[59]

The study and practice of both faiths' teachings were part of temple doings. Bible studies were held on Wednesday and Friday

---

*The use of "G-D" as substitution for the name of the Creator is done as a sign of respect in compliance with Jewish law.

nights, and the Jewish Sabbath was observed from Friday to Saturday evenings. Every Saturday at 4:20 p.m. temple members read the Old Testament, while on Sundays they consulted the New Testament at the same hour. The temple stressed that although cannabis was a divine gift that aided their spiritual practice, it was not itself a deity, and the biblical God and his Son would always be the focus of worship and devotion.

A self-confessed "Jew for Jesus," Rubin emphasized that the primary mission of the temple was compassion, since "G-D is Love (1 John 4:8)." As part of this mission of kindness, the temple's dispensary sold medical cannabis at an affordable price to its clientele, many of whom were cash-strapped cancer patients or disabled people. To Rubin and the temple, it was both their constitutional right and their sacred duty to use and distribute the plant for both physical and spiritual healing of all peoples, whatever their faith.

Unfortunately, the local law didn't agree. Shortly after the temple's founding, the LAPD decided that the Judeo-Christian faith it practiced wasn't a "real" religion, and therefore the First Amendment protection it claimed for cannabis use was null and void. Cops busted Rubin in November 2006, and the married father of seven and registered Republican spent the next few years in and out of L.A.'s jails and courts, fighting an array of charges and suing the city for violation of his religious rights. He even ran for mayor of Los Angeles to publicize both his legal plight and the healing powers of cannabis and came in seventh in a field of ten candidates.

At present, the temple is active mostly online, where it hosts videos of Rubin's sermons and raises money by selling e-coins and NFTs. Rubin told me that he still conducts Bible studies with temple faithful but is careful to hold them in discreet private spaces, much as a first-century Christian pastor would in Rome. With cannabis now fully legal in the Golden State, the temple founder remains confident that he'll soon be able to emerge from the catacombs and spread the message of God's love and the life-changing powers of cannabis openly in the City of Angels.

TEXAS LSD CULT

In the July–September 1970 issue of the *Journal of American Folklore*, scholars Richard Bauman and Neil McCabe described a Dallas-based underground spiritual organization that used LSD in its rituals.

The two academics reported that the nameless group had been active in Dallas since the mid-1960s, and that it employed a transcendent and monistic theology influenced by Hindu and Buddhist concepts, and a rite-of-passage initiation for its members reminiscent of the ancient mystery schools. Its aim was to bring initiates into a "mystical merging of the self with some universal and unitary principle and the attainment of a totally new and non-rational perspective on existence."[60]

Prospective members had to be at least twenty-one years of age, prior LSD users, and interviewed and approved by the group leader. Once qualified, the prospect was instructed in the finer points of Zen, yoga, and self-hypnotism, and led through at least one acid session to determine the proper dosage for the initiation ceremony.

The ceremony, which seemed to be the cult's only collective rite, took place in the basement of a member's house. Initiates were taken into an upper room, dosed with acid, and then led through a series of yogic and self-hypnotic exercises to prepare themselves for the ceremony. Meanwhile, the congregation, which included the leader and his wife, twelve elders, and a small choir, assembled in the basement and celebrated an opening liturgy. Eventually, the initiate was led downstairs, and the main rite began.

Although the ritual itself was a secret, the group did reveal part of its litany to Bauman and McCabe. The litany was largely based in writings from the Upanishads and the Zen mystics that emphasized the death of the ego, the unity of all existence, and the Clear White Light and the Void that could be attained by sincere seekers.

As students of folklore, the authors were most interested in how the litany parodied common proverbs, such as "Boys will be boys," and "Live and let live," to illuminate and explain the psychedelic experience. The readings, alternately recited by the sect leader and the chorus, told the initiate that "Void will be Void," and urged them to "Live and yet die, die and yet live," and to go with the flow, "Out of sight, out of sight, Mind," to that nameless place where being and nonbeing were one, and the seeker could die in ego and be reborn in spirit.

Since Bauman and McCabe as outsiders were forbidden to witness the whole rite and were mainly concerned with the folkloric aspects of the litany, their article revealed little else about the group. Information on it from other sources seems nonexistent, and the group is almost certainly long defunct, its lysergic rites now lost save in the distant memories of its still-living initiates.

TRANS HUMAN CHURCH OF ENLIGHTENMENT

In the early 2000s this Toronto-based group launched a website named the Spice. It claimed to be dedicated to "a scientific approach to spirituality" based in transhumanism—a philosophy popular among techies and science-fiction enthusiasts that seeks to enhance and extend human life and expand consciousness by developing cutting-edge health and communication technologies.

The Trans Human Church of Enlightenment drew on its theology from the writings of one Greg Adams. A "philosopher, inventor, artist, scientist, computer geek, consultant, husband, and plain simple person,"[61] Adams maintained his Art of Perception website to disseminate his "Adams Unification Theory of Quantum Cosmology," along with other pieces about spirituality, philosophy, economics, and politics. A philosophical libertarian, Adams ran both his personal site and the church's for "the open exchange of thoughts, beliefs, and ideas" about the nature of enlightenment with fellow seekers.

The church named a mysterious substance it called "spice" as its sacrament and represented itself as the foremost authority on it. For $120 CAN, interested parties could order a gram of spice, which contained roughly fifty-five doses of the chemical. Once the gram was shipped out, the customer was considered a member of the church, and a communicant in their search for better living through psychedelic chemistry and transhumanist technology.

According to a reporter for *The Entheogen Review,* spice was the chemical compound 2C-I (2,5-Dimethoxy-4-iodophenethylamine). A phenethylamine first synthesized by legendary entheogenic chemist Alexander Shulgin, 2C-I was legal in Canada at the time of the church's founding, and popular in the European and North American rave scenes. Listed as a Schedule I drug in the United States because of its chemical kinship to amphetamines, 2C-I, known in the rave world as "Smiles," has been implicated in the deaths of at least three American users, including *Sons of Anarchy* actor Johnny Lewis. The church probably intended to head off its Canadian prohibition by declaring it a religious sacrament, much in the manner of other sects discussed in this volume.

Ironically, the church was busted by the Canadian government not for its spice sales, but for unauthorized use of the country's Coat of Arms on its website. The Dominion finally got around to prohibiting 2C-I along with various related compounds in 2016, but by then the church had long since stopped advertising its chemical wares, and its modest internet presence can only be found today as archived web pages.

UNIVERSAL LIFE CHURCH OF CHRIST LIGHT

Ira Mullins was a devotee of the *Urantia Book,* a famous "channeled" work by an unknown author that proffers "enlarged concepts and advanced truth" about the origins of Earth and the Universe, the nature and doings of God, and the life of Jesus. A former Rosicrucian Fellowship member who'd been dissatisfied with that group's ascetic path to higher consciousness, Mullins claimed that while reading the *Urantia Book* under the influence of cannabis, peyote, and LSD, he entered a transcendental state of "total and complete union with God and his Lord and Master, Jesus."

In the early 1970s Mullins and his wife founded the Universal Life Church of Christ Light on his property in Mendocino County, California, to create a sacred community based on the vision. The sect was a congregation of Kirby Hensley's Universal Life Church, a nondoctrinal mail-order ministry that has ordained millions of would-be clerics for free since 1962, and chartered thousands of nontraditional fellowships under its corporate aegis. Although the ULC forbids its congregations to use their religious status to challenge drug laws, a few of them have nonetheless attempted to organize entheogenic circles in the mother church's name.

Universal Life Church of Christ Light members lived on the Mullins' property in tipis. There they worshipped by sitting in a circle, sharing sacramental cannabis, chanting the om mantra, reading passages from the *Urantia Book,* and meditating on the attributes and teachings of the Christ. Mullins later claimed he'd held at least a thousand of these ceremonies on the land.

Things went bad on May 30, 1972, when one church member, angered that the Mullinses had banned him from the land for his excessive boozing, led a warrant-bearing sheriff's deputy to a cannabis crop on the property. Busted and eventually convicted for cultivation, the sixty-year-old Mullins protested that both his First and Fourth Amendment rights had been violated; he maintained that the cannabis plants were "an object of worship and a sacrament of his church, essential to an exclusively religious ritual," and that the raid on his property constituted an unreasonable search and seizure.

In *People v. Mullins,* the Court of Appeals ruled that the church head's religious-freedom argument had no merit based on *People v. Woody* and similar cases and cited other rulings that justified the raid. His conviction upheld, Mullins and his sect disappeared from public view.

UNIVERSAL ORTHODOX DIOCESE

On December 12, 2008, Gregory Karl Davis, a former Anglican monk, was asleep in a cave at Negril Beach, Jamaica. Suddenly a voice awoke him and told him that the biblical Tree of Life was the cannabis plant.

Inspired by the revelation, he returned to his home in Atlanta, Georgia. There, he discovered the works of Polish anthropologist Sula Benet, who theorized that the true "holy anointing oil" in biblical times was made of cannabis, or *kaneh bosm,* which she claimed was later mistranslated as "calamus" in Exodus 30:23. Based on the data, Davis realized that cannabis oil was the charismatic element that cleansed a baptized person from sin and allowed them to partake of the Christian sacraments.

Davis believed that he was commissioned to reestablish the true, cannabis-oil-using Christian faith and founded the Universal Orthodox Diocese. According to its website, the diocese "proclaims the Evangel of Revelation 14:6, 7, that Jesus is the Anointed physically with KNH BSM (canna spice or cannabis) in fulfillment of all the law and the prophets as King like Saul and David, as are all Christian kings, together with Haile Selassie the First. And that KNH BSM (canna spice or ganja) cures all cancers and is the Tree of Life in Revelation, and the leaves of the tree were for the healing of the nations."[62]

The diocese saw its mission "to provide this (God given herb agriculturally processed by Rastaman as sacrament and medicine), in obedience to our religious duty owed to the indigent and helpless men, women and children of our fallen world for their spiritual and physical healing."[63] Its theology combines the mystic writings of Christian visionary Emanuel Swedenborg, the practices of the Ethiopian Orthodox Tewahedo Church, and the Rastafari revelations of Emperor Haile Selassie as a divine leader and ganja as a holy sacrament.

The Right Reverend Davis claimed episcopal authority to lead the sect not by way of Christian apostolic succession, but through a series of initiations involving such disparate entities as the Atlanta Boy Choir, the nontrinitarian Church of God International, and "Almighty God, to be His Servant to form Order for the New Church age of the Holy Spirit." He ran the diocese as a *corporation sole*—a legal entity that allows an individual to control a nonprofit religious body without bylaws, a board of directors, or other organizational complications.

A self-proclaimed "Doctor of KNH BSM," Bishop Davis also promoted the healing properties of cannabis oil. Through a charitable organization, he produced a low-THC version of the oil, which he distributed to patients who carry a Georgia State medical-marijuana card. However, he was not averse to consuming the herb in other forms; Bishop Davis believed that the various New Testament passages about Jesus appearing in "clouds" meant that the Christ literally manifests in cannabis smoke.

Not surprisingly, Bishop Davis was largely condemned by the few mainstream Christians who took note of his ministry. Orthodox Christians especially took a dim view of his Eastern church title and vestments, and declaimed his cannabis-centric ministry, and his generally heterodox public pronouncements and eccentric image.

Although he managed a data-rich website, and posted prolifically on cannabis-related internet forums, the bishop seemed to gain few real-world followers beyond Alabamans Brenda and Bruce Shoop. When the two anointed Universal Orthodox Diocese missionaries ran afoul of drug laws in 2008, they failed to persuade a court that their cannabis-centric religious practices were valid. Still, Bishop Davis continued his online campaign to convince Christendom that anointment with cannabis oil was the key to a reformed and revitalized faith, until his death in July 2022. Although the church's website is still active, its future as a religious organization is unknown.

WAY OF INFINITE HARMONY

For thousands of years, the Chinese have used cannabis for both medicinal and ceremonial purposes. In the Gobi Desert and elsewhere across the vast country, archaeologists have uncovered tombs of shamans, nobles, and warriors containing offerings of marijuana buds, which date back to around 500 BCE, the era of Confucius and Lao Tse.

To the ancient Chinese the Princess Magu, "Immortal Xu Miao" (Infinite Harmony), was the Goddess of Cannabis. One of the Taoist Immortals, Magu always appears in the guise of a teenage girl, and is often accompanied by cranes and deer, or depicted holding peaches or wine—the symbols of eternal life.

Magu's worship in the modern West has been established by the Way of Infinite Harmony. An internet-based group, the Way describes itself as "a Taoist sect based on the Immortalization of Her Holiness Princess Magu, Goddess of Cannabis, [that aims] to attain the Tao (achieve Enlightenment). It is our belief that Cannabis is the key to understanding the Self and achieving true internal cultivation, as shown to us by Her Holiness."[64]

The sect's scriptures are contained in Way of Infinite Harmony, a self-published book that reprints legends and stories of Princess Magu, many of which appear in English for the first time. Followers of Magu are also advised to read the key works of the Taoist canon, such as the *Tao Te Ching, Zhuang Zhou, Liezi, Huahujing,* and the *Wenzi.*

To Magu's devotees, the Magu Xian Shou is the most sacred of all Way scriptures. It is the story of how the Goddess gave cannabis wine to the Queen Mother of the West to ensure the matriarch's longevity

Fig. P2.4. Princess Magu, the Taoist Goddess of Cannabis
Photograph courtesy of the Museum of Warsaw.

and demonstrates that the deities recognize that the Path of Magu—the Way of Infinite Harmony—is a path to the Eternal Tao. Devotees chant the words "Magu Xian Shou" as a mantra and believe that meditation on the chant and the story bring one closer to attaining the Tao and knowing the Self.

Other than "Cannaisseur," a medical-marijuana patient and YouTube poster who has described his devotion to Magu in online videos, the Way of Infinite Harmony seems to have no visible followers beyond the anonymous founder. Nevertheless, the THC-Taoist sect continues its mission as both a modern Western take on the ancient Chinese traditions, and an heir to the far older path of enlightenment, and union with the One, through chemical ecstasy.

ZIDE DOOR CHURCH OF ENTHEOGENIC PLANTS

This sect based in Oakland, California, made headlines in the summer of 2020, when cops raided their warehouse-based church. According to official sources, the lawmen confiscated over $200,000 worth of cannabis and psilocybin mushrooms—the Zide Door's declared sacraments. Weeks later, founder Dave Hodges defiantly reopened the space, and began a freedom of religion legal war with the City of Oakland.

Hodges, a longtime activist in the Bay Area's medical-marijuana scene, first conceived the group after a high-dose psilocybin trip, where he experienced the Power that had first made itself known in humanity's shaman-haunted past. Hodges calls this maximum-strength sacrament a "god dose," and the church's website offers practical advice for trippers who ingest these super-sized supplements.

The church also endorses "the advanced entheogenic use of cannabis" to develop insight into oneself and one's circumstances. "Once someone learns to focus their inner eye," says church doctrine, "cannabis allows them to use it to understand life, the world and the teachings from the spirits that communicate through mushrooms and other entheogens."[65]

Conveniently enough, the church offers psilocybin 'shrooms and cannabis to its members, which Hodges estimates number in the tens of thousands. Its website offers free memberships to all adult visitors who agree with its principles, provide a government ID, and can describe why they want to join. The site also dispenses dosage and trip information not only to god-dose cosmic explorers, but to casual microdosers as well.

An allied nondenominational interfaith organization, the Church of Ambrosia, functions as the sect's more theoretical arm. Not to be confused with Texas's Amanita-oriented Ambrosia Society (see page 259), the church's website posits that not only religion, but human communication itself, evolved from primates' experiences with psychedelic mushrooms—the "fruit of the Tree of Knowledge" that pushed the species into an intimate but strained fellowship with God, far beyond the lordly innocence of the beasts of the field. The church maintains that microdoses and god doses alike "help you connect with who you truly are and what exists beyond," and may even make you smarter by building new neural pathways in the brain.

Until COVID-19 struck, the church held services every Sunday at 4:20 p.m., where the sacraments were distributed and shared. Cannabis and psilocybin continue to be available for walk-ins, so long as they're verified church members.

The Zide Door is a vital part of a Bay Area culture already friendlier to entheogens than perhaps any other part of North America. When the church was busted, Oakland had already legally decriminalized psilocybin; the cops used the building's unlicensed vending and health complaints about sacramental pot smoke as the rationales for the raid. Even then, the charges didn't stick.

Just a year later a bill advanced through the California Assembly to legalize small doses of not only psilocybin, but mescaline, LSD, MDMA, and DMT statewide. Activist group Decriminalize California went one step further than this and supported a proposition that would essentially legalize psilocybin in any quantity for adult state residents, stressing the "spiritual, religious" nature of the magic-mushroom experience.

Slowly, the third millennium world was discarding the antientheogen prohibitions of the previous age. Sects dedicated to their use will continue to emerge and serve communities of seekers pursuing this most primal and powerful form of spiritual experience.

PSYCHEDELIC SECTS

From Prehistory into the
Third Millennium

In the end, what are we to make of the sixty-odd churches, circles, sects, and cults covered in these pages?

Are they, as their critics often charge, nothing more than gaggles of drug-sodden thrill seekers and social misfits hiding behind spurious rationales about "consciousness expansion" and "freedom of religion"?

Or are they legitimate, if unorthodox, spiritual organizations that are rooted in a primal human need to experience ecstatic and transcendent states, and that are carrying on the ancient shamanic and sacramental practices of religious traditions from around the world?

In the title of a 1971 booklet, the controversial guru Rajneesh (a.k.a. Osho) called LSD "a Shortcut to False Samadhi [meditative enlightenment]." The title seemed to sum up the attitudes of many orthodox religionists from Eastern and Western paths toward the use of entheogens. Divine consciousness, they maintain, can only be achieved through intense spiritual work, usually accompanied by the renunciation of earthly concerns and pleasures, and often taking a lifetime or more to realize. To them, taking drugs only produces a short-term, crude counterfeit of the truly spiritual transcendent state, and bears as much resemblance to the mysticism of the saints and bodhisattvas, as masturbation does to tantric sex.

For the most part, the psychedelic religionists have taken such criticisms in stride. They assert that entheogenic rapture is physiologically and psychologically indistinguishable from the altered states of consciousness created by intense prayer, meditation, fasting, and other more socially acceptable forms of religious devotion, and can produce the same lasting positive effects as the ascetic religious paths. Certainly, the testimony of countless individuals in both traditional societies and the postwar West, who've found in the hallucinogens transformative spiritual experiences that eluded them in other faiths or practices, must count for something as well.

The psychedelic religionists also point to the consistent presence of consciousness-altering chemicals in the history of global religions. From the mysterious Soma of the Hindus to the hemp seed the Buddha consumed each day, to the sacramental wine of Judaism and Christianity, to the hashish indulgences of the Ismaili Muslim warriors, divine intoxication in one form or another appears repeatedly as part of the human spiritual experience. And for shamanic traditions the world over, psychoactive plants and fungi are key elements in the quest to attain transcendent consciousness.

Although persecuted and driven underground by churches and states who saw their entheogenic practices as satanic and subversive, shamans, witches, curanderos, alchemists, and others nevertheless tended the hidden flames of psychedelic gnosis through the centuries. As biologists, anthropologists, and adventurers began to examine the mysteries of psychoactive substances during the twentieth century, the hidden flames began to flicker anew in Western academia and bohemia, breathing fresh air and drawing scientists and seekers alike to their light.

Nowhere were these mavericks more faithfully represented than in North America. For four centuries the United States and Canada had absorbed waves of missionaries, pilgrims, and religious dissenters of all kinds who saw in the New World the place where they would create the New Jerusalem promised by prophecy, according to their own lights. It was only natural that in a land of constitutionally protected religious freedom and diversity, the rediscovery of "plant shamanism" would take the form of churches and sects devoted to the sacramental use of the entheogens.

Appropriately enough, the phenomenon began with the continent's indigenous peoples. When peyote spirituality began to spread among an American Indian population beaten down and demoralized by centuries of colonialism and conquest, it was organized as an incorporated church under the First Amendment guarantees of religious freedom. But that freedom wasn't always acknowledged by the courts, and the Native American Church spent eight decades fighting for the right to ingest a plant whose usage predated the American government by millennia. By the mid-nineties, it emerged victorious, a symbol and beneficiary of constitutional protections for dissident and minority faiths.

The dozens of psychedelic religions that appeared in the Native American Church's wake used similar religious-freedom justifications but represented a very different form of North American spiritual tradition. From the earliest days, the continent had birthed new sects and cults that reflected both the experiences of New World peoples and the unorthodox visions of their founders and followers. Groups ranging from the Mormons and the Pentecostals to tiny cults led by eccentric preachers and self-proclaimed prophets grew up wild and strong in American soil, each adding its own color and pattern to the human religious tapestry.

During the sixties rapid changes in Western social norms altered traditional definitions of what *clergy, churches,* and *religions* themselves were. In contemporary North America, the changing definitions began to be reflected in both court decisions and popular opinion, as increasing religious diversity widened the scope of spiritual possibility and practice for millions.

Communities that gather privately and approach the Divine with the aid of the "plant teachers," are migrating from the fringes toward the mainstream, and finding greater legal and social tolerance for their activities than did their predecessors. Nowhere is this more apparent than in the appearance of legal public spaces dedicated to psychoactive spirituality. Barring a neo-prohibitionist backlash, it's almost certain that such spaces will continue to emerge in entheogen-friendly locales across the continent.

From indigenous prehistory to a century of First Amendment controversies and court battles, to the twenty-first century's psychedelic renaissance, it's been a long, strange trip for the entheogenic sects. And it shows no signs of ending any time soon.

PSYCHEDELIC SUBSTANCES AND THEIR ASSOCIATED SECTS

*An * indicates the primary sacrament of a group
that uses multiple substances in its practices.*

2C-I (2,5-DIMETHOXY-4-IODOPHENETHYLAMINE)

Trans Human Church of
　Enlightenment

5-MEO-DMT (SEE BUFOTENINE)

Acacia

*Oratory of Mystical Sacraments

AMANITA MUSCARIA

*Ambrosia Society

Oratory of Mystical Sacraments

AYAHUASCA

*Arizona Yage Assembly

*Ayahuasca Healings

Church of Gnostic Luminism

Oklevueha Native American Church

Oratory of Mystical Sacraments

Soul Quest Church of Mother Earth Inc.

Temple 420

BUFOTENINE (5-MEO-DMT)

Church of Gnostic Luminism

Church of the Toad of Light

CANNABIS

American Council of Internal Divinity

Brotherhood of Eternal Love

*Chicago Jazz Cannabis Circle

Church of Cognizance

Church of Gnostic Luminism

Church of the Golden Rule of Charity

Church of Naturalism

Church of the Realized Fantasy

Church of Sunshine

Church of the Universe

*Ethiopian Zion Coptic Church

Farm, The

*First Church of Cannabis

CANNABIS (CONT.)

*Hawai'i Cannabis (THC) Ministry
*Healing Church, The
*International Church of Cannabis
Lazy Nickels
Neo-American Church
New American Church
*New World Church
Oklevueha Native American Church
Oratory of Mystical Sacraments
*Pot Illuminati
Psychedelic Venus Church
Religion of Drug
Shiva Fellowship
Shivalila
Universal Life Church of Christ Light
Universal Orthodox Diocese
Way of Infinite Harmony
*Zide Door Church of Entheogenic Plants

DPT (N,N-DIPROPYLTRYPTAMINE)

Temple of the True Inner Light

HAWAIIAN WOODROSE SEEDS

Church of the North American Shamans

LSD (LYSERGIC ACID DIETHYLAMIDE)

American Council of Internal Divinity
*Brotherhood of Eternal Love
Church of Gnostic Luminism
*Church of the Golden Rule of Charity
*Church of Naturalism
*Church of Sunshine
Dog Commune
League for Spiritual Discovery
*New American Church

Psychedelic Peace Fellowship
Psychedelic Venus Church
Servants of Awareness
Shivalila
*Texas LSD Cult

LYSERGIC MORNING GLORY SEEDS

Church of the North American Shamans

MDA (3,4-METHYLENEDIOXYAMPHETAMINE)

Temple of the True Inner Light

MDMA (3,4-METHYLENEDIOXY-METHAMPHETAMINE)

New World Church

MESCALINE

Church of the Awakening
Church of Gnostic Luminism
Church of Sunshine

PCP (PHENCYCLIDINE)

New American Church

PEYOTE

American Church of God
*Church of the Awakening
Church of the First Born
Church of the North American Shamans
Ghost Clan
Grady Peyote Group
Native American Church
Native American Indigenous Church
*Neo-American Church
*Oklevueha Native American Church
Oratory of Mystical Sacraments
Peyote Way Church of God

PSILOCYBIN

Church of Sunshine

Church of Gnostic Luminism

*Church of the North American Shamans

Church of the One Sermon Divine
    Assembly

Fane of the Psilocybe Mushroom Association

International Copelandia Church of God

New World Church

Oklevueha Native American Church

*Oratory of Mystical Sacraments

*Zide Door Church of Entheogenic Plants

SALVIA DIVINORUM

Church of the Divine Sage

Church of Gnostic Luminism

Church of the North American Shamans

*First International Church of Salvia
    Divinorum

SAN PEDRO CACTUS

Church of the North American Shamans

Oklevueha Native American Church

Oratory of Mystical Sacraments

SYRIAN RUE

*Oratory of Mystical Sacraments

TOBACCO

Church of the North American Shamans

UNSPECIFIED

Church of the Psychedelic Mystic

Fellowship of the Clear Light

Paleo-American Church

VARIOUS LEGAL PSYCHOACTIVE SUBSTANCES

Church of the Tree of Life

NOTES

Because hyperlinks do not always remain viable, we are no longer including URLs in our resources, notes, or bibliographic entries. Instead, we are providing the name of the website where this information may be found.

CHAPTER 1. THE NATIVE AMERICAN CHURCH

1. El-Seediab, "Prehistoric Peyote Use," 238–42.
2. Furst, *Hallucinogens and Culture*, 13.
3. The 1918 Articles of Incorporation of the Native American Church are available on the Prairie Creek Settlement website.
4. Blair, "Habit Indulgence in Certain Cactaceous Plants Among the Indians," 1033–34.
5. People v. Woody, 61 Cal.2d 716 (1964).
6. American Indian Religious Freedom Act Amendments of 1994, H.R.4230, 103rd Cong. (1994).

CHAPTER 2. THE CHURCH OF THE AWAKENING

1. Aiken, "The Church of the Awakening," 172.
2. Aiken, "The Church of the Awakening," 172.
3. Aiken, "Can Drugs Lead You to God?"
4. Aiken, "The Church of the Awakening," 165.
5. Melton, "Affirmations: Church of the Awakening," in *American Religious Creeds*, 100.
6. "Delic Missionaries Bring Clear Light Here," *Berkeley Barb*, October 21, 1966, 4.
7. "Delic Missionaries Bring Clear Light Here," 4.
8. Merton to Aiken, August 14, 1967, "Merton's Correspondence with Aiken, John W., Dr.," The Thomas Merton Center at Bellarmine University, Louisville, Ky.
9. Department of Justice, Bureau of Narcotics and Dangerous Drugs, Depressant

and Stimulant Drugs, "Use of Peyote for Religious Purposes," 35 Fed. Reg. 14789, 14792 (September 23, 1970).

10. Department of Justice, "Use of Peyote for Religious Purposes," 35 Fed. Reg., at 14793.

11. Department of Justice, "Use of Peyote for Religious Purposes," 35 Fed. Reg., at 14793.

12. Kennedy v. Bureau of Narcotics and Dangerous Drugs, 459 F.2d 415, 417 (9th Cir. 1972).

CHAPTER 3. THE PEYOTE WAY CHURCH OF GOD

1. Eric Tsetsi, "A Remote Arizona Church Offers Followers Peyote-Induced Psychedelic Trips," *Village Voice,* January 8, 2014.

2. Coogan, *Dreamer of the Day,* 424.

3. Walter Bowart, "Psychedelic Reservations," *East Village Other,* March 15, 1966, 6.

4. People of the State of Colorado v. Mana Pardeahtan, Criminal Action no. 9454, Denver County Court, June 27, 1967.

5. "Detailed Chronology of Events in the History of the Peyote Way Church," Peyote Way (website), accessed September 25, 2022.

6. "Word of Wisdom," section 89, Peyote Way (website), accessed September 25, 2022.

7. "What We Believe," Peyote Way (website), accessed September 25, 2022.

CHAPTER 4. THE OKLEVUEHA NATIVE AMERICAN CHURCH

1. Sarah Laskow, "In 2016, the 'First Legal Ayahuasca Church' Got Shut Down. Was It a Scam—or a New Religion?" Atlas Obscura (online), September 16, 2016.

2. "The Making of a Seminole Medicine Man," Native American Churches (website), accessed September 25, 2022.

3. "Clifford 'White Buffalo Man' Jake: Healing and Blessing," Native American Churches (website), accessed September 25, 2022.

4. Oklevueha Earthwalks Native American Church of Utah Inc., Federal ID #841402813, available on the Prairie Creek Settlement website, accessed September 25, 2022.

5. Chen Cho Dorge, "Native American Church Oklevueha NAC Will Protect You," (blog post), DMT Nexus (website), February 28, 2011.

6. Hailey Branson-Potts, "Topless Carwash Raises Cash for Deputies Wounded in Gun Battle at Rastafarian Pot Farm," *Los Angeles Times,* September 9, 2019.

7. Karina Brown, "Native American Church Resists Pot Enthusiasts," *Courthouse News Service* (website), April 19, 2016.

8. Brown, "Native American Church Resists Pot Enthusiasts."

9. "National Council Does Not Condone Faux Native American Churches or Marijuana Use," Indian Country Today (online), last updated September 13, 2018.

10. Brown, "Native American Church Resists Pot Enthusiasts."

CHAPTER 5. THE LEAGUE FOR SPIRITUAL DISCOVERY

1. Greenfield, *Timothy Leary*, 72.

2. Greenfield, *Timothy Leary*, 103.

3. Leary, *High Priest*, 25.

4. Greenfield, *Timothy Leary*, 113.

5. Greenfield, *Timothy Leary*, 184.

6. Greenfield, *Timothy Leary*, 184.

7. Leary, *High Priest*, 253.

8. Leary, *High Priest*, 256.

9. Greenfield, *Timothy Leary*, 187.

10. "Statement of Purpose of the International Federation for Internal Freedom," Chartered Board of Directors of IFIF, January 24, 1963, in Penner's (ed) *Timothy Leary: The Harvard Years*.

11. "Statement of Purpose," IFIF, January 24, 1963.

12. Greenfield, *Timothy Leary*, 212.

13. "Millbrook Summer School Psychedelic Courses," Castalia Foundation, n.d.

14. "Millbrook Summer School Psychedelic Courses," Castalia Foundation, n.d.

15. "Timothy Leary Interview" *Playboy*, September 1966, 100.

16. Leary, *High Priest*, 320.

17. Leary, *Start Your Own Religion*, 3.

18. "Straits Leery of Leary League," *Berkeley Barb*, December 16, 1966, 2.

19. Wilson, *Cosmic Trigger*, 41.

CHAPTER 6. THE NEO-AMERICAN CHURCH

1. "The Neo-American Church Catechism and Handbook: A Review by Timothy Leary," in Kleps's, *The Boo Hoo Bible*, 208.

2. Kleps, *Millbrook: The True Story*, 12–13.

3. "Membership Application," The Original Kleptonian Neo-American Church, n.d., in Kleps's *The Boo Hoo Bible*, 218.

4. Kleps, *The Boo Hoo Bible*, 3.

5. Narcotic Rehabilitation Act of 1966: Hearings Before a Special Subcommittee of the Committee on the Judiciary, Second Session, 89th Cong. 413 (1966) (statement of Arthur Kleps, Director, Neo-American Church, Morning Glory Lodge, Cranberry Lake, N.Y.).

6. United States v. Kuch, 288 F. Supp. 439, 444 (D.D.C. 1968).

7. Kleps, *Millbrook: A Narrative*, 90.

8. Ed Dwyer and Robert Singer, "Art Kleps, Chief Boo-Hoo, Neo-American Church," *High Times*, March 1976, 21.

CHAPTER 7. THE BROTHERHOOD OF ETERNAL LOVE

1. Tendler and May, *The Brotherhood of Eternal Love*, 63.

2. Schou, *Orange Sunshine*, 32.

3. Tendler and May, *The Brotherhood of Eternal Love*, 65.

4. Tendler and May, *The Brotherhood of Eternal Love*, 65.

5. Tendler and May, *The Brotherhood of Eternal Love*, 65.

6. Tendler and May, *The Brotherhood of Eternal Love*, 67.

7. Black, *Acid: The Secret History of LSD*, 21.

CHAPTER 8. SHIVALILA

1. Yablonsky, *The Hippie Trip*, 43.

2. Yablonsky, *The Hippie Trip*, 43.

3. Salisbury and Lorenz, *Gridley Wright: Confessions of a Yogi in Bali*, Audio CD.

4. Salisbury and Lorenz, *Gridley Wright*.

5. Children's Liberation Front, *The Book of the Mother*, 16.

CHAPTER 9. THE CHURCH OF NATURALISM

1. Rolfe, *Fat Man on the Left*, 91.

2. "Head News," *East Village Other*, September 29, 1970, 21.

3. Cross, "Chicago's Improbable Drug Rescue Team," 44.

4. Cross, "Chicago's Improbable Drug Rescue Team," 44.

5. Lande, *Mindstyles, Lifestyles*, 273.

6. Rolfe, *Fat Man on the Left*, 84.

7. Rolfe, *Fat Man on the Left*, 92.

CHAPTER 10. THE CHURCH OF THE TREE OF LIFE

1. Gottlieb, *Legal Highs*, vii.

CHAPTER 11. TEMPLE OF THE TRUE INNER LIGHT

1. Billy Gram, "The Psychedelic Church," *Yipster Times*, Fall/Winter 1975, 14.

2. Gram, "The Psychedelic Church," 14.

3. Native American Church of New York v. U.S., 468 F. Supp. 1247, 1249 (S.D.N.Y. 1979).

4. Gorman, "Divine Smoke and God's Flesh: Psychedelics and Religion," *High Times*, 41–44, 75.

5. "Report: Church Lures Converts with 'Designer Drug,'" *United Press International* (website), July 2, 1988.

6. Gorman, "Divine Smoke and God's Flesh," 41–44, 75.

7. Mac Hinelf, "The Temple of the True Inner Light," Trance Am (website), August 29, 2020.

8. "The Serpent," Temple of the True Inner Light, Psychede Tripod (website), accessed September 25, 2022.

9. "The Signs and 'Near Death' Experiences," Temple of the True Inner Light, Psychede Tripod (website), accessed June 23, 2021.

10. Lyttle, "Drug Based Religions," 271–84.

CHAPTER 12. THE SHIVA FELLOWSHIP

1. "Shiva Missionary and Cop Go Up in Cloud of Smoke," *Berkeley Barb,* June 14–20, 1968, 7.

2. Art Johnston, "Kick Out the Jams! The Jungle Is Ours!" *Berkeley Barb,* March 14–21, 1969, 11.

3. Willie Minzey, "Shiva Head," *San Francisco Good Times,* June 26, 1970, 12.

4. Mother Boats, "10 to Life for Willie," *Berkeley Barb,* June 18–24, 1971, 2.

CHAPTER 13. THE PSYCHEDELIC VENUS CHURCH

1. *Venereal Missal,* Psychedelic Venus Church, n.d., 3.

2. Sides, *Erotic City,* 71.

3. *Venereal Missal,* 3.

4. *Venereal Missal,* 4.

5. Graysmith, *Zodiac Unmasked,* 143.

CHAPTER 14. THE ETHIOPIAN ZION COPTIC CHURCH

1. Middleton, *Ganja Warrior Priest,* 159.

2. Middleton, *Ganja Warrior Priest,* 213.

3. "Holy Smoke," *60 Minutes,* CBS News, October 28, 1979.

4. Carl Hiaasen, "The Law and Brother Louv," *Miami Herald,* August 2, 1981, 314.

5. Olsen v. DEA, 878 F.2d 1458, 1463 (D.C. Cir. 1989).

6. Tod Mikuriya, "Judge Ruth Bader Ginsberg—So much for the First Amendment," Drug Library (website), accessed September 25, 2022.

CHAPTER 15. THE CHURCH OF THE UNIVERSE

1. Loehndorf, "The Canadian Inquisition."

2. Assembly of the Church of the Universe, "FAQs," IAMM (defunct website), accessed September 25, 2022.

3. Assembly of the Church of the Universe, "Church Credo," IAMM (defunct website), accessed September 25, 2022.

4. Loehndorf, "The Canadian Inquisition."

5. Watts, "Bongos, Cymbals, Bells Herald 'Ecstasy Mission' for Church's Birthday," 15.

6. "Hamilton to Consider Creating Nude Beach," *Windsor Star,* May 7, 1999, 23.

7. Tracy Gordon, "Cannabis is 'our cross, tree of life,' say accused pot priests," *Religion News Service* (website), April 13, 2010.

8. Michelle DiPardo, "Church Allegedly Dealt Pot," *National Post,* October 28, 2006, 14.

9. Dan Nolan, "Pot Advocate Walter Tucker Dies at 79," *Hamilton Spectator,* April 26, 2012.

10. Teviah Moro, "Michael Baldasaro, Hamilton's High Priest of Pot, Dead at 67," *Hamilton Spectator,* June 9, 2016.

CHAPTER 16. THE HAWAI'I CANNABIS (THC) MINISTRY

1. "Holy Herb Sacrament—The Religion of Jesus Church," Salvation Anointed (website), accessed October 17, 2022.

2. "THC Ministry: The Hawai'i Cannabis Ministry," THC-Ministry (website), accessed January 15, 2021.

3. Cozad, *God on High,* 63.

4. Cozad, *God on High,* 64.

CHAPTER 17. THE INTERNATIONAL CHURCH OF CANNABIS

1. "The Basics," Elevationists (website), accessed September 25, 2022.

2. "The Basics," Elevationists (website).

3. "F.A.Q.," Elevationists (website).

CHAPTER 18. AYAHUASCA HEALINGS

1. *The Letters of Allen Ginsberg,* 232.

2. Rose, "America Is Getting Its First Legal Ayahuasca Church."

3. "Legal Ayahuasca Retreats in America—ONAC—Ayahuasca Healings Church," Ayahuasca Healings Church (website) available on Web Archive (website), accessed December 8, 2015

4. "Legal Ayahuasca Retreats in America—ONAC—Ayahuasca Healings Church," Ayahuasca Healings Church (website) available on Web Archive (website).

5. "Legal Ayahuasca Retreats in America—ONAC—Ayahuasca Healings Church," Ayahuasca Healings Church (website) available on Web Archive (website).

6. Capps, "Cult Leader or Religious Savior?"
7. Christina Callicott, "Pandora's Brew: The New Ayahuasca, Part 5," *Savage Minds* (blog), March 4, 2017.
8. Callicott, "Pandora's Brew."
9. Callicott, "Pandora's Brew."
10. "If You Could Change ANYTHING In Your Life . . . What Would You Change?" Your Highest Truth (website), accessed September 25, 2022.
11. Russell Hausfeld, "Ayahuasca Healings' Trinity de Guzman Calls Coronavirus 'A Necessary Purge,'" Psymposia (website), March 25, 2020.
12. Sarah Laskow, "In 2016, the 'First Legal Ayahuasca Church' Got Shut Down. Was It a Scam—or a New Religion?" Atlas Obscura (online), September 16, 2016.

PART II. MINOR SECTS

1. Ambrosia Society, "About Us," Ambrosia Society (website) available on Web Archive (website), accessed October 23, 2022.
2. Arizona Yage Assembly et al. v. Barr et al., Case no. 3:20-cv-03098 (N.D. Cal. May 5, 2020) 17.
3. Wilson, *Sex and Drugs,* 98.
4. "Church of Cognizance," Dan Mary (website), accessed September 25, 2022.
5. "Dale R. Gowin," Smash Words (website), accessed September 25, 2022.
6. "The Luminist League," Luminist (website), accessed September 25, 2022.
7. "The Luminist Manifesto," Luminist (website), accessed September 25, 2022.
8. "Church of the Divine Sage," Divine Sage (website), accessed September 25, 2022.
9. "Church of the Divine Sage."
10. Smith, "A Negro Peyote Cult," 448–53.
11. "Entheogens and Freedom of Religion," *The Entheogen Review, Complete 1992–2008,* available on Archive (website), accessed October 11, 2021.
12. Lewis, "Church of the One Sermon," in *The Encyclopedia of Cults, Sects, and New Religions,* 212.
13. Lyttle, "Drug Based Religions," 271–84.
14. Sager, "The High Life and the Strange Times of the Pope of Pot," 69, 75.
15. Lyttle, "Drug Based Religions," 217–84.
16. Most, *Bufo alvarius,* 14.
17. Jacquelynn Powers Maurice, "Mike Tyson 'Died' while Tripping on Psychedelic Toad Venom," *New York Post,* November 16, 2021.
18. Robert Gehrke, "The Long, Strange Trip of Steve Urquhart, from GOP Lawmaker to Founder of a Church of Magic Mushrooms," *Salt Lake Tribune,* September 7, 2020.

19. "Who We Are," The Divine Assembly (website), accessed September 25, 2022.

20. "Legal Worship," The Divine Assembly (website), accessed September 25, 2022.

21. Steve Urquhart, "The Legality of Psychedelic Churches," The Utah Bee (website), accessed October 23, 2022.

22. "The Fane of the Psilocybe Mushroom," The Fane (website) available on Archive Today (website), accessed September 25, 2022.

23. "Fane Charter," The Fane (website) available on Archive Today (website), accessed September 25, 2022.

24. "The Sacrament," The Fane (website) available on Archive Today (website), accessed September 25, 2022.

25. "Fane Membership," The Fane (website) available on Archive Today (website), accessed September 25, 2022.

26. Niman, "Out to Save the World."

27. Gaskin, *Cannabis Spirituality,* 40.

28. Gaskin, *Cannabis Spirituality,* 59.

29. "'Clear Light' Sought for LSD Religionists," *Berkeley Barb,* June 17, 1966, 2.

30. The First Church of Cannabis, "Deity Dozen Pathways," Cannaterian on Facebook (website), accessed September 25, 2022.

31. John Sinclair, "Sacramental Herb," *Detroit Metro-Times* (online), May 25, 2011.

32. J. Christian Greer, "Sisters of the Psychedelic Revolution: A Conversation with Leni Sinclair and Genie Parker," online lecture, Center for the Study of World Religions: Transformation and Transcendence (website), November 18, 2020.

33. Adam Woodhead, "How Hippies Turned a College Town into 'The Dope Capital of the Midwest,'" *VICE* (online), May 22, 2019.

34. "Zenta Rocks Labor Temple," *Ann Arbor Sun,* May 31, 1974, 18.

35. Stuart, "Entheogenic Sects and Psychedelic Religions," 17–24.

36. In re Grady, 39 Cal. Rptr. 912 (Cal. 1964).

37. *The Lazy Nickels Action Philosophy,* 16.

38. *Completely Sirius for Once: A Lazy Nickel Manifesto* I, no. 1.

39. "Mission Statement: Native American Indigenous Church (NAIC)," SomaVeda (website), accessed September 25, 2022.

40. "Native American Indigenous Church," SomaVeda (website), accessed September 25, 2022.

41. "Join NAIC Tribal Organization!" SomaVeda (website), accessed September 25, 2022.

42. Lyttle, "Drug Based Religions," 271–84.

43. Lyttle, "Drug Based Religions," 271–84.

44. Jay Leiderman, "Summaries of Religious Use of Marijuana Cases," Jay Leiderman (website), accessed February 11, 2020.

45. "Oratory of Mystical Sacraments," Oratory of Mystical Sacraments (website), accessed September 25, 2022.

46. "About," Oratory of Mystical Sacraments (website), accessed September 25, 2022.

47. "About," Oratory of Mystical Sacraments (website), accessed September 25, 2022.

48. "About," Knights of Acacia (website), accessed September 25, 2022.

49. Feirtag, "Religion: Freaks Worship, Gods Inscrutable," 6.

50. Steven Hager, "The Hippie Ten Commandments," Steven Hager (website), November 2, 2011.

51. Burke, "Princess Leda's Castle in the Air," 104–11.

52. Michael Itkin, "Psychedelic Peace Fellowship: Affirmation of Purpose," Self-published, October 17, 1966.

53. Itkin, "Psychedelic Peace Fellowship: Affirmation of Purpose."

54. Elcock, "High New York," 200.

55. Conversation with the author, August 5, 2019.

56. *Revelations of Awareness* #98-6, issue no. 500, 3.

57. "Subject (Thank God for the Hippies)," *Revelations of Awareness* #77-11 (1977), 2.

58. Josh Adler, "Florida's Ayahuasca Church Wants to Go Legal," *VICE* (online), September 20, 2017.

59. Cozad, *God on High,* 46.

60. Bauman and McCabe, "Proverbs in an LSD Cult," 318–24.

61. "About AOP," Art of Perception (website) available on Web Archive (website), accessed August 9, 2013.

62. "Claim of Right Reverend Gregory Karl Davis," Universal Orthodox (website), accessed September 25, 2022.

63. "Claim of Right Reverend Gregory Karl Davis."

64. "About," Way of Infinite Harmony (website), accessed September 25, 2022.

65. "Zide Door," Zide Door (website), accessed September 25, 2022.

BIBLIOGRAPHY

"2C-I," *EROWID Vaults,* accessed March 17, 2020.

60 Minutes. "Holy Smoke." XII, No. 7, Aired October 28, 1979 on CBS News.

"$40,000 Bail Set for Calif. Fugitive." *Burlington Free Press,* May 25, 1985, 17.

Abrams, Robert. "Script for the Cataclysm." In *Twenty-Minute Fandangos and Forever Changes: A Rock Bazaar,* edited by Jonathan Eisen, 3–18. New York: Random House, 1971.

Adams, Barry. "Creative Philosophy and Sociology of the Law of Peace: Legal HipStory for Religious Use Defense under Religious Freedom Restoration Act." Bliss Fire's Legal Hipstory (website), Accessed March 11, 2019.

Adler, Josh. "Florida's Ayahuasca Church Wants to Go Legal." *VICE* (online), September 20, 2017.

Aiken, John W. "Can Drugs Lead You to God?" *FATE* 16, no. 5, issue 158, May 1963.

———. "The Church of the Awakening." In *Psychedelics: The Uses and Implications of Hallucinogenic Drugs,* edited by Bernard Aaronson and Humphry Osmond, 165–81. Garden City, N.Y.: Anchor Books, 1970.

———. *Explorations in Awareness.* Socorro, N.Mex.: Church of the Awakening, 1966.

———. *Explorations in Awareness: Finding God by Meditating with Entheogens.* Berkeley, Calif.: Ronin Publishing, 2016.

Aleisa, Mark, and Tim Evans. "Who Is First Church of Cannabis Founder Bill Levin?" *IndyStar,* June 27, 2015.

Anderson, Edward F. *Peyote: The Divine Cactus.* Tucson: University of Arizona Press, 1980.

Applebaum, Jerry. "Marijuana Church Opens Oct. 30." *Los Angeles Free Press,* October 10, 1969, 6.

Babs. "Psychedelic." *San Francisco Good Times,* Vol. 3, No. 34, August 28, 1970, 7.

Baghavad Gita. Translated by Swami Prabhavananda and Christopher Isherwood. New York: New American Library, 1972.

Barbour, John. "'Family of 30' Struggles to Find a New Way." *Arizona Daily Star*, March 29, 1970. Section C, 3.

Barmann, Jay. "Oakland Police Raid Church That Was Allegedly Selling Mushrooms and Weed to Congregants." *SFist,* September 1, 2021.

Baum, Julia. "San Jose Moves to Shut Down Two Churches Selling Marijuana." *San Jose Mercury News,* November 17, 2017.

Bauman, Richard, and Neil McCabe. "Proverbs in an LSD Cult." *Journal of American Folklore* 83, no. 329 (July–Sept. 1970): 318–24.

Beck, Garrick. *True Stories: Tales from the Generation of a New World Culture.* Bloomington, Ind.: iUniverse, 2017.

Black, David. *Acid: The Secret History of LSD.* London: VISION, 1998.

Blair, Thomas S. "Habit Indulgence in Certain Cactaceous Plants Among the Indians." *Journal of the American Medical Association* 76, no. 15 (9 April 1921): 1033–34.

Blake-Hannah, Barbara. "Remember the Coptics?" Academia (website), accessed December 26, 2021.

Blomquist, Hakan. "The Riley Crabb Correspondence." UFO Archives (blog), accessed February 2, 2021.

Blumberg, Antonia. "Step Inside The Technicolor World Of The International Church Of Cannabis." *Huffpost,* April 21, 2017.

Brand, Stewart. "Indians and the Counter-Culture." *Clear Creek* 2, no. 18 (December 1972): 34–37.

Breese, Kim. "Walter Tucker: Caretaker for God." *Conestoga College SPOKE,* January 9, 1994, 12.

Bridges, Virginia. "Judge Dismisses Woman's Religious Drug-Use Argument." Alabama Press-Register available on Web Archive (website), June 20, 2008.

Brown, Karina. "Native American Church Uneasy with New Influences." *Courthouse News Service,* April 18, 2016.

———. "Native American Church Resists Pot Enthusiasts." *Courthouse News Service*, April 19, 2016.

Burke, Thomas. "Princess Leda's Castle in the Air." *Esquire,* March 1970, 104–11.

Burnett, John. "Christie Is Again Denied Freedom." *Hawaii Tribune-Herald,* December 12, 2010, 1.

Calabrese, Joseph D. *A Different Medicine: Postcolonial Healing in the Native American Church.* Oxford, UK: Oxford University Press, 2013.

Calabrese, Maria. "'Reverend' Seeks to Set up Compassion Club." *North Bay Nugget,* November 28, 2002, 1.

———. *The Long Watch: A Little before, a Whole Lot during, and a Sliver after Life in a Psychedelic Church.* Whittier, Calif.: Spiraling Books, 1987.

Call, Jack. *Life in a Psychedelic Church.* Self-published, 2020.

Campbell, Colin. "Set Our Pastor Free." *San Francisco Good Times,* May 14, 1971, 1.

"Candidate Charged." *Kingston Whig-Standard,* September 18, 1975, 31.

"Cannabis Minister Roger Christie Sentenced to Five Years." *Big Island Now,* April 28, 2014.

Capps, Reilly. "Cult Leader or Religious Savior? This Pro-drug Exile Is Being Called Both." *Rooster,* October 7, 2016.

Carl Olsen's Marijuana Archives. Drug Library (website), accessed December 27, 2021.

Chacruna Institute for Psychedelic Plant Medicines, and Allison Hoots. *Guide to RFRA and Best Practices for Psychedelic Plant Medicine Churches.* San Francisco: Chacruna Institute for Psychedelic Plant Medicines, 2021.

Cheneviere, Hokulani. "Roger Christie, Hawaii's Medical Marijuana Political Prisoner." Medical Marijuana 411 (website), accessed January 12, 2022.

Children's Liberation Front. *The Book of the Mother.* Bakersfield, Calif.: Children's Liberation Front, 1977.

Ching, Harold. "Very Simply, He's Running for Senate." *Honolulu Star-Bulletin,* September 11, 1974, 83.

Christie, Roger. "Christie Encourages Support for Bill Urging Feds to Release Him Before Trial." *Hawai'i News Daily,* April 7, 2013.

"Church Founder Held." *Sault Star,* June 18, 1986, 14.

"'Church' Holds Nude Olympics." *Ottawa Citizen,* July 27, 1982, 6.

"Church Ministers Fined $500." *Brantford Expositor,* October 8, 1981, 2.

Church of Cognizance. "Church of Cognizance Introduced." n.d.

Church of the Tree of Life. *The First Book of Sacraments of the Church of The Tree of Life: A Guide for the Religious Use of Legal Mind Alterants.* San Francisco: Tree of Life Press, 1972.

Church of the Universe, The. IAMM (defunct website), accessed January 22, 2022.

"'Church of the Universe' Founder Walter Tucker Dies at 79." *The Record,* April 27, 2012.

"Church of the Universe Holding 'Nude Olympics'." *Brantford Expositor,* July 14, 1989, 9.

"Church of Universe Minister Gets Two Years." *Sault Star,* December 1, 1994, 19.

Churchill, David. "Common Guy Baldasaro Wants Your Vote, Not Money." *Hamilton Spectator,* July 28, 2014, 5.

Collins, Don. "Church of the Universe Lights up Congregation." *Calgary Herald,* March 23, 1983, 89.

"Comin' Down." *The Seed,* August 15, 1969, 6.

"Completely Sirius for Once: A Lazy Nickel Manifesto I," No. 1. State College, Pa.: Buffalo Thunder Cabal, n.d.

Coogan, Kevin. *Dreamer of the Day: Francis Parker Yockey and the Postwar Fascist International.* Brooklyn, N.Y.: Autonomedia, 1999.

"Cosmic Awareness: Bob Dobbs Interviews David E. Worcester." *Paranoia Magazine Web Supplement,* Five Bodied (website), July 2008.

"Court Rejects All Arguments." *Regina Leader-Post,* January 23, 1980, 42.

Cox, Billy. "A glimpse of the revolution." *Herald-Tribune,* March 22, 2020.

Cozad, Laurie. *God on High: Religion, Cannabis, and the Quest for Legitimacy.* London: Lexington Books, 2018.

Critchell, David. "Showtime's Mr. Bong." *GQ,* July 11, 2006.

Cross, Robert. "Chicago's Improbable Drug Rescue Team." *Chicago Tribune Magazine,* September 21, 1969, 44.

———. "The Immortals: LSD and the Hippie Life in Chicago." *Chicago Tribune Magazine,* August 20, 1967, 20.

"Crown's Remarks Cause Mistrial." *Brantford Expositor,* June 20, 1979, 10.

"CryptoBeast #22: Mana the Man of Mystery Part 2, with Special Guest Carl Hassell." YouTube (website), accessed July 10, 2021.

Dass, Ram, and Ralph Metzner. *Birth of a Psychedelic Culture: Conversations about Leary, the Harvard Experiments, Millbrook, and the Sixties.* Santa Fe, N.Mex.: Synergetic Press, 2010.

de Guzman, Trinity. "My Humble Confession." Ayahuasca Healings (website), June 28, 2018.

"Delic Missionaries Bring Clear Light Here" *Berkeley Barb,* October 21, 1966, 4.

DiPardo, Michelle. "Church Allegedly Dealt Pot." *National Post,* October 28, 2006, 14.

The Divine Assembly (website), accessed January 2, 2022.

Dobruck, Jeremiah. "Costa Mesa Marijuana Raid Hit Native American Church, Not a Dispensary, Lawyer Says." *Los Angeles Times,* February 4, 2016.

Eason, Brian. "Colorado Rejects Late Attempt to Bar Pot Use in Churches." *Denver Post,* April 20, 2017.

El-Seediab, Hesham R., et al. "Prehistoric Peyote Use: Alkaloid Analysis and Radiocarbon Dating of Archaeological Specimens of *Lophophora* from Texas." *Journal of Ethnopharmacology* 101, nos. 1–3 (3 October 2005): 238–42.

Elcock, Chris. "High New York: The Birth of a Psychedelic Subculture in the American City." Ph.D. diss., University of Saskatchewan, 2015.

Elevationists Unite! on Denver Like a Local Tours (blog), accessed December 12, 2021.

Enos, Leonard. *A Key to the American Psilocybe Mushroom.* Lemon Grove, Calif.: Church of the One Sermon, 1970. (Revised, 1971).

"Entheogens and Freedom of Religion." Entheogen Review available on Archive (website), accessed October 11, 2021.

Ethiopian Zion Coptic Church (website), accessed December 26, 2021.

"Ex-Candidate Gets 60 Days on Gun Count." *Ottawa Journal,* November 13, 1975, 68.

Feirtag, Michael. "Religion: Freaks Worship, Gods Inscrutable." *The MIT Tech,* December 18, 1969, 6.

Fong-Torres, Ben. "Sit-In Starts Again." *San Francisco State College Golden Gater,* April 20, 1965, 1.

Fortin, Jacey. "Marijuana on Religious Grounds? A Cannabis Church Opens in Denver." *New York Times,* April 20, 2017.

Furst, Peter. *Hallucinogens and Culture.* Novato, Calif.: Chandler & Sharp, 1976.

Gardner, Martin. *Urantia: The Great Cult Mystery.* Amherst, N.Y.: Prometheus Books, 2008.

Gaskin, Stephen. *Cannabis Spirituality.* New York: High Times Books, 1996.

Gatehouse, Jonathon. "Pot Activists Send Sample to Health Minister." *National Post,* October 13, 1999, 8.

Gehrke, Robert. "The Long, Strange Trip of Steve Urquhart, from GOP Lawmaker to Founder of a Church of Magic Mushrooms." *Salt Lake Tribune,* September 7, 2020.

Geoghan, Clara. "Inside Elevationism, the Practicing Religion at the International Church of Cannabis." *Westword* (website), December 1, 2020.

Ginsberg, Allen. *The Letters of Allen Ginsberg.* Edited by Bill Morgan. Boston: Da Capo Press, 2008.

Gorightly, Adam. "Fred Crisman and the Servants of Awareness." *Historia Discordia,* October 9, 2019.

Gorman, Peter. "Divine Smoke and God's Flesh: Psychedelics and Religion." *High Times,* January 1990: 41–44.

Gottlieb, Adam [John Mann]. *Legal Highs.* Berkeley, Calif.: Ronin Publishing, 1994.

Gram, Billy. "The Psychedelic Church." *Yipster Times* 3, Issue 3 (Fall–Winter 1975), 14.

Gray, Stephen, ed. *Cannabis and Spirituality: An Explorer's Guide to an Ancient Plant Spirit Ally.* Rochester, Vt.: Park Street Press, 2017.

Graysmith, Robert. *Zodiac Unmasked: The Identity of America's Most Elusive Serial Killer Revealed.* New York: Penguin, 2007.

Greenfield, Robert. *Timothy Leary: A Biography.* New York: Harcourt, 2006.

"Group Plans Charter Challenge." *North Bay Nugget,* August 9, 2007, 2.

Hager, Steven. *Magic, Religion, & Cannabis.* CreateSpace, 2015.

hairy ass. "The Laid, Laid Show." *San Francisco Good Times* 4, No. 28 (September 17–30, 1971), 21.

Hall, Bill. "The Death-Dancer's Cult." *CSC Nusletter* VI, No. 4 (October 1980): 9–10.

"Hamilton to Consider Creating Nude Beach." *Windsor Star,* May 7, 1999, 23.

Hanna, Jon. "Sources." *The Entheogen Review* 14, no. 1 (Autumnal Equinox 2005): 122.

"Hart to Heart." *The Aberee* 11, no. 6 (October 1964): 2.

"Harvard Student: 'No-Smoking Law Restrains Religion.'" *United Press International* (website), February 16, 1987.

Hausfeld, Russell. "Ayahuasca Healings' Trinity de Guzman Calls Coronavirus 'A Necessary Purge.'" *Psymposia.*

"Head News." *East Village Other,* September 29, 1970, 21.

Hecht, Peter. "California's Cannabis Priestess Arrested on Felony Charge." Leafly (website). "Hemp Store Declares Itself Holy Smoke Mission of God." *The Colonist,* March 21, 1998, 41.

Hiaasen, Carl. "The Law and Brother Louv." *Miami Herald,* August 2, 1981, 314.

"'High Priest' of Pot Given Year in Jail." *Los Angeles Times,* February 15, 1972, 21.

Highpine, Gayle. "The 'Legality' of Ayahuasca Churches Under the Oklevueha Native American Church." Bia Labate (website), accessed December 12, 2021.

Hinelf, Mac. "The Temple of the True Inner Light." Trance Am (website), accessed June 24, 2021.

Hirschfelder, Arlene, and Paulette Molin. *Encyclopedia of Native American Religions.* New York: Facts on File, 1992.

"Holy Pot Smoker Jailed Despite Vow." *Red Deer Advocate* (Red Deer, AL), June 9, 1984, 7.

Hudson, J. Hamilton. "How Can You Drink Ayahuasca Legally in the U.S.?" Chacruna (website), accessed December 20, 2021.

Indian, John. "Bum Trip at Acid Rescue." *The Seed,* August 1, 1969, 5.

"Indian's Religious Rights Ruled Violated by Drug Ban." *The Daily Sentinel,* June 28, 1967, 16.

Innes, Stephanie. "Pot Church Takes a Hit." *Arizona Daily Star,* July 9, 2006, 1.

Jaeger, Kyle. "California Bill To Legalize Psychedelics Possession Advances Again, With New Amendments That Add Limits." Marijuana Moment (website), accessed September 12, 2021.

Jay, Karla. *Tales of the Lavender Menace: A Memoir of Liberation.* New York: Basic Books, 2000.

Johnston, Art. "Kick Out the Jams! The Jungle is Ours!" *Berkeley Barb,* March 14–21, 1969, 11.

Kastl, Albert J., and Lena Kastl. *Journey Back: Escaping the Drug Trap.* Chicago: Nelson-Hall, 1975.

Kerr, Keoki. "Officials Unveil Hawaii Marijuana Case." Cannabis Culture (website), accessed December 1, 2021.

Kinney, Robert. "Mothers of Shivalila: Changing Societal Values." *State Hornet* 30, no. 64 (May 16, 1978): 12.

Kleps, Art. *The Boo Hoo Bible.* San Cristobal, N.Mex.: Toad Publishing, 1971.

———. *Millbrook: A Narrative of the Early Years of American Psychedelianism.* San Francisco: Original Kleptonian Neo-American Church, 2005.

———. *Millbrook: The True Story of the Early Years of the Psychedelic Revolution.* Oakland, Calif.: Bench Press, 1977.

La Barre, Weston. *The Peyote Cult.* 5th ed. enlarged. Norman: University of Oklahoma Press, 1989.

Lacy, Suzanne. "Prostitution Notes." In *Veiled Histories: The Body, Place, and Public Art,* edited by Anna Novakov, 147–70. San Francisco: San Francisco Art Institute/Critical Press, 1997.

"Land Boom Special!" *Divine Toad Sweat,* December 1977, 1.

Lande, Nathaniel. *Mindstyles, Lifestyles.* Los Angeles: Price/Stern/Sloan, 1976.

Lander, Devin. "Start Your Own Religion: New York State's Acid Churches." *Nova Religio* 14, no. 3 (2011): 164–80.

Lasko, Sarah. "In 2016, the 'First Legal Ayahuasca Church' Got Shut Down. Was It a Scam—or a New Religion?" *Atlas Obscura,* September 16, 2016.

The Lazy Nickels Action Philosophy. Los Angeles: Buffalo Ghost Dance Productions, n.d.

"The Leader of a Religious Order that Smokes Marijuana" *United Press International,* (website), September 14, 1982.

Leary, Timothy. *Flashbacks.* Los Angeles: J. P. Tarcher, 1983.

———. *High Priest.* Berkeley: Ronin Publishing, 1995.

———. *Start Your Own Religion.* Millbrook, N.Y.: League for Spiritual Discovery, 1966.

Leary, Timothy, Richard Alpert, and Ralph Metzner. *The Psychedelic Experience: A Manual Based on the Tibetan Book of the Dead.* New York: Citadel Press, 2003.

Lee, Martin, and Bruce Shlain. *Acid Dreams: The CIA, LSD, and the Sixties Rebellion.* New York: Grove Press, 1985.

Leiderman, Jay. "Summaries of Religious Use of Marijuana Cases." Jay Leiderman (website), accessed February 11, 2020 (article no longer available).

Lemons, Steven. "Arizona's Marijuana-Worshipping Church of Cognizance Seeks a Legal, Spiritual High." *Phoenix New Times,* March 6, 2009.

Lewis, James R., ed. *The Encyclopedia of Cults, Sects, and New Religions.* 2nd ed. Amherst, N.Y.: Prometheus Books, 2002.

"Links to Occult Eyed in Dancer's Death." *Rockland Journal-News,* Feb 23, 1992, 77.

Loeffler, Jack. "Headed Into the Wind." *El Palacio,* Summer 2017.

Loehndorf, Dan. "Dreams of a Hemp-Based Community." Cannabis Culture (website), December 15, 1994.

——. "The Canadian Inquisition: A History of the Church of the Universe." *Cannabis Culture,* Summer 1997.

"Lord Shiva on Trial." *San Francisco Good Times,* May 7, 1971, 10.

Lyttle, Thomas. "Drug Based Religions and Contemporary Drug Taking." *Journal of Drug Issues* 18, no. 2 (1988): 271–84.

"Man Tells Judge his Drug Need is Religion-Based." *Windsor Star,* May 16, 2002, 17.

Mann, John. *The Book of Sacraments: Memorial Edition.* Berkeley, Calif.: Ronin Publishing, 2015.

Marijuana and the Bible. The Ethiopian Zion Coptic Church, 1980.

"Marijuana Appeal Put on Hold." *Calgary Herald,* December 22, 1982, 14.

"Marijuana: Its Cosmic Significance, Physical Effects, and Other Interesting Information on the Subject (Thank God for the Hippies)." *Revelations of Awareness* #77-11 (1977).

"Marijuana Jails Four in Burlingame." *San Mateo Times,* November 17, 1966, 41.

Marriott, Alice, and Carol K. Rachlin. *Peyote.* New York: New American Library, 1971.

Marshall, Sue. "Pot-Sex Church Celebrates Hedonism." *Los Angeles Free Press,* March 13, 1970, 19.

Matlock, Staci. "Ghost Clan Cuts Fence 'To Defend Community Rights.'" *The Taos News,* July 10, 1997, 10.

——. "Ghost Clan Ready to Sue over Ute Mountain Access." *The Taos News,* August 22, 1996, 8.

——. "Ute Mountain Ranch Owner Sues Three Men for Trespassing." *The Taos News,* June 18, 1998, 10.

McLintock, Barbara. "High Priest of Pot Loses His Licence." *Vancouver Province,* June 14, 1998, 18.

Medrano, Kastalia. "Welcome to the International Church of Cannabis." Inverse (website), accessed November 29, 2021.

"Mellon Millions Underpin Artistic Endeavor near Tucson." *Arizona Republic,* March 1, 1970, 216.

Melton, J. Gordon, ed. *American Religious Creeds.* Vol. 3. New York: Triumph Books, 1991.

———. *Melton's Encyclopedia of American Religions.* 8th ed. Detroit: Gale, 2009.

"Men Arrested for Mailed Pot." *National Post,* May 24, 2000, 5.

"Merton's Correspondence with Aiken, John W., Dr." Merton (website), accessed September 12, 2020.

Middleton, Clifton Ray. *Ganja Warrior Priest: Genesis.* Self-published, 2021.

Miller, Melanie J., et al. "Chemical Evidence for the Use of Multiple Psychotropic Plants in a 1,000-Year-Old Ritual Bundle from South America." *PNAS* 116, no. 23 (June 4, 2019): 11207–12.

"Minister Jailed." *North Bay Nugget,* May 3, 1983, 2.

Minzey, Willie. "Shiva Head." *San Francisco Good Times,* Jun 26, 1970, 12.

———. "Thinking Plant." *San Francisco Good Times,* Oct 9, 1969, 5.

"'Missionaries' Fraud Trial Starts." *Brantford Expositor,* June 6, 1979, 14.

"Missionary for Toad Venom Is Facing Charges." *New York Times,* February 20, 1994.

Mitchell, Thomas. "International Church of Cannabis Stung by Undercover Denver Police on 4/20." *Westword,* July 20, 2017.

———. "Cannabis Church, City Attorneys Dig in for Trial Over Misdemeanors." *Westword,* January 20, 2019.

———. "Jury Finds Cannabis Church Founder Guilty in 4/20 Party Case." *Westword,* February 1, 2019.

Morang, Joe. "Seize Five Youths at Drug Center." *Chicago Tribune,* March 1, 1971, 26.

Moro, Teviah. "Michael Baldasaro, Hamilton's High Priest of Pot, Dead at 67." *Hamilton Spectator,* June 9, 2016.

Most, Albert [Ken Nelson]. *Bufo alvarius: The Psychedelic Toad of the Sonoran Desert.* Denton, Tex.: Venom Press, 1984.

"Muggles Jug Pat Ward Pal." *New York Daily News,* January 5, 1956, 485.

Muneta, James D. "Peyote Crisis Confronting Modern Indigenous Peoples: The Declining Peyote Population and a Demand for Conservation." *American Indian Law Journal* 9, no. 1 (2020): Article 6.

Musers, John [Evan Eyerick]. *Lazy Nickels Information Booklet.* Laguna Beach, Calif.: Self-published, n.d.

Naumetz, Tim. "Grass-roots Candidate Flying High." *Ottawa Citizen,* July 17, 1998, 3.

Nelson, Nick. "Medicine Man." *Provo Daily Herald,* May 22, 2005, 1.

The Neo-American Church Catechism and Handbook. Millbrook, N.Y.: Kriya Press, 1967.

Niermann, Ingo. *The Curious World of Drugs and Their Friends.* London: Turnaround, 2008.

Niman, Michael I. "Out to Save the World: Life on the Farm." *High Times,* February 1995.

"Nine Members of the Jamaica-based Ethiopian Zion Coptic Church." *United Press International* (website), June 19, 1981.

Nolan, Dan. "Pot Advocate Walter Tucker Dies at 79." *Hamilton Spectator,* April 26, 2012.

"North Coast Residents Indicted by Grand Jury." *Ukiah Daily Journal,* Sept. 16, 1984, 2.

"Nude Promoters Charged." *Owen Sound Sun Times,* January 5, 1978, 13.

O'Connor, James. "Grow Pot to Save Trees, Urges Reefer Reverend." *Winnipeg Sun,* August 27, 1990, 6.

Olin, William F. *Escape from Utopia.* Rolling Hills, Calif.: B. L. Winch Associates/Jalmar Press, 1980.

Oppenheimer, Mark. "As a Religion, Marijuana-Infused Faith Pushes Commonly Held Limits." *New York Times,* July 20, 2013.

Penner, James, ed. *Timothy Leary: The Harvard Years.* Rochester, Vt.: Park Street Press, 2014.

Paxton, Ryan. "Smokin' Platform." *Humber Et Cetera,* November 23, 2000, 10.

Pedersen, Joe Mario. "DEA Denies Central Florida Church's Request to Use Drug for Religious Purposes: Report." *Orlando Sentinel,* June 23, 2021.

Peters, George. "A Study of Psychedelic Drug Users." *Journal of Orthomolecular Medicine* 2, nos. 2–3 (1970): 103–7.

"Peyote Legal in Colorado." *The East Village Other,* July 15–30, 1967, 17.

Poland, Jefferson [Clitlick]. "Making Mince Meat of Minzey." *Berkeley Barb,* August 10–16, 1973, 8.

Poland, Jefferson, and Sam Sloan, eds. *The Sex Marchers.* Los Angeles: Elysium, 1968.

"Police Fondled Brother, Jury Told." *Edmonton Journal,* June 12, 1979, 10.

"Police Prod Parkside Prelate Praying for Peace." *Berkeley Barb,* June 7–13, 1968, 10.

"Pot Advocate Jailed Six Years, 34 Days on Sex, Drug Convictions." *Nunatsiaq News,* June 7, 2012.

"Pot Appeal Snuffed Out." *Times Colonist,* January 23, 1980. 39.

"Pot 'Minister' a Murderer." *Vancouver Province,* July 7, 1993, 5.

"Pot-Smoking Clergy to Get Back Their Stuff." *Sault Star,* September 21, 2000, 6.

Powers Maurice, Jacquelynn. "Mike Tyson 'Died' While Tripping on Psychedelic Toad Venom." *New York Post,* November 16, 2021.

Pratt, Steven. "Teen-Age Girl's Nine-Day Trip on Drugs." *Chicago Tribune,* February 1, 1971.

"Protestors Launch Complaint." *North Bay Nugget,* May 27, 1999, 5.

Psychedelic Peace Fellowship. "Affirmation of Purpose." October 17, 1966.

Rager, Joshua. "Peyote and the Psychedelics: 20th Century Perceptions of the Religious Use of Psychoactive Substances." *Denison Journal of Religion* 12, no. 3 (2013): 1–15.

"Rare Indian Drug Nabbed in Spa 'Party-House' Raid." *Desert Sun,* May 28, 1962, 1.

Ray, Karla. "No Charges after Death Investigation at Ayahuasca Church." WFTV (website), October 14, 2018.

"Report: Church Lures Converts with 'Designer Drug' Jay Leiderman (website).'" *United Press International* (website), July 2, 1988.

"Report of Experiment with MDMA. Date: December 22, 1980." Isomer Design (website), accessed January 8, 2021.

"Rev. Minzey Faces Life for Pot Sacrament." *Berkeley Barb,* May 14–20, 1971, 7.

Rigal-Cellard, Bernadette. "An Analysis of the Peyote Way Church of God in the Legal Field." A paper presented at CESNUR 2004 international conference, Baylor University, Waco, Texas. June 18–20, 2004.

Rodrigue, Daniel. "The Story Behind a 1984 Hallucinogenic Pamphlet from Denton Is Just as Trippy as Its Subject." *Dallas Observer,* April 13, 2021.

Rolfe, Lionel. *Fat Man on the Left: Four Decades in the Underground.* Los Angeles: California Classics, 1998.

Rose, Nick. "America Is Getting Its First Legal Ayahuasca Church." *VICE* (online), December 11, 2015.

Roszak, Theodore. *The Making of a Counter Culture.* New York: Double Day, 1969.

Rubin, Craig. *9021GROW.* Beverly Hills, Calif.: 2000 BC, 2005.

Ryder, Turk. "Double Murder on Satan's Six Acres!" *Official Detective* 54, no. 3 (March 1984).

Sager, Mike. "The High Life and the Strange Times of the Pope of Pot." *Rolling Stone,* June 13, 1991.

Sahagun, Louis. "Why Are Some Native Americans Fighting Efforts to Decriminalize Peyote?" *Los Angeles Times,* March 29, 2020.

Salisbury, David, and Keith Lorenz. "Gridley Wright: Confessions of a Yogi in Bali." Gridley Enterprises, 2002. Audio CD.

Schou, Nick. "'Hippie Mafia' Hash Smuggler Arrested." Accessed September 5, 2021.

———. *Orange Sunshine: The Brotherhood of Eternal Love and Its Quest to Spread Peace, Love, and Acid to the World.* New York: Thomas Dunne, 2010.

"Sex Drug Cult." *Berkeley Tribe,* November 28–December 5, 1969, 3.

"Shiva Missionary and Cop Go Up in Cloud of Smoke." *Berkeley Barb,* June 14–20, 1968, 7.

Shlacter, Barry. "Cult Leader is Dead, But His Followers Refuse to Mourn." *Santa Cruz Sentinel,* March 12, 1980, 40.

Sides, Josh. *Erotic City: Sexual Revolution and the Making of Modern San Francisco.* New York: Oxford University Press, 2009.

Smith, Huston, and Ruben Snake. *One Nation under God: The Triumph of the Native American Church.* Sante Fe, N. Mex: Clear Light, 1996.

Smith, Maurice G. "A Negro Peyote Cult." *Journal of the Washington Academy of Sciences* 24, no. 10 (October 15, 1934): 448–53.

Sogol, Pierre [Frederick Wolf]. "Aquarius Rising." Unreleased film, 1967.

Stafford, Peter. *Psychedelics Encyclopedia.* Los Angeles: J. P. Tarcher, 1983.

"Statement of the National Council of Native American Churches Concerning the Proliferation of Organizations Appropriating the 'Native American Church' Name with No Ties to the Indigenous Worship of the Holy Sacrament Peyote." Native American Rights Fund (NARF) (website), accessed December 23, 2021.

Stewart, Omer C. *Peyote Religion: A History.* The Civilization of the American Indian Series, Vol. 181. Norman: University of Oklahoma Press, 1993.

———. "Peyotism in California." *Journal of California and Great Basin Anthropology* 8, no. 2 (1986): 217–25.

"Straits Leery of Leary League." *Berkeley Barb,* December 16, 1966, 2.

Stuart, R. "Entheogenic Sects and Psychedelic Religions." *MAPS Bulletin* 12, no. 1 (2002): 17–24.

"Student Pleads Guilty to Rape; Sent to Topeka." *Manhattan Republic,* April 13, 1955, 1.

"Supreme Court Won't Hear Case of Pot-Smoking, Self-Styled Clerics." *Sault Star,* May 2, 2009, 14.

Tabachnik, Sam. "Future of Public Pot Smoking in Denver May Be Impacted as International Church of Cannabis Co-founder Heads to Court Tuesday." *Denver Post,* January 26, 2019.

"Teen's Death Inquiry Set." *Chicago Tribune,* May 19, 1970, 18.

Teeter, Donald E. *Amanita muscaria: Herb of Immortality.* Manor, Tex.: Ambrosia Society, 2005.

Tendler, Stewart, and David May. *The Brotherhood of Eternal Love.* London: CyanBooks, 2007.

Testimony to the Psychedelic (The Newest Testament to the Light). New York: Temple of the True Inner Light, 1981.

Thomas, Bob. "Indian Gets Inspiration in Designs of Antiquity." *Arizona Daily Star,* December 6, 1960, 13.

Thorne, Harris. "Another Win for Religious Use of Psychedelics: New Hampshire v. Mack." Harris Bricken (blog), accessed April 20, 2021.

Tibbetts, Janice. "Nudist Reverends Support Smoking the 'Holy Plant.'" *Windsor Star,* September 8, 2003, 11.

"Topless carwash raises cash for deputies wounded in gun battle at Rastafarian pot farm." *Los Angeles Times,* September 9, 2019.

"Tucker loses another legal battle." *Regina Leader-Post,* February 18, 1980, 53.

Tuohy, John. "First Church of Cannabis wins IRS nonprofit status." *IndyStar,* June 2, 2015.

"Two Are Arrested Here at Park 'Free Pot Party.'" *New York Times,* Sept 3, 1974, 31.

U.S. Department of Health, Education, and Welfare. Food and Drug Administration. Notices of Judgment under the Federal Food, Drug, and Cosmetic Act. Drugs and Devices, Issues 7121–8240. Washington, D.C.: Government Printing Office, 1964.

Unger, Brent. "The Ganja Man." *News Herald Lifestyle,* September 4, 1994, 1.

Universal Orthodox Church (website), accessed February 11, 2021.

Urquhart, Steve. "The Legality of Psychedelic Churches." *The Utah Bee,* Accessed January 1, 2022.

Watts, Richard. "Bongos, Cymbals, Bells Herald 'Ecstasy Mission' for Church's Birthday." *The Colonist,* June 11, 1996, 15.

Wei, Ma Guang. *Way of Infinite Harmony: Faith of Her Holiness Princess Ma Gu, Goddess of Cannabis.* N.p.: Way of Infinite Harmony, 2013.

"Welcome to the Religion of Jesus Church." Hialoha available on Web Archive (website), accessed February 1, 2021.

Wells, Walter. "History of the Ethiopian Zion Coptic Church." Self-Published, n.d.

"Whee Willie Rafted Away in the Raw." *Berkeley Barb,* April 18–24, 1969, 3.

"White Men Witness Indian Peyote Rites." *Saskatoon Star-Phoenix,* October 15, 1956, 15.

"Wilbur Minzey, Film Engineer." *The Signal,* January 7, 2000, 3.

Wilson, Robert Anton. *Cosmic Trigger: The Final Secret of the Illuminati.* New York: Pocket Books, 1977.

———. *Sex and Drugs: A Journey Beyond Limits.* Las Vegas, Nev.: Falcon Publishing, 1987.

———. "Timothy Leary and his Psychological H-Bomb." *The Realist,* no. 52, August 1964, 1, 17–20.

Woodhead, Adam, "How Hippies Turned a College Town into 'The Dope Capital of the Midwest.'" *VICE* (online), May 22, 2019.

"Witness: Gold Lured Brothers." *Montreal Star,* June 8, 1979, 26.

Wright, Gridley. "Strawberry Fields Forever. . . ?" *Los Angeles Oracle,* August 1967, 35.

Wright, Gridley. *Shivalila: Social Culture Based on LSD Research.* San Francisco: Children's Liberation Front, 1978.

Yablonsky, Lewis. *The Hippie Trip.* New York: Pegasus, 1969.

Young, Gord. "'Church' Lights up for Cannabis Day." *North Bay Nugget,* July 3, 2003, 3.

INDEX

Note: Page numbers in *italics* reference photographs.